DISCOVERING THE BIBLICAL WORLD

Revised Edition

DISCOVERING THE BIBLICAL WORLD

HARRY THOMAS FRANK

Revised Edition

Edited by James F. Strange

HAMMOND INCORPORATED   MAPLEWOOD, NEW JERSEY 07040

Above: Alabaster relief from Assyrian palace at Nimrud. The figure offering the libation cup is Asshurnasirpal II, a contemporary of Omri.

Title page illustration: The Dead Sea

Scripture quotations, unless otherwise noted, are from the Revised Standard Version of the Bible, copyrighted in 1946, 1952 and © 1971 by the Division of Christian Education, National Council of the Churches of Christ in the U.S.A. and used by permission.

The spellings of personal names and geographical place names which appear on the maps and in the text of this book are those used in the Revised Standard Version of the Bible.

DISCOVERING THE BIBLICAL WORLD.
Revised edition
Entire contents ©Copyright 1988, 1975 by HAMMOND INCORPORATED

Library of Congress Cataloging-in-Publication Data

Frank, Harry Thomas.
    Discovering the Biblical world.

    Bibliography: p.
    Includes index.
    1. Bible—History of Biblical events.   2. Bible—History of contemporary events.   I. Strange, James F. II. Title.
BS635.2.F7   1987   220.9'5   86-14963
ISBN 0-8437-3628-3 Hardcover edition
ISBN 0-8437-3627-5 Deluxe edition
ISBN 0-8437-3626-3 Softcover edition

Printed in the United States of America

Preface to the Revised Edition

There is a sense in which it is impossible to edit anyone else's writing, for it is as personal as one's face. I certainly felt that way as I slowly unpacked my mental chisel and mallet and examined Harry Thomas Frank's text of "Rediscovering the Biblical World." Upon careful inspection, it loomed just a bit larger than life, and I paused to wonder.

My mind slipped back to more than fifteen years ago, to Tel Ta'anach in Israel. There Tom Frank and I struggled across the recently plowed top of the ancient mound and talked about Paul Lapp's excavations there and Tom Frank's role in them. Our conversation, though punctuated by heavy breathing from laboring across fresh furrows, moved afield to the story of Deborah, to the Megiddo plain and the fearful portrait of Armageddon in the New Testament book of Revelation, and to other matters that the setting, the bright sun, and the balmy weather suggested. I was struck with Tom's intensity about the Biblical story, his mastery of the details of the narrative, and his commitment to retelling it. I wondered if he would get that retelling into print.

Of course he did. And now, years later, after the book has had wide readership and Tom has left us, I have taken on the task of remodeling certain points of his prose. The job has been deceptively simple in concept, but remarkably difficult in execution. I have simply endeavored to bring Tom Frank's text up to date, to omit some repetitions, to correct a few items, and to interleave some recent archaeology, so that this book could offer an up-to-date, imaginative tour of the Biblical story, a story that has shaped western intellectual history so powerfully. At the same time I wanted the text to continue to offer an accurate sense of the land itself that is the setting for this story. I hoped that the prose could remain vigorous, forceful, and yet simple.

I now offer this text to the reader with all its remaining cracks and fissures, for none of us produce perfect prose. On the whole it belongs to Tom Frank. Here and there one can find the evidence for my mason's chisel. It is now a cooperative offering. I hope Tom approves.

January 1987   J. F. Strange

A footed lamp from the period of the Hebrew kings.

CONTENTS

The mound of Tell el-Hesi. Archaeologists at work in southwest Israel. Tell el-Hesi, one of the first mounds to be excavated in Palestine, is thought to be the site of Biblical Eglon, a Canaanite royal city taken by Joshua.

1 RECOVERY OF ANCIENT LIFE

The silent breeze becomes almost audible as it dances among the leaves of infant olive trees and stirs up a miniature whirlpool of dust here and there. Gleaming in the brilliant sun, the stones of a cyclopean bulwark are proud, unyielding as they have been for thousands of years. In the center of what had once been a city, intersecting walls outline a great temple, and in its forecourt is a large standing stone, a curious altar, perhaps a place of sealing covenants. Quite nearby a whitewashed, domed structure, a medieval Arab tomb protects a shrine much older — nothing less than the reputed grave of Joseph, Patriarch of Israel. A little farther along in this direction an unfinished Orthodox church's mournful uncovered enclosure offers what shelter it can to a deep well, one where it is said Jesus talked with a disreputable Samaritan woman. On the other side of the ruined city, alongside the road toward the Jordan River, a magnificent tomb has been found which had collapsed sometime in the past seventeen hundred years. When the soil was removed in 1972 eight superb Roman coffins were exposed.

The sights and sounds of the present intrude rudely upon the past. The mind, dwelling on ancient things, becomes aware once more of life around it. A mechanic's angry hammer is heard urging a recalcitrant tire upon a rim. Laughing children are playing tag among the trees. In the distance a horn announces that someone is in a hurry here at Balata where the highway from Nablus to Jerusalem turns sharply south and rushes through the valley. Towering high above and flanking this striking spot are Gerizim and Ebal, two mountains which have looked down upon scenes ancient and modern and have remained silent and majestic, one smiling, the other frowning, both knowing.

Has it not always been thus in this strange land, this Holy Land, this place peculiarly blessed and cursed? Has there been a time here when men did not know a more antique era, when they did not struggle with the present and look to the future? Did not Abraham pause here between the two mountains? Is this not where Joshua urged men to "choose the Lord?" Before these heroes of Israel, hundreds of years before them, the Canaanites built this place. After them the kings of the Hebrews came, once even making this the capital of Israel. And did not this place defy other Jewish kings, until in 107 B.C. one of them made an end to it?

This is Biblical Shechem. Like so many other places in the country it reminds the sensitive visitor of how the ancient and the modern lie close to each other in this land. And — if we have eyes to see — it reminds us of something else too, something very important. For these ancient stones, laid bare by the archaeologist's skill, speak not of dead peoples and civilizations but of life itself. Everything that is recovered from bygone days tells us of life. A city wall or a comb, a broken pot or a fragile scroll — it does not matter how small, how seemingly insignificant or how sensational — everything had behind it some intelligence, some purpose, some need, some desire.

We are entirely too used to museums and to their "priceless" artifacts set in deathly silent galleries. Ancient or modern, culture has always been a fabric woven of purposes and cross-purposes, designed by fundamental human needs, colored by hope and flawed by envy. There never has been such a thing as a "dead civilization," for wherever men and women have been born, lived and died there

The fortress—temple at Shechem, probably the scene of Joshua's covenant (Joshua 24:1-28) was built around 1650 B.C. and with modifications continued in use throughout the Period of Judges.

9

has been that constant struggle with nature and neighbor, that continuing effort to find the right relationship with each. What the historian and the archaeologist seek to do today is not to provide museums with new prizes, but to bring alive the kind and character of life that was lived in a given place at a given time. Evidence is sometimes meager and often controversial, yet with due caution and a certain audacity the effort at historical reconstruction must be made. And it should be done with a sense of the feel, the taste, the smell of life. Here archaeologists have been invaluable. Not the dashing adventurers they are often made out to be, these patient, skilled and occasionally plodding men and women have made it possible in a sense to walk in the past along ageless streets within hoary walls. Often this is a story of kings and priests, since they are the ones who have left most of the written records, palaces and temples. But we know of humble people too. We can walk through their houses, see how they slept, ate, worked and played; we know what kind of grains they grew, how they processed them and made their tools and clothing. We know much of how they worshiped and how they were buried. The last two centuries have seen great strides in our appreciation of ancient times, not least because the archaeologist has been able literally to write history from the soil where no documents exist and to place written records into a living context. History, it needs to be remembered, has never been dead. It is we who have failed to understand that it is always alive.

At no point have we moderns been more guilty of deadening the ancients than in the case of those characters, cultures and causes spoken of in the Bible. So often the Bible is seen as some sort of fossil, something that is not now and never has been alive. Reasons for such a view are many and varied, but most focus upon its holy character. Many people seem to think or at least to act as though the Bible if seen as living drama will somehow diminish as Sacred Scripture. Such a view could hardly be more mistaken historically or theologically. The Bible, is to be sure, a peculiar piece of literature compounded by many types of writings from countless hands over hundreds of years. It is, moreover, not a history book nor, as is sometimes thought, the story of a people. It is about God and his dealings with men. Yet the unique perspective which it takes says that God deals with people in human situations. Thus the Bible is not a dehistoricized myth, but a vibrant, exciting drama of life. Those who would make it a sacred fossil have missed not only its historical virility, but also its central theological thrust.

Archaeologists working in the Middle East in the past century and a half have made phenomenal strides in recovering previously unknown or dimly perceived cultures and in the process have placed the Bible in a living context. This recovery followed two overlapping tracks: the decipherment of ancient languages and the development of adequate field skills for excavation. The solution of these twin problems began in Egypt. In 1799 Napoleon's engineers, while digging a fort near one of the mouths of the Nile in the western delta at a place called Rosetta, found a stone inscribed in three languages which were recognized as Greek, demotic (a cursive writing used in Hellenistic Egypt) and hieroglyphics (a form of writing characteristic of more ancient Egypt). The same text was in all three languages. Since Roman times scholars had been aware of the vast amount of hieroglyphics written literally all over the surviving ancient buildings beside the Nile. But the knowledge of how to read this partly phonogrammic, partly ideographic writing had been lost. Now, with the aid of this chance discovery, scholars had a solid grip on unraveling the mysteries of this language and thus laying open a massive library of information. By 1822 the task was far enough advanced to allow more widespread translation of ancient Egyptian texts to begin. It was not until the last quarter of the nineteenth century that scientific grammars began to appear.

The Rosetta Stone, unearthed by French troops during Napoleon's Egyptian expedition of 1799. The name Ptolemy in the cartouche below was the first clue to deciphering Egyptian hieroglyphics.

P T O L M Y S

About the same time, in 1884 to be exact, a monumental step was taken in the development of archaeological field technique. It was in that year that Sir Flinders Petrie began to excavate at Naucratis. The significance of this work cannot be recognized unless one understands the nature of ancient sites in the Middle East. They were occupied for hundreds and in some cases thousands of years. Numerous disasters befell these cities over the years — including war, plague, fire, earthquake. In the absence of huge machines able to level the sites before beginning new constructions occupational debris tended to build up layer by layer. On occasion this debris reaches astonishing depths; fifty or sixty feet is not uncommon. As the archaeologist works back through these layers he contends with a cultural upside-down cake, the top being the most recent and those near the bottom of the mound the earliest. To compound the matter it is not only possible but likely that numerous rebuilds have taken place within a given major layer and that stones from an earlier period were used in later construction. Moreover, a layer from a given period is not likely to have a consistent depth within itself. It was Petrie who first came to grips with these problems and laid the sure foundations for adequate field technique. With him excavation in the Middle East takes a significant turn, away from treasure hunting and toward the recovery of ancient life.

At Naucratis Petrie noted that each layer had its own distinctive pottery and that the shape, decoration and techniques of manufacture were clues to dating. Earlier, excavating at Troy in western Turkey in 1870, Heinrich Schliemann had suggested that successive cities on a given site might be completely separated by destruction levels. Combining the insights from Naucratis with this, in 1890 Petrie began to dig at Tell el-Hesi in southwestern Palestine. This extraordinary Englishman whose active career spanned seventy years had introduced sequence dating based upon pottery fragments, one of the most durable artifacts of man; every site is full of such material.

Early lithograph of the mound of Tell el-Hesi excavated by Sir Flinders Petrie. Petrie's work here in 1890 was a turning point in scientific archaeology.

This important methodological discovery was not lost upon one young American scholar in spite of the fact that numerous established scholars of the day thought it a waste of time. W. F. Albright was that American. Among experts in his scholarly field he had no peer. With typical thoroughness he surveyed other archaeological work to see how stratigraphic excavation, as this technique came to be called, could be improved. George A. Reisner, another American had been working under Petrie's influence in Egypt. He was the first to use meticulous recording techniques and extensive photographic records. All of these things Albright brought together at Tell Beit Mirsim in 1923. Meanwhile Albright continued to refine sequence dating based upon pottery.

Only two years later, in 1925, the Oriental Institute of the University of Chicago mounted the most massive assault on an ancient site yet seen in the Middle East. The site was Megiddo, prominent in the Biblical narrative and conspicuous on the southern edge of the Plain of Esdraelon. J. H. Breasted, who conceived this venture, brought together leading field archaeologists from The United States and Britain. C. S. Fisher, who had previously dug at Samaria, was the director. Stratified excavation reached its pre-Second World War zenith at Megiddo when the archaeologists made clear their intent to strip the mound level by level. Innovations were tried including the first use of aerial photography. Careful work, meticulous recording and interpretation by the latest methods revealed not only portions of remarkable cities from Israelite monarchical times, but also beneath it a number of extraordinary Canaanite cities, including one Early Bronze Age town which was well conceived along lines that would please even the most modern city planner. Even earlier ruins from Chalcolithic times were found. However, even the vast resources of talent and money available to this excavation did not allow the stripping of the mound. As we now know this was fortunate, since archaeological methodology still had considerable refinement ahead, and indeed we are now aware that portions of explored archaeological sites ought to be left untouched so that earlier results can be checked by later and more sophisticated techniques.

During the Second World War large-scale excavation came to a halt in the Middle East, but important work did not cease altogether. It was during this time that Nelson Glueck was making his extensive surveys of the Transjordan, both as a contribution to the Allied war effort and to increase scholarly knowledge. After the war, attempts to get back into the field on a major scale were understandably slow and were further hampered by unrest in the area. But by 1952 a team from the British School of Archaeology in Jerusalem headed by Kathleen Kenyon had tackled Tell es-Sultan — Old Testament Jericho. While her results, reported later in this book, surprised and even shocked many, her major contributions to our current story were truly epoch-making advances in stratigraphic excavation techniques. Building upon earlier work and upon insights of her teacher, Sir Mortimer Wheeler, she introduced a number of refinements, including a new type of grid system which meant that the mound would be dug in squares as over against attempts to strip a site or, as the French had been doing following an older German method, tracing walls to reveal buildings. Miss Kenyon's system provided right-angle banks of dirt called *balks,* in which the occupational history of the structure against which they stood could be read. This and other advances also allowed her to identify foundation trenches, thus correctly interpreting earlier stones used in later construction.

While work was still going on at Jericho, an American dig was begun at Shechem under the direction of G. Ernest Wright, who learned field techniques in the 1930s at Beth Shemesh. The latest techniques were employed and methodological perfecting continued. In addition, Wright undertook to train a younger generation of talented field archaeologists, many of whom are currently directing their own excavations in the Middle East under the aegis of the American Schools of Oriental Research in Jerusalem.

While this long but steady development of field technique was going on, significant movement was being made in the recovery of ancient languages and dialects of Syria-Palestine. This was spurred particularly by the discovery of a large library of Canaanite materials at Ugarit in Lebanon in 1929. At the same time Albright and others were seeking to perfect sequence dating based on pottery. In 1948 radiocarbon dating was introduced. While its plus or minus 10 percent error is often too large to aid significantly in dating later materials, its use has revised all ideas of earlier chronology.

We have so far neglected Mesopotamia, the valley between the Tigris and Euphrates rivers. Today it is hard to realize that two hundred years ago we had virtually no detailed knowledge of ancient life in this valley. What has been found there since 1842 is little less than spectacular. It was in that year that Paul Botta, French Consul in Mosul, let it be known that he was in the market for antiquities. In attempting to trace the source of some particularly attractive tiles, he found Khorsabad. The tiles were from the royal palace of Sargon II (722-705 B.C.), conqueror of Samaria and destroyer of the Kingdom of Israel! Even in its ruined state the structure was breathtaking in its beauty, with high walls covered by paintings, reliefs and mosaics in rich colors, and with monumental winged-animal statues guarding the gates.

Human-headed winged lion from the palace gate of the Assyrian king Asshurnasirpal II, a contemporary of Elijah. It lay buried for some twenty-six centuries until its recovery in the nineteenth century.

The imagination of Henry Layard, a virtually penniless Englishman, was fired by Botta's discovery. Layard came to the "land between the rivers" and twenty miles from Mosul dug into a large mound. The very first day he came down upon another palace, and on the next day he found yet another monumental building with walls seven feet high covered from floor to roof line with beautifully carved reliefs. This was Nimrud, ancient Calah, an Assyrian capital whose main palace was built by Asshurnasirpal II (ca. 883-859 B.C.). By 1849 Layard, flushed with success, came to the mound just across the river from Mosul. Before long he had laid bare the palace of Sennacherib and had identified Nineveh, so feared and hated by ancient contemporaries. The walls of this city were seventy-five feet high, double brick thirty-two feet thick, and protected by fifteen gates with a moat seventy-five feet wide. Many of the buildings of the city were decorated with glazed polychrome tiles whose colors were still vivid when Layard first gazed on them. They often featured deep blue, a color still prominent on decorative tiles in the Middle East.

In the palace at Nineveh was a library, apparently placed there by Asshurbanapal, Sennacherib's grandson. Still arranged neatly according to subject matter, these cuneiform tablets contained a broad survey of the knowledge of that day. But, as in Egypt previously, who could read this ancient language, this chicken-scratch made on wet clay with sticks? The problem of decipherment was solved in much the same way as in Egypt. Twenty-six miles from Kermanshah there is a large carving high up on a sheer rock face. It was ordered cut there by Darius the Great (522-486 B.C.) to celebrate his successful struggle to bring the fragmented Persian Empire back together following the death of Cambyses II. Like the Rosetta Stone it was written in three languages. Dangling from ropes high above the valley floor, Henry Rawlinson, a major in the British army assigned to the East India Company, managed to copy a vast amount of text. This wedge-shaped cuneiform material was extremely difficult to figure out, but with persistence and patience Rawlinson was able to unravel the meaning of some four hundred lines of Old Persian.

When, a short time later, a tablet containing ideogrammatic script was found it was possible to correlate it with the syllabic materials. With this in hand a Babylonian grammar was produced over the next half century. But this is arduous work and continues today.

Thus, then, in the past century and a half the Ancient Near East has emerged from relative obscurity. Many devoted people have worked with patience, often under hardship, to recover languages, to develop field techniques, to survey, explore and make accurate maps. Problems of dating have been tackled, debated and in some cases solved. Today the task continues on an accelerated basis. We would be mistaken to think that the great days of Middle Eastern archaeology are over, however. Popular imagination may never again be aroused as it was by the discovery of the tomb of Tutankhamun or the chance find of the Dead Sea Scrolls. We may not again see the likes of an Albright or even a Petrie, but many gifted young archaeologists are in the field today at more sites than ever. Work is severely limited by lack of funds, since it is the spectacular, not the lengthy, patient, unsung work often with no guarantee of great finds, that attracts money. Still the work goes on and our knowledge of the life of the ancient Middle East grows. It not only goes on, it expands. The work of the departments of antiquities of countries such as Cyprus, Egypt, Israel and Jordan continues with a faster pulse than ever before. And the American Schools of Oriental Research has through the late 1960s and early 1970s expanded its activities into Saudi Arabia, Cyprus, Yemen and along the Euphrates as well as undertaking a larger role in Israel and Jordan.

Small stone stele shows Asshurbanapal, founder of the library of Nineveh, carrying bricks. The cuneiform inscription proclaims his architectural activities.

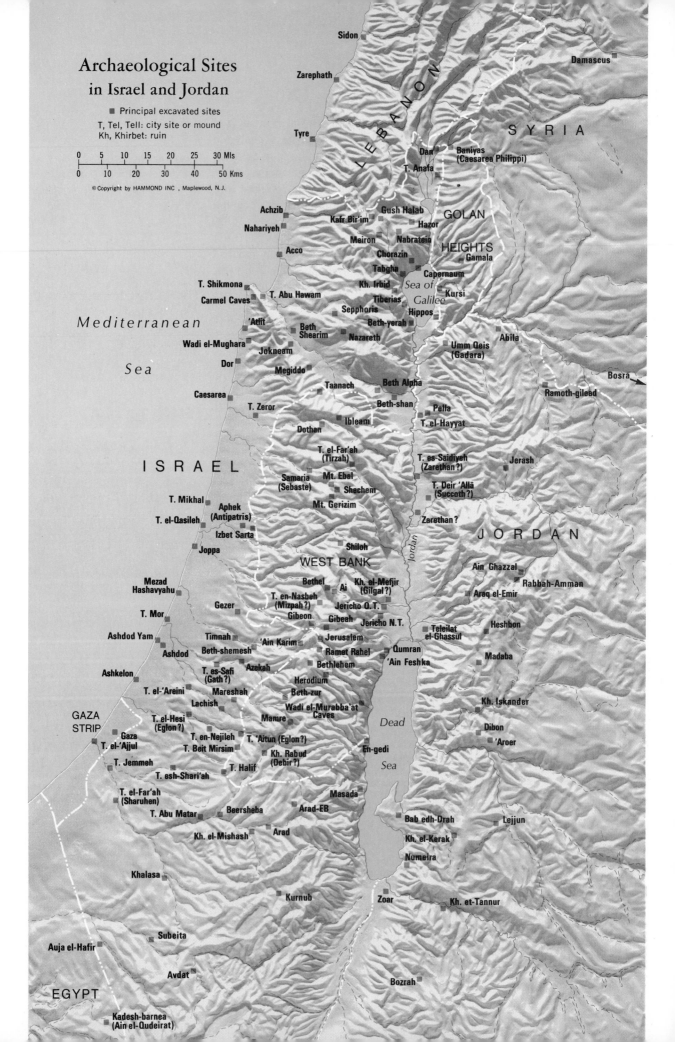

Archaeological Sites
in Israel and Jordan

■ Principal excavated sites
T, Tel, Tell: city site or mound
Kh, Khirbet: ruin

0 5 10 15 20 25 30 Mls
0   10   20   30   40   50 Kms

© Copyright by HAMMOND INC., Maplewood, N.J.

Mediterranean

Sea

ISRAEL

GAZA
STRIP

EGYPT

LEBANON

SYRIA

GOLAN

HEIGHTS

Sea of
Galilee

WEST BANK

JORDAN

Jordan

Dead

Sea

Sidon
Zarephath
Tyre
Damascus
Dan
T. Anafa
Baniyas
(Caesarea Philippi)
Achzib
Nahariyeh
Kafr Bir'im
Gush Halab
Hazor
Meiron
Nabratein
Acco
Chorazin
Gamala
Tabgha
Capernaum
Kh. Irbid
Kursi
T. Shikmona
Tiberias
T. Abu Hawam
Carmel Caves
Sepphoris
Hippos
'Atlit
Beth-yerah
Beth
Shearim
Nazareth
Abila
Wadi el-Mughara
Jokneam
Umm Qeis
(Gadara)
Dor
Megiddo
Caesarea
Taanach
Beth Alpha
Bosra
T. Zeror
Beth-shan
Pella
Ramoth-gilead
Dothan
Ibleam
T. el-Hayyat
T. el-Far'ah
(Tirzah)
Samaria
(Sebaste)
Mt. Ebal
T. es-Saidiyeh
(Zarethan ?)
Jerash
Shechem
T. Deir 'Alla
(Succoth ?)
T. Mikhal
Mt. Gerizim
Zarethan ?
T. el-Qasileh
Aphek
(Antipatris)
Izbet Sarta
Joppa
Shiloh
Ain Ghazzal
Bethel
Kh. el-Mefjir
(Gilgal ?)
Rabbah-Amman
Mezad
Hashavyahu
Ai
T. en-Nasbeh
(Mizpah ?)
Gezer
Gibeon
Jericho O.T.
Areq el-Emir
Gibeah
Jericho N.T.
T. Mor
Heshbon
Jerusalem
Teleilat
el-Ghassul
Ashdod Yam
Timnah
'Ain Karim
Ramet Rahel
Qumran
Madaba
Ashdod
Beth-shemesh
Bethlehem
'Ain Feshka
Ashkelon
Azekah
T. es-Safi
(Gath ?)
Herodium
T. el-'Areini
Mareshah
Beth-zur
Kh. Iskander
Lachish
Wadi el-Murabba'at
Caves
T. el-Hesi
(Eglon ?)
Mamre
Dibon
Gaza
T. en-Nejileh
T. 'Aitun (Eglon ?)
En-gedi
'Aroer
T. el-'Ajjul
T. Beit Mirsim
T. Jemmeh
Kh. Rabud
(Debir ?)
T. Halif
T. el-Far'ah
(Sharuhen)
T. esh-Shari'ah
Masada
T. Abu Matar
Beersheba
Arad-EB
Bab edh-Drah
Lejjun
Kh. el-Mishash
Arad
Kh. el-Kerak
Numeira
Khalasa
Zoar
Kh. et-Tannur
Kurnub
Subeita
Auja el-Hafir
Avdat
Bozrah
Kadesh-barnea
(Ain el-Qudeirat)

The pioneers did their work exceedingly well, and many have entered into the fruits of their labors.

Among those who have entered into these fruits and who are themselves laboring are archaeological volunteers. Until 1955 excavations in the Middle East tended to depend upon local native labor. When he undertook to excavate at Masada, however, Yigael Yadin of Hebrew University in Jerusalem issued an international call for volunteer help. Of course, Yadin had a core of professionals, but he needed a good deal more manpower. The response to his invitation was overwhelming. Thousands from twenty-eight countries applied. Far from being paid, these people had to pay their own way to Israel. Volunteer help is now used on a number of Israeli excavations, but the idea was picked up and developed by several digs in Israel sponsored by the American Schools of Oriental Research. The Gezer Expedition was the first to turn from the idea of a purely professional work force to a training dig to seek to instruct the volunteers in various phases of excavation technique. When the Joint Expedition to Tell el-Hesi went into the field for the first time in 1970 it did so with two purposes: "to recover the occupational history of one of the most famous sites in Israel," and "to offer students, younger scholars and others an opportunity to obtain field experience in archaeology under the direction of talented teachers and skilled archaeologists." The now completed work at Khirbet Shema', Meiron, Gush Halav, Nabratein and Caesarea, and ongoing work at Sepphoris and Tel Miqne, all projects of the American Schools, employ the same volunteer concept. In addition to professional field archaeologists these digs are also staffed by specialized geologists, biologists, anthropologists, ethnologists, potters, surveyors, photographers, artists and even computer experts. The volunteer groups are made up of undergraduate and graduate students, professors, ministers, rabbis, teachers, businessmen and persons retired from various professions. All must be at least eighteen; the oldest so far was seventy. A total group, professionals and volunteers, may range from thirty to one hundred and twenty.

One of the more obvious gains of all this long development in archaeology has been an extensive recovery of the Biblical context. This is to be seen both in our present knowledge of surrounding and often more antique cultures (the Hebrews were relative latecomers to the ancient scene) and in specific materials bearing directly on certain Biblical passages or events. For example, among the tablets Layard recovered from Nineveh was one containing a portion of an account of a deluge bearing close resemblance to the flood story told in Genesis. Subsequent discoveries of other portions of this tablet and other inscriptions from Mesopotamia have established that this is a very old story indeed, dating back in written form to at least 1800 B.C. and in oral form far older than that. When and how the Hebrews came in contact with the story is not clear, but this and other evidence points to the Mesopotamian origins of the Hebrews and shows earlier forms which they took and used for their own purposes. Likewise, other recovered documents such as the *Wisdom of Amenemope* from Egypt and the *Code of Hammurabi* from Babylon show striking parallels to certain passages in Proverbs and Leviticus respectively. Such discoveries in no way diminish the religious value of the Bible, but go far to show the Hebrews in living dialogue with their neighbors.

The same is true of certain artistic and architectural materials. The parallel between ivory decorations found at Samaria and Megiddo and those found elsewhere in the Middle East, as at Nimrud, Damascus and various sites in Lebanon, again shows the Biblical story in a dynamic context. This is further born out by the specific Biblical statement that Solomon, among others, hired Tyrian architects and builders to construct his new Jerusalem.

Typical Day at an Archaeological Excavation

4:00 A.M. — Rising bell

4:30 — Light breakfast

5:00 - 8:30 — First session of work on the site: digging, sifting, hauling dirt and stones, field analyses; survey team examining nearby area; specialists and recorders at work in camp.

8:30 — Second breakfast

9:00 - 1:00 — Second session of work on the site.

1:00 — Lunch

2:00 - 3:00 — Rest

3:00 - 5:30 — Study of problems in field and camp; washing and "reading" of pottery; balk drawing; clean up camp.

5:30 — Showers, wash clothes

6:00 — Dinner

7:00 - 8:00 — Evening lecture; free time for relaxation, letters, music; staff reviews the day and plans for next day.

9:00 P.M. — Lights out

Clay tablet from Nineveh contains an account of a legendary flood similar to that told in Genesis.

15

Obelisk of Shalmaneser III found at Nimrud commemorates his victories west of the Euphrates. Among the monarchs doing obeisance is Jehu of Israel.

But the recovery of the Biblical context never stops, and the finds can open up new vistas for understanding the Bible. For example, in 1974 Italian archaeologists working in the dusts of Tell Mardikh in northern Syria discovered a royal archive in a hitherto unknown palace that dated between 2600-2250 B.C. The archive is now known to count 17,000 clay tablets, about twenty percent of which are written in a language never encountered before. The texts and other finds establish that Tell Mardikh is none other than ancient Ebla, known from other ancient texts, though its location had always escaped detection.

Now it is clear that ancient Eblaite is a Semitic language, kin to Hebrew and Canaanite, though written in cuneiform ideogams. Proper names commonplace in the Hebrew scriptures seem to have been found in the Eblaite tablets, suggesting that these names have a history in northern Syria. It is even possible that religious and other institutions known in the Bible and in Canaanite civilization may be reflected in these early documents. If so, then the history of the region — and the context of Abraham — must be rewritten to reflect these finds.

Likewise records of non-Israelite monarchs found elsewhere throw new light on situations or events mentioned or in some cases merely suggested in the Biblical narrative. A recovered text of Shalmaneser III tells of the 2,000 chariots and 10,000 foot soldiers Ahab the Israelite was able to employ against him on the battlefield at Qarqar in 853 B.C. The Black Obelisk of this same Assyrian king gives us the only contemporary picture we have of a Hebrew monarch, and in so doing reflects the devastating effect of Jehu's revolt and its destruction of the Omride house in Israel. Ahab may have been able to put massive armaments in the field against the Assyrians, but Jehu is shown on his hands and knees bowing as a vassal before this same Shalmaneser.

The capture of Samaria in 721 B.C. and its aftermath are described in the annals of Sargon II, recovered from the palace at Khorsabad; and Sennacherib's Prism, found at Nineveh, tells how he shut up Hezekiah, King of Judah, in Jerusalem "like a bird in a cage." This refers to events of an Assyrian campaign in 701 B.C. which included the siege of Lachish, one of the southern fortresses protecting Judah's capital. When Layard unearthed Sennacherib's throne room in 1849 he found a large relief on the wall depicting the siege, capture and destruction of Lachish. And from Lachish itself has come dramatic evidence of a later attack on that fortress. The famous Lachish Letters, eighteen inscribed potsherds found in the rooms of the demolished city gate there, are from a signal post linking Lachish with Azekah, another of the fortresses guarding this frontier. "The signal fires of Azekah can no longer be seen," says one of these writings on potsherds. This meant that Lachish was next, and then only Jerusalem remained. The year was 586 and the days of the Kingdom of Judah were numbered.

Illustrations could be multiplied, but need not be done so here. Most such matters bearing upon the Biblical story are included within these pages.

Before turning to that narrative, however, we must consider no matter how briefly the complex and controversial question of the relationship between archaeology and the Bible. This is really a question about history and the Bible. The issue is made difficult by the fact that Biblical writers see the historical process as a medium through which and in which God reveals himself and accomplishes his purposes. Moreover, while the Bible is not a history book, there are large sections devoted to historical narration and the general thrust of the book is or appears to be sequential. If these two matters— the theological and the sequential narration — are separated they can be dealt with more easily.

The theological view that history is a medium of revelation is one with which the archaeologist *as* archaeologist cannot deal and the historian *as* historian cannot verify. To say that God is acting in history is a confession of faith and as such can be pointed to and explored by the historian. But as the cause of events it can neither be affirmed or denied by the historian, who must work within his own framework. And for that matter so must the theologian. This seems to mean, among other things, that the recovery of various details of ancient life which tend to confirm the historical narrative of the Bible do not at the same time "prove" the worth of Sacred Scripture for faith. Faith, in a Biblical sense, would appear to arise on a different basis. God, in short, is neither affirmed nor contained by historical methodology.

But there is certainly a large and important area in which the work of archaeologists and historians is related to the Bible. If, for example, the recovery of ancient Middle Eastern life had shown that the Biblical writers were either incorrect in what history they do report or had sought to falsify it, there would be serious repercussions concerning the veracity of other Biblical statements. Just the opposite has in fact happened. Archaeological recovery of ancient life has tended at point after point to show with what faithfulness the Biblical writers recorded contemporary events. This indicates that the Bible as a primary historical document is a trustworthy guide to those events and situations which it describes. This does not, it needs to be repeated, speak about the Bible as a faith document. Faith is its own justification.

The archaeologist recovers the raw data of history and interprets it in light of other excavated materials. As a historian the archaeologist may also begin to piece together the ebb and flow of events in light of economic, political, social and other causes and effects. An archaeologist who is also a theologian may deal with a very different kind of causation attributed to events by Biblical writers, who saw the world dominated by the active presence of God.

It may seem arbitrary to some to make such a sharp distinction between these three roles: archaeologist, historian and theologian. There is, of course, overlap, since the historian, to interpret correctly, must be sensitive to the kind of material being studied. For example, one who has no feel for the theological nature of the Bible is unlikely to understand its historical value. The archaeologist, on the other hand, while having a vast store of knowledge from many disciplines, cannot be influenced by historical theories or theological positions. Of the three roles, that of the archaeologist is perhaps the most neutral, yet it does not exist in isolation. At the same time it is very important to keep these three roles separate to preserve both the proper character of the Bible as a faith statement inviting others to that same faith and of scholarly historical reconstruction which must be as objective as possible.

With these things in mind we turn to the story narrated in Scripture.

Stylistic changes in everyday pottery such as oil lamps help date excavated materials. The four-spouted lamp (left) is from Patriarchal times; the Herodian lamp (right) is typical of Jesus' day.

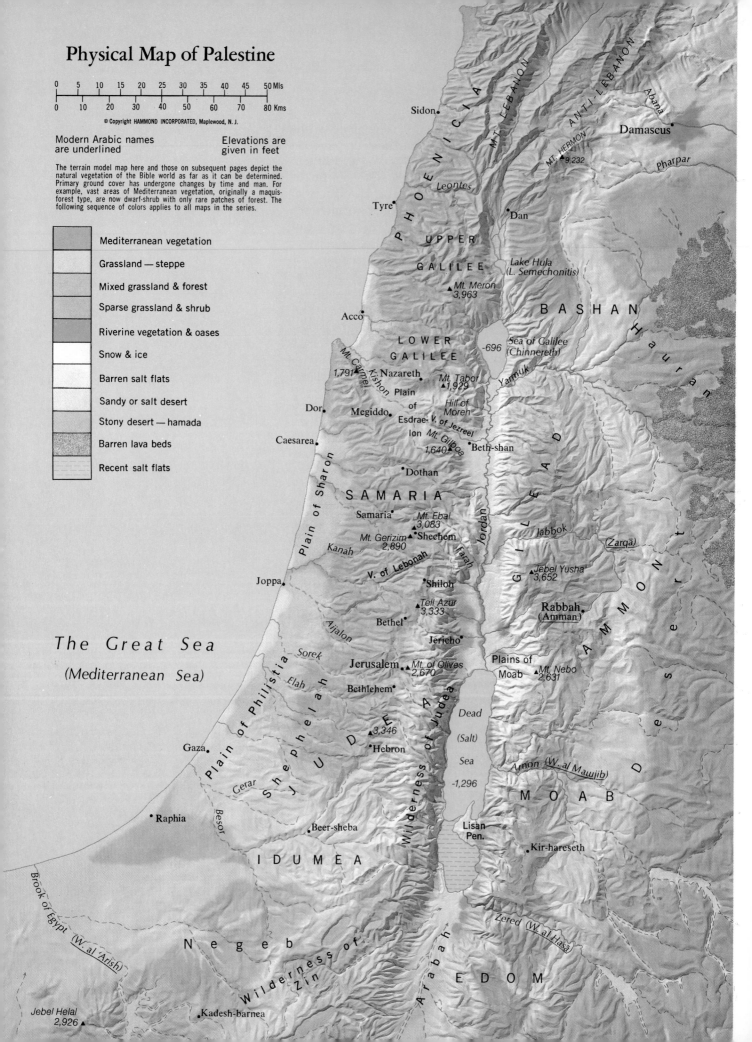

Physical Map of Palestine

0 5 10 15 20 25 30 35 40 45 50 Mls
0   10   20   30   40   50   60   70   80 Kms

© Copyright HAMMOND INCORPORATED, Maplewood, N.J.

Modern Arabic names
are underlined

Elevations are
given in feet

The terrain model map here and those on subsequent pages depict the
natural vegetation of the Bible world as far as it can be determined.
Primary ground cover has undergone changes by time and man. For
example, vast areas of Mediterranean vegetation, originally a maquis-
forest type, are now dwarf-shrub with only rare patches of forest. The
following sequence of colors applies to all maps in the series.

Mediterranean vegetation

Grassland — steppe

Mixed grassland & forest

Sparse grassland & shrub

Riverine vegetation & oases

Snow & ice

Barren salt flats

Sandy or salt desert

Stony desert — hamada

Barren lava beds

Recent salt flats

The Great Sea

(Mediterranean Sea)

Sidon

Damascus

P H O E N I C I A

MT. LEBANON

ANTI-LEBANON

Abana

MT. HERMON
9,232

Pharpar

Tyre

UPPER
GALILEE

Dan

Leontes

Lake Hula
(L. Semechonitis)

B A S H A N

Acco

Mt. Meron
3,963

LOWER
GALILEE

Sea of Galilee
(Chinnereth)

-696

Hauran

Mt. Carmel
1,791

Nazareth

Kishon

Mt. Tabor
1,929

Plain
of

Hill of
Moreh

Yarmuk

Dor

Megiddo

Esdrae-
lon

V. of Jezreel

Mt. Gilboa
1,640

Beth-shan

G
I
L
E
A
D

Caesarea

Dothan

S A M A R I A

Jordan

Jabbok

Zarqā

Samaria

Mt. Ebal
3,083

Mt. Gerizim
2,890

Shechem

Kanah

Farah

Jebel Yusha
3,652

Plain of Sharon

V. of Lebonah

Joppa

Shiloh

Rabbah
(Amman)

A
M
M
O
N

Tell Azur
3,333

Bethel

Ajalon

Sorek

Jericho

Jerusalem

Mt. of Olives
2,670

Plains of
Moab

Mt. Nebo
2,631

Bethlehem

Elah

Plain of Philistia

Shephelah

J
U
D
E
A

Wilderness of Judea

Dead
(Salt)
Sea
-1,296

Gaza

Gerar

3,346

Hebron

Arnon (W. al Maujib)

M O A B

Besor

Raphia

Beer-sheba

Lisan
Pen.

Kir-hareseth

I D U M E A

Brook of Egypt (W. al 'Arish)

N e g e b

Wilderness of Zin

Arabah

Zered (W. al Hasa)

E D O M

Jebel Helal
2,926

Kadesh-barnea

2 HOLY LAND HORIZONS

The Holy Land is full of meaning for Jews, Christians and Moslems. This land and its peoples were the objects of the Patriarchs' travels, the prophets' pleadings and the priests' supplications. Here David ruled, Solomon built and the Assyrians and Babylonians destroyed. In those hills and valleys the Maccabees struggled heroically and successfully against the Syrian Greeks, and their latter-day successors, the Zealots, fought as heroically yet vainly against the might of Rome. The lakeside and hills of Galilee echoed to the words of the Man of Nazareth, and the dust of the Samaritan roads measured his stride as he was drawn inexorably toward Jerusalem. It was also to Jerusalem, according to tradition, that Mohammed later came to pray, and it was from here that he sprang into heaven to talk with God. So many memories and so much meaning for so much of mankind, past and present, are drawn from and packed into the Holy Land.

It may be one of the ironies of history that this place which has been the setting of enormously significant events should itself be tiny. Palestine, to use the common name that transcends and includes political, religious and cultural distinctions over many centuries, is at the eastern end of the Mediterranean Sea. Its historical function has been as a land bridge between Asia and Africa. The earliest known great urban cultures arose on the flanks of Palestine, one in Mesopotamia, that fertile area lying between the Tigris and Euphrates rivers, and a second in Egypt on the banks of the Nile. An arc can be traced between ancient capitals beginning at the Patriarchal city of Ur near the Persian Gulf and moving northwest to Haran and then south by southwest through Syria and Palestine until one comes finally to the broad, black land of the Nile Delta and Egypt, which stretches like a narrow fertile ribbon along the Nile. This half-moon of arable land which is surrounded by bleak desert and high mountain is known as the Fertile Crescent. From that point where it breaks out of the Lebanon Mountains near Dan below Mount Hermon to the place where it is swallowed up by the desert south of the springs of Beersheba, it is just over 150 miles long. This is Palestine. The average width of this "bridge," bounded on the west by the sea and on the east by the massive earthquake scar we know as the Jordan Valley, is about 45 miles. The total land area is approximately that of New Hampshire. Apart from the Canaanites none of its peoples exercised much cultural influence in the Ancient World. Except for a flicker of time under David and Solomon the area had little influence on the changing of empires. Yet out of this minute space, having little cultural or political impact, have come spiritual forces that have decisively shaped the course of history.

It is difficult for one who has not spent much time in the land to appreciate its extraordinary contrasts. The green hills of Galilee, which are capable of producing two crops a year, seem worlds away from the shimmering golds and browns of the harsh desert south of Hebron in Judea. There are no rivers of agricultural importance; the creek beds, dusty in summer, capture the runoff of winter rains and can become terrifying torrents of water. Land burned and parched most of the year is ablaze with color when the spring

Goats deep in the central hills of Samaria. This forbidding area, crisscrossed by small, deep valleys, has ever been the habitat of shepherds.

flowers appear. In this compact area stark hills suddenly give way to lush valleys. And everywhere, especially in Samaria and the Judean highlands, there are stones, boulders and rocky outcroppings, ever a challenge to the farmer, ancient and modern.

Yet the geography of the area, so important for the events which took place there, is easy to remember. The Holy Land is divided into three zones north to south and four west to east. North to south there are Galilee, Samaria and Judea; west to east the divisions are the coastal plain, the highlands, the Jordan rift and the Transjordanian heights.

Galilee is divided into two parts: Upper and Lower Galilee. Upper Galilee played a small role in Biblical history. It is a mountain plateau between 2,000 and 3,900 feet above sea level which abruptly breaks the Lebanon and Anti-Lebanon mountain ranges. The highest peak in Palestine is in Upper Galilee. Mount Meron (Jebel Jermaq) rises to 3,963 feet but does not compare with the Lebanons, which tower between 6,000 and 10,000 feet. In Biblical times Upper Galilee was heavily forested; still its valleys provided easy west-east access from Tyre and Sidon to Damascus. This was not only a factor in the economic prosperity of these cities but also partly explains why the northerners sought tenaciously to hold the region against the Israelites. In this area are Abel-beth-maacah, a crossroads and cultic center; Dan, one of the royal cities of Jeroboam; and Caesarea Philippi, a New Testament city. These as well as Merom and Hazor have a place in the Bible story. But on the whole the region was inaccessible to peoples living to the south.

Indeed, in the Bible "Galilee" almost always refers to Lower Galilee. This is exclusively so in the New Testament. Lower Galilee, the plateau area south of a line drawn from Acco to the northern end of the Sea of Galilee, rarely exceeds 1,500 feet above sea level. It is an extremely attractive and fecund region, having for centuries provided olives, wheat and grapes, the staple foods of Biblical times. Its most significant feature is a great valley running northwest by southeast from the Bay of Haifa to the Jordan River. This broad valley, known by its Greek name of Esdraelon, produces marvelous crops of wheat and is the breadbasket of Palestine. In its center, where it is almost fifteen miles wide, sits rounded Mount Tabor, majestic in its solitude. Some say this is the scene of Christ's Transfiguration. Biblical memories, in fact, haunt the valley. The villages and towns in the north of the valley were the locale of most of the ministry of Jesus. Here are Nazareth, Cana and Nain — Jewish centers in the midst of a largely Gentile population. A little farther northeast is the Sea of Galilee, a breathtaking blue basin twelve miles long and six miles wide whose surface is 696 feet below sea level. On its western or Galilean shore are Capernaum, Magdala, Chorazin and other towns known to the Gospels.

South of the valley, literally ringing its southern rim, are the "cities of the plain," important in the Old Testament. Among them are Megiddo, Taanach and Ibleam. The major coast road from Egypt, the Way of the Sea, turned inland through a pass between Megiddo and Taanach in order to bypass Mount Carmel and give access to the valley and to roads northward. This pass, fought over from pre-Israelite days to the First World War, is dominated by the mound of ancient Megiddo, known in Rev. 16:16 as Armageddon.

In the southeast Esdraelon is joined to the Jordan Valley by the three-mile-wide Valley of Jezreel. In a little over ten miles this valley drops rapidly from 300 feet above sea level to some 820 feet below sea level at the point where it joins the Jordan rift. The southern rim of this corridor is formed

The Plain of Esdraelon looking north toward Mount Tabor.

by Mount Gilboa where Saul and his sons were slain, and at the southeastern end is Beth-shan, where the Philistines hung the fallen king's headless body on the city walls. At the other end of this little valley, commanding a spectacular view of the rapid fall in elevation, is Jezreel itself, the winter home of the Israelite Omride kings, where Jezebel met her terrible death.

Until recent times swamps and their accompanying diseases were a problem in the Plain of Esdraelon. Rain runs off the surrounding hills onto the poorly drained floor of the valley. The River Kishon, scarcely more than a stream most of the year, further contributes to the marshy character of the central and northwestern portions of the plain, as Sisera found on one famous occasion in a battle with Deborah (Judges 5:19). Another matter which some considered unfortunate, but others prized highly, is the fact that the valley was a broad highway running from the center of Canaanite culture north of Mount Carmel (where Tyre and Sidon are located) right into the heart of Israel. Along this route came trade and ideas and people, not all of which were welcomed by those such as Elijah who struggled to keep Israelite religion free from foreign elements.

Samaria, the central hill country, is, like Galilee, divided by nature into two distinct areas. The northern part is lower than the southern and, although crisscrossed by extensive valleys, is less fruitful than the higher plateau to the south. The valleys do have the advantage — or disadvantage! — of making communications easy. It was this ease of movement combined with the security of the forest that early drew numbers of people to this part of the hill country. Indeed, ancient urban development was widespread in northern Samaria. Many famous cities grew up at the junction of major roads: Tirzah at the head of the Wadi Farah which gave access eastward to the Jordan Valley and the heights beyond; Dothan on the Plain of Dothan which leads northward into the Esdraelon; Shechem, the oldest and most important of all, which commanded the strategic east-west pass between Mount Ebal and Mount Gerizim. Curiously, none of these cities was easily defended. It was not until the founding of the city of Samaria in the ninth century that a truly formidable fortress controlled a major route in the area. Samaria was also the only city in Palestine originally founded by Israelites.

The southern plateau of Samaria is mountainous and rises to over 3,000 feet near Bethel. Both on the east and the west, however, the edges of the plateau are deeply scarred by creeks which in the winter cause heavy erosion. These difficult approaches offered military security. Moreover, until into the Biblical period, the steep hills and valleys were heavily forested. As trees were felled and land gradually laid open the area became famous for its crops. The soil of southern Samaria, among the most fertile in the land, produced bountiful harvests of grains in the valleys, and the denuded, terraced hillsides became renowned for their olives.

Among the more important Biblical centers in this area are Shiloh and Bethel. It was in Shiloh that the Israelites kept the Ark of the Covenant. And it was at Bethel, on the main north-south highland road that Jeroboam built one of his two royal shrines, the one at which Amos was later to prophesy.

Judea is a place of startling contrasts. The fertility of its soil, particularly at its highest elevation around the ancient capital, Hebron, is so striking that the Bible speaks of it as "the land of milk and honey." The reference is not to cows and bees, but to the nectar of grapes and to other crops which flourished in abundance. On the other hand, the desolation of the Wilderness of Judea, that desert east of the watershed, is unspeakable. In less than

The verdant Esdraelon Valley with the Galilee hills in the background. This "breadbasket" of the ancient Holy Land also served as a highway for the influx of new peoples and ideas.

A cluster of dates suggests the richness and plenty of well-watered date palm plantations such as those at Jericho.

21

fifteen miles the elevation drops more than 4,000 feet. The soft limestone is shredded by canyons, some quite deep, as the winter rains race toward the Dead Sea. At hardly any time in its history has this area supported human settlement. From time to time it has sheltered rebels of various kinds, and monks as well as shepherds who still lead their flocks through the sparse country in search of food. Here David fled Saul. Here Bar-Kochba's few remaining men hid from the relentless Romans. Here the monks of Qumran hid their precious scrolls which were found almost twenty centuries later.

Nature has not provided a very clear dividing line between Judea and Samaria. The line is mostly political, although a small strip (about ten miles north to south) settled by the tribe of Benjamin, lies beween the two. Structurally, however, it is a part of Judea and forms a sort of west-east route from Beth-horon through Jerusalem down to Jericho. This is virtually the only such route in the region, and fortress Jerusalem commands it at that point where it crosses the north-south road running down the spine of the highlands. This means that Jerusalem, although less than ten miles from Samaria, is the strategic center of Judea. Hebron, farther south, is the geographic center, but it never had the crucial importance of Jerusalem.

Towns and villages strung out along these various routes have played an important role in Biblical history. Between Beth-horon and Jerusalem are the cities of the Gibeonites, who tricked Joshua into an alliance. Four miles south of Jerusalem is Bethlehem, and only a few miles farther along the highland road is Hebron. Eighteen miles south of Hebron, where the rainfall is greatly diminished and the land semiarid, is Beer-sheeba, an outpost at the edge of the Negeb Desert.

The northern Negeb as it gives way to the foothills of Judea.

22

Unlike Galilee and Samaria, Judea was relatively isolated in Biblical times. Flanked on two sides by harsh desert and on the other two by mountainous country inhospitable to armies, the people of the area needed only to fortify certain passes and valleys to their northwest and southwest. This Solomon undertook to do on a vast scale.

East to west the Holy Land divides into four natural zones: the coastal plain, the highlands, the Jordan rift and the Transjordanian heights. The most prominent feature of the Palestinian coast is Mount Carmel, a limestone promontory which projects like a thumb into the Mediterranean Sea. Carmel, where Elijah contested with the priests of Baal, breaks the coast into two parts. North of the mountain high cliffs reach to the rocky coastline, and there are many inlets which provided adequate and occasionally good harbors for the small merchantmen of ancient times. Seaports with vast commercial connections grew up. Among these were Tyre, originally an island, and Sidon, the home of Jezebel. This area north of Mount Carmel was the heart of Phoenician culture and had widespread influence in the Ancient Near East, including the early centuries of the Hebrew monarchy. The most famous export of the area was purple cloth, the dye of which was made from seashells unique to the coast there. So rich was this color that from that day to this purple has signified royalty.

South of Mount Carmel the coastline is smooth all the way to Egypt and the coastal plain rises gradually into the gently flowing foothills. There are no natural harbors worthy of note. At Joppa a series of rocks formed a basin of sorts, but in anything but the gentlest winds these same rocks became a hazard to the unwieldy ships. Joppa — and thus Palestine — was bypassed by ocean trade. The Mediterranean, a broad avenue of commerce for so many ancient peoples, was a barrier to the inhabitants of Palestine.

Twenty miles south of Mount Carmel the narrow coastal lands of Dor open into the wider Plain of Sharon. In Old Testament times Sharon attracted few settlers. The sea washed up vast amounts of sand. Mouths of the small rivers choked, waters backed up and the land was swampy. Moreover, there were thick forests of stout oaks. The Way of the Sea turned inland at Beth-dagon, ran through Aphek, then northward to Yehem and the pass between Megiddo and Taanach. It thus effectively bypassed Sharon. By the time of the birth of Jesus the swamps had been drained and Herod the Great had built his wonderful artificial harbor at Caesarea. The area became an economic asset and was famous, as it still is, for its orange groves.

The Valley of Aijalon, at the southern extreme of the Plain of Sharon, provides access through the hills to Beth-horon and thence by a circuitous route south and eastward to Jerusalem and Jericho. It was here that Joshua and his Hebrews defeated a coalition of five kings while the sun stood still. South of this valley the coastal district is known as the Plain of Philistia. Unlike Sharon this area was densely populated in Biblical times, partly because of its generous fields of barley and wheat, and partly because the Way of the Sea, the most lucrative trade route between Egypt and Mesopotamia, ran through it. After the thirteenth century B.C. this plain was the seat of Philistine power.

Inland from the Philistine plain are the gently rolling hills of the Shephelah. This was the main area of contention between the Hebrews and the Philistines, and it was from this direction that Jerusalem, and thus the heart of Judea, was most open to attack. Here in the valleys of the Sorek and of Elah, Samson contended against his enemies and David fought Goliath. And also in this

The smooth shoreline and low coastal plain are broken by rocks at ancient Joppa (now Jaffa) and buildings at the modern city of Tel Aviv.

area the Israelite kings beginning with Solomon, or perhaps David, built and sought to maintain a fortification line anchored in great walled cities such as Libnah, Azekah and Lachish.

The Shephelah is attractive to the eye, and its gentle hills were in Biblical times, as today, very productive. Its dense population settled there for strategic reasons, but also for its grain, wine, olives and sycamore trees. It was also coveted as a buffer zone between the weakest point in Judah's defenses and the cities of the Philistines, which had no mountains to protect them. The hills themselves are of chalk and soft limestone. The more rounded hills of the eastern part are covered by a hard layer of lime and are less suited to agriculture.

In ancient times the Brook of Egypt, just below Gaza, marked the southern end of the Philistine plain and also the border between Palestine and Egypt. The distance from Mount Carmel to the Brook of Egypt and thus the length of the Palestinian coastal plain is a little over one hundred miles.

The central highlands of Palestine encompass both the hill country of Samaria and the hill country of Judea. These are part of a larger range of mountains running from Syria into the Sinai Peninsula and forming the western side of the Jordan Valley. From the lofty plateau of Upper Galilee there is a drop of almost 1,000 feet, sometimes by sheer cliff, to Lower Galilee. The land drops still more as the hills of Galilee slope down to the great plain. South of Jezreel the hills rise quickly again into the central highlands. A few miles from Dothan the height reaches 2,500 feet. Venerable Shechem, from very early times controlling the most important crossroad in Palestine, is nestled between Mount Ebal, 3,083 feet, and Mount Gerizim, 2,890 feet. The views from these mountains and others in the highlands is spectacular. Below lie green and brown valleys dotted here and there by square, flat-topped houses huddled together to form villages; more rarely a clump of trees is seen on a distant hillside. To the east, through the haze, the land plunges abruptly into the violet depths of the Jordan trench and toward the red-walled hills of Gilead which rise beyond. To the west, twenty-five miles away, is the shimmering Mediterranean, the sun reflecting off its waters like so many thousands of pieces of tinfoil dancing in the wind. Even from so low a hill as that of Samaria, 1,443 feet high, the sea is visible. It is said that in New Testament times mariners making their way through the azure blue waters just off the coast could see clearly the gleaming white temple to Augustus, which Herod the Great caused to be built on the summit of Samaria.

The land continues to rise, sliced here and there by splendid valleys, some of which, like Lebonah, were important parts of the stage on which the Biblical drama was played out. Around Hebron the highlands reach their highest plateau, over 3,300 feet, and begin their descent into the arid Negeb.

Because the Palestinian highlands are so narrow and because they form the western edge of the lowest geological rift on the face of the earth, they have a curious feature on their eastern side. The land falls off suddenly from the relatively cool and green uplands into a formidable, almost impenetrable wasteland and then into the rift itself. This precipitous drop east of the watershed is accompanied by staggering erosion, lack of trees, bushes and a rapid buildup in heat as one gets nearer the Jordan River and the Dead Sea. The Wilderness of Judea is the most terrible example of this sort of region in the entire country.

The central highlands were the first part of the land to be settled by the Hebrews and remained the heartland of Israel throughout the Biblical period. Along the ridge of the mountains was a road which ran from the Plain of Esdraelon to Hebron and beyond to Beer-sheba. In its course were many of

The Sea of Galilee, its surface 696 feet below sea level, lies between the rounded hills of Lower Galilee and the more abrupt slopes of the Transjordanian heights.

the great Biblical cities: Dothan, Samaria, Shechem, Shiloh, Bethel, Mizpah, Ramah, Jerusalem. For the most part the modern paved highway follows the route of the ancient way and at no point is ever far from it. While flanked by two more important trade routes of olden times, the Way of the Sea through Philistia and the King's Highway in Transjordan, the central highland road which made its way along the hills and through the valleys following the water divide gave Israel easy internal communications. Just before the time of Jesus, when the conflict between the Samaritans and the Jews became open hostility, many Jews of Galilee ceased to use this direct highland road to Jerusalem and traveled instead by a longer, much more difficult route through Transjordan. This way, bypassing Samaria, entered Jerusalem from the east and gave to Bethany a place of importance which it did not have before and has not had since.

The Jordan rift valley contains three lakes joined together by one of the most celebrated, if actually insignificant, rivers in the world — the Jordan. The river rises from various springs in the general region of snowcapped Mount Hermon (9,232 feet). Among these springs Dan and Paneas were particularly famous in Biblical times. Dan is the site of the northernmost of Jeroboam's two royal shrines. Excavations presently underway at Dan have unearthed the road into Jeroboam's city as well as the cultic center itself. Paneas is the Caesarea Philippi of the New Testament, the city near which Jesus withdrew with his disciples. It is no wonder that Jesus chose this place as a retreat for rest and reflection and for private instruction to his intimate circle of followers. One of earth's true garden spots, the abundant woods around Dan and Paneas are laced by numerous sparkling streams whose cold waters leap over rocks and occasional waterfalls until they come together to form the shallow, swift flowing Jordan.

Snow covers the slopes of Mount Hermon for most of the year. The summit is 9,232 feet above sea level.

A few miles south of Dan, the Jordan River flows into the Hula Basin, a marshy depression with a small lake at the southern end. The marshes have recently been drained and only a remnant of Lake Hula remains. The elevation of the watercourse here is 220 feet above sea level. In the next ten-mile section before the river enters the Sea of Galilee the valley floor drops 916 feet. The Sea of Galilee, around whose shores Jesus conducted the greater part of his ministry and from whose fishing boats he called many of his disciples, is scarcely mentioned in the Old Testament. The basalt rock which forms its basin apparently did not hold much attraction for Hebrew farmers, and it is well known that the ancient Israelites, aside from perhaps the tribe of Asher, were not highly skilled sailors. South of the Sea of Galilee the Jordan River winds its tortuous way some seventy miles through semijungle and marsh, dropping a final 600 feet before emptying into the Dead Sea.

In some places the Jordan Valley is as narrow as five miles and in others, near the southern end, as wide as fifteen miles. But its character does not change for its entire length. The river itself, only about seventy miles long as the crow flies, is actually over three times that long as it winds its serpentine way back and forth over the valley floor. On both sides it is enclosed by a narrow band of damp thickets which quickly give way to desolate badlands. At a few points the river inches near cliffs which occasionally collapse, effectively blocking the shallow stream for a time.

One of the sources of the Jordan River at Dan below Mount Hermon. From here the Jordan snakes its way downward through the great rift to empty into the Dead Sea 1,296 feet below sea level.

This kind of terrain made communications and trade with the Transjordan extremely difficult. Only at three places are there convenient — possible! — ways across the valley. About fifteen miles south of the Sea of Galilee the rift narrows somewhat where the Valley of Jezreel joins it from the west.

25

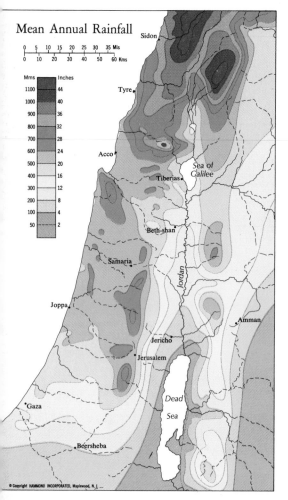

Mean Annual Rainfall

Here the great fortress of Beth-shan guarded the crossing and the entrance to Jezreel. A second crossing occurs a little below the middle of the rift. Here the Wadi Farah affords easy access from the Samaritan highlands, and the River Jabbok, descending from the east, provides a highway up the heights. The countryside in the vicinity offers little to support life, and no important city, ancient or modern, has ever stood in the immediate area of this crossing. Today the strategic Damiya Bridge spans the river at this point.

The most famous crossing of the Jordan is just north of the Dead Sea. Here the valley broadens considerably and for the most part its wind-eroded floor looks like something out of a science fiction movie. But there are two other more important points which should be noted. First, both the eastern and western hills can be fairly easily climbed here. To the west is Jerusalem. To the east is Amman, ancient Rabbah, long the chief city of Transjordan. Second, the freshwater springs which line the western shore of the Dead Sea extend into this region, and there is one of amazing output — Ain-es-Sultan, also known as the Spring of Elisha. For thousands of years this remarkable spring has watered a lush oasis widely known for its dates and bananas. It was hard by this spring that the oldest city in Palestine, perhaps the oldest in the world, came into being. This is Jericho, and Jericho grew and profited from the ford at the Jordan, now the site of the Allenby (Hussein) Bridge.

At the end of its winding journey the Jordan River empties into the Dead Sea, whose surface, at 1,296 feet below sea level, is the lowest spot on earth. The Lisan, a boot-shaped peninsula extending from the shore two-thirds of the way down its eastern side, divides the sea into two parts. The northern portion, about thirty miles long and slightly less than ten miles wide, is very deep — over 1,300 feet. The southern portion, on the other hand, is so shallow that it has recently dried up over most of its fifteen-mile length. Geologists believe that this part was dry land once before within the span of human memory. Indeed, the Biblical account of the destruction of Sodom and Gomorrah (Genesis 19:24-28) may well reflect memory of the moment when those cities disappeared beneath the waters at the southern end of the Dead Sea. As late as 1846 there was a ford across the Dead Sea very near the western tip of the Lisan, where the sea is only two and one-half miles wide. The striking fortress-mountain of Masada, the Gibraltar of the Dead Sea, commands the western end of this ancient ford.

High cliffs dominate both shores of the sea. On the east they come right up to the water but are pierced by several narrow gorges, the most spectacular

Temperature, rainfall, and relative humidity for selected stations

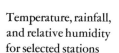

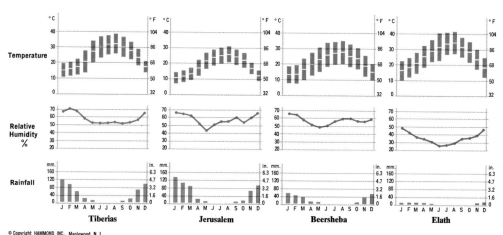

26

of which is that of the Arnon River. None of these gorges is passable, however, and movement from the sea up to Moab above is both arduous and unprofitable. Only near the Lisan is easy movement possible. Along the western shore, on the other hand, the cliffs are set back from the water's edge and the clear, fresh springs which dot the shoreline of the saltiest body of water on earth are joined by a road. One of these springs, Ain Feshkha, provided the basis of life for the famous Jewish monastic community at Qumran.

About midway down the western shore is another and more famous spring, that of En-gedi, The Spring of the Goats. In any setting En-gedi would be extraordinary but, pressed between the starkness of the Wilderness of Judea and the deathly solitude of the sea, its cool, bubbling waters tumbling over waterfalls are spectacular. "My beloved is to me a cluster of henna blossoms in the vineyards of En-gedi," says the poet of the Song of Songs (1:14) comparing his beloved to the beauty, pleasure and richness of the En-gedi oasis.

Today children frolic in the cool waters beneath the waterfalls of En-gedi, celebrated in the Song of Songs.

In contrast to the life-giving springs on its perimeter, the water of the Dead Sea itself is heavy, often motionless. The lack of any natural outlet except evaporation has caused the water to have an extremely high salt content. Indeed, the Bible refers to it as the Salt Sea. So high is this content that no marine life can exist in it, and the bather playing on its smooth surface finds his buoyancy so great that he cannot penetrate far beneath that surface. The water is, however, a rich source of minerals. Men of Biblical times extracted salt and gathered bitumen from the waters and seashore. Today various salts, including potash, are gathered in large quantities. This is particularly so near the shallow southern end of the sea where there are large, man-made evaporating pools. This strange body of water, devoid of life and seemingly useless, has become one of the major sources for minerals in modern Israel. It also provides one of the most breathtaking sights in the Holy Land. Its deep blue waters give way to aqua and then bright green below the Lisan. Sheer cliffs burned by the sun raise their sandy brown and magenta heights. Here and there a spring will intrude a speck of green. And almost always heat haze hangs over all, turning the farther hills shades of violet.

The Dead Sea near its southern end. Crystalline formations of salt and heavy concentrations of potash have been a source of wealth for centuries.

South of the sea the rift broadens and continues for one hundred hot, desert miles to the Gulf of Aqaba. This part of the rift, known as the Arabah, has little rainfall, no rivers and few springs. It was an important and much fought over region nonetheless. There were three reasons for this. First, it contains abundant deposits of copper; it was — and is — the center of extensive mining activity. Second, various trade routes, especially those from Arabia, passed near or through the Arabah. Third, at its southern end is the Red Sea port known in the Bible as Ezion-geber. All these prizes were sought after and were the causes of continuous strife between Israel and Edom. Solomon was able to secure effective control over the area and exploit its resources. He based a fleet on Ezion-geber and from there sought trade with East Africa, importing apes and baboons as well as gold and silver into Israel. Possession of the actual and potential riches of the Arabah was one of the major factors in Solomon's wealth. Hebrew kings after him sought to emulate his policies south of the Dead Sea. Some succeeded partially; most failed completely.

The Transjordanian heights are not a part of Palestine proper. (Palestine, west of the Jordan River, is called Cis-jordan to distinguish it from Transjordan.) Yet these high tablelands east of the river played an important role

27

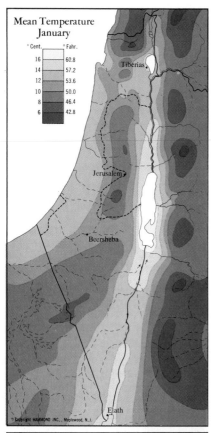

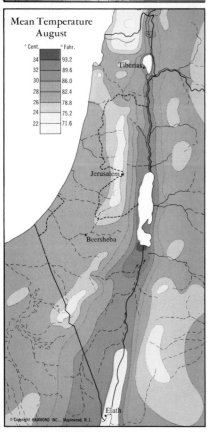

in the Bible story. The King's Highway ran along these heights. It was one of the two most important trade routes across the bridge between Asia and Africa, and it was coveted by Israel. The land over which it passed is high, sometimes rising above 5,600 feet and seldom lower than 2,300 feet above sea level. When one remembers the depth of the Jordan rift below sea level, the towering eastern cliffs become truly imposing. Their loftiness produces up to thirty inches of rain a year, and winter snows driven by icy winds whipping off the eastern deserts often block valleys. During the transitional seasons searing winds from the east can burn a path, destroying all before them and filling the air with dust. In spring and early summer, however, the fertile, well-watered ground produces abundant crops of various grains. To the east, where the plateau begins to fade into the seemingly endless desert, flocks of sheep and goats are driven before their nomadic masters. So it has been since Biblical times, when this area was famous for its crops, its flocks and its fierce men of the desert.

Four major rivers, the Yarmuk, Jabbok, Arnon and Zered cut deeply into the limestone of the heights, gathering up the winter waters from the very edges of the desert and dumping them into the Jordan River and Dead Sea. In antiquity two of these rivers formed natural boundaries: Bashan was north of the Yarmuk, and Edom was south of the Zered. Between these two were Gilead and Moab with no natural line dividing them. This was a source of continual strife between the Israelites, who once held effective control over Gilead, and the Moabites, who coveted the land.

Bashan, the northernmost part of the Transjordanian heights, lies just east of the Sea of Galilee, stretching from the Yarmuk almost to Damascus. This region benefits from the absence of western rain-blocking hills and the presence of the Hauran rise (Jebel ed Druze) to the east. The basalt slopes of the Hauran cut off scorching desert winds and allow rain-bringing west winds to reach Bashan. This and the fertility of the soil have long given Bashan a reputation for its grain and cattle (Deuteronomy 32:14). Indeed, so well known were the fat, waddling cattle of this country that Amos could sarcastically use this image to describe the lazy, prosperous women of Samaria, the "cows of Bashan" (Amos 4:1).

Bashan was, of course, a prized area in ancient times. But its isolation made invasion difficult and it enjoyed long periods of independence. Foreign rule came mostly from Damascus. Israel was able to hold parts of Bashan only occasionally. Even in the time of David the Israelites were unable to extend their sovereignty over the whole of this country.

South of the Yarmuk was Gilead, spanning the heights almost the entire eastern length of the Jordan Valley. The River Jabbok, which divides the area in two, provided the Israelites easy access from the highlands of Samaria. Near the Jabbok was the city of Mahanaim, a prominent site in the Biblical story from the time of David until the fall of the northern kingdom. It was traditionally a place of refuge for Hebrew kings who, for one reason or another, had been driven from their own country.

Gilead is the only region of Transjordan the Israelites were able to hold for long periods of time. Easy to reach, this land was similar to the hill country of Samaria, and the Israelite farmer who settled here could grow wheat and olives and produce wine from grapes. He was thus able to follow a familiar pattern of life. But the Hebrews in Gilead had to contend with the Ammonites, a desert people who established themselves in eastern Gilead after the fifteenth century B.C. The Ammonites, with their capital at Rabbah (New Testament Philadelphia, modern Amman), often successfully challenged Israelite rule east of the Jordan River.

Moab was a small kingdom, squeezed between Gilead in the north and the Zered in the south. This includes the entire eastern shore of the Dead Sea. But the heights beside the sea rise 4,300 feet above the water's surface. They are steep, wild in their sandstone configurations and inhospitable to the point of being unable to support human life. Moab is thus reduced to a small strip hardly thirty-five miles wide before its fields slip into the desert and become indistinguishable from the burning sands. Nonetheless, this tiny area, often diminished by loss of its northern portion around Mount Nebo and Heshbon, was a tenacious foe, and before the coming of the Romans few conquered and held it. Second Kings 1 and 3 tell of Israel's attempts to subdue the area. Interestingly, there is a Moabite parallel to some of the events described. While the Biblical writers put the best face possible on an Israelite military defeat, the Moabite Stone, found at Dibon in 1868, shows that the attempt to take that Moabite capital ended in utter disaster. At stake in the war was control over the King's Highway.

Edom, south of the Dead Sea, was Israel's implacable enemy. The Arabah, with its mines and trade routes, was the prize. There was little else of value in Edom. The desolate heights along the eastern side of the Dead Sea continue southward into Edom and, although the scenery is one of beautiful and even fantastic rock formations, there is little to encourage a settled population. Throughout antiquity, into and through Roman times, the peoples of Edom remained close to the desert: mobile, spartan, fierce. Petra, the rose red city south of the sea, became a place of great beauty and wealth in New Testament and later times. But all was based upon semi-piratical control of the southern end of the King's Highway. The Nabateans, who occupied Petra among other places, were skilled engineers and trapped desert rains behind dams, funneling them through channels into cities and onto fields. But the demise of Nabatean power and the breakdown of irrigation systems quickly returned the Arabah and the Negeb to their forbidding state.

A unique feature of Biblical religion is its stress on the importance of places as arenas of God's actions. Other religious writings may say that the divine is known by disclosures made in mythical time in the abode of the gods. The Bible, on the contrary, insists that God discloses himself in the lives of ordinary men and in places all can visit. Abraham at Hebron, Jacob's wrestling with an angel at the ford of the Jabbok River, Joshua's battle in the Aijalon Valley, David wandering a shepherd across the hills of Judah and as king in Jerusalem, the Babylonians before Lachish, Jesus' birth in Bethlehem — all religious events which the Bible identifies with specific places. *Who?* and *Where?* — not *What?* and *Why?* — are the Biblical questions. And the answers have to do with a people and a land. Not any people, but God's Chosen. Not any land, but the Holy Land.

The Arabah provided an easy north-south route in Biblical times, and contained invaluable copper mines.

Petra's houses, tombs and temples were carved out of solid rock by the Nabateans. This beautiful city flourished between 200 B.C. and A.D. 100.

Statue of a Sumerian priest from
Khafaje. The petaled kilt-like skirt
and clasped-hands pose are typical of
votive statues of the first dynasty of Ur.

The Mesopotamian homeland, a scene on the
outskirts of Baghdad. Life as it is
lived today on the banks of the Tigris
retains a semisedentary flavor.

3 ISRAEL'S EARLIEST MEMORIES

When the time came for Israel to set down an account of its origins, the writers did so by reciting from oral tradition the stories of the wanderings, lives and faith of its Patriarchs — Abraham, Isaac, Jacob and Joseph. The writers, while affirming that for Israel the creative impulse lay with God, record the germinal events in the lives of the Patriarchs. Such are the events which shaped the people of Israel: Abraham's faith in God's promises, Isaac's contending twins, Jacob's struggle with an angel and Joseph's miraculous rise to power in Egypt. In many and varied tales about wandering herdsmen a single theme emerges: God, out of his faithfulness, has created a people unto himself. So Israel understood its origins.

This is, of course, a theological understanding of Israel's earliest memories. And it is this theological reason which was responsible for preserving these stories for many centuries and for passing them on in oral and written form. The Bible is first and foremost a book about God, his will and his actions. Yet, as we observed earlier, God's will is never abstract and is always, from a Biblical point of view, acted out in the affairs of men. This means that while the Bible is indeed a religious statement it is also full of history. Thus we must read the Bible both theologically and historically at the same time. With this in mind, what then can we say about Israel's earliest memories?

It is clear that Israel understood its origins, however obscure in detail, to lie in the north, in Mesopotamia. This is the land from which Abraham came, and it was to that place that he sent seeking wives for his sons. Moreover, many of the stories which circulated around Hebrew campfires and later found their way into the Bible are unmistakably Mesopotamian in their form. This is particularly true of those stories in the opening chapters of Genesis in which ancient Israel confesses its faith about the creation of the world and the significance of man. Furthermore, the laws by which the early Hebrews governed themselves are closely paralleled by law codes and legal practices which archaeological discoveries have shown were in use in ancient Mesopotamia.

Frieze from Sumerian temple at Tell el-Obied shows cows being milked and butter being made. Shell and limestone figures in black bitumen. First half of the third millennium B.C.

It is also clear that Israel understood its forefathers to have been shepherds, semi-nomads who drove their flocks before them as they traversed the Fertile Crescent before finally settling in Canaan. Yet the story begins not in the desert, but in one of the greatest of the early cities — Ur. "Terah took Abram his son and Lot the son of Haran, his grandson, and Sarai his daughter-in-law, his son Abram's wife, and they went forth together from Ur of the Chaldeans to go into the land of Canaan; but when they came to Haran, they settled there" (Genesis 11:31).

Ur was an ancient and important city in lower Mesopotamia long before the young Abraham wandered its maze of streets. Like many before him, he could watch at the docks as sun-blackened sailors struggled to load and unload ships that had come up the Euphrates River from the broad waters of the Persian Gulf. In ancient days the river came right up to the towering walls, and children running along the massive bulwarks, fifty to ninety feet wide, could peer down from the battlements on a wonderful scene. Filled by the

The ziggurat at Ur with flight of steps restored. Only the lower platform of the original three-tiered monument survives.

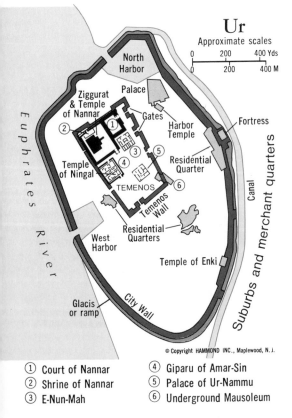

① Court of Nannar
② Shrine of Nannar
③ E-Nun-Mah
④ Giparu of Amar-Sin
⑤ Palace of Ur-Nammu
⑥ Underground Mausoleum

warm breezes, sails of varied and vivid colors contrasted sharply with the dull brown houses and lush green fields that stretched in every direction toward the horizon. Lining the river, tall palms swayed to a curious rhythm, while in the distance men splattered with mud were at their never ending job of keeping the irrigation canals clean and free flowing. Commerce and agriculture — these had been the lifeblood of the Sumerian city for centuries before the Hebrew patriarchs appeared.

Today the visitor to Ur is overwhelmed by the desolation of the place. Already in decline before Abraham's time, Ur suffered a fatal blow some five hundred years before the birth of Jesus, when the Euphrates disastrously shifted its course eleven miles eastward. The city, once a thriving metropolis, was finally abandoned. Irrigation canals as well as the old riverbed itself choked and filled as the relentless desert reclaimed all. Even the enormous ziggurat, that great three-tiered brick tower which had dominated the city for almost two thousand years, came to be little more than a mound in an endless grainy sea. Such was the sight that greeted the archaeologists when they came to that seemingly unpromising site. Yet in 1854 J. E. Taylor, British consul at Basra, recovered documents there establishing beyond question that this was once-glorious Ur. Even more startling was the work of Leonard Woolley and his colleagues from 1922 to 1934. From the hot, dusty mounds at Ur they excavated an awareness of the everyday life of one of the greatest commercial centers of antiquity.

Ur stood on a promontory between the Euphrates and a navigable canal and thus had two harbors. Unfortunately, the architects and engineers of Ur, deprived of stone, were forced to use mud brick and burnt brick. They therefore had to depend on massiveness for effect, and as a result, the city possessed a very stolid look. At its height some thirty-four thousand people lived in the four square miles within its walls. The suburbs, merchant quarters and other areas of metropolitan Ur pushed the total to over a quarter of a million persons. But the inner city was the vital center. Standing on a raised platform, the irregular, oblong inner city was surrounded by soaring burnt-brick walls. A steep ramp, or *glacis*, which descended twenty-five feet to the river both defended and supported the massive walls.

The surrounding fields interlaced with life-giving veins of clear water were necessary to the life of the city but did not account for its wealth or importance. Ur was a major manufacturing and commercial center. The abundant harvests provided for the laborers, artisans and merchant princes. But the pulse of the city and the sources of its treasures lay in its industry. Archaeologists at Ur found widespread evidence of home industries. A small family might form a manufacturing unit. There were numbers of much larger factories as well, turning out the woolen textiles for which the city was famous. As one might expect, there was a flourishing merchant class engaged in the shipment and transshipment of goods. Water transportation was cheap. More expensive donkey caravans fanned out in every direction. A bill of lading from about 2040 B.C. shows the cargo of one ship from the Persian Gulf to have included copper ore, gold, ivory, hardwoods, diorite and alabaster. Some of these items are not found in the Gulf region and suggest that Ur traded with a very wide area. Indeed, the workshops of Ur used lapis lazuli from the Pamir mountains beyond Persia, and jewelry from Ur has been found in the Nilgiri hills of southern India!

The houses of Ur were normally two-storied. On a hot night the family might sleep on the flat roof protected from the early morning sun by an awning. From the outside the mud brick houses presented a solid facade without windows — perhaps a measure of protection against the narrow, unsanitary

32

streets. But on the inside rooms surrounded an open courtyard which could often be pleasant with its brick paving and drains that collected rainwater into the middle of the square. Many of the houses excavated at Ur contained private chapels for the household gods, calling to mind the story of Rachel's stealing the *teraphim* from her father's house (Genesis 31:19-55). Written texts recovered at Nuzi, also in Mesopotamia, show that possession of these clay statues conferred rights of inheritance on the holder. It is easy to understand why Laban and his kinsmen pursued Rachel and Jacob with murderous intent.

When Abraham left Ur in his father's train, he was part of a general migration of peoples who moved through Mesopotamia sometime after 2200 B.C. Two centuries earlier Ur had lost its political influence and its economic domination of the lower plain. There was, moreover, a general collapse of urban culture over much of the Fertile Crescent. Times were not so good for merchants and caravaneers, and this group may well have included Terah, Abraham's father. Haran, in the northern reaches of the valley, offered greater opportunities and to this place Terah came with his clan. There they stayed until the father died. Abraham, now head of the clan and free to follow his own designs, turned south.

Molded Babylonian votive plaque of early second millennium B.C. is suggestive of the household gods referred to in Genesis 31:19.

By what routes and at what pace Abraham moved we are not told. The Bible says merely that Abraham with his retinue came to the land of Canaan, "to the place at Shechem" (Genesis 12:6). It is interesting to speculate as to Abraham's probable route into Canaan and to Shechem. From Haran he could have moved directly south to the oasis of Tadmor (Palmyra) and then on to Damascus. From Damascus Abraham, moving southwest, could have used the crossing on the Upper Jordan to enter Canaan by way of Hazor. Other routes are possible, however, such as a route that went through Ebla and Kadesh to Damascus.

Ebla, incidentally, had been a commercial center greater than Ur between 2600 and 2250 B.C. Recently 17,000 clay tablets were discovered at Ebla that chronicle the growth and destruction of a mighty Semitic city about the time of Abraham. It is too soon to say whether this city played a role in the Abraham cycle in Genesis, but some have seen King Ebrun of Ebla as the same as the Eber of Genesis 10:21-25.

Shechem was an important cultic center and the most strategic city in northern Canaan, although not the largest. From time to time it had opposed the will of its Egyptian overlords. On occasion it had paid dearly, as its excavated damaged gates still attest. Apparently Abraham did not tarry long at Shechem, nor even in Canaan. After brief sojourns near Bethel and at Moreh, famine drove him into Egypt where the ever faithful Nile offered food for his flocks.

Clay tablet from Ebla, circa 2400 B.C. It utilizes the cuneiform script developed by the Sumerians but is written in an archaic Semitic language.

Abraham was a man of considerable means even before he entered Egypt. His household included not only his own array of servants — slaves in his tents, shepherds, herdsmen, armed retainers — but also those of his nephew, Lot. Missing from his train was that which he most desired: a son and heir. Sarah was barren.

Yet Sarah and her barrenness provided an occasion for a considerable increase in Abraham's wealth. In Egypt he passed off his apparently beautiful wife as his sister. She was, in fact, his half sister (Genesis 20:12), and more than once he sought to ingratiate himself with kings by allowing her to enter their harems. In Egypt pharaoh showered Abraham with riches until he discovered the infamous deception. With indignation he caused the desert chief-

The traditional tomb of Joseph at Shechem. According to Joshua 24:32 the Israelites brought the bones of this Patriarch here and not to the family tomb at Hebron.

tain to be driven from the land. But Abraham was allowed to carry with him "his wife and all that he had."

Abraham — "very rich" — returned to the place near Bethel where he had previously established an altar. This feature of the story seems to indicate something which appears elsewhere in the Patriarchal narratives as well as in other nomadic societies. Clans or groups of clans established cultic centers to which the scattered parts of a group would return seasonally. In keeping with desert ways these altars were open; that is, they were not surrounded by defensive walls. Clans seem also to have had specific places at which various members, especially chiefs, were buried even if they had died far away. This may explain why Jacob's body was returned to Canaan for burial (Genesis 49:28-50:14), and why Joseph's embalmed body was kept for many years until it too could be returned to Canaan (Genesis 50:25; Exodus 13:19). Hebron seems to have been such a burial ground. There in the Cave of Machpelah, Abraham and Sarah were buried, as were Isaac and Jacob. Joseph rested finally at Shechem probably because the invading Hebrews who bore his body with them were centered around Shechem for some time before they were able to penetrate, much less control, the Hebron area.

Archaeologists have found shrines and burial grounds whose strange features may be accounted for by the practices just mentioned. At Tell Deir 'allā (Biblical Succoth) just east of the Jordan River there is a large open shrine. Its excavators have argued that it is a nomadic cult site at which the scattered clan gathered in the winter when it came from the cold highlands into the warm valley. According to this view it needed no walls, since holiness was its protection. In the eastern Lisan by the Dead Sea there is the largest ancient cemetery yet found in the Near East. It lies beside the silent ruins of a walled city called by the same name as the cemetery, Bab edh-Dhra. Yet the cemetery is curiously much too large for the Bronze Age city. Could this be a nomadic burial ground in use for thousands of years? Certain historians of religion believe that the origins of the Passover ritual lie in these nomadic habits, and some hold that the God of Abraham, Isaac and Jacob was a clan deity associated with a nomadic shrine.

Abraham's riches now worked against him. So great were the flocks tended by his herdsmen and those of his nephew that the foliage on the hills around Bethel failed them. Sheep and goats seem to be able to live on almost nothing, but with cattle it is a different matter. Strife broke out. Herds were attacked and the men of Lot fought with those of Abraham as each sought pasturage for their beasts. Abraham intervened with his nephew, suggesting that for the sake of peace between kinsmen they should separate. Lot was given his choice of grazing lands and chose to go east, in the vicinity of Sodom. Abraham turned to the west and settled at Mamre near Hebron.

Things went well with Abraham, and he prospered. But Lot was caught in a war between rival kings, captured in Sodom and taken with his goods northward beyond Damascus. When Abraham heard of this he gathered his 318 "trained men" and quickly moved north to Dan. There he divided his force and struck in a two-pronged attack. He rescued not only Lot and his goods, but other booty which had been taken from Sodom as well as "the women and the people" (Genesis 14:16).

The presence of so large a body of military men whom Abraham could muster quickly raises questions not only about the extent of his riches, but also about the nature of his work. W. F. Albright suggested that Abraham owned caravans plying their trade along donkey trails between Canaan and

34

Egypt. To Albright's mind such a person, and *only* such a person, would be likely to have 318 armed retainers on immediate call. In recent years several archaeologists, notably Nelson Glueck, identified a number of previously unknown caravan way stations in the Negeb Desert and across the Sinai. We have long known about the more famous trade routes, such as the Way of the Sea, but it now appears that there was a larger number of routes than was previously suspected. This knowledge, coupled with our awareness that Hebron and Beer-sheba (where Abraham is also said to have lived) were key commercial centers on one end of the trade routes, increases speculation about the commercial side of Abraham's life.

However he made his living Abraham was surrounded by wealth and its attendant reputation. The man had all his heart could desire — except that which he desired above all, a son and heir. According to the custom of that day were he to die childless all his power and possessions would pass to his chief servant, one Eliezer of Damascus. But there was another custom which allowed a barren wife to give her handmaiden to her husband in order to provide an heir. So Sarah gave Hagar the Egyptian to Abraham "and he went in to Hagar, and she conceived" (Genesis 16:4). Sarah's ill feelings toward Hagar hardly decreased after the birth of the child, a son called Ishmael. Worse, when God fulfilled his promise to Abraham and Sarah bore a son, Isaac, Sarah prevailed upon the distraught Abraham to drive Hagar and his own teenage son into the desert. Hagar, despairing, fled south through the heat below Beer-sheba, fearing all the while for the life of her child. Miraculously, both were spared. The boy grew into a man, a man of the desert, wise in the ways of the sands and expert with the bow. He took an Egyptian as wife and dwelled in the Wilderness of Paran. Today Bedouin tribes of the south claim descent from Abraham through Ishmael.

Under the cool oaks at Mamre in the luxurious tents of his parents, the child Isaac became all the more precious in the eyes of his father. And the Lord said to Abraham, "Take your son, your only son Isaac, whom you love, and go to the land of Moriah, and offer him there as a burnt offering upon one of the mountains of which I shall tell you" (Genesis 22:2). Heavy in heart but unswerving in faith, Abraham journeyed for three days with two of his servants and with his young son. Then they came to the place. Tradition locates this sacred spot as none other than the present site of the Dome of the Rock in Jerusalem, the hill on which Solomon built his Temple of the Lord. Leaving his servants behind, the old man and the lad climbed the mount. There they built an altar and laid the wood. Curiously the child looked about for the sacrifice. "Father," he asked, ". . . but where is the lamb for a burnt offering?" Then Abraham bound his boy upon the altar and raised the sacrificial knife in his hand. At the last moment the testing of the Patriarch of Israel was ended and a ram caught fast in a nearby thicket was substituted for the child through whom God's promise of a people was to be realized.

Abraham returned home rejoicing in God. And he lived with Sarah until her death, whereupon he buried her in the Cave at Machpelah. After her death he married Keturah, about whom we know nothing except that she and Abraham had six sons. It is through these that the Arabic tribes trace their ancestry to the Great Patriarch. Before his own death Abraham sent these sons away, perhaps both to save them from Isaac and to guarantee an undisputed family succession. The old man settled everything upon Sarah's son, including God's promise of land and people. In Abraham's death his sons Ishmael and Isaac were momentarily united as they lay their father beside

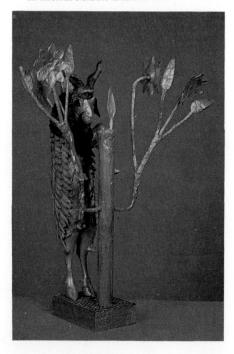

Ram of gold, silver and lapis lazuli is a rare masterpiece from the cemetery of Ur. Often called "a ram in a thicket" in parallel with Genesis 22:13, this statue from the first half of the third millennium B.C. more likely represents the tree of life with a ram, a common motif in ancient Middle Eastern art.

The geographical setting for much of the Biblical narrative is within that half circle of arable land known as the Fertile Crescent. In the east the arc follows the alluvial plains of the Euphrates and Tigris rivers. It widens as one moves northwest through grassland and steppe, then turns southwest at the Mediterranean coast and continues as a narrow belt through Phoenicia and Palestine. The arc ends in the green ribbon of the Nile. Rainfall, always scant and seasonal in the Middle East, has changed little since the beginning of the Biblical era. Cropland and grassland areas remain much as they were in Abraham's day and the extent of desert is unchanged. Forests, however, have been slowly cut back by man so that today large expanses of mountain forest or wooded areas of the Mediterranean type are scarce.

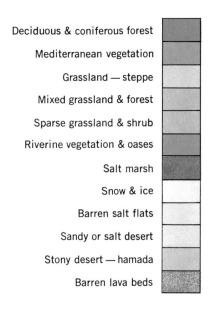

Deciduous & coniferous forest	
Mediterranean vegetation	
Grassland — steppe	
Mixed grassland & forest	
Sparse grassland & shrub	
Riverine vegetation & oases	
Salt marsh	
Snow & ice	
Barren salt flats	
Sandy or salt desert	
Stony desert — hamada	
Barren lava beds	

Wall painting from tomb at Beni-hasan
depicts Asian peoples, probably
Amorites, entering Egypt about 1900 B.C.

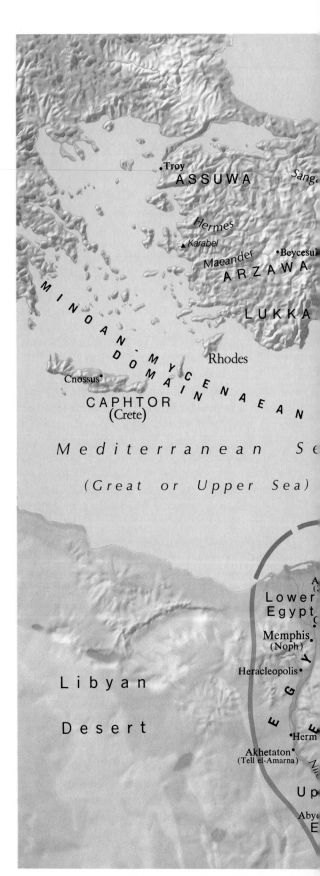

Black Sea

CAUCASUS

Caspian Sea

KASHKA

Halys

Alaca Huyuk

Hattusas

Ankuwa

Cyrus

Mt. Ararat

Araxes

URARTU

HITTITE

Kanish

Tuz

EMPIRE

(HATTI)

HURRIANS

(HORITES)

L. Van

L. Urmia

TAURUS MTS.

Kizzuwatna

Malataya

MITANNI

Haran

Tell Halaf

Tigris

Tepe Gawra

MEDIA

Mersin

Carchemish

Paddan-aram

Washuk-kanni

Tell Brak

Nineveh

Arbela

Alalakh

Haleb

ASSYRIA

Calah
(Nimrud)

ZAGROS

Ugarit

Ebla

Asshur

Jarmo

Ecbatana

GUTIUM

Tepe Siyalk

Hamath

Nuzi

ASHIYA,
ITTIM
(Cyprus)

Arvad

Qatna

Kadesh

Tadmor

Mari

Euphrates

Diyala

MOUNTAINS

Tepe Giyan

Gebal
(Byblos)

Damascus

Agade?

Eshnunna

Akkad

KASSITES

Sidon

Sippar

BABYLONIA

Susa

Tyre

Hazor

KEDAR

Cuthah

Kish

Dor

Megiddo

Babylon

Nippur

ELAM

Joppa

Shechem

Isin

Gaza

Jericho
Jerusalem

Sumer

Lagash

Beer-sheba

Hebron

Erech

Larsa

Kadesh-barnea

Ur

Eridu

Sinai

MIDIAN

Dumah

ARABIA

Persian

Gulf

(Lower

Sea)

Tema

The Ancient World
at the Time of the Patriarchs

Route of Abraham and the Patriarchs
(Early 2nd Millennium B.C.)

Areas of influence of major
powers about 1350 B.C.

Red Sea

Dedan

Dilmun?

No
bes)

0   50   100   150   200   250Mls

0   50   100   200   300   400Kms

© Copyright HAMMOND INCORPORATED, Maplewood, N.J.

Haram el-Khalil at Hebron. In spite of medieval minarets and crenelations, Herod's enclosure wall around the traditional burial place of Abraham and Sarah is still clear.

his much-loved Sarah. Today the traditional site of the Cave of Machpelah is covered by a great mosque. This stately building, still preserving the magnificent structure Herod the Great built to honor the holy site, is known by the Arabs as *el-Khalil,* "The Friend" — for Abraham was "the friend of God."

Isaac is unusual in that, with one exception, the stories about him in the Bible are dominated by other people. When this child of the promise is almost sacrificed, it is to test the faith of his father. The poignantly beautiful tales of how he came to wed Rebekah celebrate her sense of destiny and her independence of action, a trait which pervades and decisively shapes the Isaac stories. With the birth of contentious twins to the once apparently barren Rebekah the narrative focuses upon the two sons, Esau and Jacob. Only in the account of Isaac's refuge from famine in Gerar and his subsequent dealings with Abimelech is Isaac dominant (Genesis 26). Certainly among the Patriarchs of Israel, Isaac is the least significant.

Yet he has his importance. Israel remembers its foundations in God's promise to Abraham, and Isaac is not merely the inheritor of that promise but the one who dramatically passes it on. Unlike his father, who reacted to his wife's barrenness by seeking solutions based upon contemporary custom, Isaac resorted to prayer with diligence and patience. After twenty years the Lord was gracious to him and "granted his prayer, and Rebekah his wife conceived." The two children strove together within their mother — a sign of things to come.

When the time arrived Rebekah brought forth sons, the first very red and covered with hair, the second a fair child who held fast his brother's heel. The older was named Esau, "hairy," and the younger Jacob, "he who seizes the heel." Later Esau was to make a bitter pun on Jacob's name when he said, "Is he not rightly named Jacob? For he has supplanted me these two times" (Genesis 27:36). This refers to Jacob's grasping, his overreach by means of which he had taken that not rightfully his. In the end Jacob stole not only Esau's birthright, but the father's blessing upon the elder son as well.

Differences between the two, so pronounced at birth, increased as the brothers steadily advanced into manhood. Esau is the swarthy man of physical action, stalking beasts across field and through forest with devil-may-care courage. Fresh game and daring exploits doubtless suitably embroidered in the telling won the heart of his father for this son who lived today to the full, taking little thought for the morrow. But Rebekah loved the quiet Jacob, who preferred the cool of the tents to the challenge of the fields.

On one famous occasion the hunter returned from the fields ravenously hungry. Jacob was cooking pottage but refused to give any to his brother unless . . . . His price was high. He wanted nothing less than the birthright of his elder brother! This entitled him not only to a double portion of the inheritance, but also to eventual leadership of the family. Esau considered the dangers he faced; on any day he could be struck down by one of the wild animals he pursued. A bird in the hand, he reasoned, is worth two in the bush. He well might not outlive his father, but he was hungry. "Jacob said, 'Swear to me first.' So he swore to him, and sold his birthright to Jacob. Then Jacob gave Esau bread and pottage of lentils, and he ate and drank, and rose and went his way" (Genesis 25:33-34).

The fatal day came. Isaac, nearly blind and expecting death, sent Esau into the field to hunt down and prepare yet one last meal. Then, he said he would give Esau the blessing. Rebekah, overhearing, sent for Jacob and together they deceived the old man. While Esau was stalking game Isaac groped in near darkness to touch the son who was before him. The voice was Jacob's. But ah yes, he was hairy like Esau, not smooth like Jacob. "Are you really my son Esau?" "I am." Then the shrewd old man told his son to come near and kiss him. The smell was the smell of Esau's clothing. This was the final proof. Through dim eyes the Patriarch could not see the sorry spectacle before him: Jacob's smooth flesh covered by skins of young goats and wearing Esau's best garments. So his father blessed him, and the younger son fled before the hurrying steps of Esau coming to kneel before his aged father.

White-hot enmity between the twins could scarcely be disguised and Esau began to plot Jacob's murder. Again, Rebekah intervened, intending to send Jacob far north to her brother Laban, who dwelled at Haran. Isaac, however, had to be persuaded to allow the one to whom the land had been given to leave. How to do this? Had not Abraham sent to Haran to find a wife for Isaac, a woman of their own people and not one of these Hittites and Canaanites among whom the Patriarchal clan now lived? Should not he do the same for Jacob? With this argument Rebekah further deceived Isaac, hiding her true motives. So Jacob went to his uncle Laban. And Esau, twice stung, went to another uncle, Ishmael, and married his daughter Mahalath. But this union drew Esau and his descendants further away from his family, for his cousin-wife was three-quarters Egyptian. The light falls increasingly and then exclusively upon Jacob.

Journeying northward from Beer-sheba Jacob took the mountain road and spent a night at the Canaanite shrine of Luz, a few miles north of Jerusalem. He laid his head upon a stone to sleep and dreamed one of the most famous dreams in history. A ladder reached from earth to heaven. Angels were ascending and descending on it, and God himself appeared. He was, he said, the God of Abraham and Isaac, and he repeated to Jacob the promise of land, people and prosperity. Israel thus remembers that Jacob was confirmed the inheritor of the promise and blessing given to him by Isaac. In spite of the way in which Jacob came by the promise, the blessing once given could not be recalled, and it was confirmed by no less than God himself.

Jacob rose early in the morning, still awed by the experience of the night. Before continuing his journey he set up the stone which had served as his pillow and consecrated the pillar with oil, calling the place by a new name, Bethel, "the house of God."

At the end of his long and eventful journey Jacob came to the region of Haran. While seeking his uncle he accidently met his cousin Rachel, whom he loved at once. The young man bound himself to his uncle for seven years as an indentured servant with the understanding that at the end of that time Rachel would be his wife. Laban agreed. Jacob served him for the allotted time, only then asking for his well-won wife. Through deceit Laban married Leah, Rachel's older sister, to Jacob. For once the wily one was cheated. With Leah came Zilpah as handmaiden. But Jacob's heart still yearned for Rachel, his first and apparently only love. Once again he bound himself to his uncle for seven more years. But this time he was to be wed to Rachel first and then serve his time. Laban agreed and Rachel came into Jacob's house along with her handmaiden Bilhah.

By these four women Jacob became the father of twelve sons from whom the twelve tribes of Israel are said to be descended. Leah was the mother of Reuben, the oldest, as well as of Simeon, Levi, Judah, Issachar and Zebulun. From Zilpah come Gad and Asher. Bilhah, given by the barren Rachel to her

A modern Bedouin woman. Some scholars think that Bedouin life today still resembles that of Patriarchal times with its emphasis upon strict morality and hospitality.

Jacob and His Descendants

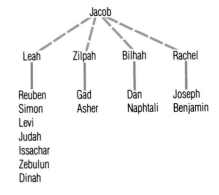

Jacob

Leah	Zilpah	Bilhah	Rachel
Reuben	Gad	Dan	Joseph
Simon	Asher	Naphtali	Benjamin
Levi			
Judah			
Issachar			
Zebulun			
Dinah			

husband in a scene reminiscent of the story of Hagar and Abraham, bore Dan and Naphtali. With mounting anguish Rachel watched this parade of sons. In the rivalry with her sister all of the advantage seemed to be with Leah. Anguish turned to bitterness and bitterness to reproach of her husband, and Jacob's anger clothed Rachel. It was not until after the birth of Dinah, Jacob's first daughter and Leah's seventh child, that "God remembered Rachel, and God hearkened to her." She brought forth a son and called his name Joseph. Later, in Canaan, she was to die in childbirth giving her husband his last son, Benjamin.

After the birth of Joseph, when Jacob had been with Laban for twenty years, he wished to take his family and return to Canaan. Under the careful eye of Jacob, Laban's wealth had increased substantially. Now Jacob wanted his share. Indeed, he wanted the best of everything, merely pretending to desire but a pittance to sustain his family and allow him a beginning in Canaan. He made a bargain with Laban, one which Laban thought could be used to cheat Jacob and give him even less than he appeared to ask for. Laban was hopelessly outmatched. He once tricked his young nephew in the matter of Leah, but this time Jacob had carefully set his snare. He "grew exceedingly rich, and had large flocks, maidservants and menservants, and camels and asses." Jacob has taken all that was our father's," said Laban's sons, "and from what was our father's he has gained all this wealth" (Genesis 31:1).

For the second time in his life Jacob had to flee. While Laban was in the fields shearing his animals, Jacob's flocks were streaming across the Euphrates heading south. Unknown to either of the men Rachel had stolen the family household gods. By the third day Laban and his sons knew all and were in full pursuit. Traveling without slow moving flocks they were able within a week to catch Jacob on the Gilead heights. Bitter accusations ensued on each side. In the end they agreed to a covenant between them. Today the words of that covenant are widely used by lovers, but between Laban and Jacob there was no love lost. The Lord watch between you and me, when we are absent one from the other" is a modern English translation (Genesis 31:49). The original has a much different tone, however. It is something like this: "God keep his eye on you when I am not around to do so." This, not the more romantic version, catches something of the enmity that had poisoned the relationship between Laban and Jacob.

Some days later Jacob with his family, his servants and his flocks began to descend from the Transjordanian heights by that ancient way leading from Mahanaim through the Jabbok cleft into the Jordan Valley. To the west the Wadi Farah offered a way into the Samaritan highlands. Jacob was soon to set foot once more on the promised soil.

What a sight it must have made with hordes of goats and sheep strung out along the hot, dusty, tan pathway. On every side the agile beasts would be going up and down the steep hillsides and along the narrow zigzag paths that only goats and sheep seem to be able to negotiate. In the center of the steeply sloping valley was the camel train. Splendid, tinkling, with the sun illuminating its bright colors, this slow moving, rocking procession bore Jacob's wives, their handmaidens and the children along with such movable wealth as did not walk on four feet. Near the bottom of this almost five-thousand-foot descent Jacob paused and gave the command to divide his flock into two groups. He was about to meet his brother Esau after twenty years. "If Esau comes to the one company and destroys it," he reasoned, "then the company which is left will escape."

Following the way of the sheep has been an honored profession in the Middle East since time immemorial. Sheep and goats furnished many of the basic necessities of life such as food, shelter and clothing.

Jacob took two other precautions. First, he sent some of his servants ahead bearing impressive gifts for his estranged twin. Second, having seen his entire train safely over the River Jabbok, probably at a crossing very near the modern highway, he stayed behind to pray, reminding God of his promises now that he was about to enter the land. He also besought deliverance from the terrible vengeance of Esau, ever the man of action. Jacob found himself in the presence of an angel and they wrestled the night through. The Patriarch's leg was injured, still he gained the upper hand and would not let the other go until he had received a blessing. Just as dawn lightened the sky above the lofty heights and began to bathe the great valley floor to the west, Jacob received not only a blessing but a new name as well. "Your name shall no more be called Jacob, but Israel, for you have striven with God and with men, and have prevailed" (Genesis 32:28).

Limping off in the full light of a new day Israel went forth into Canaan to meet his brother. Esau had also prepared. He came with four hundred men. His intentions were clear. Fear rose in his brother's breast, but Jacob-Israel went forward bowing himself seven times to the ground. They faced each other at a distance. Suddenly Esau ran forward, embracing and kissing Jacob, and they wept tears of joy. All was harmonious when the brothers separated this time. Yet they met again only to bury their father.

Jacob now wandered through Canaan in a series of adventures: avenging the defilement of Dinah at Shechem, worshiping at Bethel, burying Rachel at Bethlehem, where her tomb is still to be seen (Genesis 35:16; but see 1 Samuel 10:2). At last he arrived at Hebron to be united briefly with his venerable father, somewhat surprisingly still alive. It was not long, however, before Isaac rested with Abraham and Sarah in the Patriarchal sepulcher.

It would seem now that Jacob, home from his Mesopotamian adventures and come into the family fortune, would be able to withdraw to the kind of life that originally appealed to him. But a quiet life was not to be. The family seethed with animosity. It came to rest upon the seventeen-year-old Joseph, specially favored elder son of Rachel. While his much older half brothers roamed the highlands following their father's flocks and protecting his interests, Joseph treated these hardworking men with disdainful abandon. He whispered malicious tales about his brothers in his father's ear. Arrogantly he paraded Jacob's partiality. While they dressed in the short, sleeveless tunic common in that day, Joseph was adorned in a brightly colored flowing robe with long sleeves. This garment became a symbol both for Joseph and for his brothers.

At last came a chance for revenge. Camped on the Plain of Dothan they saw the brightly colored robe approaching. Joseph had been sent to find his brothers. They seized him, cast him into a pit and debated the merits of his murder. A passing caravan bound for Egypt decided the heated discussion. The lad was spared, but only because his brothers could both be rid of him and turn a profit at the same time. So Joseph was sold into slavery. His coat dipped in blood was shown to his father as evidence of his death.

Still more grief was to come. In the next years the crops became thin; grazing land for the flocks more difficult to find. Worse, the rusty hills and brown fields did not turn green in the spring and no grain waved in the gentle breezes. Bony animals stumbled, fell and began to die. The always difficult land became hostile, and Jacob turned his eyes toward Egypt as countless herdsmen had done from time immemorial during famine in Palestine. He sent several of his sons southward to buy grain.

Bedouin shepherds, however wealthy, did not often receive an audience

This modern Yemenite Jew from the desert near Beer-sheba is reminiscent of the Patriarchal figures of ancient Israel.

with the Grand Vizier of Egypt. But there they were, Jacob's sons, standing before the second most powerful man in the land, with his fine linen robe, his gold chain around his neck and the pharaoh's signet on his finger. And how roughly he treated them, almost accusing them. It seemed strange that although they had an interpreter he appeared to understand their private conversation. His interest in their family was inordinate and he demanded to see their youngest brother. He retained Simeon as a hostage before releasing the others upon their promise to return with Benjamin. Jacob, upon hearing of this, would not risk Benjamin.

Yet the time came when the grain bought in Egypt was no more. Hard famine was upon the land. "Go again," said Jacob, "buy us a little food." But now his sons would not go again without Benjamin because of the stern warning given them by the Grand Vizier: "You shall not see my face unless your brother is with you."

The Grand Vizier was, of course, none other than Joseph. How had this slave risen to such power in Egypt? To Israel's theological memory the answer is clear: God favored Joseph and even evil directed toward him worked for his benefit. But such memories are preserved in earthy stories full of intrigue, passion and not a little suspense. All is set against a background of splendor accurately mirroring what historians and archaeologists know about the antique land along the Nile in the eighteenth to sixteenth centuries B.C.

A striking young lad, handsome in body as well as mind, Joseph was sold to Potiphar, captain of pharaoh's guard. Obvious ability was recognized and he soon became chief steward of the house. But Potiphar was not the only one to notice the attractive newcomer. "Lie with me," said the captain's wife. Day after day she besought him. Enraged at his constant rejections she falsely accused him of seeking to seduce her.

Even in prison his talents found work. For over two years he oversaw the other prisoners. So it seemed he might live out the rest of his life until one night when the pharaoh had a disturbing dream. None of his legion of magicians and astrologers could offer a satisfactory interpretation. Then it was that his cupbearer remembered a young Hebrew in prison who had once correctly interpreted dreams. Seven years of famine will follow seven years of plenty, said Joseph, deciphering the mysterious scenes which the Egyptian king had beheld in his sleep.

It was for this service as well as his proven administrative ability that Joseph now became the second greatest power in the land. His chariot went about directly behind that of pharaoh himself, but Joseph's word carried its own authority.

It might well be asked if the elevation of a foreigner — particularly a despised sand dweller — is historically credible especially among the proud Egyptians. The question is complicated by the fact that we have no direct extra-Biblical references to any of Israel's Patriarchs, including Joseph. Yet there is one period in Egyptian history when the rise of such a Semite to power in Egypt is not merely possible, but even likely.

The position of the Thirteenth Egyptian Dynasty was usurped about 1640 B.C. by a highly disciplined group of invaders using a new weapon — the chariot. With the mobility and swiftness afforded by these platforms for archers, the Hyksos swept out of the north, down the Palestinian coast and right onto the Egyptian throne. For over two and one-half centuries the entire eastern Mediterranean coast was nominally under the control of these Semitic conquerors. Yet they were but a veneer, a warrior aristocracy who affected neither local culture nor religion. At

The Great Pyramid of Cheops reflected in floodwaters of the Nile. The period of pyramid building ended at least five centuries before the time of Joseph.

site after site in Palestine and Egypt, archaeologists have shown that for this period native cultural development continued unbroken. Military innovation was the foreigners' contribution. In addition to the chariot they also introduced a new type of city wall.

To Egypt they also brought something else previously unknown. A foreign dynasty, especially one including those whom the Egyptians derisively called sand dwellers, was unheard of and deeply resented. "Sand dwellers" refers to nomadic shepherds, such as Jacob's family. The Hyksos, although later called shepherd kings by the historian Manetho, were likely not shepherds at all. It was their Semitic background and the Semite identification with herding that may have led to this understanding of Manetho's phrase. At any rate, the time of the Hyksos conquest of Egypt fits with the portion of the Patriarchal Period in question, and the inclusion in government of a fellow Semite of considerable talent is completely reasonable from a historical point of view.

This must remain conjecture, but it is not unfounded guesswork. Moreover, there can be little doubt that the emotional scenes when Joseph revealed himself to his brothers and bade them bring their father to share his station and plenty are woven on an Egyptian tapestry. As Israel remembers the stories about Joseph it faithfully preserves the essentially Egyptian stage on which they were played out. Interwoven with Egyptian threads are nomadic strands. Joseph requested and received permission from the pharaoh to take his father's body to Canaan to bury it in the family tomb at Hebron. When Joseph died his body was embalmed to keep it until it too could be taken back.

So it was that Jacob and his clan came to dwell in Hyksos Egypt. Their black tents dotted the lush grazing areas of the northeastern delta and sheep and goats ranged widely. This "land of Goshen" was ever the envy of nomadic herdsmen. And it had become the home of those who basked in the reflected glory of the Grand Vizier and his memory.

Now there arose in Egypt a pharaoh "who did not know Joseph" (Exodus 1:8). This was probably Ahmose, founder of the Eighteenth Dynasty. He had mastered the art of the chariot and could meet the hated foreigners on their own terms. The Egyptian people rose with him and Hyksos power was broken, not only along the Nile, but everywhere. He knew not Joseph. He cared little about the privileged place the long dead Grand Vizier's people held in the land. To the Egyptians' natural repulsion to shepherds (Genesis 46:34) was added the fact that these particular people were a reminder of foreign domination. They were aliens, unwanted aliens, fit only to work on those building projects that would erase the memory of generations of shame and celebrate the emerging glory of a new Egypt.

For the people of Jacob, the tribe of Joseph, a new era opened and they entered "the house of bondage." A long night stretched before them.

Brickmaking in ancient Egypt, from the drawing of water (left) to plumbing the laid walls (lower right). These captives of Thutmoses III performed the same work required of the Hebrews in Egypt.

Canaanite ivory figurine with glass eyes, from Megiddo (c. 1350-1150 B.C.). Carved ivory was widely used in the Ancient East to decorate furniture, and that was likely the function of this woman with a staff. See Amos 6:4.

4 LIFE IN ANCIENT CANAAN

While the Hebrews in Egypt languished under the whips of cruel task-masters, the culture and economy of Canaan were recovering from the havoc caused by nomadic waves that had swept over the land several centuries earlier. Sometime before 2300 B.C. shepherds in ever increasing numbers drove their flocks over the northern hills, into the central highlands and gradually encroached upon the fields and fertile valleys that supported the life of the cities. In addition to the problem of dwindling food supplies urban centers faced a slackening in vital trade. Highways became dangerous; paths winding through narrow valleys offered excellent opportunities for hillside shepherds turned part-time robbers. Eventually peoples of the hills and peoples of the towns and cities came to fight random pitched battles, and the life of the cities was gradually extinguished as Canaan entered its "dark age."

It is an old and oft repeated drama — the shepherd against the agriculturalist. This note is sounded in the Cain and Abel story and is well known from the frontier days of the American West. In Canaan at the turn of the second millennium before Christ it brought to an end the first great period of one of the oldest civilizations of mankind, that of the Canaanites.

Jericho, deep in the Jordan Valley a few miles north of the place where the river empties into the Dead Sea, had been a fortified city as early as 5200 B.C. Excavations by Briton Kathleen Kenyon in 1955-1956 found a massive, round stone tower. This is a part of the fortification of this most ancient settlement. Men had not yet mastered the art of pottery — and it was a couple of thousand years before they did — yet their engineering skill as shown by the Jericho tower was remarkable. Still the time of true urban culture had not yet come. The stout, early walls of Jericho could not hold back various peoples who forded the Jordan nearby, and the city's fortunes waned. Curiously, the people who seem to have introduced pottery at Jericho were far from skilled in engineering and architecture. Their homes were ill-protected squalid huts.

In the middle of the fourth millennium — around 3500 B.C. — an urban culture began to rise in Canaan. At about the same time high civilizations appeared along the Nile and between the Tigris and Euphrates. Archaeologists have discovered that these three contemporary centers of city life — the earliest known — were independent but not unrelated. That is, each seems to have arisen from its own impulses and followed separate lines of development. In addition, there are evidences of cross-cultural influences, although the significance, not to say the very existence of these, is debated among scholars. For instance, it is not clear whether Mesopotamian architectural and engineering designs and skills were an impetus in Egypt before consolidation took place along the Nile in the fabled Third Dynasty. Many who argue that this is so point to the step pyramid of Giza as evidence. This second-oldest piece of monumental architecture in the world (after the Jericho tower) is similar in some respects to the ziggurats of Mesopotamia, and its stones appear to have been cut to resemble mud brick, the common building material of the rockless Land of the Two Rivers. Some interesting evidence from this same

Pre-pottery Neolithic tower at Jericho. This massive stone tower, some 30 feet in diameter, was once part of an extraordinary defensive system. It is the oldest known monumental structure in the world — over eight thousand years old.

45

Agricultural implements from Neolithic times; the stone adze and sickles have flint blades for a cutting edge.

Farming in early times was at first limited to turning the earth with a wooden hoe. Crude ploughs pulled by oxen or donkeys were a later development. Egyptian tomb painting c. 1420 B.C.

period was discovered eight miles north of Jerusalem in the summer of 1971. An American team led by Joseph Callaway found what may be a temple on the summit of Ai, famous for its prominent place in the Biblical account of the conquest of Canaan by the Hebrews. If the building did not actually serve Egyptian deities, there is no doubt that the large structure was built according to Egyptian standards and that pottery found in it dates the ruin to the first or second Egyptian dynasty. While Mesopotamian influence may be seen in the step pyramid, none is discernible in the Ai building from the same period. Yet the mass movements of peoples in those days certainly were scattering ideas and techniques widely across the Fertile Crescent, and no one structure will show them all.

The impetus for the rise of urban civilization in the Middle East in the fourth millennium lay in events which had been unfolding over many thousands of years. These events are known as the Neolithic Revolution. Whenever cultural development reaches the Neolithic, or New Stone Age (and it occurred at different times in different geographical settings around the world), a radical change takes place in the manner of life. Domestication of animals and harvesting of planted crops gradually replace hunting wild beasts and gathering random grains as staple food supplies. These things are necessary in order for people to be able to settle in one place and stay there. Thus the first part of the Neolithic Revolution, the domestication of animals and crops is the necessary prerequisite of urban life. From the evidence now available, it appears that this step in Palestine first took place on the slopes of Mount Carmel and in the Lower Jordan Valley.

Hunters and foragers roamed Palestine some half million years ago. Skull fragments and crude tools found deep in the Jordan Valley indicate the presence of early man there before that rift valley reached its present depth. But by 10,000 B.C. the process of the Neolithic Revolution was underway there. Scattered across the hills and valleys of Palestine were numerous small pre-Canaanite villages. More likely than not everyone in the settlement was related to the oldest male as chief of the family grouping. Their homes were little more than round holes in the ground, perhaps as much as fifteen feet in diameter and covered with a thatched roof. In spite of the prized but roughly cultivated fields nearby, these village dwellers maintained a high degree of mobility. Often when the harvest was gathered they would move on with their flocks, either to return to this spot or seek another when the season for planting came again.

A consequent development from the tame animals and planted fields of the Neolithic Revolution was writing. When people settle down it soon becomes important to keep track of what portion of the land belongs to whom. And when the community learns to produce a surplus beyond its immmediate needs it can barter this for another community's surplus of something else. There is obviously a need to keep track of all this. Writing met these needs, and its appearance near the end of the fourth millennium B.C. marks the beginning of true urban civilization with its artisans and commercial life.

Writing apparently began among the Sumerians, the first city dwellers of Mesopotamia. Another and dissimilar system of writing was shortly in use in Egypt. The Canaanites, middlemen between two great commercial centers, followed the Mesopotamian pattern but with many Egyptian loanwords. It is from Canaanite refinements of language that we inherited our alphabet.

By 8000 B.C. the Neolithic Revolution was in its final phase. And by 5000 B.C. there was a walled city north of the Dead Sea. Yet it was not until about 5,500 years ago — the twinkling of an eye in the story of man — that culture as we understand it today began to appear. The people who founded this culture in Palestine were the Canaanites. Relatively sophisticated by 3200 B.C., their manner of life remained unbroken until nomadic hordes began to overwhelm it around 2300 B.C. This period of almost a thousand years is known as the Early Bronze Age.

The distinctive characteristic of Early Bronze Age Canaan was the walled city. On the edge of almost every large fertile valley in early Canaanite Palestine towering walls surmounted a prominent hill. At the entrance to every valley that served commerce — Jezreel, Farah and Sorek, among others — were massive walls of cities. Where trade routes intersected and at particularly strategic points with sufficient water supply it was the same thing: mud brick, stone and baked brick forming defenses, making spheres of influence, staking out permanent claims. So it was at Hazor, Megiddo, Shechem and Jebus.

Behind the walls narrow, cobbled streets ran with abandon in all directions, following little predetermined course. Those who hurried along them seemed to move through a maze of walled alleys as characterless two-storied houses on each side presented a windowless countenance. Yet the interior of many of these houses was pleasant enough, with fruit or vine in the small open courtyard and drains from the flat roof depositing rainwater in jars below. The poor did not live as well, yet their houses often had two rooms and always the traditional flat roof where the family could sleep on very hot nights, with a vine or rush covering overhead to deflect the heat of the early morning sun.

When the sun rose the city came to life. Large wooden gates opened and farmers left the protection of the walls to walk to the surrounding fields and vineyards where they were to labor until dusk. Tradesmen and others jammed their burdened donkeys into narrow gates — some just wide enough for a beast with a sack on each side! — and into the growing hubbub of the streets. Tumult grew as one neared the marketplace, focal point of activity. Merchants' hands flailed endlessly in the air as they bartered. Grain, wine and fruits were to be found in abundance. Here and there women with young ones in tow paused to look longingly at new ornaments on display: shell earrings, a fiancée necklace, silver bracelets and more rarely a gold ring. The women were soon about their business again, however, weaving rough cloth in their homes or grinding grain between two basalt stones.

At the shrine — and there was at least one in every city — worshipers entered the first of three rooms or chambers that made up the temple. They bore small bowls filled with cereal or wine or olive oil. In the middle room they placed these on low benches along the walls where priests picked them up to present them before the deity in the holy of holies, the third or inmost chamber. This room was usually square, dimly lit if lighted at all, and had red paint on the walls. In its rear wall was a small niche whose use is unknown to us.

These cities were jealous of their fields, their commerce, their command of a portion of the trade routes. They also displayed a fatal weakness common to Canaanites of all periods and the reason for their eventual political demise. They could not unite. As was true of classical Greece, geography militated against coalition of the Canaanite cities. In the central highlands around 1200 B.C. there was a confederation of five cities in a limited area, but this was the exception. Valleys and hills made communication difficult, even more so in a time when walking was the normal mode of movement. Diverse elements within the population also had an impact. Hittites, Horites and others living

Canaanite incense stands made in the form of houses. From the Early Bronze Age.

Cult mask of the Late Canaanite Period was found in a potter's workshop at Hazor.

This Early Bronze Age Canaanite altar at Megiddo continued in use through the Biblical Patriarchal period. Over 26 feet in diameter and 4½ feet high this "high place" was a forerunner of the shrines condemned by Israel's prophets.

among the native people contributed to disunity. Finally, there seems to have been a fierce sense of independence among the Canaanites, a loathing to yield authority. So they traded with each other suspiciously and went to war among themselves incessantly. While culture reached a relatively high level and trade expanded, lack of concerted effort, failure to make common cause in using meager resources and intermittent fighting combined to keep the Canaanites from their potential. In the end they were spectators while two more tightly organized peoples, the Philistines and the Hebrews, struggled for control of the land.

But that was not to be until a thousand years later. Meanwhile, as increasing numbers of nomadic shepherds overspread the country, trade slowed and ceased; cities declined and some were even abandoned. The nominal Egyptian overlords had their own domestic troubles, and the imperial designs of the Mesopotamian powers had not yet come to flower. For four hundred or more years, from about 2300 B.C. until at least 1900 B.C. if not later, Canaanite Palestine was a stagnant backwater.

Slowly the cities began to revive, larger and stronger than before. Stick plowpoints scraped the surface of the long-neglected fields to receive seed again. In early summer barley and wheat once more appeared in the fields beneath the great stone walls. Disunity continued. Even so, caravans once more moved with ease across the land. Egypt and Mesopotamia enjoyed prosperity, and this was almost always good for the commerce of the bridge lying between these giants. Even the coming of the Hyksos did not retard the recovery of Canaanite life. These hard-driving charioteers from the north held very loose military control.

By the time the Hyksos were driven from Egypt and their power broken everywhere, Canaan had fully emerged from its dark age. At Hazor in the north the largest walled city in ancient Palestine grew richer from caravans moving along the highway to and from Damascus. Farther south on this road, where it pierced the mountains and emerged by the sea, the cities of Megiddo and Taanach stood along the route, taking tribute from passing merchants and keeping a wary eye on each other. At Ashkelon, Gaza and Eglon in the south, Bethel, Gibeon and Ai in the central highlands, Shechem, Dothan, Ibleam farther north — all over the land it was the same. The people flourished.

It would be wrong, however, to describe this period, the Late Bronze Age (ca. 1550-1200 B.C.), as a time of peace and untroubled prosperity. Intercity strife, always cherished by the Canaanites, grew more intense. One of the reasons for this was quite likely the return of prosperity itself. After a long period of commercial drought there were fortunes to be made. The greater the portion of trade routes a city could control or influence, the greater the income. Booty from war was an important source of wealth, and prisoners were a major supply of slaves and source of labor.

Some have suggested that the Egyptians, whose emerging New Kingdom Empire now actively included Canaan, encouraged division among the Canaanites in order to keep them too weak to rebel. It is true that the Egyptians maintained garrisons, often Nubian mercenaries, at strategic locations through the country. But these were not for the purpose of pacifying the land, nor for interfering with local culture, religion or even politics. On occasion these soldiers did see to it that the Canaanite princes were able to maintain themselves in power against marauding bandits, who seemed to have been particularly strong in the Shechem region. But the major purpose of these

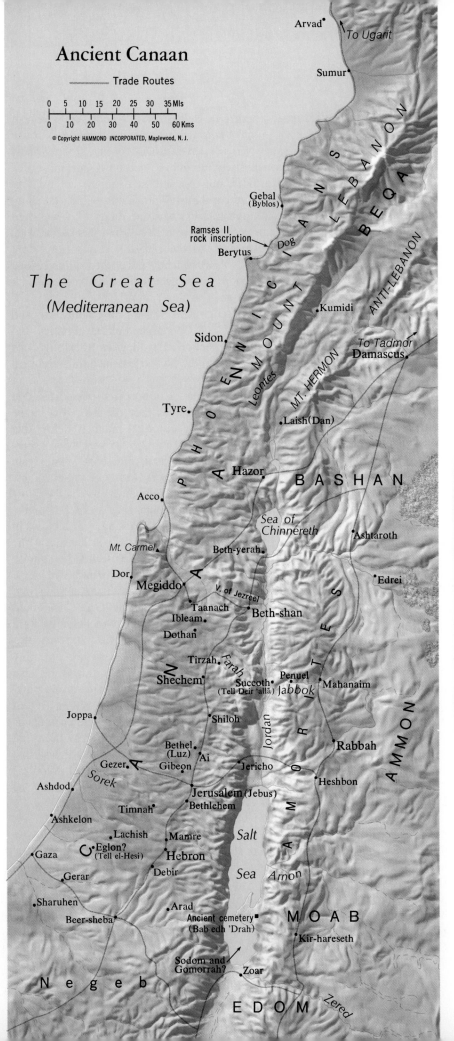

Ancient Canaan

―――― Trade Routes

0 5 10 15 20 25 30 35 Mls
0 10 20 30 40 50 60 Kms

© Copyright HAMMOND INCORPORATED, Maplewood, N.J.

The Great Sea
(Mediterranean Sea)

Arvad *To Ugarit*

Sumur

Gebal
(Byblos)

Ramses II
rock inscription
Berytus

Dog

L E B A N O N

B E Q A A

A N T I - L E B A N O N

Kumidi

Sidon

To Tadmor
Damascus

P H O E N I C I A

M O U N T

Leontes

MT. HERMON

Tyre

Laish(Dan)

Hazor

B A S H A N

Acco

Sea of
Chinnereth

Ashtaroth

Mt. Carmel

Beth-yerah

Edrei

Dor

Megiddo

V. of Jezreel

Taanach
Ibleam

Beth-shan

Dothan

A M O R I T E S S

Tirzah

Farah

Penuel
Mahanaim

Shechem

Succoth
(Tell Deir 'alla)

Jabbok

Joppa

Shiloh

Jordan

Bethel
(Luz)
Ai

Rabbah

A M M O N

Gezer

Gibeon

Jericho

Sorek

Jerusalem (Jebus)

Heshbon

Ashdod

Bethlehem

Ashkelon

Timnah

Salt

Gaza

Lachish

Mamre

Eglon?
(Tell el-Hesi)

Hebron

Gerar

Debir

Sea

Arnon

Sharuhen

Arad

M O A B

Beer-sheba

Ancient cemetery
(Bab edh 'Drah)

Kir-hareseth

N e g e b

Sodom and
Gomorrah?

Zoar

Zered

E D O M

Canaanite anthropomorphic vase with
exaggerated features found at Jericho
dates from about the seventeenth
century B.C.

49

Canaanite bichrome jug of the time of the Biblical Patriarchs, from Ajjul. This type is native to Cyprus and its presence in Middle Bronze Age Canaan indicates early commerce with the islands of the Great Sea.

Egyptian garrisons in Canaan, whether at Beth-shan, Megiddo, Ashkelon or elsewhere, seems to have been to make sure the heavy taxes demanded by the pharaoh were paid. At the same time, the presence of foreign troops, badly paid, poorly led and without much discipline offered certain opportunities for the more unscrupulous native princes, not to mention a number of military governors. Extortion and bribery were constant handmaidens of high taxation. What was paid into the Egyptian king's treasury was one thing, what was paid into the pockets of the devious was another. Frequently during this period rival princes accused each other of disloyalty to the pharaoh and sought more troops to destroy the king's enemies. Not infrequently the enthroned god along the Nile was petitioned for more troops to protect against mercenaries previously sent, or even against the Egyptian governor himself!

So jealousy, intrigue, accusations, tough soldiers, grasping politicians and strife were a part of a "Golden Age" of Canaanite culture. Politics and government were ever the failing of these people. But they had their successes too, and these lay in the fields of commerce, the plastic arts including architecture and in religion.

Much had been said about the overland trade routes that passed through Canaan and also about the economic opportunities they offered. Now in the Late Bronze Age another broad avenue of commerce opened before the Canaanites, or at least some of them. North of Mount Carmel a broken shoreline furnished the growing number of Mediterranean merchant vessels safe harbors and a chance to replenish their meager stores. Many of these shallow draft boats were powered by rowers — often slaves chained to their oars — and a square sail located amidships. In basic design they were not unlike Egyptian ships which had plied the Red Sea for a thousand years. Now, in harbor after harbor north of Mount Carmel, their masts shook angrily at the clouds as the little boats rocked back and forth. In their low-ceiled holds were amphoras filled with wines from various island and mainland vineyards, grains of many kinds and perhaps more luxurious items then coming into vogue: carved ivories from Egypt, fine pottery from the Greek Isles and splendid purple cloth from that portion of Canaan which the Greeks were coming to call Phoenicia, "the land of purple."

Several of these harbors were especially well endowed by nature. Not only did they offer protection against Mediterranean storms, but they were also joined to Damascus and Mesopotamia beyond by overland roads easily passable and relatively safe. For these reasons among others Tyre, Sidon, Byblos and Ugarit became great trading ports, polyglot, wealthy, noisy and cosmopolitan. In their turn Canaanite ships dropped anchor along the Iberian coast and in Sardinian waters, trading the products of Mesopotamian and Palestinian fields and craftsmen for iron ore. Cyprus was an object of Canaanite colonization as Carthage in western North Africa was to be centuries later. In the Black Sea and along the Nile Canaanite faces were well known.

Gradually, as peoples north of Carmel looked more and more to the sea and increasingly assumed a new role in the life of the Ancient East, their differences from Canaanites south of Carmel became more pronounced. It was in the affluent ports that Canaanite civilization reached its zenith in the Late Bronze Age. South of Carmel the inland cities shared in the rising tide of prosperity but remained dependent upon an agricultural base. Distinctions between them and the northern ports grew, so much so that the people of the ports are now commonly called Phoenicians to distinguish them from the other Canaanites.

In Phoenicia architecture and stonemasonry reached a state of perfection hardly equaled elsewhere in the ancient world. Those rulers who could afford it brought craftsmen from the coast to design and build their royal structures. So it was that Solomon implored Hiram, king of Tyre, to send men to construct the major buildings of emergent royal Jerusalem. Solomon's Temple was the finest example of a well-known Canaanite design, and there is little wonder that craftsmen from the north would use vast amounts of cedar from the Lebanon Mountains in this sanctuary as well as in Solomon's palace. If the most perfectly preserved example of the extraordinary skill of Phoenician stonemasons is to be found today at Samaria among the ruins of the royal palace of Omri and Ahab, it is because these kings also employed Tyrian and Sidonian architects and builders.

The interiors of these spectacular buildings also displayed the conception and execution of Phoenician artistic genius. Vivid evidence of this has been discovered in this century. While the vicissitudes of history and countless wars have obliterated, perhaps forever, any evidence of Solomon's Jerusalem, Samaria remains a fertile field for archaeologists. Digging at this ancient capital of north Israel in 1912 American scholars found numerous pieces of exquisitely carved ivory, some whole, but most broken. These were the remains of decorations from chairs, tables, beds and walls and were mute evidence of the sacking of the palace by plundering Assyrians in 721 B.C. Since 1912 archaeologists working in Mesopotamia have found similar ivories at sites of royal residences of kings of Assyria and Babylon. Some of these carvings appear to have been booty taken from a prostrate Damascus in the ninth century B.C. Recovered ivory objects bear striking Egyptian artistic influence. Raw material is known to have come from African elephants and to a certain extent from limited herds in Mesopotamia. Yet Canaan itself was a major source of these finished ivories.

Literature also flourished in the great seaports. Mention has already been made of the fact that it is to the Canaanites that we owe our alphabet. In the

View of the harbor of Sidon.
The narrow coastal strip of Phoenicia was dotted with harbor towns which developed into great trading ports whose power, prestige and rich cultural heritage lasted into Hellenistic times.

Limestone stele from Ugarit shows Baal in his most characteristic role as the winter rain god, "the thunderer who mounts the clouds."

Semitic tongue of those people the first two letters were called *aleph* and *bet;* in Greek *alpha* and *beta*. Hence the name of the letter system. The Canaanite alphabet was in use by traders in the eastern Mediterranean as early as 1500 B.C. The exact relationship between the language of the Canaanites and that of the later Greeks is much disputed today. But few will deny that there is an important connection.

Attached to the palaces and temples of these Phoenician cities, as elsewhere in the Ancient East, were libraries and scribal schools. At Ugarit (near modern Beirut) a chance discovery in 1928 led to the unearthing of royal archives containing hundreds of texts. Diplomatic correspondence was there, all neatly cataloged as it had been by exacting civil servants over three thousand years ago. There were other administrative documents as well as military dispatches, private letters, lists of temple offerings, observations of the movements of the heavenly bodies and even a prescription for curing ailing horses.

Among the more interesting writings, from the point of view of understanding the Bible, are lengthy religious epics. These ancient documents, in the form in which they were found, are major literary works. It is clear that while they were being refined as literature around 1400 B.C. (the date of some of the Ugaritic materials) they are based on much older oral tradition. They are, in fact, a weaving together of many more ancient stories into a unified whole, a major epic of the people. The same process has been known in various cultures, the most ancient being the *Epic of Gilgamesh* from Babylon and that perhaps most familiar to English-speaking readers — *Beowulf*.

There are several epics from Ugarit. One tells of legendary kings, Keret and Dan'el. Another, and more important one, has to do with Baal, the fertility god, he who rides the clouds, casts the lightning and causes thunder and rain. When he is captured by Mot, god of death, rivers turn to dust, fields thirst, drought is in the land and famine threatens.

The story line of this epic is sometimes hard to follow, perhaps because we do not possess all the necessary tablets and possibly because of the ancient piecing together of various accounts. Whatever the problems and the reasons for them, it is clear that the story is a seasonal drama based on the abrupt changes and striking contrasts between seasons. Baal, bringer of fruit and vine, the one who causes the fields to be luxuriant with grain, without whom the flocks are barren, is the bearer of fertility. His consort is Anath, a perpetually pregnant virgin who is goddess both of love and war. It is she who rescues her "lord" (that is the meaning of the word *Baal)* and lover when he has fallen prey to the cunning Mot. Because of this escape from the power of death, Baal resumes his rightful place as rains fall upon the scorched earth and the browns and golds of the hills and valleys disappear in an explosion of color as flowers, grains and fruits once again grace the land.

Many other gods and goddesses appear in this epic. Most important among these is El, the high god, and his consort, Asherah. El is quite lazy, however, and although his word is undisputed among the gods and mere mention of his name enough to strike terror into the heart of even Mot, the active roles are those of Baal and Anath.

There are several curious features about this drama. One of the most striking is the fact that this is an agricultural drama preserved in the midst of a mercantile people. Perhaps this is not so surprising, however, when we recall that the epic is made up of stories centuries old, accounts which probably accurately reflected the people's beliefs long before they turned their eyes away from the fields and toward the sea. Unfortunately, not enough evidence has been recovered from these cities at the height of their commercial life to determine what the Baal ritual was like then, and thus how it was similar to and different from that shown in the epic itself.

A second curious matter, and one about which there is little question, is the difference between Canaanite religion as seen in the writings from Ugarit and Canaanite religion as reflected in the Bible. Baal is the central figure in both, and his role in both is that of a fertility god. But in the Bible his consort seems to be Asherah. Anath is hardly mentioned at all, never in direct connection with religious matters but only in place-names. El also does not appear in the same position in the drama. While a pantheon of gods and goddesses is implied in the Bible, it is not as explicit as at Ugarit.

Discrepancies between what we see of Canaanite religion in the Ugaritic writings and what we see of it in the Bible may have a number of explanations. Some scholars note that the coastal materials in their written form are many centuries older than the Biblical material in its written form. Time, they say, accounts for the differences. This may be a factor. However, the epics from the ports appear to show literary development beyond the stage of the materials in the Bible. In other words, the Bible reflects actual ritual practice, whereas Ugaritic texts appear to be dealing with the story after it has reached a classical stage in the development of literature.

Other scholars point to the widening cultural gap between the Phoenician ports and the Canaanite heartland. While agricultural rituals were losing their immediacy among a mercantile people, they continued to be believed and practiced inland where everything, including the commercial life of the cities, depended upon the regular recurrence of the early and late rains. In this living situation the rituals continued to evolve, but where they came to be considered as literary texts they became frozen in form and unchanging.

Such speculation is based on the assumption that there was once a single Canaanite myth and ritual. This is a dangerous view to take, however, particularly when we are dealing with something like Canaanite religion which has many folk characteristics. It was associated with many, many local shrines, each of which had its own provincial features. Furthermore, it existed for hundreds of years in a politically disjointed context which may have encouraged variations.

For all this, and for all the gaps in our knowledge of Canaanite beliefs and practices, it is quite clear that the religion was a fertility cult par excellence and that it was found in some form wherever there was Canaanite culture. There is also no doubt that the Biblical writers abhorred this religion and repeatedly described it as "an abomination." Their dislike for it may in part have been the more strict desert ethic in conflict with an agricultural religion which viewed sexual morality differently. But it was more than that. Canaanite religion and Hebrew faith were fundamentally different. One worshiped the forces of nature and celebrated the seasonal cycle. The other maintained that its God was beyond nature, indeed, was its creator and sustainer. If many, perhaps most of the Hebrews worshiped at both shrines of Baal and of the God of Israel and even came to confuse one divinity with the other, those who wrote the Bible neither practiced nor condoned such things. Some might believe divine will and power was seen in gentle rains and waving fields. But to the faithful in Israel the true will of the true God was known in and through history, in those events by which he was creating a people for himself.

Late Canaanite tablet from Megiddo inscribed with part of the Gilgamesh epic is further evidence that Canaan was in the cultural orbit of Mesopotamia.

5 THE EXODUS

The Exodus from Egypt — that miraculous escape from hopelessness and despair — is the central event in the life of Israel. Throughout its ancient life Israel prefaced its laws with the statement, "Remember that I am the Lord your God who brought you out of the land of Egypt," or variants of the same (see Exodus 20:2; Deuteronomy 1:30; 5:6 and others). Even today the Passover, celebrating the deliverance of Israel from Egyptian bondage, is one of the most important holy days in the Jewish calendar. When the Early Christians sought to understand the shattering experience which had happened to them in Jesus of Nazareth, one of the most widely used images was that of the Exodus. Jesus was the New Moses; the community, the New Israel. To pass through the waters of baptism was to be redeemed from hopelessness and given new life. Even outside the strictly religious traditions of Judaism and Christianity, the Exodus theme has throughout the ages been a symbol of hope and a call to action for oppressed peoples everywhere. So it was to ancient Israel, who confessed that God had done this wondrous thing and in the doing had made them a people.

The wandering Israelite Tribe of Joseph led by the aged Patriarch Jacob had fled from Canaan, where the hardships of famine had made life so difficult, to go down into Egypt. They settled in the rich grazing lands in the northeastern delta region, the Land of Goshen. There, with few changes, they continued a style of pastoral life familiar and comfortable to them. Life was, if anything, easier than it had been formerly. The land was less harsh, fertile without the endless hills and valleys of Canaan. Flocks thrived. So long as power was held by Joseph and the invading Hyksos, whom he probably served, the Hebrews received good treatment and enjoyed their new home. That at least seems to be one of the implications of Exodus 1:8: "Now there arose a new king over Egypt, who did not know Joseph." That is, a new dynasty arose which did not remember the services of Joseph and did not continue to treat his people with respect. On the contrary, this new dynasty may well have looked upon the Hebrews as allies of a hated foreign rule. This new king may have been Ahmose I, who drove the Hyksos from the throne and founded the native and eventually glorious Eighteenth Dynasty. The Hebrews, who under Joseph had served the Hyksos and who continued after his death to be favored by these fellow Semites, were now at best foreigners, at worst, enemies. Ahmose became pharaoh around 1550 B.C. The Exodus very likely took place sometime in the early 1200s, perhaps as early as 1290. The night of bondage in Egypt was as long as it was dark.

The exact date of the Exodus is unknown, nor is it likely ever to be established. It is not referred to in any Egyptian texts. Quite naturally, they took little notice of it. It was a matter of only local importance. An insignificant group of people had gotten away. They had provided a certain amount of slave labor, but there were plenty of others to press into service. The massive building projects would go on virtually uninterrupted. To the Hebrews, on the other hand, it was of fundamental importance. Yet it was not dated in any of their documents either. That it happened, not when, was the vital thing. So

Opposite:
Nile riverboat loaded with produce and oxen threshing grain. The Hebrews enjoyed their new home in Egypt until a dynastic change around 1550 B.C. Egyptian tomb painting from Thebes.

55

Limestone relief of Ramses II, pharaoh of Egypt at the time of the Exodus according to current reckoning.

An Egyptian landscape with distant pyramids rising above the verdant plain of the Nile River.

we are left to surmise on the basis of other factors what the approximate date of the Exodus might have been.

Some years ago it was fashionable to date the Exodus to the fifteenth century B.C. First Kings 6:1 says it was 480 years from the Exodus to the fourth year of Solomon's reign. This points to the fifteenth century. Moreover, the discovery of the fourteenth-century Amarna Letters, letters from vassal princes in Canaan to Amenophis IV (the famous Ahkenaton) speak of confusion in the land. The disturbance was occasioned by the relaxation of Egyptian rule coupled with marauding bands of brigands who are called "Hapiru." The Hapiru were associated in some scholars' minds with the invading Hebrews. Furthermore, Professor John Garstang, the excavator at Jericho, said that that city was destroyed in the Late Bronze Age, a time which would fit with the other evidence. This city was, of course, the one which the Bible says was the first to be taken by the Hebrews in Canaan as they marched around its walls and blew their trumpets and the walls came tumbling down. So a number of factors converged to support what seemed to be a Biblical dating for the Exodus. The suggestion was that the pharaoh of the Exodus was either Thutmoses III (ca. 1490-1435) or Amenophis III (ca. 1406-1370).

Today the picture has changed entirely. One by one the factors which pointed to an early date for the Exodus have either been called into doubt or have been shown to have nothing to do with the question. At the same time new evidence has come to light which points to a later date: the thirteenth century, perhaps early in the reign of Ramses II (1290-1224). Exodus 1:11 tells us that the Hebrews' bondage had to do with rebuilding the royal treasure cities of Pithom and Ramses. The nature of this bondage as described in Exodus 1:14 strongly suggests that, being nomads close to the building sites, these people were pressed into labor gangs. They were forced to develop the fields which would support the populations of the cities as well as to make brick out of which the splendid new royal bastions were being constructed. Archaeologically recovered history of these sites indicates that they went into decline when the Hyksos were driven from the land, but that they were rebuilt under Ramses II or possibly his father, Seti I (1309-1290 B.C.). There is also the statement in chapters 20 and 21 of Numbers that when the Hebrews sought to cross Edom and Moab they were turned back and had to make their way along the border between these lands. Again archaeological research can now tell us about the history of this Transjordanian area. It was occupied in the fourteenth century, but this population may have been nomadic or semi-nomadic. It was not until the thirteenth century that there was organized settlement. Before that time there would have been no kingdoms of Edom and Moab to refuse passage to the Hebrews. There has also come to light another written source of interest in dating the Exodus. This is an Egyptian inscription celebrating the victories of Pharaoh Merneptah in Canaan around the year 1220 B.C. This speaks of "Israel" and is indeed the oldest written mention of Israel we know. Of course, this only shows the latest date one can give for the presence of Israel in Canaan. But the date of the inscription — 1220 B.C. — is taken by some to be significant in light of other evidence. A part of that evidence, in addition to what has been mentioned, is the violent destruction of a number of Canaanite cities in the thirteenth century. Was this the work of invading Hebrews?

Clearly the question of the date of the Exodus cannot be settled decisively. Yet the weight of evidence is strong, and almost all scholars today agree upon Ramses II or possibly his father as the ruler whose heart was hardened against the Hebrews.

This question of dating such a great event is not unimportant. It is obviously important to the historian. But it is also a matter of concern for anyone who wishes to understand the theology of Israel and to seek those factors which shaped the distinctive Hebrew view of God and his relationship with men. The old view that Hebrew monotheism was really but a variation of a type of Egyptian theology which reached its culmination with Ahkenaton's worship of the solar disc has fallen along with the fifteenth-century dating of the Exodus to which such a view owed so much. Moses (and the name is Egyptian!) may have been reared in a pharaoh's household (Exodus 2:10), but historical evidence today makes it extremely unlikely that this pharaoh was Amenophis IV, the famous Ahkenaton, either when he was crown prince or pharaoh. The origins of Hebrew monotheism must be sought elsewhere, perhaps in the very Exodus experience itself. Whatever its origin, there is no doubt that much of the shape and expression of later Hebrew monotheism was the result of the wilderness wanderings and desert life of these people and their subsequent struggles against the seduction and tenacity of Canaanite culture.

So, very likely sometime in the early thirteenth century, a straggling group of nomads fled in terror and apprehension. As they moved swiftly as possible eastward, the unfinished yet splendid monuments on which they had been laboring loomed in the gray dawn behind them, visible symbols of the magnificence and power of New Kingdom Egypt, one of the greatest empires ever known to man. Seemingly powerless by comparison, the Hebrews were moving toward the water, hopefully toward the safety of the farther desert and relentlessly toward an unknown future. Their prospects were anything but bright. Very soon the escape would be known. Soldiers would be in pursuit. The women with the precious children slowed the pace. Would they be overrun by swift chariots and cut to ribbons by winged arrows and flashing swords? It was hardly a triumphal procession.

All the same the people were not without resolution. Had they not already seen wondrous things performed by this God of whom Moses and his eloquent brother Aaron had told them? Had they not in one terrible night anointed their doorposts with blood as death passed over their homes? Was not this strange man Moses with them, urging, inspiring, ever driving them forward?

Who was this Moses, this colossal man who in Israelite memory stands second only to the towering figure of David? Any student of the Bible knows that it is fruitless to seek for a biography of him. In those stories concerning Moses we have recollections of Israel's early experiences with God, and reflections of Israel's later unity projected backward into an earlier period. But as any careful reader of the Bible also knows, the texts still convey something of the man himself, his personal magnetism and daring, his ability to persuade and to lead, his people's admiration and fear in his presence, his fierce anger and occasional violence and, above all, his unfailing faith in God. And something else comes through too — a pervading sense of overweening presumption upon God. It is this which leaves Moses an old man standing on Mount Nebo gazing into, but forbidden to enter, the Promised Land.

One of the curious things about the Hebrews' memories of their great men is the fact that they preserve an awareness that they were, in fact, men. Men flawed. The temptation to glorify their heroes was always present, as it is among all peoples. But it is the Hebrews themselves who tell about the cunning of Isaac, the baseness to which David could — and often did — stoop and the pride of Moses.

Twin pillars at Karnak are decorated with papyrus and lotus motifs as symbols of Upper and Lower Egypt.

Egyptian chariot with horse and waiting charioteer incised in limestone from the time of Akhenaton.

All the same, Moses was a man set apart by God for his own purposes; namely, to take the family that had gone into Egypt and to make of it a nation. The story of Moses' miraculous escape from watery death in his infancy (Exodus 2:1-10) reminded the faithful that this human was no ordinary mortal. He could and at least twice did converse face-to-face with God. On the first occasion Moses was a fugitive from Egyptian justice, fleeing to the land of the Midianites after he had killed an Egyptian overseer. There, as he wandered more or less aimlessly among the hills following his father-in-law's sheep, he came upon an astounding thing. Before his very eyes a bush was burning, but was not consumed by the flames. Such a thing would indicate to the ancient mind the presence of the divine, and this Moses understood as he removed his shoes so as to stand in reverence on holy ground. Here Moses is confronted by God, who says, moreover, that he is the God of the Fathers, of Abraham, Isaac and Jacob. There is more. For the first time a man hears the awesome name of God. This name which is revealed to Moses still baffles, and it is not possible to translate it meaningfully into English, or into any language. In ancient Hebrew there are no vowels, but scholars have proposed that it might sound something like *Yahweh*. What does this mean? The best guess is that the word may have to do with the verb *to be* and might be translated "I am who I am," or "I will be what I will be." In truth no one really knows how or even whether to translate it. The name itself is so holy that to this day no Orthodox Jew will take it upon his lips. It was this name that fell upon the ears of Moses, and with the name came the charge to return to Egypt, weld together the people and bring them safely out of bondage into a land which God would show them.

Risking all, Moses stood before the Egyptian monarch demanding (!) his people's freedom and their right to leave the country. Unflinching he stands in the midst of a frightened people who are on the verge of panic with the dark waters before them and pursuing Egyptians behind them and commands his people to "stand still and see the salvation of the Lord." And miraculous it was.

> Sing to the Lord, for he has triumphed gloriously;
> the horse and his rider he has thrown into the sea.
> (Exodus 15:21)

Even today, in translation, this song of Miriam, Moses' sister, conveys the stunned sense of the impossible having happened as well as the overwhelming joy of the Hebrews. Somehow, someway, they had gotten safely across the water in time. The chariots bogged down, horses and riders sank in the mud and the waters closed over the Egyptians. "Sing to the Lord." This was his doing. This group of nobodies with no apparent strength were free from the greatest power on earth. Hopelessness had been redeemed by faith and by a willingness to act on the basis of God's promises. It was a lesson the Hebrews would sorely test over the centuries, but one which was burned deeply and indelibly into their consciousness.

The place of this miracle was not, as is commonly thought, the modern Red Sea. In order to cross at this point the fleeing Hebrews would have to have gone south for hundreds of miles over exceedingly difficult terrain, and all the way within the boundaries of Egypt proper. No, they moved eastward as quickly as they could in order to remove themselves from pharaoh's power. The eastern border of Egypt was guarded by a string of fortresses to the north and the Bitter Lakes to the south. This line ran along the present route of the

Suez Canal. Either unwilling or unable to challenge the fortresses, the Hebrews took their chances on crossing the lakes. These are called *Yam Suph* in Hebrew. This may mean Sea of Reeds or Sea of Weeds but certainly does not indicate the present Red Sea. At one time, however, the term "Red Sea" may have indicated not only that large body of water far to the south, but the Gulf of Suez and its marshy connections northward to the Bitter Lakes as well. At any rate, it seems that it was here, in the eastern marshes of Egypt, that the Hebrews in flight were saved from disaster; a salvation they attributed to God's aid.

Once safely across the water they were in the Sinai. Specifically, they found themselves in the Wilderness of Shur. No one really knows what direction the Hebrews took from here. At least four paths lay open to them. Directly ahead was the Road to Shur which led northeastward to Beer-sheba. This may have been the ancient way over which Abraham earlier had plied his donkey caravans. Further north along the coast was the *Via Maris,* the famous Way of the Sea, one of the greatest and most heavily traveled trade routes in the Ancient East. To the south was yet another major trade route, the one that penetrated the heart of the Sinai Peninsula, joining Egypt with Arabia and passing through Ezion-geber, near modern Elath, at the northern end of the Gulf of Aqaba. The fourth way which lay before them was not a trade route. Almost due south was the road that led to the rich mines of Sinai, from which, as inscriptions still in place there show, Egyptians had been taking precious copper and turquoise since as early as the First Dynasty (ca. 3100 B.C.). It is this which is the traditional route of the Exodus. Unlike the other three roads farther north, this one offered relative safety, partly because there were only enough soldiers there to keep the road open, and partly because of its increasing isolation as it plunged deeper and deeper into the wastes of the peninsula.

And the Sinai is for the most part waste. It has never supported a settled population. There is desert; there are vast trackless areas of scrub brush with boulders strewn about countless years ago by volcanoes whose now-smokeless jagged peaks seem to glare menacingly at any unfortunate enough to be moving through the heat and dust of that vast desolation. Infrequently, from place to place, life-giving water bubbles to the surface, date palms flourish and the weary traveler can find genuine refreshment and rest. Sometimes these places are little more than waterholes usable in the winter, but there are oases like Feiran which to the parched and sunbaked voyager must appear as only a little less than the Garden of Eden.

Through this inhospitable land the Hebrews struggled. After they had been about fifty or sixty miles and a month and a half in this land food ran low, then ran out. Deep in the Sinai, just beginning to ascend the uplands of the lower peninsula, the Hebrews remembered Egypt, "the fleshpots of Egypt." By comparison even that looked attractive: "And the whole congregation of the people of Israel murmured against Moses and Aaron in the wilderness, and said to them, 'Would that we had died by the hand of the Lord in the land of Egypt, when we sat by the fleshpots and ate bread to the full; for you have brought us out into this wilderness to kill the whole assembly with hunger'" (Exodus 16:2-3).

Rephidim, which they now approached, was beyond Dophkah (Serabit el-Khadim?) where excavators have found much evidence of ancient Egyptian mining operations. This includes a large temple, a number of stelae and remarkable writings from various dynasties, including attempts by Semitic slaves

The deeper one penetrates the Sinai the more welcome becomes the occasional oasis such as Wadi Feiran shown here.

Manna, used to feed the Israelites in Sinai, came from the tamarisk tree. The honey-sweet substance is produced by scale insects which feed on the sap of the tamarisk.

The Exodus

→ Traditional route of the Exodus
┅► Unsuccessful invasion of Canaan
— Trade routes

20 40 60 80Mls
0   40 80 120 Kms

© Copyright HAMMOND INCORPORATED, Maplewood, N.J.

The Great Sea
(Mediterranean Sea)

Tyre
To Damascus
BASHAN
Acco
Hazor
Sea of Chinnereth
Mt. Carmel
Madon
Ashtaroth
Dor
Megiddo
Edrei
Taanach
Beth-shan
Jordan
Jabbok
Shechem
Aphek
AMMON
Joppa
Shiloh
Rabbah
Gezer
Bethel Ai Jericho
Heshbon
Ashdod
Jerusalem
Mt. Nebo
Ashkelon
Lachish
Salt
Dibon
Gaza
Eglon? Debir Hebron
Sea
Arnon
Raphia
Beer-sheba
Arad
MOAB
Hormah
Kir-hareseth
Jebel Madurah
Zoar
Zered
Negeb
Wilderness
Lje-abarim
of Zin
Bozrah
Kadesh-barnea
Oboth
Punon
Sela
Jebel Harun

Lake Sirbon
The Way of the Sea
Brook of Egypt
Pelusium (Sin)
Baal-zephon Zilu
Tanis
Ramses
The Way of the Sea
Goshen
Wilderness of Shur
Jebel Helal
Pibeseth (Bubastis)
Pithom Succoth
The Way to Shur

Nile Delta

EGYPT
Bitter Lakes
Heliopolis (On)
Wilderness
of
Etham
Wilderness
of
Paran
Great Pyramids
Memphis (Noph)
Mitla Pass
Sinai
Peninsula
Lake Moeris
Crocodilopolis
Marah?
Elim?
EDOM
Ezion-geber
The King's Highway
Arabah
Heracleopolis

Nile
Wilderness
of
Sin
Hazeroth?
LAND
Dophkah? (Serabit el-Khadim)
Alush?
Kibroth-hattaavah?
W. Feiran
Taberah?
OF
Jebel Serbal
Rephidim?
Mt. Sinai (Jebel Musa)
MIDIAN

(Gulf of Suez)
(Gulf of Aqaba)

Akhetaton (Tell el-Amarna)
Red Sea

to simplify Egyptian hieroglyphics and reduce them to an alphabetical system. To the west on the shore of the Gulf of Suez a fifteenth-century B.C. Egyptian port has been found. As the Hebrews moved south of this point and to Rephidim in the Wilderness of Sin, they passed beyond the danger of confronting Egyptian soldiers. But they hardly passed out of all danger. It was at Rephidim that the Hebrews were attacked by the Amalekites, a fierce desert tribe from the northern Sinai who claimed nominal rights over the entire area. These hard-living, hard-fighting, camel-riding people were greatly feared. They would sweep out of the desert, attack, pillage, destroy and withdraw taking no hostages and few slaves. These were the people who fell upon the Hebrews, already sorely tried and weary. And none was more weary than Moses, who for the first time found his strength unequal to his resolve and to the task at hand. He therefore chose one of the younger men to be the warrior chieftain of Israel and to fight to save the people. This young man, Joshua, prevailed against the Amalekites. This is the first mention of Joshua in the Bible (Exodus 17:9f.), but hardly the last.

Jebel Musa, the traditional mountain of Moses, thrusts its granite mass above the Sinai plain.

From Rephidim the people moved by stages into the uplands, to the very mountain of God where there took place a monumental event which was nothing less than the constituting of Israel as God's covenanted people. They were now encamped around Mount Sinai, since early Christian times traditionally identified with Jebel Musa, fifty-five miles north of the southernmost end of the Sinai Peninsula and in the very heart of the forbidding highlands. The deeper the Hebrews penetrated these highlands and the nearer they came to Mount Sinai, the more spectacular and wilder the valleys became. The multicolored granite hills sparkle in the bright sun and the occasional scrub brush serves to reinforce the starkness. And it is quiet. Little lives in this place, and the stillness is extraordinary. Suddenly the seemingly endless ravines give way to a plain beyond which an awe-inspiring mountain of red granite rises 2,600 feet above the plateau. This is Sinai, the traditional place where God is said to have spoken with Moses and to have given to him the Ten Commandments written on two tablets of stone.

Israelite worship of a golden calf in Moses' absence reflected century-old use of this fertility symbol. The version here is the Egyptian sacred bull Apis.

The solemn cadence of the Biblical narrative tells how the people were consecrated and bounds laid around the sacred mountain lest its holiness be violated. The mysterious and threatening power of God could only be approached by priests, and they only to a certain point. Beyond that Moses and Aaron, and then Moses alone, could go. The stage was set for the supreme moment in Israel's history, the sealing of the Covenant by the giving of the Law and the constitution of Israel as God's people.

And Moses went up and was alone with God for many days.

All the while the people on the plain below were in solemn assembly — or were supposed to have been in solemn assembly. Actually, Moses was so long on the heights that the people began to be concerned at the disappearance of their leader, and then to despair. Unity shattered and the community fragmented. Many, if not all, returned to familiar and comforting patterns of bygone days. Led by none other than Aaron himself, they brought together their gold earrings and cast them into an idol, a bull. The bull had for centuries been a symbol of fertility in the Ancient Near East, and the revels of the Hebrews at Sinai on this occasion show that this is what they also understood it to be. This sorry scene, expunged from so much of Israel's later memory, which came to view the desert period as one of unblemished purity, is nonetheless preserved in that curiously honest Israelite fashion and is reported in the Book of Exodus (Chap. 32).

View from the saw-toothed summit of Mt. Sinai. For failing to heed God's word the Hebrew people were forced to wander in this stark wilderness for a generation before entering the Promised Land.

In the midst of this bacchanalian orgy Moses reappeared, bearing the sacred tablets. In fury at what his eyes beheld of his supposedly holy people, he crashed the stones to the ground and came with great anger into the camp intent upon nothing less than a blood purge. Great was the defilement and great was the punishment. Of those who did not heed Moses' call to repentance, "there fell that day of the people about three thousand men."

Once more upon the mountain Moses beseeched God to forgive his people — or else to take away Moses' life itself. And the Lord relented, and the people of Israel prayed in the doors of their tents whenever Moses went outside the camp to the Tent of Meeting where he spoke to God "face to face, as a man speaks to his friend." At length the Lord commanded Moses to prepare two more tablets. Once again he wrote his Ten Words and entered into a covenant with the people of Israel. First among those words was this: "Thou shalt have no other Gods before me." In time this became the touchstone of Israel's faith and the bedrock of Judaism and Christianity.

In the spring of the year, after many eventful months before Sinai, the Hebrews were on the move northward; northward toward the Promised Land. Deuteronomy 1:2 says that it is eleven days' journey from the holy mountain to Kadesh-barnea, the place in the southern Negeb where the people were to dwell for so long following their unsuccessful attempt to invade Canaan from the south. Surely this eleven days must refer to the progress possible to an unencumbered person moving rapidly on an uneventful journey. This human mass that now moved forward was hardly unencumbered and their passage was not uneventful.

The people moved by stages, settling eventually in the Wilderness of Paran which gives way to the Negeb. Now they were able to pursue once more the life of the desert, the Bedouin wandering with his flocks. Yet the cohesion which had been forged in the starkness and bitterness of Sinai was not lost completely. Moreover, like Middle Eastern desert peoples from time immemorial, their eyes and desires were directed toward the seemingly more prosperous agricultural area with its apparently easier life, distractions and seductions. The Hebrews looked northward, toward the Land of the Canaanites. Canaan — the Promised Land!

The springs of Kadesh, which served as the center of Hebrew nomadic life, are known to the Bible as Kadesh-barnea or Meribath-kadesh. This oasis in the Wilderness of Zin is just east of the Wadi el-Arish and some fifty miles south of Beer-sheba. It is composed of three springs, the largest of which, Ain el-Qudeirat, is the only one which flows all year round. Excavations here and in the immediate area have revealed remains of fortresses from the times of Solomon and Uzziah, indicating that these two kings may have sought to establish military and agricultural centers to develop this semiarid region.

In an earlier time, Moses, uninterested in the agricultural possibilities of his surroundings, chose a small group of men and sent them northward to spy out the land of Canaan prior to an invasion from the south. Numbers 13:20 says it was "the season of the first ripe grapes"; that is, it was late summer. The handpicked men, led by Joshua, went forth to spy, to probe and to see what they could see. And what they saw was wondrous to their eyes.

Traversing the land of Canaan they found many peoples, all of whom seemed to them large in stature and dwelling in strongly fortified cities in the midst of a country the spies described in a phrase which has become famous: "a land of milk and honey." That is, its flocks and fields were extraordinarily fruitful. As if to underline their report, the spies brought back pomegranates and figs and bunches of grapes so massive as to be carried on poles between two men. And they brought back fear. So terrified were most of the men of the advance party that they not only advised Moses to give up his scheme, but also went to their own tribes extolling the marvels of the people in Canaan and speaking about the foolishness and hopelessness of attacking them or seeking to displace them.

Alone of all the spies, Caleb and Joshua urged the people to advance northward at once and to seize that which the Lord had promised. "Let us go up at once, and occupy it; for we are well able to overcome it," said Caleb. But they and Moses did not prevail. Yet once again the people murmured against Moses and longed for Egypt rather than death in the desert or falling with their wives and children by the swords of the Canaanites. As he had done so often in the past in times of crises, Moses withdrew to the Tent of Meeting to find solace in prayer and in the presence of God. And the Lord withdrew his promise from that generation of Israel and renewed the promise of the land only with their children. As for the fainthearted fathers, they would live out their lives and die in the wilderness. Following an abortive and ill-conceived assault on the Hormah and perhaps Hebron regions of southern Canaan, the wilderness wanderings of the Hebrew people began. Indeed, a generation was to pass before the Hebrews would once more set foot upon the soil of Canaan.

The story of Israel in the wilderness, from the time of its miraculous escape from Egypt until its final and successful plunge into the central hill country of Canaan, is a curious fabric woven from the diverse and often contradictory strands of faith and rebellion. The people, blind to manifest and manifold signs from God, continually doubt the wisdom of Moses' leadership and insist rather upon their old, familiar ways which do not take account of their covenant with God nor of their new peoplehood. In practice the people hardly consider God's promises creditable. So runs the narrative. Yet pervading all is a sense of the steadfastness of God himself, who with tender care and stern discipline is teaching his people to rely utterly upon him. These themes, found in almost all of the stories from the wilderness period, interlace the accounts of the sojourn at Kadesh-barnea.

By almost any calculation the Hebrews remained at Kadesh-barnea for well over thirty years following the abortive attempt to invade southern Canaan. There Miriam, embodying in herself faith and unfaith, died and was buried. And again, in an action parallel to that which had been performed at Rephidim, Moses caused water to flow from rock and save a thirsting people. According to Deuteronomy 32:50-52, on these occasions Moses presumed on God and failed to interpret to the people the giving of the water as a sign from God. This is specifically mentioned as a reason why Moses was not allowed to enter the Promised Land.

After perhaps as many as thirty-five years at Kadesh-barnea, the Hebrews were once more on the move. They were going east or possibly even northeast. Their intention was to invade Canaan from the east, but their exact route when they began to move from the Wilderness of Zin is dependent upon where we locate Aaron's grave — a matter of some disagreement. Numbers 20:14-21 contains Moses' request to the king of Edom seeking permission to pass through Edomite territory and along the King's Highway, that great trade route which ran north and south along the Transjordanian heights. The Edomite king refused and underlined his resolve by a strong show of force. So Israel set a path to skirt the borders of Edom.

The bounty of the fields and vineyards of Canaan impressed the scouts sent out by Moses.

The mountains and high tablelands of Edom. The Israelites were denied passage through this land southeast of the Dead Sea.

We are told that at this point, just as Israel was leaving Kadesh without permission to cross Edom, Aaron died and was buried on Mount Hor. This happened only after Aaron, taken to the summit of the mount, laid his priestly garments upon the shoulders of his son Eleazer in the presence of all Israel and thus passed on the high priestly office. Where did this take place? Traditionally Mount Hor is identified with Jebel Harun, a 4,800-foot-high peak in central Edom; indeed, it is the highest and one of the most rugged of the Edomite mountains. On its summit today is a mosque containing a tomb which from antiquity has been pointed out as the final resting place of the first high priest of Israel. This site is almost certainly not the actual one. It is in the heart of a country to which the Hebrews had been forbidden entrance, and it is too high for the people of Israel to have witnessed the transference of priestly office as described in the Bible. The Jewish historian Josephus, writing in the first century, identified Hor with one of the jagged heights near Petra. In the same vicinity today local guides point out a place where water flows from the rock into an altogether pleasing pool. This, they say, is where Moses struck the rock and the water rushed forth. Jebel Madurah, about fifteen miles from Kadesh-barnea, is thought by many today to be a more likely site. But no one really knows. The name *Hor* is probably derived from the Hebrew word meaning "mountain," and thus offers no help. All else is relative speculation, as is any attempt to trace in detail the movements of the Hebrews as they made their way eventually to the encampment on the plains of Moab opposite Jericho.

But this much is clear: they moved south first and journeyed over seventy-five air miles (much longer over the rough ground) until they came to the head of the Gulf of Aqaba, to Ezion-geber. At this hoary trading center, later to be famous as Solomon's port for commerce with eastern Africa, the trade routes from Arabia joined the southernmost end of the King's Highway. From here the Hebrews moved north, at one point being forced to take a circuitous and extremely difficult route around the borders of Edom and Moab, a route which took them to the mining center of Punon (Feinan), into the area south of the Dead Sea and also through the spectacular gorge of the Zered.

At last — at long last — Moses stood with his people on the threshold of the Promised Land. From the high mountains bordering the northeastern shore of the Dead Sea there is on a clear day one of the most fantastic sights one can imagine.There, just over the edge of the bleak hills, is the deep blue, placid water of the Dead Sea. To the north, as far as the eye can see, is the valley of the Jordan River, a luscious green laid in the midst of brown and beige. And beyond the sea and to the west of the Jordan there are other hills, not quite so high as Nebo on which one is standing, but jutting up, walling in the waters and abruptly breaking the moonscape-like plain which borders the river. As the mountains rise to the west, vegetation appears beyond the terrible waste of the Wilderness of Judah, and in the heat haze the green seems to pale and to shimmer and to change configurations.

Such was the view which the tottering Moses had as he gazed into the Promised Land, a land which he desired above all to enter, but a land from which he had been barred by his sin of presumption.

Such was his view. But his vision far outran his view, and it was his vision which was to carry younger men across the Jordan.

6 SETTLEMENT IN CANAAN

For a long time it has been commonplace to refer to the Hebrew entry into Canaan as a conquest. The suggestion is that it was a well coordinated military campaign swiftly executed and replete with the siege and destruction of great cities and eventuating in the subjugation of the entire native population. This, indeed, is the impression fostered by one of the Biblical accounts. The Book of Joshua notes a three-stage military invasion. The Hebrews, according to this source, struck from the east into the highlands, there defeating a coalition of five kings. Turning south, they penetrated to the very borders of Philistia (modern Gaza) before moving far to the north to end any active opposition and reduce those major cities which might serve as the focus of resistance. So Joshua.

The Book of Judges, on the other hand, presents quite a different picture. According to this source the process took considerably longer and was compounded of a number of factors, one of which was indeed fighting. The archaeologically recovered history of Canaan tends to support this view. There was no point in the Late Bronze or Iron I periods when Canaanite life and culture suffered an irruption and dislocation of the sort that occurred at the end of the Early Bronze Age when it was overrun by desert nomads. There simply is no cultural break in Late Bronze-Iron I times. If we did not have the Bible to tell us, we would not know unequivocally that a new group of people had come into the land. This indicates that these new people were culturally assimilated to the life they found. Such a process takes a long time, and this is precisely what those narratives describing the Period of the Judges (ca. 1200-1000) tell us. Moreover, the prophets and priests of Israel struggled through the entire life of the Israelite kingdoms against the tenacious and sometimes overpowering influence of Canaanite culture and religion. The process of assimilation continued down to the Exile, and it became increasingly difficult to distinguish Hebrew elements among the more sophisticated Canaanite ones. The religions of the two people, so very different, served in the end to distinguish the genius of Israelite life. Culturally, Canaan triumphed.

It would be more fitting, therefore, to refer to the Hebrew entry into Canaan as an incursion and settlement, punctuated — perhaps in its early stages — by sieges and pitched battles, but for the most part a process of assimilation. We should also keep in mind the nature of Canaan. There was no central political unity unless it was imposed from without. Walled cities stood for the most part at the heads of major valleys which served as highways in the broken landscape. Each of these cities was surrounded by fields upon which it was dependent for food. Small villages were to be found from place to place, even in the interior of the highlands. But these inhospitable highlands, affording little opportunity then as now for raising large crops, had a very small population; mostly shepherds whose nimble-footed sheep and goats could leap among the rocks in search of nourishment. The occasional deep well provided water. Here, among the ravines and in the hills, the Hebrews settled. And it was from here that they went forth to fight the Canaanites and also to learn from them the ways of agriculture and the settled life.

Ivory box decorated in high relief with lions and sphinxes was found in the palace at Megiddo c. twelfth century B.C. This is a fine example of the richly carved ivories produced by the Canaanites.

A shofar, a type of trumpet used in ancient Israel for special religious purposes in both war and peace.

The deep excavations made at Jericho reveal ramparts and houses from very early occupation levels, but in connection with the Israelite conquest at the end of the Late Bronze Age, the archaeological evidence is scanty and inconclusive.

One of the peculiar features of the Bible, as we have noted, is its theological view of history; the idea that events in themselves and in total are means in and through which God is accomplishing his purpose. It is this which has led the writers of Joshua to compress their narrative and see the end of the matter in which, indeed, "all Israel" did come to dwell in the Promised Land. This does not mean that there is no trustworthy history in the Bible, or in the case of the Hebrew entry into Canaan, in Joshua and Judges. There is no reason to doubt the essentially correct historical impression given by the Biblical narrative as a whole. The Hebrews, camped on the Plains of Moab near the major ford of the Jordan a few miles north of the Dead Sea, crossed the river in a manner reminiscent to the Israelite mind of the crossing of the waters in the escape from Egypt (Joshua 3:1-17). At once they came to Gilgal, a very old Canaanite holy place, which in later days was to see the anointing of Saul as the first king of Israel. But now it served Israel in another way. Here, at the first shrine encountered in the Promised Land, Joshua circumcised all the men of Israel in order to consecrate the new generation for the holy tasks ahead.

At this point occurs one of the most interesting stories told in the Bible, and one which has caught popular imagination throughout the centuries. It is the capture of Jericho, the oldest known city in the world. According to the Bible, Jericho was the first city the Israelites besieged and destroyed in the Promised Land. They threw their lines around the city and, as was the practice, sought to starve it into submission. "Now Jericho was shut up from within and from without because of the people of Israel; none went out, and none came in." This could very often result in stalemate and, were the besieging forces not well prepared, they could suffer as much or more than the inhabitants of the city. What the situation was at Jericho on this occasion we do not know. But the method of final assault as described in the text is certainly unique in the history of warfare. The priests are said to have carried the Ark of the Covenant on a circuit of the walls for seven days. On the seventh day they blew their seven *shofarim,* trumpets made from rams' horns, and with a great shout of the Hebrew people the massive walls tumbled down, leaving the city defenseless. Following the sack of the city it was burned to the ground in a great conflagration.

In the early 1930s excavators claimed to have found evidence of this Israelite destruction. These findings were part of the argument for the earlier dating for the Exodus. Jericho was said to have been destroyed in the fourteenth century and showed signs of having been burned. More recent archaeological work at Jericho using newer and more precise methods of dating have shown the earlier excavators to have been wrong. Tell es-Sultan, the mound of Old Testament Jericho, is badly eroded. If there were ever any evidence of a Hebrew destruction of the site, or of any other Late Bronze or Iron I disaster there, it is now gone. What Professor Garstang and his colleagues in the 1930s thought to be fourteenth-century materials are, in fact, from the Early Bronze Age — no later than 2300 B.C.! Little remains even of the Middle Bronze city, and very little (other than one juglet and five reused tombs) from the Late Bronze Age. Archaeology can, therefore, neither confirm the Biblical destruction nor support those scholars who argue that Jericho was an insignificant and undefended town at the time of the Hebrew entry.

From Jericho the Hebrews moved west and slightly north by means of a valley rising into the central highlands. A few miles north-northeast of Jerusalem and only two miles from Bethel, this valley is commanded by extensive ruins of an ancient city known to the Bible as *Ai,* and in modern Arabic as *et-Tell.* Both the Hebrew and the Arabic mean simply "the ruin." It is at an elevation 3,200 feet above Jericho. According to Joshua 7 it was not a particularly large city in those days, nor one which the Hebrew spies in advance of the main body thought they would have much trouble in capturing. Yet the force sent against the city was repulsed with losses and sent fleeing across the hills and down the valleys. It was only then that the discovery was made that one of the Hebrews had sinned in disobeying the ban on what Jericho loot could be kept and what had to be brought to the altar of God. This man and his family were slain. Once more the Hebrews proceeded against Ai. Only this time they laid careful plans, including a feinted retreat and an ambush of the men of Ai and their allies, the men of Bethel. The plan was a complete success. Ai was captured and burned. All of its inhabitants — men, women and children — were slaughtered without quarter. Only cattle were spared.

Descriptions of this struggle on the eastern edge of the hill country are among the most lengthy of such accounts in the Bible and have a prominent place in the conquest narrative. With Ai reduced the entrance to the highlands lay open. Clearly this is the meaning of the story in Joshua 9 which tells how a coalition of four cities centered on Gibeon tricked Joshua, the Hebrew

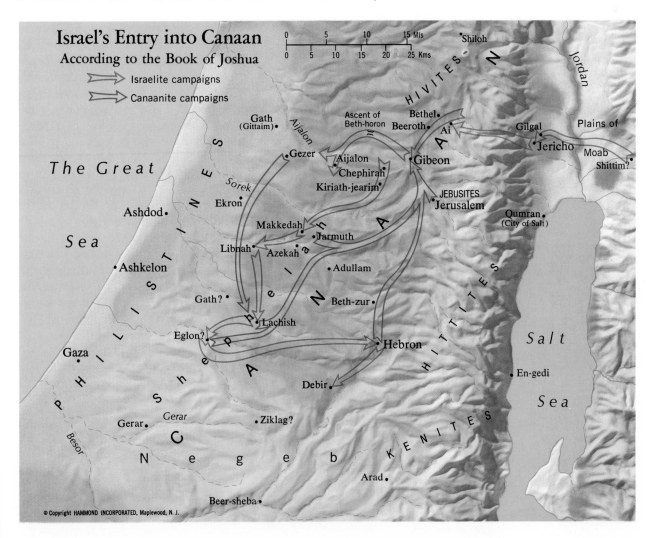

Israel's Entry into Canaan
According to the Book of Joshua

➡ Israelite campaigns
➡ Canaanite campaigns

0   5   10   15 Mls
0   5   10   15   20   25 Kms

Shiloh

HIVITES

Jordan

The Great

Gath (Gittaim)

Aijalon

Ascent of Beth-horon

Bethel

Beeroth

Ai

Gilgal

Plains of

Jericho

Moab

Shittim?

Gezer

Aijalon

Chephirah

Gibeon

Kiriath-jearim

JEBUSITES
Jerusalem

Qumran
(City of Salt)

P H I L I S T I N E S

Sorek

Ekron

Ashdod

Sea

Makkedah

Jarmuth

Libnah

Azekah

Adullam

Ashkelon

Gath?

Beth-zur

Lachish

Eglon?

Hebron

Salt

Gaza

En-gedi

Debir

Sea

Gerar

Gerar

Ziklag?

N   e   g   e   b

K E N I T E S

H I T T I T E S

S h e p h e l a h

J u d a h

Arad

Besor

Beer-sheba

leader, into an alliance when the frightening news of the destruction of Ai came to them. Yet, here again, as at Jericho, archaeology is unable to confirm the story as told in Scripture. It is not because the mound at Ai is eroded as is Tell es-Sultan in the Jordan Valley. Indeed, the large site near the modern village of Deir Dibwan is rich in remains, but these seem to be either too early or too late to fit the Biblical account. Very early in the Bronze Age there was certainly a large and apparently wealthy city at the site. There was also a small Iron Age village on the southeastern slopes of the hill. But what was there in the thirteenth century when the Hebrews are supposed to have sacked the place? Large-scale excavations in the 1930s and again in the late 1960s and continuing today have failed to find Late Bronze remains.

At nearby Bethel a thirteenth-century destruction level has been uncovered. Was this the place destroyed by this violent incursion into the hills? Is it possible that in those days the mound near Deir Dibwan was already desolate and that this accounts for the name *Ai*, "ruin"? Were traditions about Bethel and Ai confused in the retelling over the years before they were written down? We do not know and probably never shall know for sure. At any rate, archaeology, which many see as a scientific tool lending support, and in some minds therefore credence, to the Biblical story, has raised more questions than it has answered about the first two cities said to have been conquered by the Hebrews; namely, Jericho and Ai.

Yet the Hebrews did invade the land from the east, and the valley leading upward from Jericho toward Ai is the natural route into the central highlands. Once established in force at the head of that valley, these aggressive nomads were a real and present danger to the settled population. It is little wonder that the four cities immediately to the west on the crown of the mountain ridge tricked Joshua into thinking they lived a great distance away, in an area the Hebrews were not interested in, and by this means secured a covenant of peace with the intruders. When the men of Israel discovered the deception they were angered and came against the men of Gibeon and the other cities, making them slaves to cut their wood and draw their water. But they did not kill them because of the covenant that had been made.

To the south there were others who were angered by the Gibeonites. In Jerusalem and Hebron, even as far away as Lachish and Eglon near the Philistine plain, men despised Gibeon because the city had entered into a covenant with invaders of the land. Gibeon and all those who had joined in this treachery would be punished. Joshua, at Gilgal with the main body of the Hebrews, heard of the plan against his new allies and of the threat to his dominance of the central hills so lately won. In a forced night march he intercepted the men of the south near Gibeon and drove them through the mountain pass to the northwest, through that place known as the ascent of Beth-horon, and into the valley beyond. And Joshua commanded:

> Sun, stand thou still at Gibeon,
> and thou Moon in the valley of Aijalon.

Joshua 10:13 goes on to say that the sun and the moon did indeed stay their appointed journeys until the Hebrews had won a great victory, including the capture of the kings of five cities. Years ago Copernicus realized that this narrative referred not to any movement of the heavenly bodies but to the decisiveness of the victory won, in Israelite eyes, with the aid of divine help. Yet the fabric of the description and its graphic quality have made it one of the most widely known and frequently repeated of the Biblical stories.

The Book of Joshua says that now, having established a secure position in the central highlands, Joshua and his men followed their success in the Aijalon with swift vengeance upon the cities of the south. It names the places destroyed as Makkedah, Libnah, Lachish, Eglon, Hebron and Debir. Moreover, we are told that when the people of Gezer came up to aid Lachish, they were also killed, every man of them. Scholars are divided in their views about this so-called second phase of the Hebrew conquest of Canaan. First of all we should note the conspicuous absence of Jerusalem from this list. The king of Jerusalem is said not only to have taken part in the intended assault upon Gibeon and the ensuing battle in Aijalon but was pointed out as the instigator of the whole thing (Joshua 10:1). Yet Jerusalem was not taken. It resisted and maintained its fierce independence until the time of David some two hundred years later.

What of the other cities, those claimed to have been destroyed at the time of Joshua? At three of the sites — Lachish, Eglon (= Tell el-Hesi?) and Debir — archaeologists have established that there were major destructions which fit well with the approximate time of the Hebrew entry into Canaan. Work at Gezer has not shown the same thing, but then the text does not say that the city of Gezer was taken, only that those Gezerites who came out to help Lachish were slaughtered. The next question is this: who was responsible for the destruction of Lachish, Eglon and Debir?

We must remember that the Hebrews were not the only people breaking into Canaan at this time. The Philistines were establishing themselves roughly in what is now known as the Gaza Strip, and at almost exactly the same time as Joshua and his people moved in from the east. The three cities mentioned are in an area which certainly would have attracted more than passing Philistine interest. Eglon, in fact, came to be known as a major center of Philistine power. Was the thirteenth-century overthrow of these Canaanite cities the work of these newcomers, and not that of the others to the north? Or were the Egyptians, an ever present danger to southern Canaan, to blame as they sought to reassert a long-lapsed sovereignty over their former empire?

At this distance and without any clear cultural identification, archaeology cannot tell us who was responsible for a given destruction. Still, the coincidence between the Biblical narrative and available archaeological evidence is striking and must be seen as having a possible, if not a necessary, connection. One must also ask if it was possible that in this one period the Hebrews could become masters of the hill country *and* the Negeb *and* the lowlands *and* the slopes as reported in Joshua 10:40. Among other things, the stories of Samson, to which we shall turn shortly, suggest not.

What about the campaign in the north, the third phase of the conquest according to the Book of Joshua? Following his successes in the south, Joshua moved far to the north, beyond the Sea of Galilee, and defeated a coalition of Canaanite kings by the Waters of Merom. As a result of this battle the great city of Hazor fell into Israelite hands and was utterly destroyed (Joshua 11:1-15). Archaeological work which has been going on in Galilee since 1955 has thrown some interesting light on this matter. In the first place, Hazor, once a proud city of some two hundred acres, the largest in Canaan, was indeed destroyed by fire at approximately this time. The site was not rebuilt until over three hundred years later when the Israelites placed a modest fortress on the brow of the acropolis. In the interim, on top of the charred ruins of the palace of the Canaanite king and other splendid buildings, there were rude huts erected by a people whose culture was inferior to that which had been over-

Excavators at Hazor have uncovered the palace of the Canaanite king who tried too late to form a coalition to oppose the Israelites in the far north.

Copper tools and weapons like the Early Canaanite curved knife and spearheads shown here did not have the strength and cutting edge of iron weapons introduced by the Hittites.

Bronze figurine of a young bull found at a cult center on a hill near Mt. Ebal; circa 1200 B.C.

thrown. Debir, in the south, shows a similar history. Were the conquerors of these places desert folk who had not yet come to terms with the more sophisticated culture of Canaan?

This brings us to the second point about recent excavations in Galilee. As has already been suggested, the Canaanites were mainly agriculturalists, which in those days meant that they dwelled in cities and villages situated on easily defended hills beside fertile valleys. The higher hills, penetrated only with effort, chopped up by seemingly interminable ravines and offering little opportunity for crops, had a sparse population. Yet it was precisely this area that was most attractive to the Hebrew pastoralists. They could not effectively challenge Canaanite power on the plains. The Canaanites' mastery of the bow, their swift chariots and above all their ability to work with iron made them a formidable foe. Furthermore, the lightly armed guerrilla fighters from the hills could scarcely have the discipline to meet an organized frontal attack. No, the mountains suited not only their way of life, but also their military abilities at the time. In the mountains where chariots and frontal attacks counted for nothing, they could wreak havoc on any who challenged them. Besides, what would they have known of city life and farming had they been immediately successful in conquering the cities and the fertile plains? The example of Hazor's decline, already described, may furnish an answer.

In the 1970s an Israeli archaeologist working in the Galilee hills found extensive evidence of many small fortified villages from the Period of the Judges. These contained a type of pottery seemingly unrelated to Canaanite types. This is almost sure evidence of new peoples. At first this appeared to be a type of pottery related to known forms from farther north, from what is present-day Syria and even beyond. Yet this does not now seem the case. The pottery may be Hebrew, and may help explain what was probably going on in northern Galilee in the conflict between the pastoralist and agriculturalist.

In 1983 an Israeli archaeologist working on top of Mount Ebal near ancient Shechem discovered a great outdoor altar constructed of unhewn stones and earth. It stood in the midst of roughly circular walls that served to isolate it from its immediate environment. Its associated pottery dated it to the twelfth century B.C. This may be the very one mentioned in Joshua 8:30. As though this were not enough, an accidental discovery of a bull figurine at an open air sanctuary atop a hill some ten kilometers north of Mount Ebal helped to round out a picture of Israelites worshiping in partially assimilated Canaanite forms in the tribal territory of Manasseh.

If one can correctly assume that the Book of Joshua has compressed the entire process and if one keeps in mind the fact that all of those who later came to be known as Israel did not participate in the Exodus, then the process becomes clearer. It would seem that there were people living in the land who might be said to be related ethnically to those Hebrews who had been in Egypt and who broke into the central highlands of thirteenth-century Canaan. These people from an earlier wave had coexisted with the Canaanites for many generations, coming out of the hills from time to time harassing the city dwellers. Now, as those who had come in from the eastern desert solidified their hold on the central highlands and began to spread northward, they encountered their kin, so to speak. Shechem, the most important city of the north brought into the Hebrew fold through a covenant and not by fighting, was probably a part of this process (Joshua 24). As we know from fourteenth-century Egyptian texts Shechem was for many years a city with a non-Canaanite population and

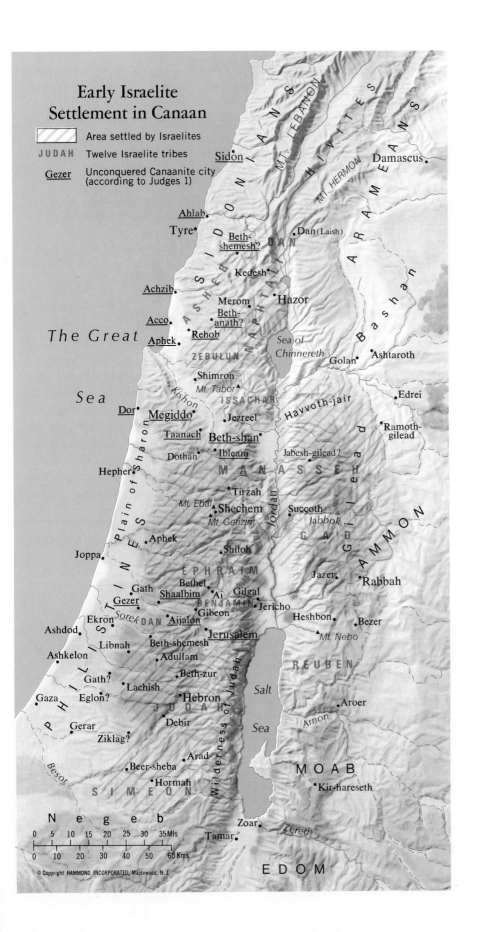

Early Israelite Settlement in Canaan

▨ Area settled by Israelites

JUDAH Twelve Israelite tribes

Gezer Unconquered Canaanite city
(according to Judges 1)

SIDONIANS
MT. LEBANON
HIVITES
MT. HERMON
ARAMEANS

Sidon
Damascus

Ahlab
Tyre
Beth-shemesh?
Dan (Laish)
DAN

Kedesh

Achzib
Merom
Hazor
Bashan

Acco
Beth-anath?
Rehob
Aphek
ASHER
NAPHTALI
ZEBULUN

The Great
Sea of Chinnereth
Golan Ashtaroth

Shimron
Mt. Tabor
Edrei

Sea
ISSACHAR
Havvoth-jair
Ramoth-gilead

Dor
Megiddo
Jezreel

Kishon
Taanach
Beth-shan
Jabesh-gilead?

Dothan
Ibleam
MANASSEH

Hepher
Gilead

Tirzah
Mt. Ebal
Shechem
Succoth
Jabbok
AMMON

Plain of Sharon
Mt. Gerizim
Jordan
GAD

Aphek
Shiloh

Joppa
EPHRAIM
Jazer
Rabbah

Bethel
Gath
Ai Gilgal
Shaalbim
BENJAMIN Jericho
Gibeon
Heshbon
Bezer

Ekron
Sorek DAN Aijalon
Ashdod
Jerusalem
Mt. Nebo

Libnah
Beth-shemesh
REUBEN

Ashkelon
Adullam
Beth-zur

Gath?
Salt
Lachish
Hebron
Sea

Gaza
Eglon?
JUDAH
Aroer

Gerar
Debir
Arnon

Ziklag?
Wilderness of Judah

Beer-sheba
Arad
MOAB

Hormah
Kir-hareseth

SIMEON

N e g e b
Zoar
Zered

Tamar

0 5 10 15 20 25 30 35 Mls

0 10 20 30 40 50 60 Kms

© Copyright HAMMOND INCORPORATED, Maplewood, N.J.

EDOM

was considered to be the focus for brigandage which afflicted the central part of the country. Over the years — perhaps a couple of generations — the Hebrews began to infiltrate the hills of Galilee and to strengthen their brothers' relative position. At first it was imperceptible, then increasingly and alarmingly evident. Too late the king of Hazor awoke to the danger and sought to rally his allies against the Israelites.

Thus what we have in the so-called conquest of Canaan is a lengthy and complex process compounded of fighting, assimilation, coexistence and doubtless many other factors not entirely evident to us today. It was not, it seems safe to say, the lightning military campaign depicted in the Book of Joshua. The first chapter of Judges says that after the death of Joshua most of the major Canaanite cities were still unconquered. Among these it lists Debir, Hebron, Bethel and their territories. Moreover, in the years following the death of Joshua there appeared among the Hebrew tribes charismatic leaders who arose in response to clashes with the Canaanites. Deborah, a prophetess from the Ephraim hills, was such a person. She rallied the northern tribes of Zebulun and Naphtali near Mount Tabor on the great plain and to the astonishment of all offered battle to the Canaanite general Sisera and his previously invincible chariots. It was unheard of for the men of the hills, however large their number, to throw themselves before the wheels of the Canaanites. Yet near the Kishon, the stream that winds its marshy way through the plain, Deborah committed her men against those of Sisera. Fortuitously, or as the Israelites saw it — by an act of God, there was a cloudburst. The chariots, "nine hundred chariots of iron," bogged down. In a moment the agile and lightly armed guerrillas were upon them. Sisera, leaving his immobile vehicle and fleeing on foot, left the field and the victory to Deborah. He came at length to the tent of Heber the Kenite, who, we are told in the narrative, was at peace with Jabin, the king of Hazor, the same one, interestingly enough, who was said to have been killed by Joshua (Joshua 11:10). Heber's wife, Jael, invited Sisera to rest himself and to sleep in safety. And when he was asleep she drove a tent peg through his head. So the victory was complete. "Then sang Deborah and Barak the son of Abinoam on that day:

'That the leaders took the lead in Israel,
that the people offered themselves willingly,
    bless the Lord!
Hear, O kings; give ear, O princes;
    to the Lord I will sing,
I will make melody to the Lord,
    the God of Israel. . . .'"

Mount Tabor where the forces of Deborah gathered to give battle against the army of Sisera. A torrent turned the Esdraelon Plain into a quagmire, making the Canaanite chariots ineffective (Judges 4:6f).

This Song of Deborah, quoted here only in its opening stanza, is generally regarded as the oldest extant lengthy piece of Hebrew literature (Judges 5). It extols the people of Israel for their victory and above all gives thanks to God who gave them strength in the hour of trial and divine aid in the form of the torrent Kishon.

From the south, from the gentle, verdant foothills forming the frontier between what became Judah and Philistia, there are other stories, stories without a victorious ending for the Hebrews, stories about Samson, a man of strength, a man of God, a man of playful foolishness and terrible vengeance. His extraordinary physical power as well as his exploits with women were renowned in the towns, villages and valleys of southwestern Canaan. His power, we are told, came from his having been dedicated to God by a Nazirite vow before he was born. Among other things this vow prohibited him from cutting his hair. Thus when Delilah, a temptress from the valley of Sorek, had him sheared at the bidding of Samson's enemies the man who slew a thousand with the jawbone of an ass (Judges 15:14f.) was helpless. No more would he confound the Philistines with his riddles, anger them by burning their ripe fields by novel methods, or carry off the gates of their cities. In the darkness of the blind he would trod endlessly around and around as he took the place of an ox at the grinding wheel. Insults and the sting of the whip fell equally upon his back. But in the dimness of the prison mill and in the darkness of his despair, his hair was growing again. Thus when the Philistines gathered in the Temple of Dagon to offer sacrifices of thanksgiving for the capture of Samson and to make sport of him, the Israelite was able to push apart two of the pillars and bring the roof crashing down in his final vengeance (Judges 16:23-31).

The pristine folk quality of these stories about Samson is still evident in spite of later editing and inclusion in the theological epic of Israel. Samson is still a buccaneering kid whose play is tempered by sharp and serious conflict. And the frustration in the stories comes through, too; the frustration of the Hebrews in their dealings with the Philistines and in their attempts to dislodge them.

From the Period of the Judges, therefore, we have the exploits of two leaders of Israel dealing with their neighbors, Canaanite and Philistine. Both are essentially local conflicts, involving those Hebrew tribes directly affected. Samson was a loner, but his adventures summed up much of the experience of the tribes of Judah and Dan. Deborah led Zebulun and Naphtali against Sisera and had help from Issachar, Machir, Ephraim and Benjamin. But Judah, unaffected by what went on in the north, sent no aid, nor did Dan or Reuben for much the same reason. Only a few tribes, such as Asher, had long and peaceful relations with their neighbors. The Hebrews, it would seem, were not ready for unity.

Turbulence in Canaan was the order of the day, turbulence compounded by the entry of the Hebrews from the east and the Philistines from the southwest; turbulence compounded by the removal of imposed external political unity, the only kind the Canaanites ever knew. Throughout the Ancient Near East the Late Bronze Age was a period of upheaval and confusion. There was momentary weakness in the north, in Mesopotamia, and in the south once-glorious Egypt had yet to recover from an almost fatal invasion of Sea Peoples. The effect of all this within the narrow land bridge joining Mesopotamia and Egypt can be imagined. In the midst of this chaos, as the Hebrews later saw it, God was working to weld a new unity and to deliver the land into their hands.

Philistine anthropoid coffin from Beth-shan.
The distinctive features of such coffins
have helped archaeologists identify
Philistine sites.

Aerial view of the mound of Beth-shan.
After the defeat of the Israelites by
the Philistines, the bodies of Saul and
his sons were displayed on the walls
of Beth-shan.

7 THE FOUNDING
OF THE ISRAELITE STATE

The two centuries which Biblical historians know as The Period of the Judges, roughly 1200 to 1000 B.C., saw the growth in Canaan and consolidation in power of the two groups which had invaded that unhappy land in the turmoil of the Late Bronze Age. The Israelites, as we have seen, were spreading over the hills and highlands and by a variety of means were challenging the Canaanites, even in some of their stronger citadels. But in their organization the Israelites were still basically tribal, jealous of the rights of their elders and caring little for the struggles of brother tribes removed from them by distance. In the absence of a king and a strong central government there was intertribal warfare. In this Benjamin was almost eliminated. And relative chaos seems also to have been the rule of the day in interpersonal relations as well: "In those days there was no king in Israel; every man did what was right in his own eyes" (Judges 17:6). There were abortive attempts to correct this state of affairs, but they failed in the case of Gideon for theological reasons and in the case of Abimelech because ambition and pride were all too obvious motives. So Israel remained united only by the most tenuous bonds and fragmented for the most part by tribal loyalties and the pressing tasks of making a home in a new land.

Unity of purpose and the ability to work together was, on the other hand, one of the bases of Philistine strength. The Philistines were one of the tribes of Sea Peoples who caused such havoc in the eastern Mediterranean near the end of the Late Bronze Age. As early as the reign of Pharaoh Merneptah (ca. 1224-1214 B.C.) some groups from the northeastern Mediterranean region had allied themselves with the Libyans and unsuccessfully attempted an invasion of Egypt from the west. A proud boast of Merneptah which has come down to us notes the fate of that attempt. Much more serious was the invasion a generation later, in the time of Ramses III. The Egyptian victory at the Battle of the Nile is immortalized in reliefs on Ramses III's sanctuary at Medinet Habu.

According to the Bible (Amos 9:7) the Philistines were from Caphtor, the ancient name for Crete. Some scholars argue that the name Caphtor also refers to the southern coast of modern Turkey, to that region known as Cilicia. Evidence from Greek epic poetry and Philistine material remains in Israel suggest that, if these people did not actually come from the mainland, they had close contact with its culture. The three-man chariots they used are similar to those of the Hittites, and their preference for fierce hand-to-hand combat as well as their advance skills in metal working show affinities with mainland Asia Minor. Yet once these people settle in the land to which they eventually give their name — Palestine — their way of life comes more and more to resemble that of the Canaanites. The earliest Philistine remains at Ashdod, for example, bear unmistakable evidence of Aegean origin. Their mud brick houses are of several rooms, and one shows the open court so familiar in proto-Greek civilization. Numerous small objects including a gold disc with Aegean decorations have also been recovered, along with distinctive painted pottery prominently featuring fish and bird motifs of the Cypriot type.

Philistine pottery; the shapes and painted decorations betray the possible Aegean origin of the Sea Peoples.

It was on the walls of Medinet Habu that Ramses III celebrated his victory over the Sea Peoples in the Battle of the Nile. The feathered headdress is thought to identify Philistines.

A little over a century later Ashdod shows a considerable blending of Philistine and Canaanite elements. The houses are simpler, usually of one room and built after the native mode. Bird and geometric designs decorating pottery are still clearly Philistine, but forms and techniques are now Canaanite. Fertility figurines, well known in Canaan at this period, are also in abundance, but they may have been sculptured bases for goblets of a type found in Greece and on Rhodes and, therefore, should not necessarily be taken as an indication of Philistine adherence to Canaanite religion. But the prominent role of Dagon in Philistine life (Judges 16:23) shows that in religion, too, Canaanite ways were making significant inroads. On the whole late tenth- and ninth-century Ashdod is a blending of cultures and shows that the Philistines had settled firmly.

How did they come to be in the land? The answer may be found somewhere in the aftermath of the Battle of the Nile and the ensuing foreign policy of Ramses III. Our ability to fill in details is, unfortunately, minimal for lack of information. This much seems clear: following the battle Ramses wished to reestablish Egypt's colonial domination to the northeast, in Canaan. But Egypt's power was not equal to its ambition. The truth is that Egypt was itself vulnerable having spent its power in repelling the Sea Peoples. Either the Philistines settled in the Gaza Strip, the traditional staging area for assaults upon Egypt, and could not be dislodged, or the pharaoh proposed that they go there. The former is probably the case, but however they got there they ended up in an alliance with the Egyptians. Philistia served not only as a sort of buffer state north of the Brook of Egypt but also supplied mercenaries for Egyptian garrisons in the interior of Canaan. Philistine remains from Beth-shan, particularly the large and distinctive anthropoid coffins, underline this latter function.

It is also evident that the Philistines maintained their own independence of action. They based themselves on a pentapolis; Gaza, Ashkelon and Ashdod were on or very near the sea, while Gath and Ekron were slightly more inland. All benefited by proximity to the Way of the Sea, the great trade route that followed the coastal plain. Each city had its own king who was head of civil, religious and military matters, but one city was the leader of the league and in times of war coordinated the activities of all. At first this was Gaza's role, and later Ashdod and then Gath became the capital. The story of Samson's destruction of the temple at Gaza contains something of Israelite fear and hatred of this Philistine confederation.

If one basis of Philistine power was unity of action, the others were monies derived from trade, metalworking skills and military techniques. The reliefs at Medinet Habu show the distinctive battle dress of the Philistines: their clean-shaven faces, close-fitting helmets decorated with a circle of reeds (feathers?), their short kilts with armor for the upper body. Armament consists of long, narrow knives, a spear and a circular shield as distinguished from the elongated Egyptian variety. What these people do not have are bows. They prefer close combat to the long-range duel of arrows. At the Battle of the Nile, as at Agincourt many years later when the English longbow cut down the French knights, the bow proved decisive. Yet if the description of Goliath's fearsome armor is typical (1 Samuel 17:5-7), the Philistines did not learn the lesson of their defeat in the delta.

Part of the terror which Goliath held for the Israelites, in addition to his huge size, was the quality of his weaponry and the superiority of his iron spearpoint over the copper weapons of the Israelites. The Philistines had mastered the art of working with metals. It may well be that they learned this craft from the Hittites, who once held a monopoly on iron in Anatolia. This accounted in part for Hittite domination of that area. Now the Philistines sought to emulate the method and seek the same sort of superiority in Canaan. First Samuel 13:19-22 tells us that the Israelites had no smith and that the Philistines did not allow them one lest, on the pretext of sharpening plows, they should make swords and spears. The same passage also mentions that only the leaders of Israel had iron weapons. The clear implication is that the soldiers in the ranks were armed with bronze, and hence the military advantage lay with Philistia.

The founding of the Israelite state lay in the situation just described; namely, the spreading influence and power of the Israelites and the military superiority of the well-organized Philistines. In the end the native Canaanites, ever unable to unite, played little or no role in the matter. The Philistines moved into the vacuum left by Egypt with ambitions of their own. It seems that while they did not occupy the highlands they did establish effective points of control over major arteries. More and more they came into conflict with the Hebrews, some of whom had nationalistic aspirations of their own. At length the Philistines struck a disastrous blow at the heart of Israelite strength. From their camp at Aphek on the western edge of the highlands they poured into the valley leading to Shiloh, the central Israelite shrine in the Ephraim uplands. There Samuel had lived with the aged priest Eli, and there was located the Ark of the Covenant. The Israelites drew up in battle formation at Eben-ezer, only about two miles from Aphek but blocking the way into the valley. Furthermore, they sent up to Shiloh and had the Ark brought down to lead them into battle. It led them to slaughter. This first major engagement with the Philistines ended in an Israelite disaster. The victorious army swept on and leveled Shiloh. The Ark was captured in the field and taken to the Philistine cities where it was displayed as booty and was presented in the temples of the gods. But when plagues broke out they took it to Beth-shemesh to prevent it from becoming once more a rallying point for the scattered Israelites.

Shiloh, the resting place of the Ark of the Covenant and the most important of the Israelite shrines during the Period of the Judges, was already a famous ruin by the time of Jeremiah (Jeremiah 7:12,14).

This was certainly one of the low points of Israel's early history. But the loss of the battle and of the Ark, even the destruction of Shiloh and the death of Eli did not mean the loss of the war. While the Philistines could press on with their plan of dividing the country in half and could take renewed hope in the potentially successful outcome of this venture, they could not occupy or closely control the highlands, nor could they expect to deal effectively with the Israelite tribes in Transjordan.

Transjordan was itself presenting the Israelites with grave problems, however. The Hebrews, who had once come from the deserts and put pressure on the city dwellers, now found themselves in the reverse situation as desert marauders besieged Jabesh-gilead. People of the tribe of Gad were shut up in the city by Ammonites who had long claimed the region. The king of Ammon agreed to lift the siege on condition that he would be allowed to put out the right eye of every man of the city. A week to consider this cruel choice and a chance at hope, that was the request of the starving people. And they sent messengers across the Jordan seeking deliverance.

At Gibeah, three miles north of Jerusalem, word of the situation at Jabesh-gilead came to Saul, a strapping young warrior who was at that moment ploughing his fields. Sometime earlier to rally Israel during the crisis of leadership which followed the debacle at Eben-ezer and the destruction of Shiloh, Samuel had anointed Saul. When Samuel poured oil over the head of the tall, handsome Saul he pronounced these words: "Has not the Lord anointed you to be prince over his people Israel? And you shall reign over the people of the Lord and you will save them from the hand of their enemies round about" (1 Samuel 10:1). This was a private ceremony. Saul was not proclaimed to the people nor by the people. At best he was king without a country and without clear prospects for securing one.

But now came the opportunity in Transjordan. At once Saul slew his oxen and sent portions throughout Israel calling for men to rally to him and to the defense of Jabesh. It was ancient custom to receive a piece of sacrifice as a call to war, but just to make sure that he got the desired response Saul added the warning that "whoever does not come out after Saul and Samuel, so shall it be done to his oxen!" And they rallied and marched with haste to Jabesh-gilead, falling upon the Ammonites in the early morning hours. They fought through the heat of the day until the opposing army was scattered and the city delivered.

Samuel now publicly proclaimed Saul king, and at the old man's direction they all traveled south to that sacred spot just above the Dead Sea where Israel had first consecrated itself in the Promised Land. And there, at Gilgal, "they made Saul king before the Lord."

There is a curious feature in this story of how Israel came to have its first king. Early in the story, at the time when Israel first asks for a king and before Saul has entered the picture, there is opposition. The detailed criticism of kingship (1 Samuel 8:11-18) would appear to be a bitter reflection on the excesses of Solomon's rule. Its insertion by the writers of the Bible into a premonarchical discussion underscores their desire to show that there was opposition to temporal kingship from the very beginning. Before Saul was anointed, and well before his victory at Jabesh led to his public proclamation, there were those in Israel who argued that they already had a king. That king was none other than God, he who had saved them from their enemies in the days since the miraculous crossing of the waters on the flight from Egypt. An earthly king and a temporal state were therefore blasphemous things and a denial of the basic faith of Israel. This view, which has never been completely absent from Israelite thinking since those days, is still to be found among some more orthodox Jewish groups.

But practical politics triumphed over theological arguments. Saul was king. His first accomplishment as monarch was perhaps his greatest: he had united all the Hebrew tribes. Whether the man made history, or history the man, may be argued here as with other great figures. But the simple fact was that the Philistine threat to the Hebrews had become total. No longer could individual tribes or groups of tribes say that the fate of another group somewhat geographically removed was no concern of theirs. Tribal loyalties would remain and councils of elders would continue to hold power. Old ways and old centers of authority would continue, but for the moment they were submerged by a greater necessity — survival in the face of the already demonstrated and ever mounting Philistine threat. And there is another simple fact; there was in this situation a man equal — or *almost* equal — to it.

Before continuing the story of the struggle of these two essentially outside groups for hegemony in Canaan, we ought to ask how Saul fared as king. This question is more deceptive than it may appear. First of all, we do not know how long Saul reigned. The passage that gives the length of his reign is corrupt (1 Samuel 13:1). He either was king for two, twelve or twenty-two years. (The figure of two years is almost certainly incorrect.) In the second place,

At Gibeah the remains of Saul's fortress-palace (background) are surrounded by later construction (foreground). The rude simplicity of Saul's capital contrasted sharply with Solomon's projects in Jerusalem only a few years later.

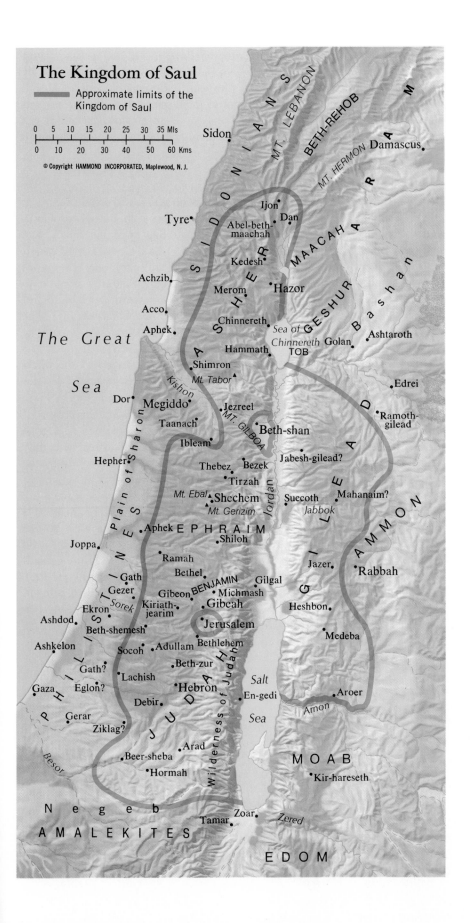

The Kingdom of Saul

Approximate limits of the
Kingdom of Saul

0 5 10 15 20 25 30 35 Mls
0   10   20   30   40   50   60 Kms

© Copyright HAMMOND INCORPORATED, Maplewood, N.J.

Sidon

Damascus

MT. LEBANON

BETH-REHOB

MT. HERMON

Tyre

Ijon

Dan

Abel-beth-maachah

MAACAH

Kedesh

Achzib

Merom

Hazor

GESHUR

Acco

Chinnereth

Aphek

Sea of Chinnereth

Golan

Ashtaroth

Bashan

Hammath

TOB

Shimron

Mt. Tabor

Edrei

Dor

Megiddo

Jezreel

Taanach

MT. GILBOA

Beth-shan

Ramoth-gilead

Ibleam

Jabesh-gilead?

Kishon

Hepher

Thebez

Bezek

Plain of Sharon

Tirzah

Mt. Ebal

Shechem

Succoth

Mahanaim?

Mt. Gerizim

Jordan

Jabbok

Aphek

E P H R A I M

Shiloh

Jazer

GILEAD

AMMON

Joppa

Ramah

Rabbah

Bethel

BENJAMIN

Gilgal

Gath

Gibeon

Michmash

Gezer

Kiriath-jearim

Gibeah

Heshbon

Ekron

Sorek

Ashdod

Beth-shemesh

Jerusalem

Medeba

Ashkelon

Socoh

Adullam

Bethlehem

Gath?

Beth-zur

Lachish

Eglon?

Hebron

Salt

Aroer

Gaza

Debir

En-gedi

Sea

Arnon

Gerar

J U D A H

Wilderness of Judah

Ziklag?

Arad

M O A B

Besor

Beer-sheba

Kir-hareseth

N e g e b

Hormah

Tamar

Zoar

Zered

A M A L E K I T E S

E D O M

The Great

Sea

S
I
D
O
N
I
A
N
S

A
S
H
E
R

A
R
A
M

N
A
P
H
T
A
L
I

P H I L I S T I N E S

79

the royal records of both Israel and Judah were lost in the destructions which overwhelmed Samaria and Jerusalem. In the third place, and perhaps most telling of all, the Biblical accounts as we have them were written either by David's men or by those in later years who were more sympathetic to David. It is not by accident that Saul's name, not to mention his exploits and accomplishments, gradually disappears from the later Biblical writings and is not mentioned at all in the New Testament. If David and his men were determined to remove their arch rival from the records they succeeded.

Yet for all this the figure of Saul emerges from the pages of Scripture as a man of energy, daring, personal courage and the ability to inspire loyalty. He is also surrounded by a pervasive aura of foreboding. This impression may be partly a result of the way the Davidic writers have cast the story: God's anointed, David, steadily rising to the throne while Saul, who has fallen from God's hand, slowly recedes. But it is also because of Saul's own mental condition. He seems to have suffered from increasingly acute paranoia. His jealous rages over the successes of the younger David were punctuated by attempts to kill the new hero in Israel. When he should have been attending to matters of state, Saul was chasing David through the wastes of the Wilderness of Judea, an area well known to the former shepherd from Bethlehem. At length the increasingly mad king drove David into the arms of Israel's enemies, the Philistines. On the night before his death we see Saul, aware of the likely fearful events of the coming day, seeking the advice of the witch of En-dor and dabbling in practices which were abhorrent in Israel.

The story of Saul is not one of failure, however, nor is it the account of a monarch slowly taking leave of his senses. For all of his periods of depression, he died on Gilboa in complete control of himself and with the dignity of the royal figure which he was. In a famous passage perhaps inspired by the account of Saul's last minutes (2 Samuel 1:1-16), Shakespeare notes of another hero: "Nothing became his life so much as his manner of leaving it." Saul died a king as he lived a king. Behind him he left solid accomplishments on which others could build. The Davidic historians would have us believe that it was David who was the great founder of the Israelite state, and David who laid the foundations and built well upon them, passing on to future generations a heritage of Israelite greatness. That David built well is beyond question. That Saul laid the firm foundations of the Israelite state seems also evident. It was Saul who united the tribes. So far as we know none rebelled against him as they were later to do against David. Nor were there intrigues against the king which caused Israelites to turn against their government and flee to Egypt, as was the case under Solomon. It was Saul who established the monarchy in Israel. So firm was Saul's work that while the religious might rail against the king and the monarchical institutions, they could think of nothing better to replace it and in the end transformed it into the very symbol of their deepest hopes — the Messiah, the heavenly king. So firm was Saul's work in this area that few, if any, objected in principle to the anointing of David and his proclamation as king. No, Saul was definitely not a weak king nor one whose accomplishments deserve the obscurity to which they have been assigned.

Saul fell afoul of the priests, and even his old friend Samuel turned against him and then abandoned him. Yet here again Saul was the pathfinder. Canaanite kings were also priests, usually chief priests. What was the role of the Hebrew king in this regard? When on one occasion Saul did act as priest and perform the sacrifices, he was scorned by Samuel and it was remembered to his

Detail from a Canaanite ivory found at Megiddo, dated 1200 B.C. It shows a local ruler on his throne. Before him are an official and a musician plucking a lyre, reminding us of David playing before Saul.

lasting shame by the Biblical writers (1 Samuel 13:5-15). Yet it might be argued that Samuel had forced Saul into this action, the action of an increasingly desperate military commander acting without precedent to follow.

But to return now to an account of the struggle between Philistine and Israelite, a conflict which was to see a dramatic reversal of roles. The Philistines might not have been fully aware of the events at Jabesh-gilead and Gilgal or they discounted their importance, for they did not move quickly to strike down the new king. Saul seems to have dispersed his followers to their homes. Perhaps this deceived his enemies. Whatever the situation, the Philistines seemed to have been lulled, and they hesitated so long that the Israelites got in the first major blow. It was struck by Saul's son, Jonathan. He swept down upon the garrison at Geba swiftly and decisively. Geba, only about three miles northeast of Saul's capital at Gibeah, guarded the southern entrance to the Michmash Pass, a strategic point which played a major role in the Philistine wars. The success of Israelite arms was widely trumpeted by Saul throughout all Israel, and the word came to the Philistines in their cities. They doubtless mustered their forces with the speed and military precision for which they were known and appeared in overwhelming force at the other end of the Michmash Pass. They were less than three miles from Geba, less than five miles from Gibeah. As word of all this spread through the valleys and across the hills, the Israelites ceased rejoicing in the exploits of Jonathan. Fear replaced joy. Caves in the limestone hills were now filled by people cowering before the sure onslaught. Even the bell-shaped cisterns cut deep into the rock to catch the precious winter rains became places of refuge. Others, not trusting to such obvious hiding places, fled with what they could carry across the fords of the Jordan and sought safety on the Transjordanian heights. Still others gathered at Gilgal around their new king, who witnessed this rapid decay of his young kingdom.

There at Gilgal he sought to rally the people and to hold the swaying loyalty of all he could. Hours stretched into days, and the days into a full week. With every passing minute a few more slipped away across the river. Still Samuel had not come to offer the sacrifices before battle. This was the occasion on which Saul took matters into his own hands. Finally Samuel came. There followed an angry scene with bitter denunciations. But in the hills the Philistines were fanning out their troops in three companies, securing the area as far as six miles north of Michmash and closing off the eastern pass through the mountains at Beth-horon. Although the train of events at this point is somewhat confused, it appears that Saul withdrew to Gibeah leaving Geba to the Philistines, who now controlled all of the major routes through the central highlands. At Gibeah the Hebrews, only six hundred in number and without the superior iron weapons of their enemies, waited. But not all.

Unknown to his father and to everyone else in the camp, Jonathan slipped away with his armor-bearer intent on nothing less than bearding the lion in his own den. He would go up to Michmash and see what a little single-handed daring would do to the Philistines. With either incredible courage or extraordinary foolhardiness Jonathan simply approached a group of hostile soldiers who were on a ridge and openly showed himself. With braggadocio the Philistines dared the young Israelite to come up the ridge. And forthwith he scampered up, using hands and feet to speed his way. His armor-bearer was right behind him, and as Jonathan smashed his enemies to the ground his servant administered the coup de grace. As others ran to the aid of their fallen comrades, Jonathan dispatched them. The advantage passed over to Jonathan as

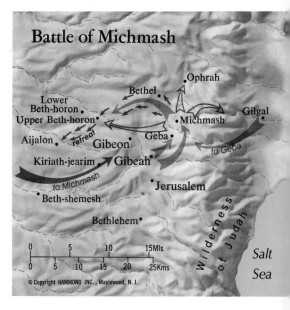

Battle of Michmash

Israelite force
Philistine force
Philistine raids

the Philistines were apparently unable to understand what was happening. There was shouting and confusion, and confusion gave way to panic. At this moment Saul, who had been with the priest seeking God's will by consulting the Urim and Thummim, came on the field with his meager force. Now everything went wrong for the Philistines. Some of the Hebrews who had been allied with them turned on them. People who had hidden in caves, cisterns and groves joined in the battle and pursued the Philistines now in full rout.

With the central highlands temporarily secure, Saul turned his attention to the farther borders of his ill-defined kingdom and warred across the Jordan against the Ammonites, the Moabites and the Edomites. In the south he fought against the Amalekites of the Negeb. But in the wars against the men of the southern desert he failed to kill their king when he had the chance. For this and other things Samuel turned more and more against the man he had singled out to be prince over Israel and had anointed with his own hands. With those same hands Samuel killed Agag of the Amalekites, Saul's prisoner at Gilgal. And Samuel and Saul departed from Gilgal enemies, Samuel to his house in Ramah and Saul to his in Gibeah scarcely two miles from Ramah.

But Samuel did not long remain in his house. Soon he was passing by Gibeah on his way south, beyond Jerusalem, to Bethlehem. There, with fear of Saul in his heart and a horn of oil in his hand, he came to the house of Jesse and asked to see his sons. One by one the old priest looked at the boys, and one by one he rejected them. Finally the youngest, who was in the field with his father's sheep, was sent for. When he came to Samuel the horn was opened and the oil poured over his head. A new king had been anointed while Saul yet rested in his palace at Gibeah. The handsome young lad with ruddy complexion and beautiful eyes who stood in the midst of his astonished brothers was named David.

Among other things David was renowned for his ability to play the lyre. As the darkening clouds of depression settled more thickly and more often upon Saul his servants thought it a good idea to bring this talented musician from Bethlehem to soothe the king's tormented mind. So much did Saul love David that the lad became the king's armor-bearer. But the military skill of the young man and his fame at having killed the Philistine tormentor Goliath filled Saul with jealousy. "Saul has slain his thousands and David his ten thousands" (1 Samuel 18:7) on the lips of the Hebrew women was not taken as a compliment by the king, but as further proof that his position was being eroded by this upstart. Yet Saul's attitude toward David was ambivalent. One day he might throw a spear at him, intent upon killing him, and the next propose that he should marry Saul's daughter and become son-in-law to the king. David might be made commander of a thousand men at one time and be saved from destruction only through the warning of Jonathan at another time. Finally Saul sent men to David's house with instructions to murder him, but Michal, Saul's daughter and David's wife, warned her husband and he fled. And he continued to flee with the help of Jonathan, who risked and received his father's wrath. David fled as far as Gath where he had to feign madness to save himself from the Philistine king of that place. Throughout the land David wandered on both sides of the Dead Sea. Whenever Saul thought he had a chance to catch David he would pursue. Once, in a cave in the Wilderness of Judah, David had a chance to kill Saul but refused to raise his hand against God's anointed. At length, in desperation David fled once more to Achish at Gath, only this time he did not pretend to be mad. On the contrary, he offered himself and the six hundred men he had gathered with him in the

Model of an Egyptian royal harp c. 1090 B.C. Little is known about the design of harps in ancient Israel, but perhaps that used by David to soothe Saul was similar to this one.

82

service of this Philistine king, asking to be sent to one of the country towns under the sway of Gath. So Achish sent him with his men to Ziklag, a place approximately halfway between Hebron and Beer-sheba. No place and no opportunity could have suited David's plans any better. From here he was able to ingratiate himself to the elders of Judah and prepare for the days when Saul would no longer sit on the throne.

And that day was fast approaching. The Philistines now determined to show their strength in the north and to follow the same design they had earlier attempted in the central hills. They would effectively cut the country in two by taking decisive command of the Great Northern Plain. They already held Beth-shan at the eastern end of the valley. Now they had to sweep that vast field and reduce any opposition which might be there. Again, as before, they massed at Aphek. This time, however, they did march north and entered the Plain of Megiddo.

Saul heard of these plans and had gathered his forces below Mount Gilboa in the Valley of Jezreel to the east and just across the flat fields from the Philistines. With a sense of impending disaster the Israelite king sought solace in necromancy the night before the battle. The witch of En-dor called up the spirit of Samuel, but as in life so in death the old man had no words of comfort for the man he had made king.

On the morrow the Philistines scored an overwhelming victory. The slopes of Gilboa ran with the blood of the finest of the young men of Israel. Saul's sons fell at his side, and an arrow pierced the body of the valiant king, seriously wounding him. In vain he begged his armor-bearer to take his sword and finish him. But the man in great fear refused this one order of his master. Finally Saul fell on his own sword, perishing along with his sons and the sons of the mothers of Israel and apparently along with the hopes for an Israelite state.

The next day, when the Philistines came to strip the bodies of those who had fallen in the battle, they came upon the bloody remains of the king and three princes. They cut off the head of the king's corpse and stripped it of armor. The armor was placed in the temple of Ashtaroth in Beth-shan while the headless body was hanged upon the walls of the city along with that of the princes. News of this atrocity reached the ears of the men of Jabesh-gilead, which is across the Jordan some ten miles from Beth-shan. They remembered their debt to Saul. And they came by night and stole the bodies from the wall, took them to Jabesh where they burned them and gave honorable burial to the bones and ashes.

In the south David was pursuing the Amalekites through the desert, seeking revenge for their raid on Ziklag. When word of the events of Gilboa reached him, he lamented for his king, Saul, and his friend, Jonathan:

> Thy glory, O Israel, is slain upon thy high places!
> How are the mighty fallen!
> Tell it not in Gath,
>   publish it not in the streets of Ashkelon;
> lest the daughters of the Philistines rejoice,
>   lest the daughters of the uncircumcised exult.
>   (2 Samuel 1:19-27)

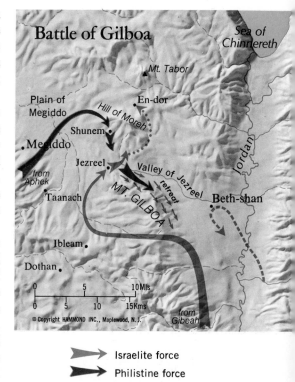

Battle of Gilboa

→ Israelite force
→ Philistine force
····> Saul's journey to En-dor
----> Recovery of the bodies of Saul and his sons

8 ISRAEL'S GOLDEN AGE

The first three-quarters of the tenth century B.C., from about 1000 to around 925, is considered the Golden Age of Ancient Israel. The period can roughly be divided in half by the reigns of David, that pious warrior who was the architect of Israel's greatness, and Solomon, that splendid autocrat who both corrupted and bankrupted that greatness. It was a time when the power struggle for the domination of Canaan came to a conclusion favorable to the Hebrews. It was also a time when the traditionally great powers in the north and south, in Egypt and Mesopotamia, had sunk to a low point and were momentarily debilitated by internal strife. Internal and external factors therefore combined to give Ancient Israel its moment in the sun. But it was not an automatic process, nor one which was achieved without struggle and a high price. Even toward the end of the process the final outcome could hardly have been imagined.

At Gilboa the hopes of Israel had been dashed. Far to the south, in the Negeb desert, David, anointed but uncrowned, was chasing the Amalekites through the desert. David had been away from his base at Ziklag. While he was actually supposed to make trouble for the Judahites on behalf of his vassal-lord, Achish of Gath, David attacked the enemies of Judah and even went as far as to send some of the spoils of his victories to the elders of Judah against the day of opportunity which was coming. This was a dangerous and bloody game David was playing. No word must reach Achish. "And David saved neither man nor woman alive, to bring tidings to Gath, thinking, Lest they should tell about us, and say, 'So David has done'" (1 Samuel 27:11).

But now Saul was dead, and the Philistines exulted. David lamented his fallen king and he set about to become king in his place. The elders of Judah, to whom David had carefully ingratiated himself, gladly received their fellow Judahite; this ruddy young man whose feats in battle had been sung in Israel, and upon whose head the revered Samuel had poured holy oil. So David went up to Hebron, the principal city of Judah, and was anointed king and ruled over the house of Judah.

Judah, the tribe that had settled in the southern hills and in the northern reaches of the Negeb, had a different history and different traditions from Israel, the tribes that had settled farther north and in Transjordan. Indeed, so strong were the differences separating these two groups that for the greater part of their existence they were in active or potential conflict. Now, with David king of Judah in Hebron, overtures were made to the northern tribes also to come forward and to recognize this Judahite as their monarch. But they were having none of it.

Abner, commander of Saul's army and probably an uncle to the late king, took Ishbosheth across the river to Mahanaim, a city of Transjordan. Ishbosheth was Saul's son, and in spite of 2 Samuel 2:10, which tells us that he was forty years old when he began to reign, he was perhaps too young to have been in the army and thus was not present at the Gilboa debacle. At any rate, he seems to have been completely under the domination of Abner, who had him anointed king over the northern tribes.

Opposite:
The Dome of the Rock in Jerusalem is the traditional site of Abraham's near sacrifice of Isaac. David purchased the land from Araunah, but it was Solomon who built the first of three Hebrew temples here. The present mosque, one of the holiest shrines of Islam, was completed in A.D. 691.

The Pool at Gibeon, part of a Canaanite water system which continued in use through the Biblical period, is 37 feet in diameter and 82 feet deep. Here the forces of David and Ishbosheth, Saul's son, fought.

Civil war broke out among the Hebrews. Both sides sent men to occupy the strategic town of Gibeon, some eight miles northwest of Jerusalem. There, around an enormous pool which is really part of an earlier Canaanite water system, a bizarre incident took place which had far-reaching consequences. The opposing forces came face-to-face, one on either side of the pool. And they sat down some thirty-seven feet apart to decide what should be done. Then Abner said to Joab, David's nephew and leader of his forces, that the young men should be allowed to "play before us." This phrase in 2 Samuel 2:14 may suggest that some sort of wrestling match or other feat of strength and skill was to determine which side was to withdraw and which was to occupy the site. Perhaps the intent was less pacific than wrestling. Whatever it was, twelve from each side came forward, and in a matter of moments dying men lay on the ground. The fierce fighting spread beyond the pool to the wine presses and groves nearby. The forces of Ishbosheth began to flee, and the pursuit was on. Asahel, a brother of Joab noted for his swiftness, pursued none other than Abner who kept warning the oncoming young man to turn back lest he be slain. But Asahel would not. When he was upon Abner the more skilled man turned and killed him with the butt end of his spear. Now Joab and his other brother Abishai pursued Abner. But near nightfall some of the Benjaminites who lived in that area rallied to Abner, and Joab stopped within hailing distance, but not close enough to engage in combat. Bitter words were exchanged, each army commander accusing the other of stirring up hatred among brethren. Joab now withdrew with his men, but the name of Abner was odious to him. The loathing which filled his heart and clouded his judgment was almost to cost David his cherished dream of kingship when the day came to avenge Asahel.

And the war dragged on from that disastrous day. We do not know how long the conflict lasted; perhaps as much as seven years, maybe even longer. During this time David's strength increased, but the forces of the house of Saul grew weaker. In the end, however, the issue was not settled on the field of battle. Abner and Ishbosheth fell out over a woman. The king's harem was inviolable. Seduction of one of the monarch's wives or concubines was tantamount to claiming the throne. Absalom understood this and used this means to publicize his own royal intentions in his revolt against David (2 Samuel 16:20-23). Whether Abner was motivated by such ambitions, or merely by lust, is not entirely clear. At any rate, he desired Rizpah, who had been one of Saul's concubines, and he took her for his own purposes. When rebuked by Ishbosheth, Abner flew into a rage. While indignantly pointing to the fact that he had kept the house of Saul safe and in power, he determined in his heart to "accomplish for David what the Lord has sworn to him, to transfer the kingdom from the house of Saul, and set up the throne of David over Israel and over Judah, from Dan to Beer-sheba" (2 Samuel 3:9-10).

Abner sent to David seeking an audience in Hebron. He also conspired with certain of the elders of Israel who, perhaps grown weary of Ishbosheth's weakness, desired David as king to deliver them from the Philistines. And Abner came to Hebron where he and David struck an agreement. Then Abner departed in peace to go north and rally Israel for the shepherd of Bethlehem. But Joab, having just returned from a raid, heard that Abner had been in Hebron and had been allowed, even encouraged to go in peace. He chastened David and made accusations against his blood enemy, apparently to no avail. Joab moved swiftly, taking matters into his own hands. He sent messengers after Abner saying that David wished him to return at once to Hebron. Joab met him at the city gate and on the pretense of wishing to speak privately drew him aside. In an instant a knife flicked forward and Asahel was avenged. But theoretically Abner had been under David's protection.

David saw the danger of the situation and was equal to it. Publicly condemning the treachery, he ordered all the people, including Joab, to gird themselves in sackcloth and mourn before Abner. In the funeral which followed David walked in the procession as the chief mourner and delivered the eulogy and then made a great show of fasting for the fallen soldier. And the people of Israel understood that it had not been the king's will that this man should die, and they were satisfied.

Meanwhile in Mahanaim Ishbosheth was seized with fear. Abner, who had been his strong arm and indeed the foundation upon which the house of Saul was built, was dead. Not only that, he died while changing his allegiance. Shock waves were felt throughout Israel. And two of Ishbosheth's tough warriors came to the king's house in the heat of the day while Ishbosheth was taking his noonday rest. There they murdered their king while he slept and beheaded him in his own bed. These two fled Mahanaim with the royal head and brought the terrible relic to David in Hebron.

Things were going splendidly for David; yet here as before with Abner and Joab a misstep could cost him everything. Clearly the two men expected a handsome reward for their great service on behalf of David. But could he condone regicide? No, he decided, he could not. Moreover, this grisly affair offered David another chance to demonstrate to the tribes of the north his kingly qualities and concern for the traditions and sensitivities of the north. The two must die. David's young men, on the king's order, killed them, cut off their hands and feet and publicly displayed these by the pool at Hebron. Ishbosheth's head was buried in the tomb of Abner, a final irony.

And the elders of Israel came to Hebron and anointed David, and he ruled over Israel and Judah. According to 2 Samuel 5:4 he was thirty years old.

David now could turn to other matters. Hebron, the natural center of Judah and its political capital for some years, was clearly not suited to be the capital of the expanded country. It was too partisan and too far south. Gibeah was more central, but it was, after all, Saul's old capital. Mahanaim was in Transjordan and in any case was more a place of refuge than a center for a kingdom. What of Shechem at the strategic center of the Ephraim hills? Whether any or all of these sites were considered we do not know. We do know that David's gaze fell upon another city, one which was more or less centrally located, easily defended and with no historical or emotional ties with either part of his new kingdom. This city was Jerusalem. It was still in the hands of the Jebusites.

"You will not come in here, but the blind and the lame will ward you off," shouted the Jebusites from the unconquered heights. Indeed, appraising the situation with a careful military eye one could see that the taunt was no idle boast. The Jebusite citadel was triangular in shape, guarded by two valleys, the Tyropoeon and the Kidron. Only on the north, where the city walls were dominated by higher ground, were extra defenses necessary. The Jebusite city tapped the Spring Gihon for its water supply. The spring at the bottom of the hill was outside the city wall, but an elaborate system of tunnels gave access from inside, thus ensuring adequate water in the event of a lengthy siege. A rock-cut tunnel, which can be entered today, ran for over 50 feet, where it was joined by a perpendicular shaft. At the top of this main shaft another tunnel led to steps to the surface. The actual distance covered by this

Jebusite Jerusalem, captured by David, occupied the Ophel ridge, the wedge-shaped promontory south of the Temple mount. The city was defended on two sides by deep valleys, the Kidron (on the right) and the Tyropoeon (now partly filled but still visible in the center of the picture).

The Ark of the Covenant in the form of a Roman wagon. From the synagogue at Capernaum.

last tunnel was about 83 feet, but the devious pattern which the workmen followed seeking softer rock carried them some 130 feet in their underground passageway. All told the water could be brought to the surface some 100 feet above the level of the spring and over 140 feet to the west. Almost three hundred years later when Hezekiah built his water tunnel in preparation for a possible Assyrian siege, he used a small portion of this earlier system.

Perhaps it was because they thought that no one could get up the perpendicular shaft joining the two more or less horizontal tunnels that the Jebusites seem not to have fortified the entrance to the system inside the city. David knew this and saw it as the weak point in Jerusalem's defenses. "Whoever would smite the Jebusites, let him get up the water shaft to attack the lame and the blind, who are hated by David's soul," shouted the king. Apparently led by Joab, the volunteers came forth and went up the shaft. David dwelt in the stronghold of the Jebusites. Jerusalem was his.

Now David did a truly exceptional thing, a thing which continues into our own day and is near the heart of Judaism, Christianity and Islam. He turned Jerusalem into a holy city. Religious fervor was blended with nationalism, producing an emotional bond which in its influence and consequences has no real parallel in history. Not only was Jerusalem to be the capital of the United Monarchy of Israel and Judah, but the Ark of the Covenant, so long a virtual captive on the borders of Philistia, was to be brought there. God's miraculous presence with his people in the wilderness and other sacred memories of most ancient Israel were to hallow this place. This was to be in deed and in fact the focal point of all of Israel's deepest meanings and affections.

Before David could carry out his intentions another and serious threat surfaced. The Philistines had heard that he had become king over Israel, and they set out to remove this king. Twice the Philistines sought to come up against Jerusalem by means of the Valley of Rephaim, in reality a hollow plain which gives access from the Wadi Serar on the Philistine plain to the central Judean highlands. Twice they came against David; twice they were defeated. Finally, with the Philistines cleared from the central highlands as far west as Gezer, the king with a great company of his subjects brought the Ark to the new capital to the accompaniment of singing and dancing. So ecstatic was David on this joyous occasion that he danced naked before the Ark, an act which led to a terrible argument between David and his wife Michal, causing David to abandon her bed and leave her childless (2 Samuel 6:20-23).

With the help of Hiram, king of Tyre, David also set about to build in his royal city and to make it a truly great one. When the fortifications were secure, Tyrian carpenters and masons built a palace for David using cedar from Lebanon. Unfortunately, only the huge platform of the public area uncovered by an Israeli expedition and a few walls from an earlier British expedition remain of David's city. Little is known about Jerusalem in this period. Yet it seems clear that David extended the city only sightly and then, as to be expected, only northward. That David had much more grandiose things in mind is shown by his purchase of the Jebusite threshing floor north of the city and by his securing of materials to build on that site a magnificent temple to the god of the Hebrews. But God, through the prophet Nathan, forbade David to build this house. No man of blood could do this lest he profane it. It would remain for David's son, Solomon, to build the Temple

There were no restraints, however, on this monarch's imperial ambitions. North, south, east and west he struck, conquering peoples, capturing land, seizing booty and laying the economic foundation for Solomon's splendor. If

The threshing floor of Araunah was set on a prominence formed by a natural rock outcrop, as in this typical threshing floor.

he did in fact take more than could be properly organized and well administered, he nonetheless held both of the major trade routes (the Way of the Sea and the King's Highway) and access to the Red Sea by means of the Gulf of Aqaba. Only in the west did he seem to be less than successful. The Philistines, while subdued, were not conquered. And it is not without interest that when Solomon married an Egyptian princess the pharaoh gave him Gezer as part of the dowry. This may only mean that the king of Egypt relinquished formal claim to this important ancient site some twenty miles northwest of Jerusalem. But given the importance of the dowry, more seems to be implied in the gift of Gezer. The fact that Israel's Philistine frontier on the southwest continued to be fortified suggests that the kingdom of David in the west displayed a more complex pattern than one is usually given to think.

Even if we grant that David had overextended himself, he nonetheless reigned in strength as king of Israel and Judah. While constant fighting went on around the fringes of his empire, David set himself to the difficult task of organizing his kingdom and building up its internal strength. He was aware of the great differences within Israel's borders — its many peoples, numerous traditions, even different religions. Saul had not been so careful about this; Solomon was to be extremely careless about these things. But David sought to erase distinctions and ease hostilities. His success was not complete. In particular the old divisions between Judah and Israel continued, and there were not a few in the north who bitterly resented this son of Jesse, this son of Judah who sat on the throne.

It is well to pause at this point and ask what kind of man David was because so much of the grief through which he and his kingdom passed in his later years seems the result of personal failure. Certainly David's character is controversial, and the matter is made no easier by the fact that the Biblical writers legendized the man and in so doing emphasized his strengths and diminished his weaknesses. Yet the fabric is still there and we can almost feel its texture. Many, perhaps most, of the great figures in history were extraordinarily complex and sometimes exhibit what appear to be and indeed may be contradictory tendencies, motives and actions. David was a prime example of this. Physical qualities had combined to cause him to be royal armor-bearer to Saul. Moreover, the story of his battle with the Philistine giant, Goliath, suggests that even as a boy his bravery was greater than that of any of the soldiers of Israel (1 Samuel 17:19-54; see also 2 Samuel 21:19). As a youth his courage had been honed by the rigors of following his father's sheep through the Wilderness of Judea east of Bethlehem, and that desolate waste had worked on his body to give him strength and striking carriage. At the same time David was recognized not merely for his martial qualities and physical prowess. As almost everyone knows the Psalms are traditionally attributed to David. This may have its basis in the young man's renown for music. So famous was he in fact that he became royal harper. And above all one must not overlook his religious devotion. Sought out as a lad by Samuel, the spiritual head of Israel in that day, he was anointed to be God's own to lead this people because of a combination of factors, not the least of which was the shepherd boy's deep piety and unswerving adherence to the God of Israel.

But when a gifted, attractive and somewhat spoiled young person becomes an adult with different concerns and new vested interests, what qualities remain? What new comes to the fore? In David's case complexity and extremes seem to be constants in his personality. We have already seen how

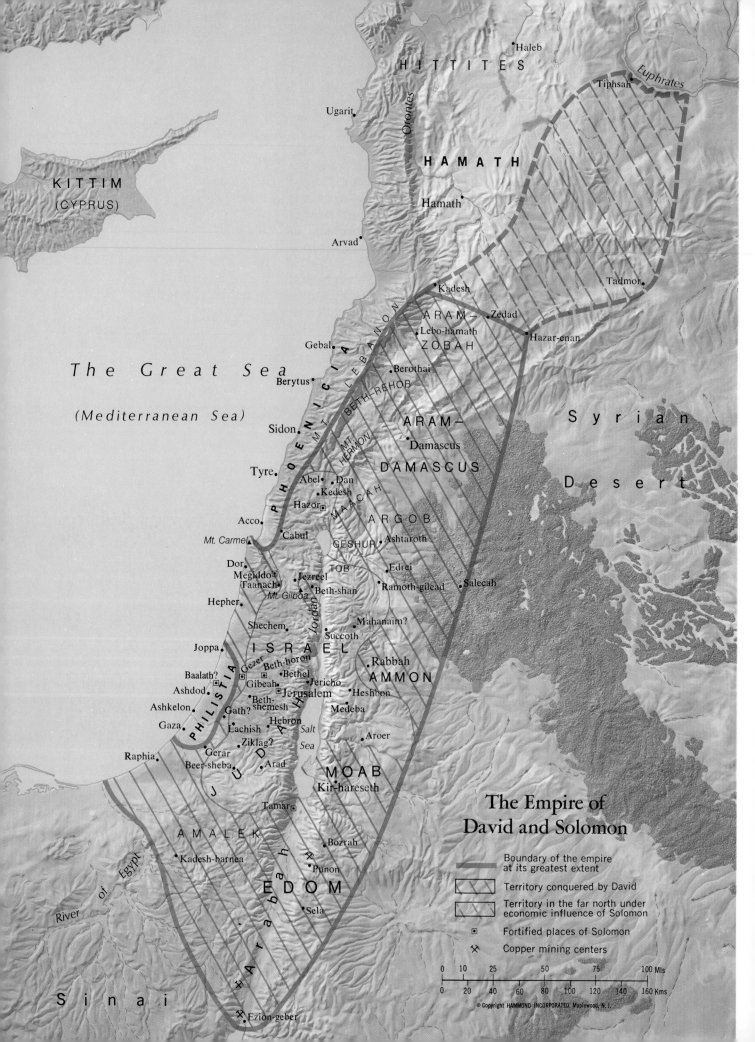

HITTITES

•Haleb

Orontes

Euphrates

Tiphsah•

Ugarit•

HAMATH

Hamath•

Tadmor•

Arvad•

Kadesh•

•Zedad

ARAM—

Lebo-hamath•

Hazar-enan•

ZOBAH

The Great Sea

Gebal•

•Berothai

BETH-REHOB

(Mediterranean Sea)

Berytus•

ARAM—

PHOENICIA

MT. LEBANON

Sidon•

Damascus•

DAMASCUS

Tyre•

Abel• Dan•

MT. HERMON

•Kedesh

Acco•

Hazor▫

MAACAH

ARGOB

Cabul•

•Ashtaroth

Mt. Carmel

GESHUR

S y r i a n

Dor•

TOB

•Edrei

Megiddo▫

Jezreel•

Ramoth-gilead•

•Salecah

Taanach•

•Beth-shan

D e s e r t

Mt. Gilboa

Hepher•

Jordan

Mahanaim?•

Shechem•

Succoth•

Joppa•

ISRAEL

Beth-horon•

Baalath?▫

Gezer▫

Rabbah

Ashdod▫

Gibeah• Bethel•

Jericho•

AMMON

•Beth-shemesh

Jerusalem•

Heshbon•

Ashkelon•

Gath?•

JUDAH

Medeba•

Gaza•

Lachish• Hebron•

Salt

•Aroer

Ziklag?•

Sea

Raphia•

Gerar•

Arad•

Beer-sheba•

MOAB

Kir-hareseth•

Tamar•▫

The Empire of
David and Solomon

AMALEK

Bozrah•

•Kadesh-barnea

✕Punon

River

of

Egypt

EDOM

•Sela

Ezion-geber✕

S i n a i

Arabah

Boundary of the empire
at its greatest extent

Territory conquered by David

Territory in the far north under
economic influence of Solomon

▫ Fortified places of Solomon

✕ Copper mining centers

0	10	25	50	75	100 Mls
0	20 40	60 80	100 120	140 160 Kms	

© Copyright HAMMOND INCORPORATED, Maplewood, N.J.

KITTIM
(CYPRUS)

ruthless he could be when at Ziklag he laid the ground for his ascension in Judah. Baseness was certainly one of the components of David's character. Nothing seemed too low for him if his personal ambitions and desires were at stake. He could commit adultery and premeditate the murder of the woman's husband, a foreigner serving loyally in the front lines of David's wars. So David and Bathsheba. He could, on the other hand, show amazing kindness to the one man in his kingdom who had a dynastic claim to the throne even stronger than David's. This potential threat, this one around whom court intrigues could and did form, was Mephibosheth, Saul's grandson, the son of Jonathan, David's dearest and lamented friend. Seemingly it was only for the sake of Jonathan that David showed this kindness; he was somewhat more careless about the other descendants of Saul (2 Samuel 21:1-9). But the point is this: David was capable of graciousness and showed it in this case and on other occasions.

He was apparently also tolerant of Canaanite ways of worship, but he did not himself either encourage these personally or by state policy and was always in his own religion deeply devoted to the god of his fathers. Indeed, the Biblical writers, struggling after David with kings who (except for three) encouraged foreign religious practices both in person and in policy, looked to David as *the* monarchical standard of piety and finally as one of the great religious examples from Israel's past.

With few exceptions everything in David's makeup seems to have its opposite. This was not true, however, of his devotion to his god, and it was not true of his failure with his children. Perhaps the oldest and best piece of historiography in the world, 2 Samuel 9-20, is an eyewitness to the reign of David; it is called his court history by some scholars. The fascination of this man is everywhere present in the strokes of that gifted ancient writer who produced this account. And nowhere is a sense of nemesis greater or portraits more pathetically vivid than in the accounts of the children of this magnificent monarch — their pride, their vanities, lusts, hatreds and self-destructive ambitions that brought tragedy to themselves and suffering to Israel. When the crown prince is killed by his half brother for raping his half sister, David does little. The murderer, Absalom, is banished — nothing more — and returns to Jerusalem, although not to court, with both intention and plan for unseating his aging and now indecisive father. And when the plot comes to fruition David and his kingdom are saved once more by Joab, older but no less single-minded. The old king staggers up the stairs of the city gate of Mahanaim sobbing, "O my son Absalom, my son, my son Absalom! Would I had died instead of you, O Absalom, my son, my son!" Hard upon the defeat of Absalom and his forces Joab rallies David to confront a new danger — the revolt of the northern tribes under Sheba, son of Bichri. Sheba chose this moment to strike while the royal armies were still wary and weakened by their dynastic struggles. But for Joab he might well have succeeded. The David of old seemed for a moment to be present once more, incisive and decisive. And the kingdom was preserved.

David's last days were full of war and court intrigue; those things he seemed never to have escaped. The Philistines were once more at his heels, and Bathsheba and her ambitions for her son Solomon were ever present. At last the old man agreed or gave in and Solomon was anointed king while David was yet alive. There was, of course, great wisdom in this. Israel had not had a dynasty. David had taken the throne from Saul's descendants. His death with a new king yet uncrowned might lead to a similar attempt by someone

Horned altar from tenth-ninth century B.C. found at Megiddo is like the altar mentioned in 1 Kings 2:28.

else, or more likely a fatal struggle among his sons. Indeed, Adonijah, an older half brother to Solomon, had already laid strong claim to the throne. But David sent Zadok the priest and Nathan the prophet down to the Spring Gihon with Solomon, and there the future splendid monarch of Israel was anointed. The succession was clear, the nation safe and the ground for true national brilliance well laid.

So David tottered toward his grave secure in the knowledge that with regard to the nation, at least, he had done his work well. The final words that are reported of him — his benediction to the coregent who would succeed him — suggest, however, that he still felt he had a few scores to settle (1 Kings 2:1-9). These he left to his son, who accomplished this and much more.

It is difficult to form any really clear picture of what Solomon was like. That he was an immensely able person there can be no doubt. Having once established himself firmly on the throne by killing his half brother, Adonijah, and all those who supported that prince's claims, Solomon set about to reorganize and tighten central control over the government of the country and to exploit the financial base which his father had left to him. David's work had been aggrandizement; Solomon's was consolidation and glorification. This involved a number of changes in policy, at least two of which were highly unpopular with various segments of his subjects. First, Solomon withdrew from some of the territory which David had taken. It was proving impossible to govern the farther reaches of empire. Although Solomon tried to keep a fortified garrison at Tadmor beyond Damascus in order to control the northern end of the King's Highway, he pulled back to what he considered secure borders and a manageable country.

A second unpopular move was to redraw the tax districts. While this may seem responsible and necessary to determine how much tax revenue the government may expect and to establish a more efficient manner of collection, Solomon drew the lines across old tribal borders. This was a direct attack on the authority of the tribal elders, those centers of power which had so long held sway among the Hebrews. Perhaps the lesson of Absalom's revolt was not lost on Solomon. Perhaps there were other motives. In any case the hand of central government was strengthened, and at the same time the local authorities became more wary of centralization.

Two other activities of Solomon proved in the end to be unpopular and, from some points of view, even disastrous. The king had a harem of one thousand wives and concubines. This meant that a very high percentage of the population of Jerusalem in Solomon's day was associated in some way with his harem, either as members of it or servants to it. It meant also that many of these wives who were foreigners worshiped their own gods. Indeed, Solomon was quite willing for them to do so and even built shrines and temples to these gods for his wives. Immediately south of the Mount of Olives is another hill, called locally The Hill of Shame, where it is said Solomon caused these places to be built.

The other activity was really a state policy, a policy related to his monumental building schemes. Press labor gangs were used. Solomon fought few wars, mostly border wars with the Edomites. There were not, therefore, large numbers of captives to use as workers. So he used the people of the country. At first Solomon seems not to have used Hebrews, only Canaanites and other non-Hebrews. This completely reversed the assimilation policy of David. But worse was to come. As Solomon's ambitions and schemes became more grandiose, the available work force proved more and more inadequate. He

Tadmor, caravan city also known as Palmyra, is associated with the empire under Solomon. The ruins are largely Roman, however.

92

began to use Hebrews in these labor gangs. But apparently only people from the north, from Israel, were used — not Judahites.

The labor policy of Solomon therefore not only discriminated among Hebrews and non-Hebrews, but in the end among Israelites and Judahites, inevitably alienating the Israelites. After Solomon's death this policy was cited to his son, Rehoboam, as one of the major grievances of the northern section of the kingdom, and it was a factor in the division of the country.

So what kind of person was Solomon? There are almost no personal stories to go on; there is nothing like the court history of David. The account of his adjudicating the case of the two women who claimed the same baby (1 Kings 3:16-28) is a part of the tradition that assigns great wisdom to this monarch. Under the same thrust the Proverbs are traditionally said to have been written by him. But little of the man comes through. He had a passion for gold, that we know, and he seems to have collected foreign women in his harem as one might bring back souvenirs from a trip abroad. He certainly was not faithful to the Hebrew god and worshiped at the shrines of a variety of gods, often playing the role of the priest. He lived in splendor not seen before in the land and not equaled again until the days of Herod the Great. Indeed, his personal magnificence and that which he bestowed on his capital city were fabled. The Queen of Sheba made a long and difficult trip to see this monarch of whom she had heard, a trip spoken of among the common people a thousand years later (Matthew 12:42). Solomon's glory was also recalled and was a standard by which to judge such things. Jesus said, "Consider the lilies of the field, how they grow; they neither toil nor spin; yet I tell you, even Solomon in all his glory was not arrayed like one of these" (Matthew 6:28-29; see also Luke 12:27).

His one great failing seems to have been that he does not appear to have counted the cost of anything. He built imposing buildings which left the country on the verge of financial disaster. Like Louis XIV of France, he employed policies supporting his personal life-style and his ambitions which were shortsighted and proved catastrophic. The cost of Solomon's reign is not to be measured in the usual financial terms, as disastrous as these were, but in political, military, social and religious terms as well. His legacy was the Divided Monarchy, two weak states contending among other equally weak states with varying degrees of success and failure over the years.

But while he reigned it was another story altogether. Egypt and Assyria were still weakened by internal dissensions. So weak was Egypt that for the first and only time the pharaoh gave the king of Israel a daughter to wife. More than that, Solomon did not give the Egyptian king a daughter in return. The petty monarchies — Damascus, Moab, Edom and others — in the land bridge between the two sleeping giants had not recovered from David's assaults and, while gaining strength, were not ready to challenge Israel on any massive scale. There were a few border problems, especially in Transjordan, but for all intents and purposes Solomon's kingdom was free not only from external strife, but also from the threat of it.

Internally, things were also pacific. The tension between north and south as well as the increased stresses resulting from various of Solomon's ill-considered policies were contained for the most part, and to our knowledge there was nothing resembling Sheba's revolt against David. Jeroboam, a military engineer in Solomon's service, had to flee to Egypt for his own safety (1 Kings 11:26-40). He was a northerner, a person of some influence there; indeed, he became the first king of north Israel in the division after Solomon's death.

Fertility figurine made from a mold found at Taanach in a late tenth-century context, roughly the time of Solomon.

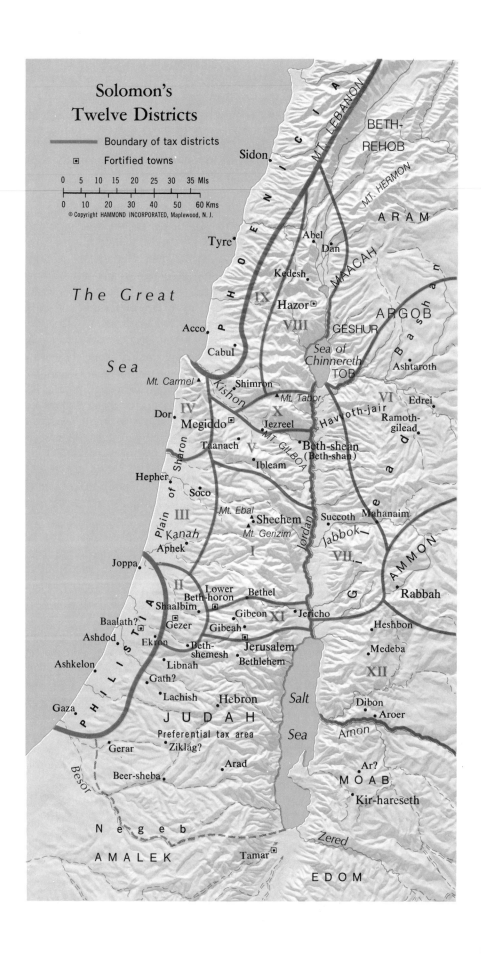

Solomon's Twelve Districts

━━━ Boundary of tax districts

▣ Fortified towns

0 5 10 15 20 25 30 35 Mls
0 10 20 30 40 50 60 Kms
© Copyright HAMMOND INCORPORATED, Maplewood, N.J.

BETH-
REHOB

PHOENICIA

MT. LEBANON

MT. HERMON

ARAM

Sidon

Tyre

Abel

Dan

Kedesh

MAACAH

Hazor ▣

GESHUR

ARGOB

The Great

IX

VIII

Bashan

Acco

Cabul

Sea of
Chinnereth
TOB

Ashtaroth

Sea

Mt. Carmel ▲

Kishon

Shimron

▲ Mt. Tabor

VI

Edrei

Dor

IV

Megiddo ▣

X

Jezreel

Havioth-jair

Ramoth-
gilead

Taanach

V

MT. GILBOA

Beth-shean
(Beth-shan)

Ibleam

Hepher

Soco

Gilead

Mahanaim

Plain of Sharon

III

Mt. Ebal ▲

Shechem

Succoth

Jabbok

Kanah

▲ Mt. Gerizim

Jordan

VII

AMMON

Aphek

I

Joppa

G

II

Lower
Beth-horon ▣

Bethel

Shaalbim

Gibeon

XI

Jericho

Rabbah

Baalath? ▣

Gezer

Gibeah

Heshbon

Ashdod

Ekron

Beth-
shemesh

Jerusalem

Medeba

PHILISTIA

Libnah

Bethlehem

XII

Ashkelon

Gath?

Lachish

Hebron

Salt

Dibon

Aroer

Gaza

J U D A H

Sea

Arnon

Preferential tax area

Gerar

Ziklag?

Arad

Ar?

Besor

Beer-sheba

M O A B

Kir-hareseth

N e g e b

Zered

A M A L E K

Tamar ▣

E D O M

94

Perhaps there is more in the story of Jeroboam's flight than meets the eye. Whatever may have been going on under the surface, Solomon's long reign nonetheless presents Israel as a secure nation, the envy of its neighbors, increasingly prosperous with a rising standard of living, a growing intelligentsia, and adventurously extending trade in almost every direction. All presided over by a splendid oriental autocrat.

The impression should not be given that Solomon's ambitious construction efforts were merely or mainly to satisfy his ego or to justify some view he held of himself. He was motivated by a concern to fortify certain strategic points in his country or along its borders. He built border fortresses, store-cities, cities for his chariots and cities for his horsemen. The Bible mentions (1 Kings 9:15) four cities that received special attention. These were Hazor, Megiddo, Gezer and Jerusalem. Major excavations have been carried out at these sites within the past ten years, and at all four archaeological work is continuing.

At three of these places — Hazor, Megiddo and Gezer — similar city gates have been uncovered, gates which seem to have been a favorite of Solomonic engineers. Unlike some other types of city gates known in the Ancient East, gates which either lapped the walls or contained ninety-degree jogs to prevent horses and chariots from dashing through a breached gate, the Solomonic structures pierced the walls directly. Apparently there were twin towers toward the outside of the gates, and six guard chambers, three on each side, just inside the wall.

Adjacent to these gates were casemate walls, in vogue at that time in Israel. Casemate walls were thought to be superior to the massive solid walls of earlier days which had proved no equal to the battering ram and scaling ladder. The casemate wall consisted of two parallel walls joined at intervals by cross walls. Behind this construction was the idea that a battering ram would not shatter these defenses, but would rather penetrate into the empty space between the walls which could be filled with dirt, stones, grain, or just left empty, depending upon an assessment of the enemy's strength and weaponry. As it turned out these casemate walls were relatively ineffectual when, after Solomon's death, the revived Egyptians swept over Israel and Judah.

The exact extent of these Solomonic cities is as yet unknown. Hazor would appear to have been a stronghold with only the highest portion of the acropolis surrounded by the casemate wall. Megiddo, which possibly had an Israelite settlement from the early days of David's reign, was somewhat larger. Perhaps the entire top of the hill was within the walls. It would seem so. At Megiddo in the winter of 1972-1973 Professor Y. Yadin showed that this site was surrounded by a casemate wall like those at Hazor and Gezer. He had earlier demonstrated that the large stable area there, attributed to Solomon, was in fact from the time of Ahab. Megiddo was an important site in Solomon's day, however, commanding as it does the pass known as Armageddon (Hill of Megiddo). This has been Palestine's Thermopylae since the day in the sixteenth century B.C. when Pharaoh Thutmoses III forced it while moving north with his army toward Mesopotamia. This was clearly a strategic point which the defense-minded Solomon was not likely to miss. Important as it was in Solomon's time, Megiddo became even greater almost a century later during the reign of King Ahab.

Gezer, we are told by 1 Kings 9:16, had been captured and burned by the pharaoh just before he gave it to Solomon as dowry for the Egyptian princess who became queen in Israel. Solomon seems therefore to have received a

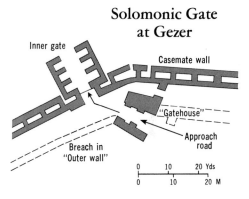

Solomonic Gate at Gezer

Inner gate

Casemate wall

"Gatehouse"

Approach road

Breach in "Outer wall"

0   10   20 Yds

0   10   20 M

Solomonic gate at Gezer with flanking guardrooms is virtually identical to Solomon's fortifications at Megiddo and Hazor.

95

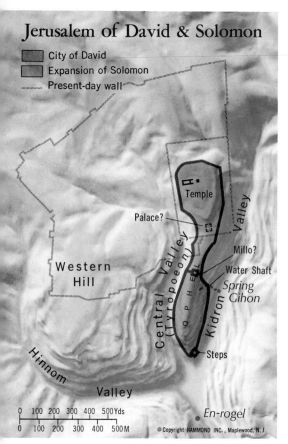

Jerusalem of David & Solomon

◼ City of David
◼ Expansion of Solomon
----- Present-day wall

Temple

Palace?

Western
Hill

Central Valley
(Tyropoeon)

OPHEL

Kidron Valley

Millo?
Water Shaft
Spring
Gihon

Steps

Hinnom
Valley

0   100 200 300 400 500 Yds
0   100 200 300 400 500 M

© Copyright HAMMOND INC., Maplewood, N. J.

En-rogel

somewhat desolated site. What he did with it we do not yet know. The marvelously preserved gateway which he built there is now visible, and the casemate wall running from it has been established by archaeologists. Beyond that the actual limits of the Solomonic town at Gezer are a subject for informed guesswork.

Jerusalem, which was Solomon's first concern and on which he lavished all the splendor at his command, is likewise a subject for informed guesswork. This does not mean fanciful mental construction, but careful reconstruction on the basis of meager evidence which is available from Jerusalem and other sites. Part of the trouble in reconstructing ancient Jerusalem of whatever period traces to the large number of sieges waged there and the consequent destruction. Another problem lies in the extensive Roman quarrying which was done at the south end of the site of the ancient city. War and quarrying, not to mention medieval and modern construction, have removed or covered much of the needed evidence for recovering ancient Jerusalem.

Yet all is not hopeless. Some things can be said, albeit with tentativeness. David's Jerusalem occupied the old Jebusite city which he had captured; namely, the southern spur of the hill between the Kidron and Tyropoeon valleys. The northern limit of this town was approximately 650 feet south of the southern limit of the great platform which is there today. It was Solomon who extended the city to the north to include the height of this ridge, a ridge dominated by the threshing floor of Araunah, which David had bought to be the site of his planned temple (2 Samuel 24: 18-25). The present massive platform, which is the work of Herod the Great, seems completely to cover the Solomonic site, whose shape and size are unknown to us.

This temple site, whatever its configuration in those halcyon days of Israel, seems to have been joined to the earlier Jebusite-Davidic city. The 1961-67 British excavations in this area found a fragmentary casemate wall which is thought to be a part of this Solomonic enclosure joining the two parts of his chief city. From 1972 the Israeli excavations in the same place disclosed a massive building about 289 by 135 feet in extent that may have been built during Solomon's reign. Benjamin Mazar has suggested that it may be the "house of Millo" mentioned in 2 Kings 12:20. It was within the newly enclosed section and certainly dominating the brow of the northern ridge that the king's palace and a temple to the God of Israel were built. Solomon's Temple, remembered with such tenacity throughout Jewish history and recalled with such fervor at the Western Wall in Jerusalem, was the crowning achievement of his reign. Actually, it might be more correct to say, based on other known examples from the Ancient Near East, that the palace and the temple were the supreme achievements of this man. It was common for great palaces to have equally splendid temples associated with them. So it was in the case of Solomon. In addition to the magnificent royal apartments (including a house built especially for the Egyptian princess), his palace had three great public chambers: the House of the Forest (of the cedars of Lebanon), the Hall of Pillars and the Hall of the Throne. The last was also called the Hall of Judgment because it was from his throne that the monarch heard cases at law and gave his decisions. An ivory throne inlaid with gold and raised six steps above the level of the floor was indicative of the decoration of this great house. Solomon even had the golden treasury of Israel made into 300 shields which he hung in the House of the Forest (1 Kings 10: 16-17).

The Temple was no less splendid, and while it may not have rivaled that built on the site almost a thousand years later by Herod the Great, it was nonetheless one of the most magnificent buildings of its day. We have two sources of information to help us reconstruct Solomon's Temple. There is a somewhat full description in the Bible (1 Kings 6:1-8:9), but its details are subject to controversy and there are many opinions. The second source is archaeology, not in Jerusalem but elsewhere. We know that Solomon hired Phoenician architects, masons and builders to construct this sanctuary. The Biblical description, whatever the difficulties with its details, strongly suggests a building not unlike those which have been unearthened in contemporary Phoenician sites. It may well have been a long, rectangular, flat and relatively low-roofed affair with three internal chambers: a porch, a nave and a Holy of Holies. The central room was about forty-five feet high. On three exterior sides were storerooms and a treasury. These were three stories high but not as high as the main building. Like other sanctuaries of contemporary design the Temple had two pillars before it, and in its courtyard there was a great altar for burnt sacrifices. There is at Tell Arad, in the northeastern Negeb, a Solomonic sanctuary whose courtyard proportions are those mentioned in the Bible of the Temple in Jerusalem. From other sites of both earlier and later date have come cult objects suggestive of those described in Scripture as having been in that great structure which once and for all changed the central shrine of the Hebrews from a wandering nomadic sanctuary to a fixed location. The building itself was monumental; so also for the Israelites was the idea which lay behind it.

Brief mention must also be made of many of Solomon's other undertakings. Almost everyone has heard of King Solomon's mines and knows of his mining operations in the Arabah, from which he got iron and copper. But his activities in the Negeb are not mentioned in the Bible, and few know that he established a number of fortifications there, some of which appear to have been centers of agricultural experimentation seeking to make the desert bloom. And of course there is the fleet which he based on Ezion-geber, near modern Elath and Aqabah. With the help of Phoenician boatrights and sailors he was able to carry on extensive trade with eastern Africa and imported into Israel — in addition to ivory, exotic woods and gold — monkeys which were favored household pets of the rich.

Solomon was glorious all right, and so was his kingdom. His sources of wealth were many: control over the two major trade routes, forced labor, commerce by land and by sea, tribute, efficient taxation and credit. Nothing was ever enough. The upkeep of the king and his retinue, including his palaces and women, was enormous. Cities sprang up out of ashes, as with Gezer, or took on new and grand appearances, as with Megiddo. And there were always the best architects, the finest masons and the most expensive materials available. All were imported, men and lumber alike. When Hiram of Tyre wished to collect some of the money Solomon owed him, the Israelite king was forced to cede territory north of Mount Carmel, one of several things for which the Biblical writers could not forgive him.

Solomon's reign was glorious, of that there can be no doubt. But characterized as it was by disregard for the jealous religion of Hebrew tradition, by excesses of spending and the injustices visited on the people in order to obtain the labor and the riches necessary to achieve this glory, Solomon's kingdom carried within it the seeds of its own destruction. And in thinking about Solomon one keeps coming back to Louis XV and life at Versailles. Perhaps the prophetic words attributed to this monarch may serve as a fitting epitaph for that famous son of David and Bathsheba: *Après moi, le déluge,* "After me, the deluge."

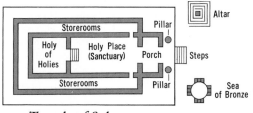

Temple of Solomon

0   10   20   30 Cubits

0   5   10   15 M

The northern shore of the Gulf of Aqabah, once dominated by the settlement of Ezion-geber where Solomon built his fleet.

9 THE TWO KINGDOMS

Solomon's kingdom barely outlived him. At his death his son and heir, Rehoboam, sought to ascend the throne of Israel and Judah. There was no difficulty in the south. The elders of Judah were no doubt pleased to anoint another native son to continue the rule which had favored Judah in so many ways. In the north, in Israel, it was a different story altogether. Before there was to be an acclamation of any son of Solomon, there must be some plain talk about certain policies of state which the men of the northern hills and valleys thought discriminatory if not unbearable. Forced labor gangs for royal building projects simply must not continue. Heavy and inequitable taxation favoring Judah would have to be modified. The new king would either have to find other ways to carry out his personal and imperial ambitions or else temper his desires. In any case, the northern tribes were clearly unwilling to bear the brunt of the monarchical burden. Underlying these real grievances was the reviving strength of the tribal elders. Solomon had not completely destroyed their power after all.

Would the elders of the north come to Jerusalem to anoint Rehoboam king? No, they would not. Would Rehoboam, yet unacclaimed king in Israel, come to Shechem to discuss matters with these elders? Yes, he would come to Shechem. This may have been in imitation of a precedent set by his father. On the other hand, Rehoboam's journey to Shechem to parley with the northern leaders may have been motivated by a desire to conciliate them. In any event, it was a confession of weakness. As the resplendent royal retinue made its slow progress through the hills of Judah and into the uplands of Ephraim, there must have been a number who awaited the king in Shechem who had their resolve strengthened and their hopes buoyed. He was coming to them!

In Egypt word of the new king's decision to go north for this meeting had reached Jeroboam, who had earlier fled from Solomon's reach because of a plot against the throne. Leaving the land of the pharaohs behind him, this ambitious northerner hurried home. He would be among those of Israel who would lay their demands before the fledgling monarch.

While the outcome of the meeting could not have been accurately predicted in advance, the acrimony which attended the sessions was perhaps inevitable. It all started calmly enough. "Your father made our yoke heavy," said all the assembly of Israel. "Now therefore lighten the hard service of your father and his heavy yoke upon us, and we will serve you" (1 Kings 12:4). Rehoboam asked for three days to consider these requests. With him were the old counselors of his father; those who, whatever their responsibility in bringing matters of state to this pass, now saw the results of Solomon's policies. They urged conciliation; ". . . speak good words to them when you answer them, then they will be your servants for ever." Unity and security in the kingdom were worth purchasing at the cost of what might be seen by some as a slight royal humiliation.

Unfortunately, also present with Rehoboam in Shechem were a group of younger men, men who had grown up with him and who now found

Opposite:
The incense stand (left) is from the time of the Divided Monarchy and is Canaanite in form. The earlier high-stemmed bowl (right) has leaf decorations thought to be similar to the adornment of columns in Solomon's Temple.

themselves with easy and direct access to the royal ear. The trappings of power, so novel and agreeable to them, were to be preserved, and there was to be no nonsense about it. "Thus shall you speak to this people who said to you, 'Your father made our yoke heavy, but do you lighten it for us'; thus shall you say to them, 'My little finger is thicker than my father's loins. And now, whereas my father laid upon you a heavy yoke, I will add to your yoke. My father chastised you with whips, but I will chastise you with scorpions'" (1 Kings 12:10-11). The people must be shown at the outset who is to rule in this land. Begin as you mean to continue. Such were the thoughts and concerns of Rehoboam's young friends. He took their advice.

After three days Jeroboam and the people of Israel came to Solomon's son to hear his answer. Hard words fell upon them, and the cry which David had heard (2 Samuel 20:1) filled the air:

> What portion have we in David?
>> We have no inheritance in the son of Jesse.
> To your tents, O Israel!
>> Look now to your own house, David.
>>> (1 Kings 12:16)

If Rehoboam meant to be a true son of his father, then he would sit on the throne of that Judahite, and on that throne alone!

The elders left Shechem — and Rehoboam. They returned to their tents firmly resolved to leave this southerner unacclaimed in the north. The die was cast, but Rehoboam had not yet exhausted his powers of "persuasion." Adoram, the taskmaster over the forced labor, was sent out to bring the people into line. He was stoned to death. The king, now near panic, mounted his chariot and made a somewhat less than stately departure for Jerusalem and safety.

Events in the north, now having been set in full motion, continued with ever accelerating speed. Jeroboam was anointed king and was acclaimed by all of the tribes of the north. Judah was alone, except for some small portions of Benjamin. As if they could gauge the intentions of Rehoboam, the people of the north raised a large army, preparing — as well they might — for what was to come. According to 1 Kings 12:25 Jeroboam also took the precaution of strengthening the fortifications of Shechem, now become the capital city of a new kingdom, Israel. Toward the end of their 1962 excavation season archaeologists of the Drew-McCormick expedition to Shechem sought to determine whether a casemate refortification of the city which they had uncovered was that of Jeroboam. They were able then to determine that it might be probable, but not certain, that their discovery was one and the same as that built by the first king of north Israel so many years ago.

An armed attack on the north, restoring the unity his vanity and immaturity had so recently shattered, was certainly what Rehoboam had in mind. In these designs he was opposed by powerful forces within his own greatly reduced dominion. Not the least of the voices in opposition were those of the prophets. During the reign of Solomon, Ahijah of Shiloh, that ancient tribal religious center of Israel, had sought out Jeroboam and designated him to lead a revolt to overthrow the grand monarch and restore worship of the true God to the land. The religious sins of Solomon were indicated by Ahijah (1 Kings 11:33) and may be spelled out in more detail in the anti-monarchy arguments now contained in the account of the anointing of Saul (1 Samuel 8:1-22; 10:17-27). There is little doubt that there was in ancient Israel a group

The East Gate at Shechem dates from the seventeenth century B.C. One of the inner orthostats was damaged in antiquity, perhaps by a battering ram. Jeroboam I strengthened the fortifications.

opposed to the institution of kingship, seeing it as both a denial of the kingship of God and also inflicting upon the people a terrible cost, religiously as well as socially and economically.

These feelings now surfaced. At this crucial moment of the division of the kingdom the prophet Shemaiah went to Rehoboam with these plain words: "'Thus says the Lord, You shall not go up or fight against your kinsmen the people of Israel. Return every man to his home, for this thing is from me'" (1 Kings 12:24). Although bitterness and what we might call border warfare went on between Israel and Judah, a full-scale war was momentarily averted. Others as well as the prophets had a hand in this. The north was, in fact, quite powerful, probably the stronger of the two, and an invasion by the south might have proved disastrous — to the south! Throughout most of their coexistence Israel was stronger than Judah and played a larger role in that small power cockpit between Mesopotamia and Egypt. And here, at the time of the division, Israel had a chance to consolidate and to solve some of the problems which were immediate.

We would do well to pause for a moment in the story and see the situation confronting the two kingdoms on the morrow of the division. Almost overnight they became petty states in the midst of a number of other small powers squabbling and constantly jockeying for advantage. The empire which David had captured and Solomon had solidified simply dropped away in the north, east and southwest. Only to the south, in the Negeb and down to the Gulf of Aqaba at Ezion-geber, does either of the two kingdoms seem to have been able to hold former imperial lands. This meant that for the moment Judah was able to control parts of Edom and retain the income from mines in the area. What happened to Solomon's sea commerce with eastern Africa we are not told. Perhaps it too was lost. Most of the other sources of income were surely lost. Control over the lucrative trade routes ceased. In Transjordan the King's Highway passed entirely out of Hebrew hands as the Israelite tribes in that area came under the sway of Damascus in the north, while to the south Moab asserted its independence. In the west the Way of the Sea, particularly that area from the Brook of Egypt perhaps as far north as Gibbethon, may have fallen completely under resurgent Philistine power. This power, while hardly such as to threaten a wholesale invasion of Judah, was enough to give trouble to the greatly weakened government in Jerusalem.

Meanwhile, the situation in the north was not much better. Israel did have some advantages in geography. Judah, huddled in the southern hills, bounded on the east by the Dead Sea, on the south by the desert, on the west and north by hostile nations was cut off from the flow of peoples and ideas. Israel, on the other hand, was penetrated to its very heartland by the Plain of Esdraelon which effectively connected the country with the flourishing Phoenician trade centers north of Mount Carmel; namely, Tyre, Sidon, Berytus and Gebal (Byblos). Israelite foreign policy shifted to take advantage of this natural situation. And the Way of the Sea still crossed Israelite territory. Its revenues were nothing compared to what they had been, but its cosmopolitan effect was still felt to a certain extent. The north was the center of the old tribal confederacy and retained some of the older traditions and practices from the time of the Judges, but its population was much less homogeneous than that of Judah. There was a significant non-Hebrew element and Phoenician influence was present and probably growing.

There were, of course, problems unique to each area. In the south Rehoboam doubtless had to deal with that national shock which comes with the sudden loss of position, but he may have been aided by the fact that the people seemed to have had no stomach for a full-scale war against the north. Perhaps Rehoboam's subjects also wished for a moment to catch their breath after Solomon's dazzling reign. What could not be postponed, however, was the question of the border between Judah and Israel. The tribe of Benjamin occupied the land immediately north of Jerusalem. The history of this tribe was a poor one, and it was in many respects the weakest of the northern group. Yet, suddenly, its territory was the most important in the land — most important, at any rate, to Judah. This narrow strip between Jerusalem and Bethel, scarcely ten miles wide, was cheek by jowl with Jerusalem! As long as this area remained loyal to Jeroboam or was under his sway Jerusalem, Rehoboam's seat, was unsafe. Rehoboam had to act in this situation and did so. The result was to make Benjamin a battleground for many years. Not until Asa, Rehoboam's grandson, was able to take Mizpah and Geba and make them into border fortresses could Judah feel secure. Israel, however, continued to hold Jericho, but the threat to Jerusalem from the east was much less than that from the north.

Jeroboam also had a multitude of problems. We have already noted that he refortified Shechem, doubtless with a view to its being his capital city. It was well suited to the purpose for many reasons. But it lacked one important thing; it was not easily defended, sitting as it does on the flat ground at the eastern end of the pass between Gerizim and Ebal. Soon the capital was shifted a few miles northeast to Tirzah. And what was the new king to do with the religious focus which David had given to Jerusalem? The people's political loyalty could not easily be distinguished from their religious attachment to that place. Jeroboam's answer was to build two new royal shrines, one in the north of the kingdom at Dan and the other in the south at Bethel. Bethel was situated on the major mountain road from the north to Jerusalem. It was, moreover, an old shrine hallowed by Jacob's vision there, and it was also near the southern border of Israel. Pilgrims headed for Jerusalem could be diverted there. It became the great royal shrine of Israel. Here and at Dan, Jeroboam placed his "golden bulls." Some may have understood these as the mounts for the invisible deity, since the image of the god riding on the back of a bull was well known in the Ancient Near East. However, judging from the consistent vitriolic attack of certain of the Biblical writers on these "sins of Jeroboam" it seems clear that many understood them to be fertility symbols.

While these two monarchs struggled with their internal problems, a staggering blow fell on them both, removing once and for all any hopes that Judah might have had of reuniting the country by force and ending any of Israel's dreams of former glories. The twenty-second Egyptian dynasty, founded by the Libyan, Shishak, sought to reestablish Egypt's colonial empire to the northeast. Shishak swept into Judah and Israel, breeching Solomon's vaunted casemate walls, burning his massive gates and overrunning his magnificent border fortresses. The Bible tells us only that Rehoboam paid an enormous tribute (including Solomon's golden shields from the Hall of the House of Cedar) to keep the Egyptian army away from Jerusalem. We are therefore dependent upon other sources to tell us the true scope of this disaster. At Karnak in Egypt there is an inscription of Shishak's mentioning over one hundred and fifty places which were said to have been taken. Even allowing for some exaggeration, there can be no doubt that Solomon's former kingdom was ravaged from Ezion-geber on the Gulf of Aqaba as far north as the Plain of Esdraelon. Even Transjordan felt the Egyptian attack. Archae-

Israelite road entering Dan. This road, perhaps constructed when Jeroboam I established a royal shrine here, turns right over an older Hyksos wall before going through the city gate.

ology tends to confirm this invasion both in scope and in detail. At a number of sites in different parts of the land artifacts or destruction layers give evidence of this disaster. Only the central hill country of Judah seems to have escaped, although archaeological work suggests that the Egyptians laid waste to the fortresses defending that area.

Both Judah and Israel were reeling. Their sole salvation seems to have been internal weakness in Egypt itself. Shishak was forced to retire and mend fences at home. Renewed dreams of another Egyptian empire in Asia retreated with him. However, he left a garrison at Gerar, and it was this group which later harassed Asa.

In the aftermath Rehoboam seems to have sought to refortify the country and in the process continued to strive with Israel over the Benjaminite area. Jeroboam had some of the same concerns, but he also had to resume the building of a new state. Of his administrative structure we know very little. He would likely have preserved as much of Solomon's elaborate structure as possible. He also continued his religio-political policies associated with the shrines at Dan and Bethel. These and perhaps other matters eventually led the religious party — the prophets and others of their persuasion — to bitter disappointment. Much of their support of Jeroboam was doubtless in the hope that the religious purity which Solomon had diluted would be returned to the land. In a situation reminiscent of Samuel and Saul, Ahijah of Shiloh rejected the drift of royal policies and broke with his king.

In addition an even more serious crisis faced Jeroboam, or rather faced the country upon the death of this first king. Could he pass on his throne to his son? Political stability and perhaps national survival were possibly at stake. David as king of Judah had been able to establish the dynastic principle. According to 2 Samuel 7, God made a covenant with David promising him and his house (that is, his descendants) the throne forever. This was celebrated in the cult at Jerusalem and is one of the reasons why Jeroboam had to break with that cult. Thus the dynastic principle was renounced by the northern tribes, and with it the Davidic covenant. Instead, they returned to an older charismatic ideal wherein the leader was designated by a prophet and acclaimed by the people. Choice thus fell upon each leader in his turn, not by accident of birth, but by divine and popular designation. Theologically and in theory it was an attractive principle. In practice it was politically disastrous. While Judah had a stable monarchy for almost the whole of its existence, Israel was unstable, with coups d'etat the rule rather than the exception. When Jeroboam passed the throne to his son, Nadab, that unfortunate monarch ruled for a year and fell in the first of many army plots. He was succeeded by his murderer, Baasha. Another precedent set by Baasha was elimination of the former royal family, in this case the descendants of Jeroboam. All of this was repeated again less than twenty-five years later when Baasha's son, Elah, was assassinated after a year in power. Baasha's family was destroyed by Zimri, Elah's murderer. Zimri ruled one week.

Zimri was an opportunist pure and simple. He seems to have had little or no backing at all. Omri, perhaps a commoner, was commander of the army in the field. He hurried to Tirzah and demanded the surrender of the regicide whose name would become infamous in Israel (2 Kings 9:31). Zimri refused and burned down the palace on top of himself. At the end of "the week of the three kings" Omri sat on the throne of Israel.

Half a century of dynastic argument and virtual civil war had left Israel practically prostrate. In the south during this time stability and safety had

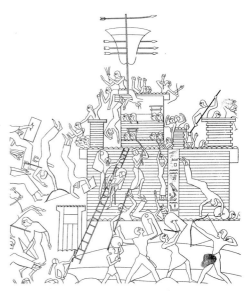

Egyptians assaulting a city, principally with the scaling ladder under the cover of arrows. The defenders seek to repel the attackers with stones, arrows and poles.

Solid mud brick wall uncovered at Tell el-Hesi may be an indication of Rehoboam's efforts to strengthen Hebrew fortifications after Shishak's invasion.

103

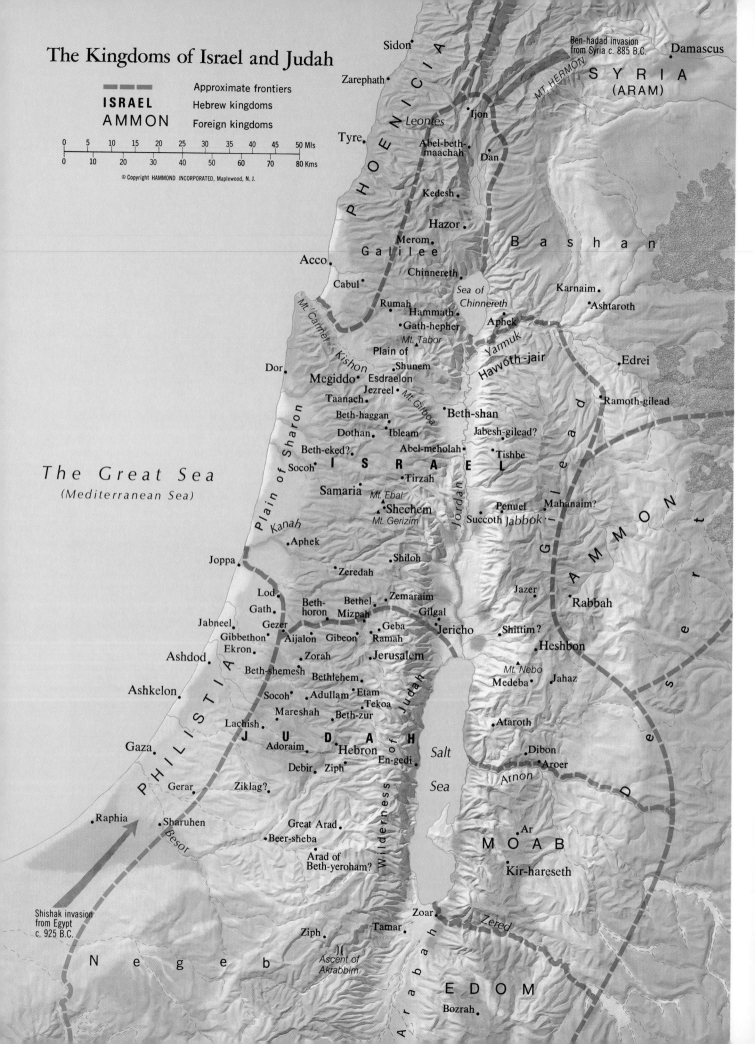

The Kingdoms of Israel and Judah

ISRAEL
AMMON

— — — Approximate frontiers
Hebrew kingdoms
Foreign kingdoms

0 5 10 15 20 25 30 35 40 45 50 Mls
0   10   20   30   40   50   60   70   80 Kms

© Copyright HAMMOND INCORPORATED, Maplewood, N.J.

Ben-hadad invasion
from Syria c. 885 B.C.   Damascus

SYRIA
(ARAM)

Sidon

Zarephath

PHOENICIA
MT. HERMON

Ijon

Leontes
Tyre

Abel-beth-
maachah

Dan

Kedesh

Hazor

BASHAN

Merom

Galilee

Acco

Chinnereth

Cabul

Karnaim

Rumah   Sea of
             Chinnereth   Ashtaroth
Hammath
Gath-hepher   Aphek
Mt. Tabor

Dor   Plain of
Megiddo   Shunem   Edrei
           Esdraelon
           Jezreel   Mt. Gilboa   Havvoth-jair
Taanach
Beth-haggan   Beth-shan   Ramoth-gilead
Dothan   Ibleam   Jabesh-gilead?
Beth-eked?   Abel-meholah
                        Tishbe

The Great Sea   Socoh   ISRAEL
(*Mediterranean Sea*)   Tirzah

Samaria   Mt. Ebal   Penuel   Mahanaim?
        Shechem   AMMON
        Mt. Gerizim   Succoth Jabbok

Aphek   Shiloh

Joppa   Jazer

        Zeredah   Rabbah

Lod   Zemaraim
        Beth- Bethel
Gath   horon Mizpah   Gilgal   Shittim?
Jabneel   Gezer   Geba   Heshbon
Gibbethon Aijalon Gibeon Ramah   Jericho
Ekron   Zorah   Mt. Nebo
Ashdod   Jerusalem   Medeba   Jahaz
        Beth-shemesh Bethlehem

Ashkelon   Socoh Adullam Etam
        Mareshah   Tekoa   Ataroth
Lachish   Beth-zur
        JUDAH   Dibon
Gaza   Adoraim   Hebron En-gedi   Aroer
        Debir Ziph   Arnon
Gerar   Salt
                         Sea
Ziklag?   MOAB
Raphia   Ar
Sharuhen   Great Arad   Kir-hareseth
        Beer-sheba
Besor   Arad of
         Beth-yeroham?

Shishak invasion
from Egypt
c. 925 B.C.   Zoar   Zered

N e g e b   Tamar
        Ziph
)(
     Ascent of
     Akrabbim   EDOM

                    Bozrah

been brought by Asa and his son Jehoshaphat. Asa had repulsed an Egyptian thrust from Gerar and driven the Egyptians south of the Brook of Egypt and out of Judah's hair for over a century. His quarrel with Israel over the Benjaminite territories and the safety of Jerusalem was solved by the simple expedient of entering into an alliance with Ben-hadad of Damascus, who did not need much excuse to attack Israel. As the Israelites pulled their forces from Benjamin and the Judahite frontier to defend Galilee from the Damascenes, Asa took Mizpah and Geba. The long-standing border question was settled. Asa also undertook a wide-ranging religious reform which was carried on by his son. He sought to remove foreign influences from the religious life of Judah and in the process probably removed many aspects of cosmopolitan life from Jerusalem. All in all Asa had brought Judah unity and had halted the downward spiral which had taken place since the disruption.

When Omri surveyed his sorry realm through the smoke of the smoldering palace at Tirzah, prospects for Israel were not bright. Upper Galilee was ravaged and open to future assaults. Former Israelite lands north of the Yarmuk in Transjordan were in Ben-hadad's hands. Judah held a firm border in the south. The economy was in collapse, or very close to it. Far to the north there were rumblings of what would eventually prove fatal for Israel — Assyria was becoming an imperial power.

For a long time, over two centuries, Assyrian fortunes had been in decline. The nadir was reached about the time David sat secure on the throne of Israel, but now Assyria was an awakened giant. Asshurnasirpal II, who was roughly a contemporary of Omri, was vigorously and rapidly reviving Assyrian strength. Using unparalleled brutality as state policy, he secured the northern reaches of his kingdom and turned his attention to the west. His armies laid waste to much of Syria, and only abundant tribute kept them from entering — and doubtless sacking — the Phoenician cities north of Mount Carmel. Thus satisfied for the moment, Asshurnasirpal withdrew. This was but the first of the seemingly interminable Assyrian campaigns across the Euphrates which took place for the next century and in the end were to destroy the Kingdom of Israel entirely. Before that fateful event, however, the Assyrian threat would produce some strange alliances among the petty states of the land bridge between Mesopotamia and Egypt, most notably involving Damascus and Israel. But for the moment Ben-hadad of Damascus could hardly have looked to Israel for solace and strength. Israel had none to offer.

The half century following the breakup of Solomon's kingdom had seen Israel engaged in an exercise in self-destruction. Now almost all it had left was Omri, an army field commander who may have been of Canaanite extraction. But what an asset this man was! Possessed of decision, dash and daring, he also had extraordinary vision. Although the Bible devotes only half a dozen verses to him and his reign (1 Kings 16:23-28), there can be little question that he was one of Israel's greatest kings, literally snatching the country from a final and fatal plunge into anarchy and disintegration. Long after his dynasty had disappeared the Assyrians still called Israel the house (or land) of Omri. This is eloquent testimony to his achievement.

How did he achieve his great work and bring the northern kingdom of Israel to the threshold of its potential greatness? He returned to the policies of Solomon: shrewd alliances promoting commerce, peace on his borders, strength beyond those borders and above all internal harmony based upon a cosmopolitan culture welcoming artisans and skilled workmen. Therefore he made peace with Judah, closing the hemophiliac wound which had so long

Samaria, "the hill of Shemer," where Omri built his royal city.

An ivory carving from Megiddo shows Egyptian artistic influence. Ivory was widely used to decorate palaces and other important buildings.

been Israel's southern border. He entered into an alliance with the Phoenicians, opening up once more trade relations which had once been a foundation stone of the economy. This alliance he sealed with the ill-fated marriage of his son, Crown Prince Ahab, to Jezebel, daughter of Ethbaal, king-priest of Tyre. In time the introduction of this strong-willed woman into the land of Israel would be regretted. For the present the Phoenician connections brought a legion of benefits. Omri also sought, with marked success, to reestablish Israelite power beyond the Jordan. He seems to have been unable to dislodge the Damascenes in the north where they held former Israelite lands. But farther south, in Moab, he was successful. The Moabite Stone which was inscribed sometime around 830 B.C. and discovered at Dhiban in the 1860s says, "Omri, king of Israel, he oppressed the land of Moab many days.... And Omri had taken possession of the land of Medeba and dwelt in it his days and half the days of his son, forty years."

As part of his new policies Omri also founded a new capital. To the northwest of Tirzah, commanding the main road from the north and thus from Phoenicia, was a solitary hill, not the highest in the area, but eminently defensible. This hill belonged to one Shemer. Omri bought it and regarded it as his private property. There, on the "hill of Shemer," he built his royal city — Samaria. This is the single example of a native Israelite city, all of the others having been of previous foundation. Yet Omri's magnificent capital can hardly be said to have been an Israelite city. Following the example of Solomon, Omri hired Phoenician architects, masons and artisans. There arose on the summit of the hill a truly splendid palace, whose masonry is among the finest extant walls from ancient times in the Middle East, and whose extraordinary interior earned the scorn of the prophet Amos, who referred to "the houses of ivory" (Amos 3:15; see also 1 Kings 22:39). Until just before the First World War this statement was thought to be an exaggeration to stress the luxury of the king and his nobles as contrasted with the poverty of the peasants. But in 1912 the famous Samaria ivories were found by excavators unearthing the ancient Israelite palace on the summit of Omri's hill. These are fragments of decorations which were attached to furniture (Amos 6:4) and perhaps screens on the walls and in the windows. Decorations of this type are still to be seen in the Middle East, although ivory has for the most part been replaced by other materials. But at Nimrud and other places in Mesopotamia where palaces of the kings of Assyria and Babylon have been dug up, large numbers of beautifully worked ivories have been found, including a massive screen which once covered an entire wall. Such was the style of these ancient monarchs, and Omri at Samaria had the means and the desire to ape that fashion.

The construction of Samaria marked a shift in Israelite foreign and domestic policy. Drift and indecision, inevitable companions of the near anarchy which had marked Israel since the collapse of Solomon's throne, were replaced by a determined policy to enrich the social base of Israelite society. This involved making the country more attractive to skilled artisans of non-Israelite background and renewing trade and cultural relations with the great Phoenician ports north of Carmel.

Strength returned swiftly. The borders were secure and previously disputed territories passed once more into Israelite hands. Economic life revived as the pulse of commerce quickened. Foreigners following trade and sensing profit played their role and were more and more to be seen in the land. The king, secure in Samaria, had reason to be pleased with his burgeoning country.

But not all were pleased. Omride policies, in the eyes of the prophets and other religionists, were succeeding all too well, and the practical results were hardly to be praised. Material prosperity, which was growing steadily, was also concentrating in the cities, making more serious the ancient division between the men of the town and the men of the countryside. The life of the rural population grew more harsh. Heavy taxes and usurious interest rates took their toll. The old Hebrew idea of inviolable hereditary property gave way to opposing Canaanite views. Smaller landholders were not only in danger of losing their property, but of being sold with their families into indentured slavery.

This growing economic crisis with its strong social implications had deep religious roots. Those whose ancestors had been under the taskmasters' whips in Egypt had strong prohibitions against slavery. And this prohibition was not merely theory, but was nourished by a heritage of desert egalitarianism and grounded in the cold realization that possession of family property was a God-given responsibility which was not to be dismissed lightly. The story of Ahab's conflict with Naboth over the latter's vineyard adjacent to the royal gardens at Jezreel is an excellent illustration of the conflict between Hebrew and Canaanite ideas and ideals about property (1 Kings 21).

A more direct religious crisis was also brewing. Solomon had built temples and shrines in Jerusalem and had dedicated many of them to the gods of his foreign wives. There was no reason why Ahab, now regnant in Samaria, should not do the same for Jezebel. The temple to Baal Melqarth which arose in the Israelite capital (1 Kings 16:32) was probably viewed by most as no more than what should be done for the queen; doubtless many for whom the religion of the Israelites was merely a veneer welcomed it. Those who objected to this and to the growing poverty in the countryside occasioned by increasing violation of what they considered sacred property rights were only religious dreamers who thought that the division of the monarchy would bring religious purity to the land. So must have thought the king and his scornful wife and others who understood the "realities" of building a viable state.

In the eyes of the pure religionists of Israel all this was bad enough; but worse — much worse — was to come. Queen Jezebel was strong-minded, tough, determined and not a little ruthless. She was moreover, like those who most deeply opposed her, a religious fanatic. It was her desire and intention to spread the cult of her god throughout the land, perhaps even wishing to make it the official religion of the royal court. At least 850 priests of Baal and Asherah dined at the royal tables and already enjoyed state sanction (1 Kings 18:19). The motley population of Israel, at best an admixture of Canaanite and Israelite, was embracing the religion of the Baals as merely another aspect of the new spirit that was upon the land. The God of the Hebrews was still worshiped, but often alongside Baal, and more and more transformed into another expression of a fertility god.

As might have been expected, extremism produced the other extreme. Opposition to Omride policies exploded in the land. It came from the edges of the desert, so long a center of the most conservative forces in Hebrew religion, and was focused squarely upon the queen and her covey of priests. The revolt was embodied in the person of Elijah.

What an extraordinary figure Elijah was. He made so profound an impression that his memory was piously preserved, heightened and interlaced with those miraculous elements which bespeak of the awe in which his contemporaries held him. A rough-cut ascetic from Tishbe in Gilead, his sparse

Gold covered statuette of Baal. Worship of the Tyrian Baal (Melqarth) was vigorously opposed by the Hebrew prophets.

body clothed in hair shirt and leather girdle, he was possessed of a single-minded fanaticism in his devotion to the purity of the religion of the God of Israel. In a society growing tolerant to the point of laxness, he was uncompromising. Israel had to choose between Yahweh and Baal.

This first of the great prophets of Israel seems suddenly to appear with a word of doom on his lips: the country is to suffer a great drought. This is divine judgment upon the people and their king for unfaithfulness. And the heavens ceased to open. The land parched while the specter of starvation hung heavy over the people. Then, in a dramatic scene, King Ahab confronted this one whom he called a "troubler of Israel." But this troubler, Elijah, flung a unique challenge. He alone would contest with the hundreds of priests of Baal. All were to gather on Mount Carmel where altars to the Hebrew God, Yahweh, and the Tyrian God, Baal, stood side by side. Each in turn was to be besought to return rain to the land.

Faster and faster the priests of Baal danced their limping dance until there was a frenzy — a wild, terrifying scene. But still no rain. "O Baal, answer us," they cried. But there was no answer. "Cry aloud," shouted Elijah with bitter sarcasm, "for he is a god; either he is musing, or he has gone aside, or he is on a journey, or perhaps he is asleep and must be awakened" (1 Kings 18:27). Frenzy grew to raving, and raving into an orgy as the pace of feet quickened and knives began to flash. The priests were slashing in the air, cutting themselves and each other. This was not uncommon in the ecstatic worship of this deity, but it availed nothing. "There was no voice; no one answered, no one heeded." All that they could do had been done, and the allotted time had run out.

Then Elijah soaked the altar of Yahweh with water three times, and when the time of the offering of the sacrifice came he prayed: "O Lord, God of Abraham, Isaac, and Israel, let it be known this day that thou art God in Israel, and that I am thy servant, and that I have done all these things at thy word" (1 Kings 18:36). As fire consumed the altar and its contents the people fell on their faces praising the Lord God of Israel and confessing that he was indeed God. At Elijah's order they arose, seized the priests of Baal, dragged them down into the valley by the Brook **Kishon** and there slaughtered them wholesale. Ahab was told by the prophet to continue the ritual and then to look out from the mountain toward the sea to the west. The seventh time he went to look a small cloud was rising and with it the promise of rain again. "Now," said Elijah, "hurriedly depart before the rains make passage impossible." And the man of God ran before the king's chariot until the gates of Jezreel.

Jezebel, hearing the excited words of her royal husband, acted with dispatch. She sent a messenger to Elijah, promising that before the new day dawned he would be like unto the slain priests of Baal. The exultant man's courage left him, and he was afraid. Southward he fled, through Judah to Beer-sheba. There he left his servant and journeyed on toward the sacred mount of God in Sinai. But after he had gone a day's journey into the wilderness, he sat down exhausted and hungry under the shade of a tree. His physical strength ebbed. Behind him his zeal for Yahweh and success in his name lay in shambles before the iron will of Jezebel. "It is enough; now, O Lord, take away my life," he prayed in this moment of spiritual and physical collapse. Sleep overwhelmed Elijah, and in his dreams an angel of the Lord appeared bidding him to eat and strengthen himself for the long journey to the holy mountain.

Air view of Mount Carmel. The Carmelite monastery at the summit marks the traditional site of the contest between Elijah and the priests of Baal.

At Sinai the revelation came to him that as long as the Omride dynasty sat upon the throne of Israel the religion of his fathers would not be secure in the land. Not in wind, earthquake, nor fire did he hear the word of God, but in a still, small voice. And in that voice he heard the words of regicide, not merely against the ruler of Israel, but of Judah and Damascus as well. Here was born the idea which, when put into reality by Elisha and Jehu, would tear the body fabric of Israel.

Ahab, meanwhile, was not without other troubles and not without success in meeting them. Ben-hadad of Syria invaded Israel, placed Ahab in a difficult position militarily and demanded heavy tribute. In desperation Ahab agreed, but then Ben-hadad raised the price. Now a fight was inevitable, and surprisingly Ahab won. Yet even in the moment of defeat the Damascene was planning another invasion of Israelite soil. It came the next year with even more disastrous results for Ben-hadad. He himself was captured in the rout of his army. Ahab, however, treated his enemy magnanimously, eventually releasing him. This was yet another cause for the conservative religionists in Israel to condemn their king. What wisdom was there in releasing this man who twice made war on Israel and would doubtless strike again.

But perhaps there was wisdom in Ahab's action. At any rate, the march of other events threw Ben-hadad and Ahab into each other's arms as they joined forces to oppose a common foe. At Qarqar in 853 B.C. the Israelites and the Syrians were part of a coalition which stopped the Assyrian juggernaut momentarily and delayed for five years the edge of the northerners' swords from their lands.

Once the massive threat from beyond the Euphrates was stayed, however, Israel and Syria once more contended for the fertile fields of Gilead. Ahab determined to take the offensive in the area of Ramoth-gilead, a key center in control of the area. As was the custom of the day he called in his royal prophets, seeking divine guidance and blessing for his intended campaign. All in chorus praised the wisdom of the monarch and assured him that divine favor would march in his ranks. Yet the king was not content with the words of his kept men. Micaiah, son of Imlah, one of the prophets of Israel, was sought out and brought to the king. When pressed he told the king of disaster that awaited him across the Jordan. For the truth this man was beaten. But Ahab did heed the words to a certain extent. In the ensuing battle he disguised himself while forcing his ally, Jehoshaphat of Judah, to wear the robes of a king into battle. But this deception did not work. A stray arrow struck Ahab. Bleeding profusely, he continued to conduct the battle until his lifeless body slumped down in his now red-stained chariot. Without accomplishing their purpose, the Israelite army with its Judahite allies withdrew, leaving the field to the enemy. At Samaria the king was mourned, while his chariot was submerged in a pool to cleanse the blood from it.

"The king is dead, long live the king." Ahaziah sat on the throne in Samaria in place of his father. The great Omrides were dead; Omri and Ahab slept with their fathers. But Jezebel lived, and her influence was hardly reduced. Indeed, her influence as queen mother seems to have been even greater than her influence when she was the monarch's wife. Elijah was quick to condemn the new king. And when Ahaziah died as a result of a fall from an upper window in the palace, Elijah turned his wrath upon Jehoram, Ahaziah's brother who succeeded him.

Jehoram was a stronger person than his brother and took steps to quell a revolt in Moab which may have broken out when Ahab died. After initial

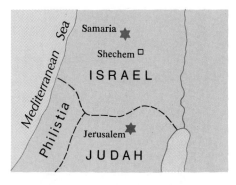

Kings of Judah and Israel
(for later kings see page 114)

JUDAH	ISRAEL
Rehoboam 922-915 ●	● 922-901 Jeroboam I
Abijah 915-913 ●	● 901-900 Nadab
Asa 913-873 ●	● 900-877 Baasha
	● 877-876 Elah
	● 876 Zimri
Jehoshaphat 873-849 ●	● 876-869 Omri
	● 869-850 Ahab
	● 850-849 Ahaziah
Jehoram 849-842 ●	● 849-842 Jehoram
Ahaziah 842 ●	● 842-815 Jehu

The Moabite Stone, found in 1868 at Mesha's capital. Carved about 840-820 B.C., it tells of the events of 2 Kings 3:4-27 and their aftermath from a Moabite point of view.

success, the Israelite army was repulsed with heavy losses, and Moab won its freedom, as the Moabite Stone tells us. In the north war with Damascus had erupted again. To the south, in Judah, Jehoshaphat had died and had been succeeded by a son whose name was also Jehoram. Like the ruler of the same name in Israel, this southern Jehoram was beset with a multitude of problems. Rebellion broke out everywhere on Judah's borders. The Judahite armies led by the militarily inept king lost Edom and with it the rich mines south of the Dead Sea as well as the port of Ezion-geber. Even some of the quiescent Philistine cities broke away. At every point the two Hebrew monarchies were being hard pressed. But at least Jehoram of Judah did not have to contend with the continuing internal conflict between Jezebel and Elijah, two worthy and unflinching opponents who were different only with regard to the objects of their devotion.

But Elijah had a plan, and he had a man. The plan was regicide and revolt, and the man was Elisha. Elisha, however, was the head of a group of prophets, not a person skilled in the military arts. But ambitious military officers are seldom hard to find, and Elisha sent a messenger to seek out Jehu, a chariot officer with a reputation for recklessness. The royal family was meanwhile at Jezreel, a royal residence near Beth-shan.

Anointed with holy oil and given the prophet's blessing — nay, order! — to go to Jezreel and seize the throne, Jehu set off to do his bloody business. The fact that this revolt was led by an army officer with apparent solid backing in the military probably shows widespread discontent in that quarter. Reverses in the wars with Damascus and Moab were in marked contrast to the victories of just a few years earlier and doubtless were blamed in many minds upon decadence and foreign ways of the privileged ruling class. Into this cauldron of disaffected strength was poured a passion of bitterness from the most extremist religious groups in the country. On the edge of the desert lived a group called the Rechabites. On principle they had entirely rejected the settled life which, in their view, brought with it the multifarious corruptions to which Hebrew religion was now being subjected. How these people viewed Omride Israel can well be imagined. Their solution was *herem,* "holy war." Their object was the wholesale sacrificial slaughter of the entire royal house, all who sided with them, served them, or in any way had anything to do with the hated dynasty and its policies. Together the alienated and ambitious military with the most conservative religionists brought upon Israel an unparalleled bloodbath and reduced the country to a level of weakness hitherto unknown.

The coup d'etat envisioned by Elijah and Elisha began as Jehu and some of his fellow officers approached Jezreel. Jehoram of Israel, recovering from battle wounds, went out with his young relative, Ahaziah, the new king of Judah, who had also taken part in the ill-fated battle near Ramoth-gilead. Ahaziah was also of Omride blood, for the two houses had intermarried. As they approached Jehu's chariot to parley, the intention of the army officers became clear. Jehoram shouted to the younger king to flee. Just then an arrow struck Jehoram, killing him instantly.

A chase ensued as the young king from the south tried to get away. There could be no thought of getting back to Jezreel. The direct way to Megiddo, a loyal and safe city, was apparently blocked. His speeding chariot went south, through the pass by Ibleam and then turned westward along the southern part of the great valley headed toward Megiddo. Near Ibleam, in the ascent of Gur, he also was struck by a flying arrow. Jehu's men were either unable to catch up to the royal vehicle or they now thought it unnecessary. This, in fact, proved to be the case. It was still over twelve miles to Megiddo. The wounded monarch hung on frantically as his chariot bumped and bounced, throwing him violently from side to side. At last Megiddo was in sight, and then he was safe inside its staunch walls. It was too late. He died shortly.

Meanwhile at Jezreel, Jehu entered the city and commanded Jezebel's servants to throw her out of a second story window. With his chariot he drove back and forth over her lifeless body and then calmly descended, entered the palace and sat down to the meal which had been prepared for her. When finally he gave orders for her to be buried —"for she is a king's daughter"— those who went to the task found that dogs had attacked the corpse leaving only the skull, hands and feet.

Samaria was now challenged by Jehu either to take up arms against him or else deliver up the heads of the princes of Israel — all seventy of them. At Jezreel Jehu received the grisly tribute which had been sent in baskets. Terror now stalked the streets of this royal town in the northern valley. Everyone who had anything to do with the Omrides — nobles, friends, priests, servants — all were taken and summarily executed. This being done the conspirators moved against Samaria. On the way they encountered by chance forty-two southern nobles and relatives of the king who were coming north to visit. These innocents knew nothing of the terrible events. They too fell victim, and their bodies were put in a pit at Beth-eked. Jehu now called forth Jehonadab, son of Rechab, to join him in the slaughter which would cleanse Israel and to aid him in the purging of Samaria. Scenes of horror, brutality and mercilessness were repeated. Cries of innocence availed nothing. *Herem!* God's honor must be avenged, his religion purified, his people made holy. A century later Hosea would recall these days as a dark blot on Israel's history.

Through trickery, deceit and with brutality Jehu spread his terror throughout the land, seeking everywhere to destroy the priests of Baal. All of this at the urging and with the cooperation of Jehonadab and in imitation of Elijah's earlier action on Carmel. But purity did not return to Israel. Jehu himself was hardly concerned with religious matters, except insofar as they aided him in taking power. From the point of view of the writer of 2 Kings Jehu's personal religion left a good deal to be desired, and the shrines at Dan and Bethel continued to function as before, earning for Jehu condemnation: "he did not turn from the sins of Jeroboam, which he made Israel to sin" (2 Kings 10:31). The revolt, which had religious instigation and support, had failed to achieve the hopes of the religionists. Jehu's strong suit was violence. For that only is he remembered.

Hittite chariot relief of the ninth century B.C. from Tell Halaf reflects a more peaceful scene than the bloody dynastic changes in Israel during the same period.

Assyrian bas-relief from Nineveh shows
Sennacherib's army assaulting the walls of
Lachish with battering rams and scaling
ladders.

10 THE END OF ISRAEL AND JUDAH

The blood purge of Baalism came at a very high price. Jehu not only got rid of the Tyrian Baal, he very nearly got rid of Israel! Indiscriminate murder in the name of God and the state left an already mixed population deeply divided. The Phoenician alliances on which so much of the Omride prosperity depended came to an abrupt end; Israelite economy began to crumble. With its young king dead at the hands of Jehu and with so many of its courtiers rotting in the pit at Beth-eked, Judah, Israel's only trusted military ally, broke the ties which Omri had carefully constructed. Hazael, who had come to power in Damascus the same fateful year as Jehu's purge, seized Israelite lands beyond the Jordan.

If anything the internal situation was the worst of it all. Social and economic abuses and the split between the cities and the countryside did not disappear with the Omrides. On the contrary, if we accept the later writings of Amos and Hosea as evidence, the matter simply continued to get worse right up to the very end of the kingdom. And what of religious reforms which were the reason for the whole thing anyway? The Tyrian Baal was gone, and with it the threat that Baalism might become the official religion of the court and perhaps even of the nation. But the local varieties of the fertility cult remained and continued without interruption. And the bitterness which was everywhere exacerbated every problem and sharpened divisions on every issue. Underlying all was Jehu's complete ineptitude. He seems to have been a singularly undistinguished monarch, unable or unwilling to come to grips with conditions which he had been primarily responsible for bringing to the land.

Perhaps it is ironic that it is of Jehu that we have the only contemporary picture of a Hebrew monarch. It came about this way. Hazael had come to power in Damascus partly because of his anti-Assyrian policies. Shalmaneser III, fully recovered from the effects of Qarqar, had campaigned across the Euphrates nine times between 849 and 841 B.C. Now he meant to punish Hazael, and he came up against Damascus. It seems that he was unsuccessful in taking the city, but he withdrew only after being paid tribute. Other kings in the area rushed to bring their gifts and hoped thus to avoid the cruel presence of the plumed helmets from the far north. Whether Shalmaneser struck a glancing blow at Israel, we do not know. At any rate, Jehu was among those who bowed themselves before the Assyrian, begging to be allowed to present gifts which had been brought for the great king. While all this is not mentioned in the Bible, it is vividly recorded on the Black Obelisk of Shalmaneser III now in the British Museum. This shaft is illustrated with scenes of the Assyrian receiving tribute. Among those pictured on his knees with his face to the ground is "Jehu, son of Omri"! What a striking difference from Shalmaneser's last contact with a Hebrew king when Ahab put 2,000 chariots and 10,000 foot soldiers in the field against him at Qarqar. It was, however, the difference between Ahab's Israel and that of Jehu.

Israel plunged into a half century of unparalleled weakness. During this time the Assyrians, occupied with their own internal problems, crossed the Euphrates only once to harass the petty nations on the Syria-Palestinian land

Panel on famous Black Obelisk from Nimrud gives us the only contemporary picture of a Hebrew monarch. Jehu, king of Israel, is shown prostrating himself before Shalmaneser III.

bridge. In a power vacuum not unlike the one which had existed during the time of David and Solomon, Damascus' fortunes were ascendant. Under Jehoahaz, Jehu's son and heir, Israel was practically a Syrian dependency. Hazael allowed the king of Israel only a small army consisting of 10 chariots, 50 horsemen and 10,000 foot soldiers. At the same time other ancient and traditional enemies took advantage of this weakness, biting off large sections of the country. Much of the seacoast was lost, and perhaps even Galilee down to the Plain of Esdraelon.

In the south Judah was not doing much better. Following the death of Ahaziah at Megiddo, the southern throne was usurped by Athaliah, an Omride princess married into the Davidic family. Her seven years as queen (the only break in the Davidic line from David to the end of the Judahite monarchy) was marked by what seems to have been an attempt to apply Omride policies to the south. But the south was a vastly different land, conservative in its ways, with a relatively homogeneous population and not blessed (or cursed!) by a geography which opened it to foreign influences. When this woman was deposed, her young son, Joash, reigned in her stead. But he was in his minority and apparently the chief priest, Jehoiada, was regent. A religious reform was carried out, seeking to rid the land of whatever success Athaliah may have had. However, when Jehoiada was dead and Joash came of age he rebelled against overmuch religiosity and became increasingly tolerant of different ideas and practices. This combined with his general ineptness eventually brought him under the assassin's blade. His reign was distinguished only by the fact that he was able to maintain himself in power for some thirty-seven years. Otherwise, Judah, ever the weaker of the two petty Hebrew states, suffered in the general decline attendant upon Israel's self-immolation and Damascus' rise to power.

Elsewhere events were afoot which would dramatically reverse this situation. In 802 B.C. Damascus was crushed by Adad-nirari III of Assyria, who had adopted the former aggressive policies of Shalmaneser III. The other petty states in the area felt the force of the blow and rushed forward with their tribute. Israel was one of these. So far as we know the Assyrian armies did not come farther south, and soon they were on their way home, drawn there by pressing needs. Assyria itself was under attack from Urartu, and this coupled with a succession of weak kings kept these armies north. Damascus, seeking to recover from this staggering blow, found hegemony over its immediate lands challenged by Hamath. Into this breach stepped Jehoash, Jehu's grandson and king of Israel.

In these shifting circumstances Israel was able to recover most of its former lands, including those beyond the Jordan. By a curious set of circumstances Jehoash also conquered Jerusalem and Amaziah, who had succeeded the murdered Joash. Amaziah had set out to reconquer Edom and with it the rich mines south of the Dead Sea. In this he was successful; indeed, his success outran his expectations and may have encouraged him to misjudge his strength. It was he who declared war on Jehoash in spite of the Israelite king's attempts to thwart such foolish action. Amaziah won the argument over whether they would have war. That was all he won. At Beth-shemesh the Judahite army was routed, Amaziah taken captive and the road to Jerusalem laid open. Jehoash took the capital, looted it, severely damaged its defensive walls and withdrew, leaving a humiliated Amaziah with his throne and little else. A conspiracy was afoot to murder this disgraced monarch. Hearing of it, Amaziah fled to Lachish near the Philistine frontier. To no avail. Assassins

Kings of Judah and Israel
(for earlier kings see page 109)

JUDAH	ISRAEL
Athaliah 842-837 ●	● 842-815 Jehu
Joash 837-800 ●	● 815-801 Jehoahaz
Amaziah 800-783 ●	● 801-786 Jehoash
Uzziah 783-742 ●	● 786-746 Jeroboam II
Jotham 750-735 ●	● 746-745 Zechariah
	● 745 Shallum
	● 745-738 Menahem
	● 738-737 Pekahiah
Ahaz 735-715 ●	● 737-732 Pekah
	● 732-724 Hoshea
Hezekiah 715-687/6 ●	*722/721 Fall of Samaria*
Manasseh 687/6-642 ●	
Amon 642-640 ●	
Josiah 640-609 ●	
Jehoahaz 609 ●	
Jehoaikim 609-598 ●	
Jehoiachin 598-597 ●	
Zedekiah 597-587 ●	

Fall of Jerusalem 587

114

caught up with him there, and Judah had a new king. He was the sixteen-year-old son of Amaziah. His name was Uzziah. In his very long reign Judah would reach heights of greatness not known since the division.

In the north there was also a new king, one who was destined to take Israel to heights of prosperity and glory. His name was Jeroboam II. We do not know half enough about this remarkable man. The Bible contains no details of his victories, only a passing reference in Amos (6:13). Yet he seems to have been a military commander of considerable ability, for he extended the borders of Israel perhaps to the limits of Solomon's kingdom. This at least seems to have been the case in the north and in Transjordan. We may infer from the Biblical accounts that he subdued Damascus (perhaps capturing the city itself) and ended Hamath's hopes for a dominion. All along the eastern side of the Jordan, Israelite strength reasserted itself, maybe even into southern Moab at the farthest reaches of the Dead Sea.

Lettering on Hebrew seal from eighth century B.C. identifies "Shema, the servant of Jeroboam."

At the same time Uzziah, in spite of his tender age, rapidly matured in the kingly arts. Having repaired the damage to Jerusalem, and having outfitted a new army by reorganization, recruitment and some sort of new siege machine he, too, undertook an aggressive campaign enlarging the horizons of Judah, physically, economically and in terms of influence and power. Among the things he did were to place experimental military-farming communities in the Negeb, to reopen the port of Ezion-geber and seek to distribute the goods of Judah's industries widely, perhaps as far as Arabia and east Africa.

Something very much akin to the Solomonic Golden Age returned to the land. Israel and Judah, extending their borders and influence in every direction, were at peace with one another. Archaeological excavations suggest that town and city life was booming amidst a growing population, which was spilling beyond former confining walls. For example, excavations in Jerusalem indicate that there was a sprawling suburb with its own defense wall and a tower on the western hill during the eighth and seventh centuries B.C. Within houses were found the bric-a-brac of everyday existence, but also clay figurines surely to be interpreted as *teraphim* — forbidden in the Bible. On the other hand, at least one potsherd from a storage jar of the period was found to be inscribed "creator of the Earth," perhaps attesting to a pious offering to be brought to the Temple. The finds reflect the mixture of superstition and faith that marks all ages, but also a robust economy. Another example is at Debir, where excavations have revealed a town benefitting from the general affluence. North and south, at the shrines of Dan, Bethel, and Arad and in the Temple in Jerusalem, priests and prophets of the state cults heralded a new age in praises to their heavenly king and devotion to their earthly monarchs. All was well, or was it?

Amidst this optimistic mood there were indications of serious trouble. Amos, in a brilliant phrase, likened Israel to beautifully ripe fruit which already had seeds of rottenness deep within. The simple fact was this: renewed prosperity had brought in its wake an exaggeration of endemic social ills. An expanding economy brought pressures to the money market and with it opportunities for fleecing the poor, the naïve and those who were economically defenseless. Small landholders, widows and orphans seem to have been choice targets of the unscrupulous. In the marketplace it was strictly "Let the buyer beware." While the state religious cults solemnly intoned the mighty acts of God in the salvation of his people and confidently, if somewhat arrogantly, entrusted the future to God's hands, fertility rites flourished throughout both kingdoms. Yahweh may have been the God of Israel, but more and more

Baal and his consort, Asherah, seemed to rule in the hearts of the people. And alcoholism was widespread; "rampant" would be a better word.

Curiously, in this situation nothing is heard from the old prophetic groups. There was no massive reaction as had been the case earlier in the north. What had happened? Had they been lulled by success in the destruction of the Omride dynasty? Or was their thinking tainted by the corruption of Yahwism which saw God's honor tied to continuation and prosperity of two petty Hebrew kingdoms? Or had the disastrous consequences of Jehu's revolt and rule in both state and religion convinced them that this path to purity was indeed deceptive? We do not know. But what did happen is very clear and represents one of the truly exceptional moments in the religious history of mankind. A series of individuals came forth, speaking in the name of the Eternal God words of condemnation and hope to a generation corrupted by its own success. In the north, in Israel, these men were Amos and Hosea. Slightly later, in the south, in Judah, it was Isaiah and Micah.

Amos and Hosea were roughly contemporaries, appearing in Israel in those twenty-five or so years just before the Assyrians destroyed Samaria — and with it Israel — in 722/721. Their writings reflect the internal conditions of the kingdom in its last days and an awareness of the black Assyrian cloud growing ever more menacing. Amos was first and is indeed the first of the great ethical prophets of Israel. He was a southerner from Tekoa, near Bethlehem at the edge of the wilderness of Judea. In his younger days he had been an itinerant farm laborer as well as a herdsman. But we must not infer from this, as so many are wont to do, that he was uninformed and imperceptive. On the contrary, nothing escaped his notice, and he went right to the heart of the matter, particularly where society and morality were concerned.

At some point Amos left his work in Judah and went north into Israel to the royal city of Bethel. There he seems to have attached himself to the national shrine, perhaps in his old capacity as a herdsman. There he also undertook his other and more important vocation as bearer of the word of God. Very well informed about international affairs, he did not hesitate to condemn Israel's neighbors (including Judah) for their sinful actions, but his most scathing words were reserved for Israel. The heart of his message was a blistering attack on the social ills of Jeroboam's kingdom:

> Thus says the Lord:
> "For three transgressions of Israel,
>   and for four, I will not revoke the punishment;
> because they sell the righteous for silver,
>   and the needy for a pair of shoes —
> they that trample the head of the poor
>   into the dust of the earth,
>   and turn aside the way of the afflicted;
> a man and his father go in to the same maiden,
>   so that my holy name is profaned;
> they lay themselves down beside every altar
>   upon garments taken in pledge;
> and in the house of their God they drink
>   the wine of those who have been fined. . . ."
>
> (Amos 2:6-8)

Thus did Amos summarize the economic, social, sexual, alcoholic and religious abuses flourishing in eighth-century Israel. And then he spelled it out

Wine press from the Medeba mosaic of the Byzantine period. The Old Testament has strongly conflicting views regarding wine which reflect both acceptance and distrust of the settled way of life.

in detail and in consequence. The priests and their worship at hallowed shrines, where they lulled the people into insensitivity with the glorious services of worship, were an object of particular vilification. Amos spoke of God's disgust with such worship, of his refusal to accept sacrifices made with the hands and not with the heart and ended with these words on false religiosity:

> Take away from me the noise of your songs;
> > to the melody of your harps I will not listen.
> But let justice roll down like waters,
> > and righteousness like an everflowing stream.
> > > (Amos 5:23-24)

The priests were not the only object of Amos' wrath. He castigated "those who feel secure on the mountain of Samaria," "who lie upon beds of ivory"; those who burden their tables with only the finest of the flocks while others go hungry; those whose idle luxury had robbed the nation of its moral fibre. Of such people his anger was greatest against the rich women of Samaria who, in this prophet's eyes, had a great price to pay for the oppression of the poor and the crushing of the needy. It was they who drove their husbands to great evils to secure more, accumulate wealth, pile luxury upon idleness. These fat "cows of Bashan" would have their day. And what a terrible day it would be when the vengeance of God would send them into captivity bound together by fishhooks. The allusion is to the Assyrian manner of stringing together prisoners.

And the justice of God would surely come upon this nation of corrupt courts, greedy merchants and its self-satisfied king. It was when Amos denounced Jeroboam and his dynasty that Amaziah, priest of Bethel, became alarmed. Was this another Elijah? Frightening memories of the Jehu business still hung heavy in Israel. But such things were far from Amos' mind. Israel was too far gone for a religious revival, or a revolt, or for anything conceived in the mind of man and executed by human hands. This arrogant nation, this proud and self-deluded people did not understand that they had offended none other than the very one "who made the Pleiades and the Orion, and turns deep darkness into the morning, and darkens the day into night." This God, not the God of a petty nation, had placed a plumb line in the midst of this people Israel. And the wall was crooked; it would not fulfill its purpose. Destruction was the only answer. Escape was possible, but it demanded repentance and a thoroughgoing reorientation. Such was unlikely; the fruit was rotten and its end was near. So Amos.

Hosea shared Amos' basic view, but his approach and the very spirit of his message were different. He was compassionate, ever pleading with the people of the northern kingdom to forsake their fertility gods who had led them into social and moral corruption and to return to a purer form of the worship of the God of Israel, as in the days of the desert wanderings. The fact that Hosea was a northerner himself (the only one of the classical prophets of the Old Testament who was) probably accounts for the compassion he shows. For Amos it was "them"; for Hosea it was "us." Moreover, while Amos for the most part attacked what he considered to be corrupt institutions — the priesthood, shrines, courts and the royal administration — Hosea evidently believed that it was the dilution of pure Yahwism by the fertility cults that was responsible for the many ills which beset the land. He determined to do a daring thing. He took the language and imagery of these cults, using them as weapons against these same cults. He spoke of Israel as an unfaithful wife

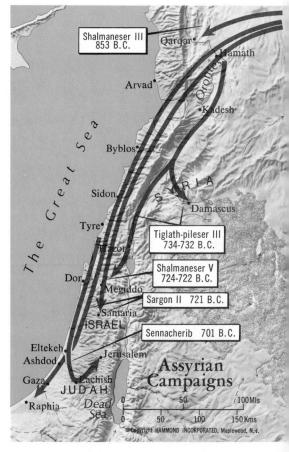

Shalmaneser III
853 B.C.

Tiglath-pileser III
734-732 B.C.

Shalmaneser V
724-722 B.C.

Sargon II 721 B.C.

Sennacherib 701 B.C.

Assyrian Campaigns

Qarqar
Hamath
Arvad
Kadesh
Byblos
The Great Sea
Sidon
Damascus
Tyre
Hazor
Dor
Megiddo
Samaria
ISRAEL
Eltekeh
Ashdod
Jerusalem
Gaza
Lachish
JUDAH
Raphia
Dead Sea
Orontes
SYRIA

0   50   100 Mls
0 50   100   150 Kms
© Copyright HAMMOND INCORPORATED, Maplewood, N.J.

seeking other lovers (the Baals) while her husband (God) waited patiently and with ready forgiveness for his wife's sincere return. Endlessly Hosea reminded the people of God's past goodness. Without letup he spoke of the heavy threat which lay over the nation. But affluence and sin walked hand in hand. The more God blessed the people, the more they turned from him. This Israel, this luxuriant vine, had a false heart. With growing despair Hosea cried out:

> Their deeds do not permit them
> to return to their God.
> For the spirit of harlotry is within them,
> and they know not the Lord.
>
> (Hosea 5:4)

Yet hope is not lost:

> Sow for yourselves righteousness,
> reap the fruit of steadfast love;
> break up your fallow ground,
> for it is time to seek the Lord,
> that he may come and rain salvation upon you.
>
> (Hosea 10:12)

Like Amos, Hosea had harsh words for the corrupt priesthood, for the dilution of justice and for the alcoholism. But he laid more stress on the fundamental cause: Israel's disregard for its covenant with God and its presumption upon God's goodness. Like Amos Hosea spoke of God's aversion to worship devoid of godly action:

> For I desire steadfast love and not sacrifice,
> the knowledge of God, rather than burnt offerings.
>
> (Hosea 6:6)

In this passage as well as others Hosea's personalism comes through, his tendency to suggest the intimate relationship of Israel with God directly. Amos had already introduced something of this sort when he said that Israel had to deal directly with God, the God who made the heavens and the earth. But Hosea's God was not so impersonal, so far removed or unfeeling in his judgment. Hosea represented God as a loving husband and again, in a very new departure from previous thinking, as a loving father desiring his son's return and grieving over his son's sins which have resulted in alienation. And alienation it was to be. The people had sown the wind; they would reap the whirlwind. Hosea like Amos saw that destruction and exile were to be Israel's lot:

> Set the trumpet to your lips,
> for a vulture is over the house of the Lord,
> because they have broken my covenant,
> and transgressed my law.
>
> (Hosea 8:1-3)

The vulture was Assyria, and it came to Samaria, perhaps in Hosea's lifetime.

After Jeroboam died, Israel's political disintegration began almost at once. Zechariah, his successor, was murdered after only six months on the throne. Shallum, the murderer, was in his turn slain by Menahem, who was able to reign for ten years. It was he who was forced to pay Tiglath-pileser III a huge tribute to keep Assyrian soldiers out of the country and to keep the borders intact. Pekahiah, Menahem's son, was the victim of yet another overthrow.

Tiglath-pileser III established Assyrian military power west of the Euphrates.

Pekah, his killer and successor, was not so successful in his dealings with the Assyrian monarch. Tiglath-pileser III lopped off Galilee and the Plain of Sharon from Israel. In addition he deported many people to the north. It was a rehearsal for worse to come. Yet Pekah clung to the throne. With increasing desperation he sought to form an alliance of small states to withstand the onslaught which all knew would come sooner or later. Rezin of Damascus joined, but Judah's Ahaz refused. Pekah and Rezin made war on Judah with the intention of replacing Ahaz with someone more amenable to their coalition. It was in this crisis that Isaiah advised his wavering monarch in Jerusalem to stand fast against the "two smoldering stumps." Isaiah was right. There was little force to back up the threat to Judah. Indeed, Israel was to last only a few more years when Hoshea, Israel's last king, mounted the throne over Pekah's bloodied, assassinated remains.

Hoshea intermittently gave tribute to the Assyrian kings, apparently paying when he felt he had to and withholding on other occasions. In the long run whether or not he paid did not really matter. It was just a matter of an Assyrian king coming along who coveted the riches of Samaria and who wished to be rid of this Israelite flea who occasionally annoyed the Assyrian elephant. Shalmaneser V was the king.

An Assyrian assault on a city. Battering ram destroys the wall while archers duel and infantry armed with spears and shields wait to dash through the breach.

He crashed into Israel, his plume-helmeted soldiers everywhere laying waste to villages, towns, cities, to fields, flocks and to people. Israel was ruined, but Samaria was still there. Shalmaneser settled down to besiege the capital city, and the wisdom of Omri's choice became clear to all. Suffering was terrible, but the hill of Shemer was not breached. Seasons changed; the siege dragged on. And then Shalmaneser died. Often in such a circumstance a siege would be lifted until succession to the throne was clear and a new monarch was firmly in control. But on this occasion the transfer of power seemed immediate and smooth. Sargon II continued to tighten the noose on Samaria. Finally, after three years the city fell, and with it came to an end this strange, violent and occasionally glorious nation of Israel, a nation that had done so much to bring about its own destruction.

In 2 Kings 17:6 is the simple statement: "In the ninth year of Hoshea the king of Assyria captured Samaria, and he carried the Israelites away to Assyria." Sargon's own records excavated at Khorsabad tell us that he deported 27,290 people and integrated fifty Israelite chariots into his own striking force. The number probably represents not only the population of Samaria, but also many people who had fled there seeking safety. They were, in any case, most of the leaders of Israel in every field. It was Assyrian policy to deport such peoples from a conquered territory and replace them with the same sort of people from another conquered area. This is the policy Sargon followed now. The leaders of Israel, of the ten tribes of the north, were taken and scattered to all parts of the vast Assyrian Empire. They had little opportunity to maintain their identity over the generations. They became "the ten lost tribes of Israel." We shall see later how Judah, also suffering exile, was able to survive because of different Babylonian policy.

Sargon II, king of Assyria, from limestone relief at Khorsabad. Sargon took Samaria in 721 B.C. He leveled the city within its walls and deported the inhabitants to Assyria.

Sargon also says that he destroyed Samaria completely and then rebuilt it "better than it was before." Excavations there tend to support this statement. At least the wholesale destruction of the place was no idle boast. Whether the Assyrian citadel outshone in brilliance the city of Omri is quite another question. But in any event, whether in luxury or in spartan military order, the Assyrians now held Israel. This meant that the southern border of the Assyrian Empire was only about five miles north of Jerusalem!

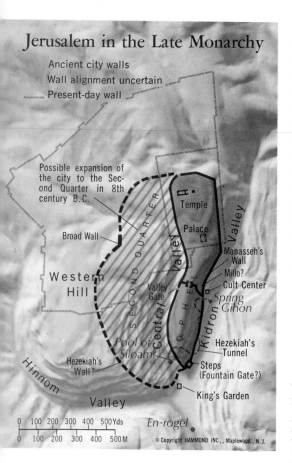

Jerusalem in the Late Monarchy

Ancient city walls
Wall alignment uncertain
Present-day wall

Possible expansion of the city to the Second Quarter in 8th century B.C.

Broad Wall

Western Hill

SECOND QUARTER

Central Valley

OPHEL

Kidron Valley

Temple

Palace

Manasseh's Wall

Millo?

Cult Center

Valley Gate

Spring Gihon

Pool of Siloam?

Hezekiah's Tunnel

Hezekiah's Wall?

Steps (Fountain Gate?)

King's Garden

Hinnom Valley

En-rogel

0 100 200 300 400 500 Yds
0 100 200 300 400 500 M

© Copyright HAMMOND INC., Maplewood, N. J.

All of these events had not been impersonally observed in Judah. Ahaz' refusal to join an alliance against Assyria was based on a sober judgment that where those people were concerned it was much better to keep a low profile and stay on the winning side. Isaiah, who had advised Ahaz' father, Jotham, counseled as much. But Ahaz went further, or perhaps he was forced to go further. He paid tribute to Assyria, which was understandable. However, he also introduced Assyrian religious practices into Jerusalem and supported cults of foreign deities. The writers of the Bible considered this merely a part of the king's personal apostasy; they conveniently overlooked the fact that Tiglath-pileser III had ordered the Judahite king to appear before him in Damascus, where instructions for the establishment of these cults were given. All the same Isaiah strongly denounced such measures. In this Isaiah, a seemingly urbane Jerusalemite, was joined by another prophet, a straight-forward, no-nonsense man of the soil from western Judah. His name was Micah. The death scene and final agony of the north had, in his view, been richly deserved. And the same would come to Judah and Jerusalem; equally well deserved. Isaiah believed that the holy hill of Zion was inviolate. Micah, on the other hand, said:

> Zion shall be plowed as a field;
> Jerusalem shall become a heap of ruins,
> and the mountain of the house a wooded height.
> (Micah 3:12)

Micah seems to have been influenced by the thought of Amos, and he condemned Judah for many of the things which had previously drawn Amos' ire upon Israel. The courts were corrupt, the priests insincere and the prophets little more than kept men. At the highest levels of government justice was perverted and little thought given to the ethical requirements of God. Worst of all, Micah said, the people "lean upon the Lord," confusing his honor with the nation's honor, assuming that no evil can befall them.

It would appear that Judah had learned very little if anything from Israel's fate. Moreover, the Assyrians were moving ever closer to Jerusalem. While Ahaz tried everything to appease them, these invaders from the north systematically reduced the fortresses guarding Jerusalem. They pushed into western Judah while strengthening their own positions in Gaza. And at Gibeah, within sight of Jerusalem, they burned the town. Smoke hanging over the Judean hills would have been clearly visible in the capital, signaling dire things to come for the royal city of David.

In these circumstances Hezekiah came to the throne in Judah. His feeling of desperation was apparently shared by many other rulers in the area. Egypt urged the petty states to combine to stay the Assyrians. There was movement in this direction, and finally Ashdod flatly refused to pay any more tribute into the treasury of the northern kings. A number of states were involved in the intrigue. Should Hezekiah commit Judah? Isaiah, for one, did not think so. He urged the king to trust in God and not in the flesh of Egyptian horses. To underline his views he paraded naked through the street of Jerusalem wearing a yoke symbolic of the plight of a prisoner of war. Thus, he said, would be the fate of Judah if it took this foolish step. Whether because of this or for some other reason Hezekiah, like the others, did not befriend Ashdod when the Assyrian army smashed it.

But there was little way Hezekiah could long avoid the Assyrians. He reversed most of his father's policies, even carrying on a religious reform and ridding himself and his city of the foreign cults which Ahaz had introduced. In those days such an act by a vassal was tantamount to rebellion. When Sargon died Hezekiah withheld tribute (2 Kings 18:7). If anybody had any doubt, this removed it. Hezekiah had prepared well for his defiance of the new Assyrian king, whose name was Sennacherib. Perhaps under the urging of Isaiah and Micah, Hezekiah seems to have taken measures to standardize weights and measures and generally to relieve some of the social ills of the state. He also took military precautions, which included not only strengthening the walls of Jerusalem, but also construction of a marvelous rock-hewn water system to serve the city if — when! — siege should come.

Pool of Siloam, Jerusalem. It was fed by Hezekiah's Tunnel, which brought water from Spring Gihon into the city. The tunnel was dug about 701 B.C.

Without an adequate supply of water an ancient city would quickly fall to attackers. In the Late Bronze Age, as we have seen, massive shafts had been dug bringing water inside the city walls at Gezer, Megiddo, Hazor and Jerusalem. Many years had now passed, however, and new measures had to be taken. At Jerusalem the configuration of the city had been radically altered. The old Jebusite system which had proved vulnerable in David's day was inadequate. Hezekiah undertook the unparalleled task of tunneling completely under Ophel ridge, some 60 feet below the surface in bed rock, in order to bring the waters of Gihon into the Tyropoeon Valley. Working in semi-darkness under extremely difficult breathing conditions the workmen tore at the hard rock with hand tools. At some points the going was too tough, and another start was made where the rock seemed less dense. Crews were working from both directions, following a winding path dictated by their ability to cut through the stubborn stone. After six to nine months of daily labor the forward men in each crew could hear the efforts of the other. In their excitement the men began to dig upward so that when they finally met they had produced something of a dam in the middle of the tunnel. This was quickly cut away, but still there was no flow. The southwestern end of the tunnel was lowered (the tunnel there is over 17 feet high), and a fall of some 7 feet had been achieved. The Pool of Siloam began to fill with precious water that was literally to be the difference between life and death for Jerusalem. The winding tunnel was 1,749 feet long — a marvel of ancient engineering.

In 1880 children playing in the waters of Siloam noticed an inscription some 20 feet inside the tunnel. It was a plaque in Hebrew put up by the builders describing the exciting moment when the two crews came together. This Siloam inscription reads as follows:

> …when the tunnel was driven through. And this was the way in which it was cut through: While…were still…axes, each man toward his fellow, and while there were still three cubits to be cut through, there was heard a voice of a man calling to his fellow, for there was an overlay (?) in the rock on the right and on the left. And when the tunnel was driven through, the quarreymen hewed the rock, each man toward his fellow, axe against axe, and the water flowed from the spring toward the reservoir for 1,200 cubits; and the height of the rock above the heads of the quarrymen was 100 cubits.

The Prism of Sennacherib, on which the proud Assyrian king notes that he had shut up Hezekiah in Jerusalem, "like a bird in a cage."

Safe behind his reinforced walls and with his marvelous water system working well, Hezekiah awaited the onslaught. It came in 701 B.C., as the poet said, "like a wolf upon the fold." Sennacherib, on a famous prism which has been found, speaks in equally florid language. He says he shut up Hezekiah in Jerusalem "like a bird in a cage." He also says that he destroyed forty-six cities of Judah, laid waste to the land, made over 200,000 people refugees (how many were killed?) and took great hoards of livestock as booty. If we may believe this Assyrian, it seems that Judah suffered a general destruction, with Jerusalem holding out virtually alone. Isaiah, who was witness to all this, tends to confirm Sennacherib's boasts when he laments the desolation of the countryside, the cities burned with fire and the fact that aliens are devouring the land (Isaiah 1:7). At the same time Micah bewails the destruction of his beloved native western Judah (Micah 1:10-15). Lachish, the major fortress protecting Jerusalem in the southwest, lay in ruins. Excavations there reveal the proportions of the disaster. Evidence of burning is widespread and one burial pit alone contained some 1,500 bodies. Yet Jerusalem held. Negotiations took place while Lachish was under siege. Hezekiah seems to have released some of the allies of Sennacherib who were held by the Judahites. But Sennacherib's envoys treacherously sought to undermine Hezekiah's popular support. Isaiah was counseling the king to surrender, but the terms were all but unconditional and Hezekiah balked at full acceptance. At this point the prophet suddenly did an about-face and sought to strengthen the king in his resolve. Perhaps Isaiah, too, was shocked by the Assyrian terms. Perhaps he sensed that Sennacherib had overreached himself. Perhaps in his heart Isaiah's firm belief in the survival of God's righteous remnant had come to mean the salvation of Jerusalem. "Like birds hovering, so the Lord of hosts will protect Jerusalem," he said (Isaiah 31:5).

And then an amazing thing happened. Sennacherib says in his annals that Hezekiah bought him off. In truth, Hezekiah did send tribute — but much later. Second Kings 19:35-36 suggests something else: "And that night the angel of the Lord went forth, and slew a hundred and eighty-five thousand in the camp of the Assyrians; and when men arose early in the morning, behold, these were all dead bodies. Then Sennacherib king of Assyria departed, and went home, and dwelt at Nineveh."

The hovering birds? The hovering birds of the Lord of hosts!

A prostrate Judah sought to pull itself together once more. Sennacherib may have withdrawn for whatever reason, but the Assyrian had no intention of allowing the measure of independence in Judah which Hezekiah desired. Tribute extracted from Judah was extremely heavy and added immeasurably to the painful pace of recovery. Hezekiah's bid for freedom had ended in unspeakable disaster. The real question was whether the nation could survive at all. Surely not if the Assyrians returned in anger.

With this in mind Manasseh, Hezekiah's son and successor, reversed the policies of his father and bound himself even closer to Assyria than his grandfather, Ahaz, had done. From all accounts, both in the Bible and in Assyrian records, Manasseh was a completely faithful vassal, sending special levies northward in addition to regular tribute, fighting alongside his liege lord against Egypt and prostrating himself before the Assyrian king to explain possible indiscretions (2 Chronicles 33:11-13). As a part of all this Manasseh gave royal sanction in Judah to the establishment and maintenance of cults to Assyrian deities. The Temple in Jerusalem became a center for worship of the astral gods. Furthermore, other religious practices which Hezekiah had sought to suppress came to the fore once more. Fertility cults flourished, with sacred prostitution even finding its way into the Temple precincts. Divination and magic, so long popular in Assyria and so strongly condemned among the Hebrews, was enormously popular in Jerusalem (2 Kings 21:6). It even seems that in Gehenna Valley, south of the city, there was a cult rite involving human sacrifice. In the midst of all this the state religion continued to honor the God of the Fathers of Israel, but this worship was now in danger of becom-

122

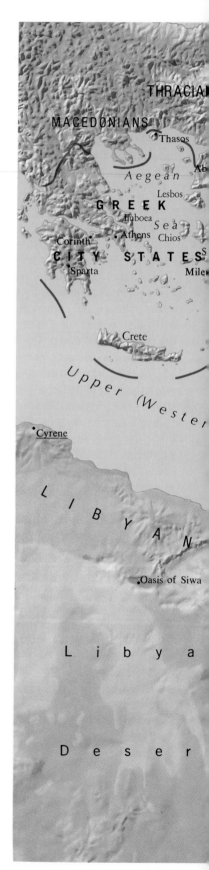

Black Sea

Sinope

Tieum

ium
Chalcedon
Astacus
zicus

PHRYGIA
MESHECH
IA

Ancyra
Gordion

L. Tuz

CIMMERIANS (GOMER)

Trapezus

CAUCASUS

Caspian Sea

L. Sevan
Cyrus

Mt. Ararat

URARTU
(ARARAT)

Araxes

Kanish

TUBAL

Togarmah
KUMUKHU

L. Van

L. Urmia
Minni

ELBURZ MTS.

Phaselis.

TAURUS MTS.
CILICIA

Musri

Melitene

Nairi

Turushpa

KUE
Tarsus

Samal
Carchemish
Arpad

Til Barsib

Haran
Gozan

Nisibis

ASSYRIA

Dur Sharrukin
Nineveh
Calah
(Nimrud)
Asshur

Arbela
Arrapkha

MADAI (MEDES)

Ecbatana

Aleppo

EMPIRE

ELAM

Phaselis

Qarqar
Hamath

Habor

Arvad

Cyprus

Tadmor

a

Sidon
Tyre

Damascus

PHOENICIA
SYRIA

KEDAR

Samaria
Eltekeh
Jerusalem
Raphia
JUDAH
trib. to
Assyria

AMMON

MOAB

Sais
Tanis
Pelusium
Migdol
Bubastis

Memphis
On

eracleopolis

o Assyria 671-651 B.C.
rmopolis

Siut

Abydos

Thebes

Syene

ETHIOPIA

ASSYRIAN

EDOM
Sela

Nile

Red Sea

Anat

Euphrates

Tigris

Diyala

Sippar
Cuthah
Babylon
Borsippa

BABYLONI

Nippur

Erech

Larsa

Ur

CHALDEANS

Pekod
Susa
(Shushan)

ARIBI

Dumah

(ARABS)

Tema

Dedan

Lower (Eastern) Sea

Dilmun
?

The Assyrian Empire

— — — Assyrian empire — c.824 B.C.

——— Assyrian empire — c.640 B.C.

Sinope   Greek colonies underlined in red

0   50   100   150   200   250Mls

0   50 100   200   300   400Kms

© Copyright HAMMOND INCORPORATED, Maplewood, N.J.

EGYPT

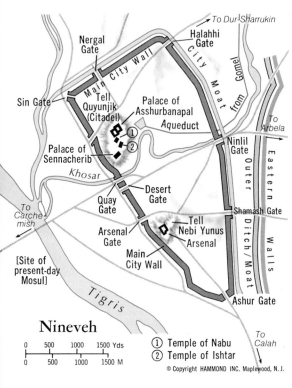

Nineveh

Nergal Gate
Halahhi Gate
To Dur-Sharrukin
Sin Gate
Tell Quyunjik (Citadel)
Palace of Asshurbanapal
Aqueduct
Palace of Sennacherib
Khosar
To Carche-mish
Quay Gate
Desert Gate
Arsenal Gate
Tell Nebi Yunus
Arsenal
Main City Wall
[Site of present-day Mosul]
Tigris
Ninlil Gate
To Arbela
Shamash Gate
Ashur Gate
Gomel from
Main City Wall
City Moat
Outer Ditch/Moat
Eastern Walls

0   500   1000   1500 Yds
0   500   1000   1500 M

① Temple of Nabu
② Temple of Ishtar
To Calah

© Copyright HAMMOND INC. Maplewood, N. J.

ing overshadowed by the other cults, and God himself was seen more and more as the head of a pantheon of divinities.

These policies may have been designed for national survival, but there were many who wondered what kind of nation it might be if it did survive. Those who spoke out against the king's policies were summarily dealt with (2 Kings 21:16). It seems that a part of Manasseh's policy was to give Assyria no reason to suspect the growth of a strong reformist and nationalistic party in Judah. The prophetic party, so violent in its reaction to Omri and so vocal in response to Jeroboam's reign, was silent. Perhaps it is more correct to say it was ruthlessly silenced.

The writers of Kings can find nothing worthy of praise in the long reign of Manasseh (some forty-five years). In their view he was a thoroughly bad king. He was, they said, worse than all the rest put together. His sins could never be forgiven. With this judgment Jeremiah agreed (Jeremiah 15:1-4).

Manasseh had preserved the nation — if little else — intact. While he was following his cautious policy toward Assyria that empire reached the zenith of its power. In so doing it overreached itself. Half a century earlier, there had been a serious revolt by the Babylonians. That uprising had been quelled but not extinguished. Egypt, which the Assyrians had subjugated only after two invasions, 671 and 663 B.C., was once more united and showing signs of independence. Everywhere the armed might which had held the great Assyrian Empire together was stretching veneer thin. There was another major revolt in Babylon. Arab tribes east of the Jordan conquered the entire area of Edom, Moab, parts of Syria and some of what had once been Israel, wrenching it out of Assyrian hands. Authority was reestablished only with the greatest effort. The colossus of the north was still on its feet, still in command, but reeling from the body blows it had taken. Sometime around 633 B.C. Asshurbanapal, a strong king who had been able to pull things together again, died. Within twenty years the Assyrian Empire — so ancient, so vast, employing terror as state policy and holding so many peoples in its awesome grasp — collapsed.

The Medes and Babylonians rose up. The Assyrians fought hard, making their enemies pay dearly for every success. But their day had been, and their hour drew ever nearer. Now the Egyptians entered the picture rushing northward with troops to shore up disintegrating Assyrian armies. Too late they realized that a weak Assyria was preferable to a strong Medo-Babylonian Empire. Nothing availed. In 612 Nineveh fell, prompting an ecstatic Hebrew poem rejoicing in the city's utter destruction. This poem has found its way into the Bible and is known to us as the Book of Nahum. Those who only such a short time earlier had been the scourge of the world fell back, reeling northward toward the city of Haran. The Babylonians swept on, and in 610 that last center of Assyrian hope fell. With Egyptian help the Assyrians vainly tried to recapture the city, and their rebuff signaled the end of a once-proud empire.

These momentous events on the vast stage of international power politics simply bypassed Judah and in the going left her free by default. Manasseh, ever faithful vassal, had been succeeded by his son, Amon, who within two years died in what may have been an anti-Assyrian plot. Josiah, an eight-year-old boy, became king of Judah. His regents apparently pursued a careful policy as events dictated. But by the time the boy was of age Assyria was no longer a threat to the country. It was no longer, in fact, able to exercise effective control over its former vassals and provinces throughout the whole of Syria-Palestine, from west of the Euphrates to the borders of Egypt. Into this void Josiah thrust the authority of a resurgent Judah. Much of the former kingdom of Israel and a great deal more fell to this energetic ruler. The limits of Josiah's kingdom are a matter of debate, but Judah seems to have reached its greatest expansion at this time.

At the same time Josiah undertook the most far-reaching religious reform ever seen in Judah. He was still a very young man, probably under twenty, yet nothing seems to have escaped his attention. One of the most important things to be done was the cleansing and refurbishing of the Temple. Manasseh had encouraged a variety of foreign cults there, including harlotry in the name of religion. While repairs were being carried out, a scroll, "the book of the law," was found. It was purported to be a sermon of Moses, and it embodied the basic reforms which many felt necessary to purify Judah. Although the view is not without its dissenters, this scroll is thought today to have been some form of the Book of Deuteronomy and to have been written by reforming priests in the time of Josiah. Deuteronomy combines pragmatic concerns with prophetic ideals. Whatever its origin, its effect on king and people was electric. Josiah commanded it to be read to the people and for the measures specified in the scroll to be carried out forthwith (2 Kings 23:21-24). Among these measures was the centralization of worship in the Temple in Jerusalem. Recently a fragment of Deuteronomy on silver foil has been found in Jerusalem. It is contemporary with Josiah or Hezekiah and may testify to the thoroughness of reforms. The renewed focus on Jerusalem meant, of course, the destruction of all those provincial shrines which for generations had been strongholds of fertility religion and focal points for the syncretism of ancient Hebrew faith. With a single stroke a problem which had exercised king, priest and prophet for centuries was solved. In 1958, at Manahat on the southwestern edge of modern Jerusalem, evidence may have been found of Josiah's destruction of these alien shrines. Masses of rocks were piled high on what seem to have been ancient altars.

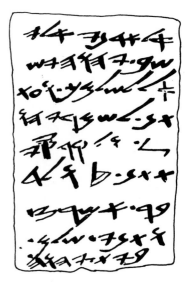

Broken pottery with writing, c. 700 B.C. from Arad, mentions "the House of Yhwh." It may refer to the Temple in Jerusalem or the recently discovered temple at Arad.

Religious reform went hand in hand with a resurgence of nationalism. Judah's star was rising. Finally there was on the throne a man who was not only a capable ruler, but one who understood from the wellsprings of his own piety the intimate connection between religion and statecraft in the Hebrew state. Although we are not informed of the later years of Josiah's rule, there seems little question that his own integrity and sense of social justice (Jeremiah 22:15-16) boded well for the nation in that interim when there was no overbearing great power to interfere. He was in all respects the right man for the right moment.

Then he made the error of becoming involved in the power game being played out on another level. In 609, as Pharaoh Neco was rushing to the aid of Assyrians seeking to retake Haran, he informed Josiah that he intended to cross Judahite territory. He was marching up the coast road and would move with his army through the pass between Megiddo and Taanach, formerly a part of Israel, but now annexed to an enlarged Judah. For reasons which we do not know Josiah forbade passage, although he was assured that the Egyptians meant only to pass on, not to tarry and pillage. At Megiddo Josiah took his stand to block Neco. It was sheer suicide. The Egyptians hardly paused and then moved on, leaving Josiah among the dead on the field. There was an extraordinary demonstration of popular passion with much wailing when good King Josiah's body was brought to Jerusalem for burial. As it turned out, it was a rehearsal for the burial of Judah herself.

Small idols such as this seventh-century B.C. Astarte figure from Lachish show the persistence of Canaanite religious cults.

Events in Judah now rushed to their inevitable and calamitous end. Within little more than twenty years Jerusalem would be a smoldering ruin, the finest of its people in exile, the monarchy a cherished memory and dreams of

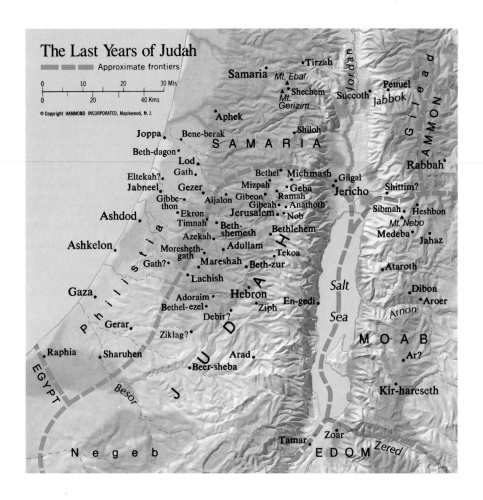

The Last Years of Judah

Approximate frontiers

0   10   20   30 Mls

0   20   40 Kms

© Copyright HAMMOND INCORPORATED, Maplewood, N.J.

glory but a flight of fancy. The monarchs who succeeded Josiah could not, had they wished, extract themselves from the turbulence of power politics as the time-honored foes, Egypt and Mesopotamia, yet again jockeyed for position with the petty states caught in the vise between them. Neco, unsuccessful on the Euphrates, summoned Jehoahaz to his headquarters in central Syria, announced to him that Jehoahaz was no longer king and deported him to Egypt. Jehoahaz' brother who took the throne name of Jehoaikim now governed Judah as an Egyptian vassal. Neco was preparing his ground for the Babylonian onslaught, and nothing shows the weakness of Josiah's expanded Judah more than the ease with which it was tossed about by the great powers. Neco wanted buffer states loyal to him. He also wanted additional sources of revenue. For four years Jehoaikim faithfully collected the heavy tribute which was laid upon Judah.

If Josiah had been the best man for one of the splendid interludes in Judah's history, this son was the very worst for a bad moment. Jehoaikim revealed irresponsibility and callousness in his decision to enlarge one of the royal palaces, the one at Ramat Rahel halfway between Jerusalem and Bethlehem. Although we are not told so, we can assume that Judah's borders had been vastly reduced and that this combined with heavy taxes for the Egyptians was playing havoc with the economy. We do know that the king had no monies in the royal treasury to pay those who labored on his house. Excoriating words flashed from Jeremiah, who in any case had no use for this man whom he prophesied would be buried like the carcass of an ass. There were bitter words for this king:

> "Woe to him who builds his house by unrighteousness,
>   and his upper rooms by injustice;
> who makes his neighbor serve him for nothing,
>   and does not give him his wages;
> who says, 'I will build myself a great house
>   with spacious upper rooms,'
> and cuts out windows for it,
>   paneling it with cedar,
>   and painting it with vermilion . . ."
> (Jeremiah 22:13-14)

A proto-Ionic capital of the type that graced the gates of the royal cities and palaces of Israel and Judah: Samaria, Megiddo, Hazor, Ramat Rahel and most likely Jerusalem and Gezer.

When archaeologists dug up this house in the 1950s, they saw the extent of Jehoaikim's work. The old royal villa had been made into a fortress palace, three hundred feet by one hundred and sixty-five feet, surrounded by a casemate wall. However, it never seems intended as a military refuge. Rather, the emphasis was upon luxury. The quality of the workmanship is superb, rivaling that of Samaria, and the excavators did find red paint on some of the stones, thus supporting Jeremiah's observation that it was painted vermilion.

In 605 B.C. the Babylonians fell on the Egyptians at Carchemish, delivering them a stunning defeat. As the men of the Nile withdrew southward, the Babylonians caught up to them again near Hamath in Syria and hammered them even worse than at Carchemish. Egyptian power in the north was crushed, and its vassals in Syria and Palestine were at the mercy of the Babylonians. Jehoaikim was quick to change his loyalties when Babylonian armies began to range along the Philistine plain and perhaps even into western Judah (Jeremiah 47:5-7; 2 Kings 24:1). The panic that gripped Judah is reflected in the first chapter of Habakkuk and at many places in the Book of Jeremiah (especially Chap. 46). Nebuchadnezzar, who had succeeded to the Babylonian throne, held Jehoaikim vassal.

But it cannot be said that Jehoaikim was a very good vassal. His real loyalties and perhaps his hopes as well lay to the south, with Egypt. Over and again Jeremiah warned against those who trusted in the flesh of the horses of Egypt, but, when in 601 the pharaoh was able to fight Nebuchadnezzar to a standoff near the borders of Egypt, Jehoaikim took the occasion to renounce his loyalty to the Babylonian. Nebuchadnezzar had only been checked, however, not defeated. In the instance Jehoaikim's decision was fatal.

It was three years before the Babylonians returned south. And when they moved, they moved directly toward Jerusalem. In the same month, December of 598, Jehoaikim died, perhaps assassinated by those who hoped that a removal of this thorn in Nebuchadnezzar's side would avert the coming blow. It didn't.

The miscalculations of Jehoaikim led the Babylonians to attack Jerusalem. Their conquest of the city is mentioned on this Babylonian chronicle.

Within three months the capital of Judah was in Babylonian hands. The eighteen-year-old king, Jehoiachin, was deposed in favor of his uncle, who took the throne name of Zedekiah. He was to be the last king in Judah. To him the Babylonians entrusted the responsibility of keeping the country quiet, pro-Babylonian (or at least neutral) and in general making himself and Judah as invisible as possible. Then the conquerors withdrew, taking with them enormous booty as well as the erstwhile young king, his mother, his anti-Babylonian advisors and many other leaders in every field of endeavor (2 Kings 24:10-17). In addition the chief fortress cities of the country had been

Revetment Wall

Judahite
Palace-Fort
Complex

Glacis

Main City
Wall

Level 3 Houses

Great Shaft

Inner Gate

Glacis

Outer
Gate

Defensive
Counter-Ramp

Revetment Wall

Roadway

Main
City
Wall

Lachish
(ca. 701 B.C.)

Assyrian
Siege Ramp

0   20   40   80 Yds

0   20   40   80 M

Lachish, the key to the southern defense of
Jerusalem. The artist's reconstruction based
on early sixth-century Assyrian reliefs.

destroyed by assault, territory had been taken from Judah and, on the whole, the economy ruined. That, thought the Babylonians, was that.

They were wrong.

Opinion varies greatly on Zedekiah. Was he weak and surrounded by men of even less character, one of the results of the deportation of the finest in Judah? Jeremiah, at any rate, held such a view of the king's advisors. But there is another view. It suggests that Zedekiah was in a very difficult position. Popular opinion had it that, had the Babylonians really been the threat they posed, they would have stayed instead of withdrawing. To test the truth of this was to invite disaster. Zedekiah faced another ambiguity. Jehoiachin was alive and well in Babylon. As excavated writings show, he was considered king of Judah and treated like the royalty he was. Did his former subjects in Judah also consider him still their legitimate king? If so, what was Zedekiah's role and authority?

Zedekiah's was not an enviable position. Then something happened that forced a choice upon him. Revolt broke out in Babylon and some of the Jewish exiles were involved. Patriotism, which had been on the rise in Judah since the Babylonians had withdrawn, reached a fever pitch. Zedekiah now invited to Jerusalem representatives of the rulers of the various states in the area. Egypt gave its full backing to this potential anti-Babylonian coalition. In the shrines and streets of Jerusalem prophets declared that God was about to break the power of Babylon and restore Jehoiachin to the throne in Jerusalem. Jeremiah violently denounced such talk as reckless and those who spoke these words as false prophets. But the tide of passion and opinion was running ever swifter. For reasons which are not known to us, this particular alliance came to nothing. Zedekiah seems to have done some hasty fence mending in the north (Jeremiah 29:3).

But by 589 Judah was again on a collision course with Babylon. We do not really know how the final break came about. There can be no doubt that nationalism had reached fever pitch in Judah and that Zedekiah was carried along by it. Egyptian urging and promises likely played their part. But few other peoples in the area seem to have been involved.

Enough was enough. Babylonia swiftly moved to erase Judah.

By the first month of 588 B.C. the leopards and wolves were prowling about the walls of a besieged Jerusalem. Other fortresses in the land, hastily rebuilt following the Babylonian invasion ten years earlier, were just as hastily reduced once more. Archaeology has recaptured one of the dramatic moments of that action. In the city gate of a devastated Lachish excavators found a series of letters written on pottery describing the last moments of Azekah, sister fortress to Lachish guarding the western approaches to Jerusalem. "We can no longer see the signal fires of Azekah," says one of the letters. Soon Lachish was in flames, and there was only Jerusalem left. In spite of Jeremiah's constant urging that the besieged city should be surrendered, the people held on with stubbornness and a determination that must have rung grudging praise from their enemies. Weeks dragged into ever more terrible weeks, and then in the summer word spread that the Egyptians were coming to their relief. It was true. Jeremiah viewed the Egyptians as the dew of the morning; much promise, but little that would be of real value. In this case the prophet was right. With surprising ease the Babylonians drove them back toward the Brook of Egypt and released their grip on Jerusalem not at all.

For another whole year Jerusalem held out. Conditions in the sealed city need not be imagined. They are spelled out for us in shocking detail:

The tongue of the nursling cleaves
　　to the roof of its mouth for thirst;
the children beg for food,
　　but no one gives to them.

Those who feasted on dainties
　　perish in the streets;
those who were brought up in purple
　　lie on ash heaps.

(Lamentations 4:4-5)

The writer of Lamentations, an eyewitness to this terrible siege, goes on to speak of how much better off are those who fall by the sword than those who endure this unfathomable suffering. "The hands of compassionate women have boiled their own children," he says (4:10). The Lord has given vent to his wrath, says this baneful message which ends on a note of despair ... "hast thou utterly rejected us? Art thou exceedingly angry with us?" (Lamentations 5:22)

In July of 587 Zedekiah sought to surrender the city and end the suffering. Once before, ten years ago, the Babylonians had treated Jerusalem with what was for those days extraordinary mercy. Not now. This time they meant to be done with the center of intrigue. Food ran out. So did the king. In the evening of the day Babylonian soldiers poured into the city, Zedekiah and some of his men fled, making for the Jordan and hoping to escape to safety in the desert. They got as far as Jericho before they were captured. Nebuchadnezzar was in Syria at his headquarters. There the Judahite and his sons were taken. No more Hebrew kings were to live in luxurious exile as Jehoiachin had done. With despatch Zedekiah was brought into the presence of the great king of Babylon, his sons were slain in his presence, and then he was blinded and dragged off northward in chains.

Jerusalem had meanwhile passed into Babylonian hands. What the Babylonians found in the city, and what they did to what they found does not require a very fertile imagination. At the same time, somewhat surprisingly, there seems not to have been any prior decision as to what should be done with the city when it fell. For a month further horrors and indignities were visited upon the sorely tried people, who must have believed that they were indeed abandoned by God himself. (Lamentations 4:9-11; 5:22). Then Nebuzaradan, chief of Nebuchadnezzar's bodyguard and thus a person of considerable importance, arrived in Jerusalem. Nebuzaradan was not a herald of good news. Upon his orders high officials of the state, and with them certain leading persons in various professions, were taken to Riblah, the Syrian headquarters, where they were executed. Others were herded together to be taken into exile in Babylonia. Jeremiah 52:29 mentions the number 832. But this doubtless refers only to adult males and likely only to inhabitants of Jerusalem. The number of deportees was much larger. Finally the walls of Jerusalem were leveled, and what remained after a year and a half of siege, a month of occupation and terror brought by Nebuzaradan, was put to the torch.

Not for the last time smoke hung heavy over the Judean hills and blew gently across the Mount of Olives. But on that day, in the heat of the summer of 587, it rose from Judah's funeral pyre. The fierceness of the Babylonian destruction has been clearly evident to archaeologists working in Jerusalem: a thick layer of ash upon floors of rooms, household goods and pottery scattered about among charred remains, and everywhere the triple-bladed, bronze "Scythian" arrowheads and a few flat iron Israelite arrowheads.

Assyrian relief shows prisoners being led off under guard. The Judahites who escaped being slain by the Babylonians were similarly herded together for exile in Mesopotamia.

129

The glazed blue walls and red figures of bulls and dragons which adorn the Ishtar Gate at Babylon have turned ochre owing to oxidation.

Among the acres of ruins of ancient Babylon lies the Southern Palace of Nebuchadnezzar, shown here. It may have been the site of Belshazzar's feast (Daniel 5).

11 EXILE AND RESTORATION

The pain-wracked processions wound their way slowly along the road that led northward from Jerusalem along the spine of the mountains. Unmitigated grief was their companion, and surrounding hills echoed to the lamentations and bitter wailings of those who, left behind, witnessed the destruction of the people of Judah. The Exile had begun as the Babylonians put into motion their policy of deporting captured peoples. Prophetic oracles, speaking of the wrath of God bringing terrible judgment upon the people, were being acted out. There was little in those hot days of the late summer of 586 B.C. on which to base much hope. And four years later in 582, when the governor, a Judahite named Gedaliah, was murdered by Judahite extremists the Babylonians were once more upon the land exercising swift justice, taking more into exile and causing still more to flee. Would Judah go the way of Israel? Like the ten tribes of the north who had been taken into Assyrian exile a century and a half earlier, would it lose its identity altogether?

Judah did survive. But the streams which emerged from this watershed were very different from the rivers of people that had poured captive into Babylon. Out of this experience, this "refiner's fire," came Judaism, a religion holding fast to its sacred traditions from ancient days, but expressing them through significantly new formulations and institutions. It was also the beginning of the Diaspora, the dispersal of a great body of Jews to places outside of Palestine. Not only were thousands carried away to Mesopotamia by the conquering armies, but hundreds, perhaps even thousands more fled Judah of their own accord, seeking safety and solace primarily in Egypt, but elsewhere around the Mediterranean as well. Jewish communities sprang up in the great cities and even occasionally far inland away from the major trade routes and the seacoasts. There was, for example, such a community on Elephantine Island in the Nile River at the First Cataract, some five hundred miles south of the delta.

It was at this time, too, that these people began to be known as "Jews." At first the term seems to have been applied to those who were of the now fallen Kingdom of Judah. But very soon it had a wider application and referred to any and all who were of Hebrew descent.

The conditions of the Jewish communities scattered around the Mediterranean and down to the Persian Gulf varied greatly. In Judah itself the situation may well have been the most desperate of all. Exact figures on the numbers of people removed from the land over the period from 598 to 582 are not available. Perhaps all told as many as fifty thousand may have been involved in forcible deportation. But remember that many others fled in the Diaspora. When we recall that the population of the country in those days was relatively small we realize what a tremendous blow this was. Moreover, according to Jeremiah 39:10 when Nebuzaradan had finished his grim work there were left in the land "some of the poor who owned nothing." To compound the problem the Babylonians, unlike the Assyrians who had earlier brought new peoples into Israel, did not move any new blood, new talent, or manpower into prostrate Judah. One scholar has estimated that of the former

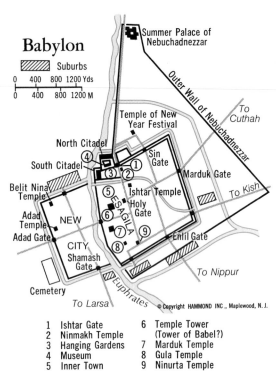

Babylon

▨ Suburbs

0 400 800 1200 Yds
0 400 800 1200 M

Summer Palace of Nebuchadnezzar

Outer Wall of Nebuchadnezzar

To Cuthah

Temple of New Year Festival

North Citadel

South Citadel

Sin Gate

Marduk Gate

To Kish

Belit Nina Temple

Ishtar Temple
Holy Gate

Adad Temple

NEW

ESAGILA

Adad Gate

CITY

Enlil Gate

Shamash Gate

To Nippur

Cemetery

To Larsa

Euphrates

© Copyright HAMMOND INC., Maplewood, N. J.

1 Ishtar Gate	6 Temple Tower
2 Ninmakh Temple	(Tower of Babel?)
3 Hanging Gardens	7 Marduk Temple
4 Museum	8 Gula Temple
5 Inner Town	9 Ninurta Temple

Model of the temple tower of Babylon.

Judahites there were only some twenty thousand left in the land; these were mostly, if not entirely, peasants. It is no wonder that archaeological excavations at various places suggest that city and even large town life ceased in Judah at this time. Jerusalem, among other cities, appears to have been uninhabited. On top of everything else, Judah's ancient enemies and more recent ones, too, moved in from every side. The Edomites drove in from the south, the Philistines from the southwest, but it was from the north that the most serious difficulties came.

A strong, if purely local group had grown up out of the ashes of what had once been the Kingdom of Israel. These people were the Samaritans. This group had resulted from the intermarriage of people left in Israel after the Assyrian deportations with new peoples whom the Assyrians had brought from other lands. They were now anxious and able to extend their influence southward, and while they seemed not interested in the wholesale annexation of Judah, which in any case might not have been permitted, they were for many years afterward concerned that no strong government be reestablished in Jerusalem. A century and a half after the Exile, Nehemiah's efforts to rebuild Jerusalem and to reestablish its authority over the area would be strongly opposed by those in Samaria.

In Babylon itself the exiles were a good deal better off than the brutal destruction of Jerusalem had presaged. Isaiah 47:6 suggests that the exiles were shown "no mercy" and that their yoke was "exceedingly heavy." From what we have seen of the siege and destruction of Judah itself we can readily agree that there is truth in this statement. Yet once the captives were in Babylon they found the situation dramatically different. The Babylonians realized that there were people of ability and training among these Judahites, and they wished to make it possible for them to contribute to local life and economy. Accordingly, as Ezekiel tells us in numerous places, the Jews were settled along the River Chebar, one of the more attractive areas of the country. There is other evidence suggesting that some of the exiles were settled in certain of the larger cities. Furthermore, unlike the earlier Assyrian policy which scattered people widely, the Babylonians allowed, even encouraged, the Jews to live together and preserve their way of life. In these circumstances more than mere survival was possible. A good life for oneself and for one's family could be had; the way into Babylonian life and society was open. Yet this invitation to prosperity held within it seeds of annihilation for the Jewish community. Many who walked through the open door into Babylonian life saw it close behind them, cutting them off from the traditions of their fathers, from their identification as Jews, from the ideas, ideals and values which had sustained their families for generations. Assimilation held its charms and its subtle finality.

While many by choice or by drift were swallowed up in the vast and grand culture in which they suddenly found themselves, others were alert to the dangers and took measures against them. These measures, as we might suspect, took various forms and were identified with differing groups. The most extreme group were those who rejected Babylonian life totally, who with hot tears remembered Zion, and who thus parading their unrequited anger and deep hostility were constant objects of Babylonian scorn. In the midst of a hundred smashed hopes and a thousand earnest prayers these peoples looked forward with eager, even malicious anticipation to the vengeance which God would pour out upon those who had dared raise their hands to defile the holy hill, Zion. Psalm 137, perhaps one of the bitterest utterances in the

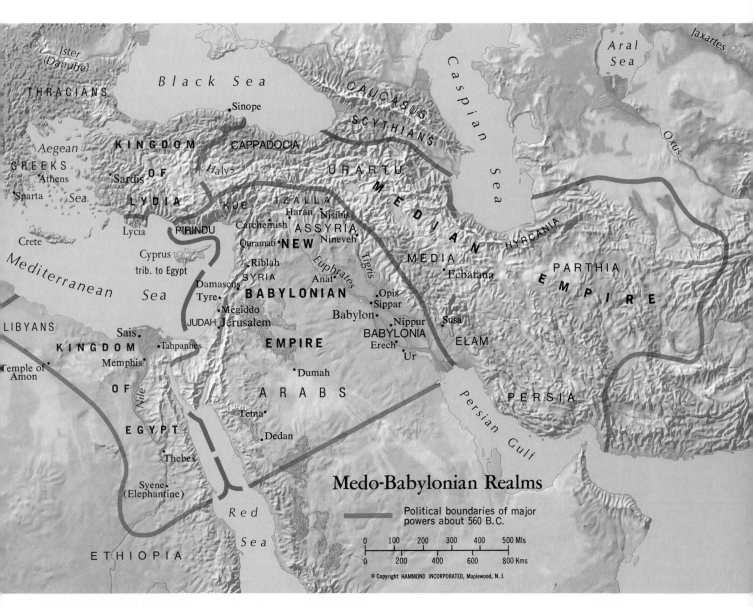

Black Sea

Caspian Sea

Aral Sea

Ister
(Danube)

THRACIANS

Sinope

CAUCASUS

SCYTHIANS

Jaxartes

Oxus

URARTU

KINGDOM

CAPPADOCIA

MEDIAN

HYRCANIA

PARTHIA

Aegean
Sea

GREEKS

Athens

Sparta

OF

Sardis

Halys

KUE

IZALLA

Haran

Njsibis

Carchemish

ASSYRIA

Nineveh

MEDIA

Ecbatana

EMPIRE

LYDIA

Lycia

Crete

PIRINDU

Cyprus
trib. to Egypt

Quramati

NEW

Tigris

Riblah

Euphrates

Opis

Mediterranean
Sea

Damascus

Tyre

SYRIA

BABYLONIAN

Anat

Sippar

Babylon

Nippur

Susa

Megiddo

JUDAH Jerusalem

ELAM

LIBYANS

Sais

EMPIRE

BABYLONIA

Erech

Ur

PERSIA

KINGDOM

Tahpanhes

Memphis

Dumah

ARABS

Persian Gulf

Temple of
Amon

OF

Tema

EGYPT

Dedan

Thebes

Medo-Babylonian Realms

Syene
(Elephantine)

Political boundaries of major
powers about 560 B.C.

Red Sea

| 0 | 100 | 200 | 300 | 400 | 500 Mls |

| 0 | 200 | 400 | 600 | 800 Kms |

ETHIOPIA

© Copyright HAMMOND INCORPORATED, Maplewood, N.J.

Head of Median guard.

Out of Media came the deliverers of
the captive Jews of Babylon. Bas-relief
shows procession of Mede guards and
subject peoples bearing gifts for the
Persian king.

133

Bible, preserves to this day the depth of the rancor of these people's feelings. Speaking of the Babylonians, the Psalm ends with these words:

> Happy shall he be who requites you
> with what you have done to us!
> Happy shall he be who takes your little ones
> and dashes them against the rock!

There is in this response to the Exile no sense of guilt for the sins of Israel and Judah; no awareness of the message of divine justice and judgment which had been on the lips of Amos and Hosea, of Isaiah and Micah. The righteousness which undergirded such a response is a self-righteousness; with bitterness compounded of a false sense of innocence, this response ignored the question of "Why the Exile?" It merely poured venom upon the Babylonians. But there were others among the exiles who were asking "Why?" Why had this awesome and far-reaching disaster fallen upon God's own people? Struggling with this profound question, the prophets, at least, came to the conclusion that the Exile was just punishment demanded by God's justice. No one, not even the Chosen People themselves, must presume upon God and upon the covenant relationship. For that relationship brings with it not privilege alone, but also responsibility; a responsibility not only to profess *mishpat* ("justice") in their worship, but to do it in their lives and to see to it that it was the informing spirit of their society. So for the prophets the Exile, in all of its horror, was not a time for despair, nor an occasion to abandon the religion of their fathers. Even as God's hand was in this punishment, so his hand would be in the redemption of a cleansed people. He would not abandon them. He was, as he had always been, faithful to his covenant obligations. The Exile would end, and with joy in their hearts and songs of praise on their lips the faithful would return to Zion.

From this point of view Jeremiah writes from ruined Zion to the exiles in Babylon. He tells them not to believe those who are predicting an immediate release and return to Jerusalem. Captivity will last for seventy years. In the meantime the people have a chance. They should not miss it.

> Build houses and live in them; plant gardens and eat their produce.
> Take wives and have sons and daughters; take wives for your sons,
> and give your daughters in marriage, that they may bear sons and
> daughters; multiply there, and do not decrease. But seek the welfare
> of the city where I have sent you into exile, and pray to the Lord
> on its behalf, for in its welfare you will find your welfare.
>
> (Jeremiah 29:5-7)

Others, too, thought that the night might be a long one and that it was vital for the community to take steps to preserve itself, not only in the ways Jeremiah had suggested, but also by bringing together the corporate memories and various traditions of the Hebrew people. The exilic period and the generations immediately following were times of extraordinary literary activity on the part of the Jews. Among other things, the great epic of the Hebrew people which comprises the core of the first six books of the Bible was reedited. And Ezekiel, a priest with the visionary gifts of a prophet, remembered the Temple and wrote down every detail he could recall. In the process he produced a matchless ideal of a heavenly commonwealth in which the people of God would dwell. At the same time he saw a resurrected Israel rising from a valley of bones, bones dried up, with lost hope, clean cut off.

A reconstruction of the Ishtar Gate at Babylon with the famous "hanging gardens" in the right background.

Yet God would cause breath to enter, sinews to appear and flesh to come upon the very symbol of death. Israel would live again, and all would know that the Lord was indeed God (Ezekiel 37). Ezekiel, moreover, agreed with Jeremiah that the covenant was not dead, but that it would have to be understood in a radically new way. The old idea of corporate responsibility and thus of corporate punishment was a thing of the past. The prophets expressed it in colorful language like this: "In those days they shall no longer say:

> 'The fathers have eaten sour grapes
>> and the children's teeth are set on edge.'

But every one shall die for his own sin; each man who eats sour grapes, his teeth shall be set on edge" (Jeremiah 31:29-30; Ezekiel 18:2).

This did not mean that for either of these prophets the community was not important. It was paramount for them and for others as well. But how could the community be preserved? Traditions were being gathered and were finding a place they had not previously occupied in the piety of the people. Various regulations which distinguished the Jews from the larger body of Babylonian life were coming more and more to the fore. Among these was an increased emphasis upon the Sabbath laws, dietary regulations and other such matters. Yet without some institution through which to express these things and around which the people could rally, all might still be lost. Among the few things the Hebrews did not have in Babylon was a temple. Whether there was a Babylonian prohibition against a practicing priesthood, or whether in the absence of a place of sacrifice the priests had little of their former function, is not clear. At any rate, the old primary religious institution was not present to the people in exile, and those who had been the leaders of the religious community could not fulfill their previous function.

Sixth-century B.C. glazed brick panel from Nebuchadnezzar's Processional Way at Babylon.

Out of this dangerous situation, by what seems to be some sort of genius, a new institution appeared, one profoundly simple and as easy to establish as it was eminently workable. It was the synagogue. It did not require a priest since it was a center for the study of the Law, that ancient revelation of himself which God had given to his people. Ten adult male Jews, that is what was required for a synagogue. But along with this a new need was felt, a need for someone whose life was devoted to a study of the Law and who could teach in the synagogue and who would instruct young Jewish boys in the Hebrew language and would read and interpret the Scriptures with them. This person was the teacher, or in Hebrew *Rabbi* (literally "my master"). Out of its own deep need the community was producing not only exceptional people such as an Ezekiel but new institutions and a new form of religous leadership. These focused on the Law.

The Law became the heart and soul of Judaism. One of the greatest hymns in the Bible, Psalm 119, is a paean of praise for the magnificent gift of the Law:

> Blessed are those whose way is blameless,
>> who walk in the law of the Lord! . . .
>
> Teach me, O Lord, the way of thy statutes;
>> and I will keep it to the end.
> Give me understanding, that I may keep thy law
>> and observe it with my whole heart.
> Lead me in the path of thy commandments,
>> for I delight in it. . . .

Oh, how I love thy law!
    It is my meditation all the day.
Thy commandment makes me wiser than my enemies,
    for it is ever with me. . . .

Thy word is a lamp to my feet
    and a light to my path.
I have sworn an oath and confirmed it,
    to observe thy righteous ordinances.
       (Psalm 119; 1, 33-35, 97-98, 105-106)

In spite of all these efforts, for all the perseverance and piety, despair stalked the homes of these exiles, and the subtle dangers inherent in the open door to Babylonian life were ever present. Not all accepted the prophetic answer to the great "Why?"—"Why had the Exile happened to them?" After a generation in Babylon there were many who still said that the gods of the conquerors were stronger than the gods of the vanquished. In this particular case the God of the Hebrews must certainly be inferior to those of the armies which had torn down the walls of Jerusalem and led its people away. This kind of thinking and the increasing pressure for assimilation produced yet another crisis among the second generation exiles. And, as before in the history of this people, an exceptional person came forth. In the long and unparalleled story of Israel there are few to match the towering figure who now addressed himself to the exiles. His lyricism, vision of God and sense of redemptive suffering are unsurpassed in Biblical literature. Musicians such as Handel and Brahms have found his words crying out to be set to music. Yet, strangely, we do not even know his name. Today his writings are attached to those of Isaiah of Jerusalem, and to many he is known as Second Isaiah. Yet this man who is responsible for Isaiah 40-55 is better served by the title: "The Unknown Prophet of the Exile."

His ministry was toward the end of the captivity, probably within the last twenty years or so. In his view the people had brought punishment upon themselves, and they had received their due; indeed, they had received double for their sins. But now the dawn for which they had been fervently looking was soon to break upon them. Words of condemnation and a call to repentance, those harsh utterances of prophets of a bygone era, were out of place in the present day. The Unknown Prophet begins his message by saying:

Comfort, comfort my people,
    says your God.
Speak tenderly to Jerusalem,
    and cry to her
that her warfare is ended,
    that her iniquity is pardoned,
that she has received from the Lord's hand
    double for all her sins.

A voice cries:
"In the wilderness prepare the way
    of the Lord,
make straight in the desert a
    highway for our God.
Every valley shall be lifted up,
    and every mountain and hill be made low;

Viewing the detail in this boldly composed Assyrian relief carving, one is reminded of Isaiah speaking about winged messengers and a mighty people whose land the rivers divide (Isaiah 18:1-2).

the uneven ground shall become level,
and the rough places a plain.
And the glory of the Lord shall be revealed
and all flesh shall see it together,
for the mouth of the Lord has spoken."

(Isaiah 40:1-5)

In lofty language unexcelled for its grandeur the Unknown Prophet attacks the suggestion that the gods of Babylon are superior to the God of the Hebrew people. The very fact of exile has itself revealed this God not to be some sort of petty divine chauvinist, caring only for the well-being of some temporary political entity. To this God nations are like a "drop from a bucket," like "dust on the scales." This divinity, creator of all that is, "measured the waters in the hollow of his hand and marked off the heavens with a span, enclosed the dust of the earth in a measure and weighed the mountains in scales" (Isaiah 40:12).

Have you not known? [asks this prophet]
Have you not heard?
Has it not been told you from the beginning?
Have you not understood from the foundations of the earth?
It is he who sits above the circle of the earth,
and its inhabitants are like grasshoppers;
who stretches out the heavens like a curtain,
and spreads them like a tent to dwell in;
who brings princes to nought,
and makes the rulers of the earth as nothing.

(Isaiah 40:21-23)

As for the gods of the Babylonians, they are the works of the hands of man; fashioned by the goldsmith and adorned with silver. They are but wood carried about from place to place on the shoulders of their devotees. Which of them answers prayer, and to whom have they come with solace? They are idols. They are "no-gods!" But who is like unto the Lord God of Israel? To whom can he be compared? The uncreated One who has created all things, it is he who is the Holy One of Israel, the Redeemer and Savior of his people.

I am the Lord, and there is no other,
besides me there is no God;
I gird you, though you do not know me,
that men may know, from the rising of the sun
and from the west, that there is none besides me;
I am the Lord, and there is no other.

(Isaiah 45:5-6)

Here, for the first time in the Hebrews' historical existence, a monotheistic argument is used against the temptations of the surrounding paganism. Again and again, the Unknown Prophet drives home the point that the Holy God of Israel is indeed God, and he alone is God (Isaiah 44:6-7; 45:6, 18, 22; 46:9). Not only so, but he will redeem his people, who should now put away their fear, renew their strength as the eagle and prepare for their joyful return to Zion.

But what of these people who are to return to God's holy hill? Are they to be the same proud, even arrogant community that presumed upon the covenant and conceived of their God in terms little larger than their political

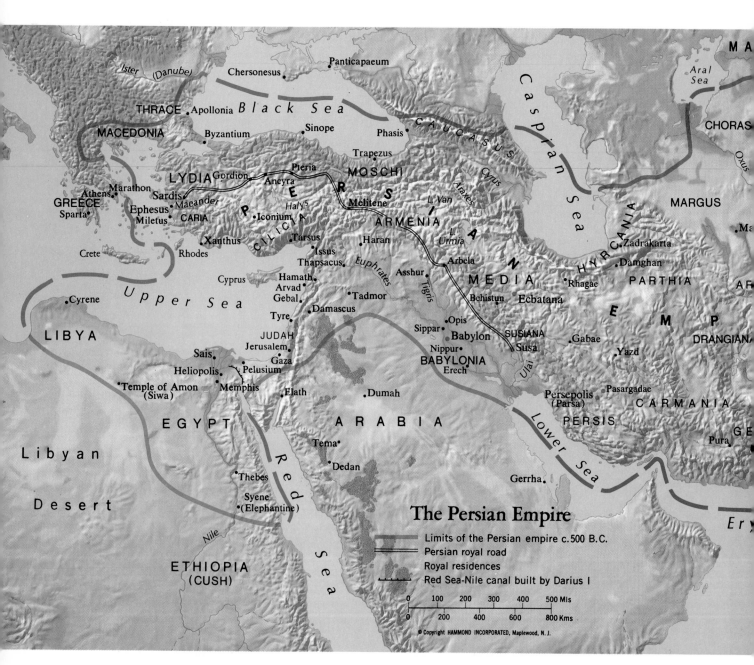

MA

Aral
Sea

CHORAS

Ister (Danube)

Chersonesus   Panticapaeum

THRACE   Apollonia   *Black Sea*

MACEDONIA   Byzantium   Sinope   Phasis   CAUCASUS   *Caspian Sea*

Trapezus   Cyrus   HYRCANIA   MARGUS

Pieria   Gordion   MOSCHI   L. Van   Araxes   Zadrakarta   Ma

LYDIA   Ancyra   Melitene   Urmia   Damghan

Athens   Marathon   Sardis   Maeander   Halys   ARMENIA   MEDIA   Rhagae   PARTHIA   AR

GREECE   Ephesus   Miletus   Iconium   Haran   Asshur   Behistun   Ecbatana   DRANGIANA

Sparta   CARIA   Tarsus   Issus   Euphrates   Opis   Gabae   Yazd

Xanthus   CILICIA   Thapsacus   Tigris   Sippar   Babylon   SUSIANA

Crete   Rhodes   Hamath   Tadmor   Nippur   Susa   CARMANIA

Cyprus   Arvad   Damascus   Erech   BABYLONIA   Persepolis   Pasargadae

Upper Sea   Gebal   Tyre   (Parsa)   PERSIS

Cyrene   JUDAH   Dumah   *Lower Sea*   Pura   GE

LIBYA   Sais   Jerusalem   Gaza   Elath   ARABIA   Gerrha   Ery

Heliopolis   Pelusium   Memphis

Temple of Amon   (Siwa)   EGYPT   Tema   Dedan

Libyan   *Red Sea*   Thebes

Desert   Syene   (Elephantine)

Nile

ETHIOPIA   (CUSH)

The Persian Empire

▬▬▬ Limits of the Persian empire c. 500 B.C.
══ Persian royal road
░░ Royal residences
┄┄ Red Sea-Nile canal built by Darius I

0   100   200   300   400   500 Mls
0   200   400   600   800 Kms

© Copyright HAMMOND INCORPORATED, Maplewood, N.J.

138

Detail of column capital at Persepolis.

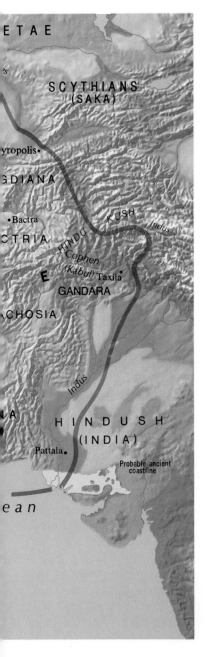

horizons? The prophet speaks to his fellow exiles, urging upon them a new idea of their place in God's purposes. In so doing he produces that for which he is justly most famous—the four servant songs of Isaiah. The best known of these begins:

> Who has believed what we have heard?
> > And to whom has the arm of the Lord been revealed?
> For he grew up before him like a young plant,
> > and like a root out of dry ground;
> he had no form or comeliness that we should look at him,
> > and no beauty that we should desire him.
> He was despised and rejected by men;
> > a man of sorrows, and acquainted with grief;
> and as one from whom men hide their faces
> > he was despised, and we esteemed him not.
>
> > > (Isaiah 53:1-3)

The identification of this "servant" is a hotly debated matter among modern scholars. From the very earliest days of the church Christians have understood these words to refer to Jesus, the Messiah of God who suffered on behalf of mankind. Such use of these exilic images is perfectly valid in light of a Christian understanding of God's redemptive purposes in history. At the same time not all scholars are agreed that the Unknown Prophet had one single person in mind when he composed these songs. Some think he had the entire community in view, and that it is the people of Israel who are to be "a light to the nations, that my salvation may reach to the end of the earth" (Isaiah 49:6). Others, while accepting the corporate interpretation of the image, reject the notion of suffering and suggest that this prophet was in fact a nationalist. Still others reject the corporate interpretation and say that this prophet had none other than Cyrus the Persian in mind. After all, argue these people, this prophet did see Cyrus as God's instrument to release the captives and restore Jerusalem (Isaiah 44:28), and he does call him the Lord's anointed, the Messiah (Isaiah 45:1).

However one understands the more difficult points in this prophet's thought, all agree that he foresaw the end of the Exile and sought to rally the people to prepare for their release from captivity and restoration to Jerusalem. Furthermore, he had correctly understood what was to be the historical role of Cyrus. Perhaps even as the Unknown Prophet spoke the short-lived Babylonian Empire began to crumble. One of the anomalies of history is the suddenness and ease with which this state collapsed. If we date its ascendancy from the destruction of Nineveh and the overthrow of the Assyrians (612) to the capture of Babylon by Cyrus (538) this Babylonian kingdom lasted only seventy-four years. It certainly was a high civilization with memorable accomplishments and there can be no gainsaying its claim to be called an empire. Yet from the outset it was disintegrating. The Medes, allies against the Assyrians, were soon at the throats of the Babylonians themselves. In the end they allied with the Persians. By 540 B.C. the situation was becoming desperate. Upper Mesopotamia was in revolt against Nabonidus, the Babylonian king, and had indeed gone over to Cyrus. Nabonidus, an extremely unpopular ruler, sought in vain to rally the people for the coming onslaught against the homeland itself. With panic spreading like wildfire, the king withdrew forces from the outlying areas and concentrated all upon the defense of his capital city, Babylon. Even statues of the gods were removed

Left:
Columns and masonry remnants are all that remain of Persepolis, the capital of the Persian Empire. The 33-acre palace begun by Darius I in 520 B.C. was burned by Alexander in 330 B.C.

139

On this clay cylinder Cyrus tells of his joyful reception in Babylon and how he set about to restore ruined sanctuaries "of the west" and to return captured peoples to their homes.

Tomb of Cyrus the Great at Pasargadae, Iran, c. 259 B.C. This conqueror of Babylon, whom Isaiah 45:1 calls "the Lord's annointed," allowed Jewish exiles to return to Jerusalem.

from provincial cities and concentrated in Babylon. The effect was hardly what Nabonidus had hoped for, but it was predictable. When the Persian armies crossed the frontier in the summer of 539 the demoralized land collapsed like a house made of cards. There were skirmishes and even pitched battles, but after the fight beside the Tigris River at Opis, Nabonidus could offer no further effective resistance. In October of 539 Gobryas, the turncoat general who had delivered Upper Mesopotamia to Cyrus, was given the honor of assaulting Babylon. But the city surrendered without a struggle.

Cyrus' orders preceded him to the city. No revenge was to be taken. The city was to have its normal life restored as quickly as possible. The gods which Nabonidus had taken from the equally well-treated provincial cities were to be restored at once. There was, above all, to be no terrorizing of the population. Indeed, Cyrus intended to change some of the policies of Nabonidus which had made him objectionable to his subjects. One can imagine the reception Cyrus received when he made his appearance in the capital a few weeks after its capture. He was not a conqueror. He was a liberator! And far from installing a foreign rule over the people, Cyrus personally took the role of Marduk, the chief god of Babylon, in the New Year Festival, thereby claiming for himself and his heirs the right to rule the Babylonian Empire by divine designation.

Within a year this beneficent and farsighted monarch had the whole of the former Babylonian Empire under his rule, and much else beside. He had already begun to implement his enlightened policy of encouraging national sentiment and local religious cults. This was a complete reversal of the Assyrians' brutal repression of nationalism and of the Babylonians' more subtle, but equally ambitious, desire to stamp out local centers of opposition. Indeed, in the very first year of his reign over his wider kingdom, Cyrus issued decrees allowing captive peoples to return to their homelands, to carry with them those religious implements which the Babylonians had claimed as booty and even provided modest amounts of money to encourage the rebuilding of local shrines. His edict ordering the restoration of the Jews to Jerusalem is found in two versions in the Book of Ezra (1:2-4; 6:3-5). This was no forced repatriation. Those who wished to stay in Babylonia were free to do so. Equally free were those who wished to return.

Shesh-bazzar, "prince of Judah," was designated to be in charge of the return, and it was to him that the sacred vessels from the Temple were entrusted (Ezra 1:8). Few joined Shesh-bazzar in the initial return, most preferring to stay in Babylonia, where by now they had sunk roots and had property that they were not willing to exchange for an uncertain future in Palestine. They were willing enough, it seems, to send an offering to aid in the rebuilding of the Temple, but there their enthusiasm for the venture ended.

The few who did return did not find the new day of Israel that had been envisioned by the Unknown Prophet, nor did their feet dance for joy while songs of mirth came from their lips. Zion lay in unspeakable ruins; ancient Judah was still much as it had been when the Babylonians departed three-quarters of a century earlier. And to their utter surprise they found themselves unwelcome. The Samaritans, who regarded the area as within their sphere of influence, did not wish them well. Nor, if it can be imagined, did the survivors of the earlier holocaust, who for several generations had struggled with the wretched land to make a bare living for themselves and their families. In the process they had taken over property which had formerly belonged to some of the exiles. Now returning families claimed their old homesteads. To complicate matters even more, the returnees regarded both the Samaritans and those who had continued in the land as religiously unclean. The Samaritans were, after all, half-breeds, not of pure Jewish stock. Hebrew worship of the sort which the peasants and others had tried to maintain had become entrenched among them, but to the returnees it was unpure, an impious farce. The joyful return so long desired and so fervently prayed for rapidly turned to gall. Anger and bitterness were on every hand, and the situation drifted toward violence.

In these circumstances Shesh-bazzar set about to rebuild the House of the Lord. Eighteen years later, however, sometime after Shesh-bazzar had disappeared from the scene, the Temple had hardly risen above its foundations. Hopes which had risen to incredible heights in 538 were dashed upon the realities in Palestine. Morale sank to its lowest point. An empty Zion hill was a fitting symbol for the whole undertaking. Surveying the wreckage of Jerusalem and the magnitude of the task at hand, the majority shared a plaintive cry: "O Lord of hosts, how long wilt thou have no mercy on Jerusalem and the cities of Judah, against which thou hast had indignation these seventy years?" (Zechariah 1:12). To keep body and soul together and to make a fresh start—these were the concerns of that tiny group huddled in the Judah hills around Jerusalem.

Then around 520 there was a new impetus. Shortly before, another and larger group had come back from Babylon. Zerubbabel, nephew of Shesh-bazzar and grandson of Jehoiachin, seems to have been their leader. At any rate, he soon emerged as head of the community, and he was a man of some force. And two new prophets had appeared: Haggai, who had a consuming passion to see the Temple finished, and Zechariah, who was concerned that the community which would worship in that house be a purified one, worthy of the messianic age which was at hand. "Is it a time for you yourselves to dwell in your paneled houses, while this house lies in ruins?" asked Haggai of those who were, at last, beginning to get on their feet. As a relative prosperity slowly began to filter through the community, the disparity between the people's new homes and the desolation on Zion was more than this sensitive spirit could bear. Is it a time for this? he asked. Zechariah, who shared this view, also was anxious that the faithful be gathered to God's holy hill to prepare for the coming of a new age. They must come back; they must come back to Jerusalem, for here God will again dwell in their midst:

> Ho! Ho! Flee from the land of the north, says the Lord; for I have spread you abroad as the four winds of the heavens, says the Lord. Ho! Escape to Zion, you who dwell with the daughter of Babylon. For thus said the Lord of hosts, after his glory sent me to the nations who plundered you, for he who touches you touches the apple of his eye: "Behold, I will shake my hand over them, and they shall become plunder for those who served them. Then you will know that the Lord of hosts has sent me. Sing and rejoice, O daughter of Zion; for lo, I come and I will dwell in the midst of you, says the Lord.

(Zechariah 2:6-10)

Persian royal tombs cut out of the rock cliff at Naqsh-i-Rustam, six miles from Persepolis.

At precisely the same time the Jewish community around Jerusalem began to stir itself, a new international crisis erupted, sending shock waves throughout the Persian Empire and doubtless beyond. Cambyses, Cyrus' son and heir, had conquered Egypt and was in Palestine on his way back to

Darius I on his throne at Persepolis with his son Xerxes standing behind him. It was during Darius' reign that the Temple in Jerusalem was rebuilt and dedicated (March 515 B.C.).

Head of Persian guard. From Persepolis.

Babylon. News came that there had been a major revolt and that a man claiming to be Cambyses' brother had taken the throne. Cambyses, who had murdered his brother some years earlier, committed suicide under circumstances which are lost to us. Darius, son of a provincial governor but of royal blood, acted with dispatch, seizing the throne in the name of the dead king, and called upon all loyal to the dynasty to rally to him. The empire was literally afire with rebellion. North, south, east and west everyone with opportunity and ambition raised armies, made claims, fanned nationalistic hopes. The Jewish community, already responsive to the messianic visions of Haggai and Zechariah, were hardly unaffected by all this. It is possible that the words of Zechariah quoted above were an appeal to the Jews of Babylon, where there was major fighting, to flee to Jerusalem for safety. It is also possible, even likely, that some of the politically reckless statements of Zechariah were in anticipation of an overthrow of Persian rule.

But Darius proved equal to the task. After two years of hard and constant fighting from one end of the empire to the other, he sat secure on his throne while his rivals were hanged, impaled, burned and generally disposed of in other ingenious ways. If he knew of the politically dangerous messianic nationalism at Jerusalem, he cared little about it, for he reaffirmed the decrees of Cyrus regarding the Jews. Archaeologists have discovered his decree among the Persian royal archives at Ecbatana.

The international crisis with its attendant messianic fervor at Jerusalem had spurred the people in their work on the Temple. In March of 515 the new structure was dedicated amid scenes of great joy and massive animal sacrifices. Yet, even as the acrid smoke of burned meat rose above the sacred site and the sounds of joyful songs resounded off the Mount of Olives, a deep disappointment settled into the hearts of the people. Darius reigned secure. Tattenai, ruler of the satrapy beyond the Euphrates (which included Jerusalem), had been not only an agent in helping to rebuild the Temple, but the one to whom the Jews of Jerusalem must give an accounting. Prayers offered in the new sanctuary included petitions for the Persian king and his sons (Ezra 6:10). The Temple stood. But it was no national shrine as had been the case prior to the Exile. It was merely a cult center, but one whose importance should not be downplayed. Whatever other function this building would or would not have, it was a—*the!*—focal point for Judaism and for over five hundred years would constitute the single visible common bond among various Jewish groups scattered widely throughout the known world.

There was still one more loss to be borne by that little community in the immediate postexilic years. The Davidic line came to an end. We simply do not know what happened to Zerubbabel. But with him ended that direct line which led back to the shepherd boy of Bethlehem who became a mighty king of Israel and founder of the line of kings that extended from around 1000 B.C. until Zerubbabel. Perhaps he died without issue. Perhaps the Persians did, after all, give some credence to the political overtones of the messianism of Zechariah and others. Perhaps the Samaritans were successful in extending their sway over the new community in one form or another. At any rate, direct rule of the Jewish community in Jerusalem passed into the hands of the high priests for over a century, until the time of Nehemiah. And with this change came a change in the nature and substance of the messianic hope. Some abandoned it completely, while others projected it into the next world. Still others conceived of it in this world's political terms, but with a heavenly figure to lead in the restoration of the fortunes of Israel. Many changes had

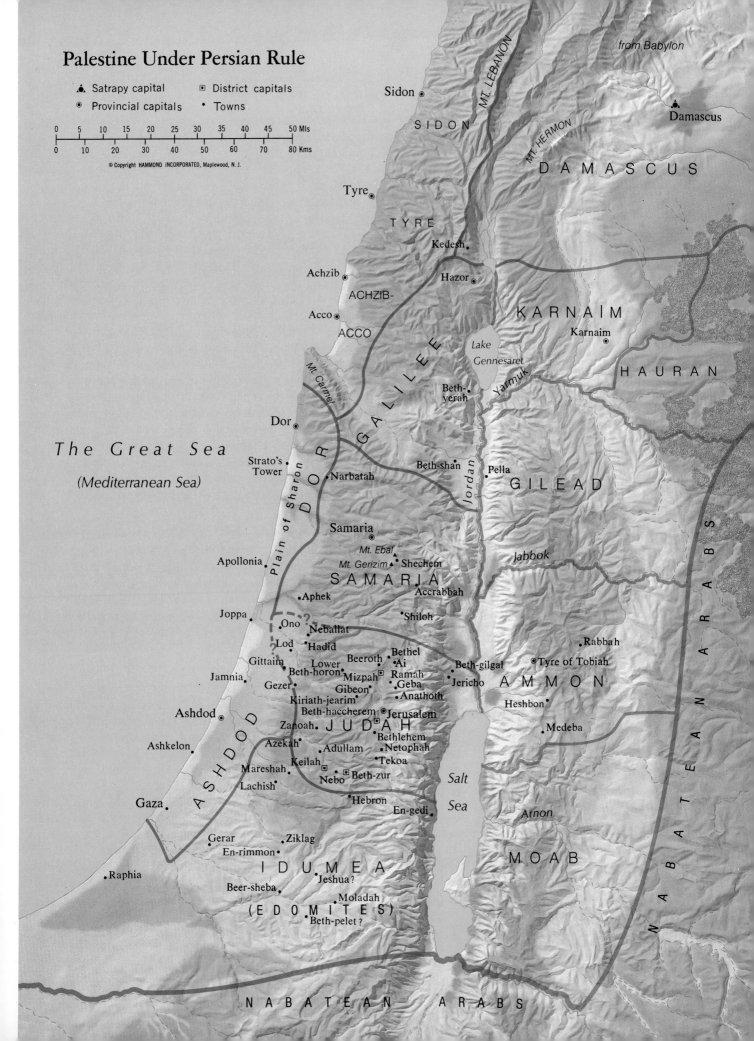

Palestine Under Persian Rule

▲ Satrapy capital ■ District capitals
◉ Provincial capitals • Towns

0 5 10 15 20 25 30 35 40 45 50 Mls
0   10   20   30   40   50   60   70   80 Kms

© Copyright HAMMOND INCORPORATED, Maplewood, N.J.

from Babylon

Sidon

SIDON

MT. LEBANON

▲ Damascus

MT. HERMON

DAMASCUS

Tyre

TYRE

Kedesh

KARNAIM

Achzib

ACHZIB-

Hazor

Karnaim

Acco

ACCO

Lake
Gennesaret

HAURAN

Mt. Carmel

GALILEE

Beth-yerah

Yarmuk

Dor

DOR

Beth-shan

Pella

The Great Sea

Strato's
Tower

Narbatah

Jordan

GILEAD

(Mediterranean Sea)

Samaria

Jabbok

Apollonia

Plain of Sharon

Mt. Ebal
Mt. Gerizim Shechem

SAMARIA

Accrabbah

Aphek

Shiloh

Joppa

Ono Neballat

Rabbah

Lod Hadid

Beeroth Bethel

Beth-gilgal

Tyre of Tobiah

Gittaim Lower
Beth-horon Mizpah Ai
Ramah
Geba

Jericho

AMMON

Jamnia

Gezer Gibeon Anathoth

Kiriath-jearim

Heshbon

Beth-haccherem Jerusalem

Ashdod

Zanoah JUDAH

Bethlehem

Medeba

ASHDOD

Azekah Adullam Netophah

Ashkelon

Keilah Tekoa

Mareshah Nebo Beth-zur

*Salt
Sea*

Lachish

Hebron

En-gedi

Arnon

Gaza

Gerar Ziklag

En-rimmon

MOAB

Raphia

IDUMEA

Jeshua ?

Beer-sheba

(E D O M I T E S)

Moladah

Beth-pelet ?

NABATEAN ARABS

N A B A T E A N   A R A B S

The ancient Jewish cemetery at Pir Bakran, near Isfahan, Iran. After the Exile the many Jews who chose not to return to Jerusalem made Persia a major center of Jewish life.

Lion and bull detail from stairway at Persepolis. It suggests the lavishness of the Persian palace where Nehemiah was cupbearer to Artaxerxes I (465-424 B.C.).

come over the community since those heady days in 538. None was to prove more profound than this.

The little community now disappears from the historian's gaze for the next three-quarters of a century. Its Jewish population seems to have continued a slow growth (Ezra 2), but to the vast disappointment of many there was no general return of large numbers of people. On the contrary, our evidence from the Diaspora at this time shows Jewish communities settling more and more into the life of their adopted lands. Yet, when trustworthy documents do become available again, the situation around 450 shows that town life is reviving in *Yahud,* as the Persians called the area. But Jerusalem, "wide and large," had few people and no new houses (Nehemiah 7:4).

And something else also appears in the mid-fifth-century Jewish community in Palestine: lethargy, monumental and eroding lethargy, invading every aspect of life public and private. The prophet Malachi complains of priests who offer blemished animals upon the altar in the Temple (1:6-14), who have debased their calling as teachers of Israel and in so doing have led many astray (2:1-9). Following the example of the priests, the people have become lax in their duty to support the Temple and its worship (3:7-10). The Lord has become weary of the words — the empty words — of the priests (2:17) and looks in vain for *mishpat* among the people. Among the people is only scandal, the scandal of intermarriage (2:11) and the scandal of divorce, because husband and wife care as little for the covenant between them as the people in general care for their covenant with God (2:13-16). Once more, as in the days of Amos and Micah, terrible words of ire fall from prophetic lips:

> For behold, the day comes, burning like an oven, when all the arrogant and all evildoers will be stubble; the day that comes shall burn them up, says the Lord of hosts, so that it will leave them neither root nor branch. But for you who fear my name the sun of righteousness shall rise, with healing in its wings. You shall go forth leaping like calves from the stall. And you shall tread down the wicked, for they will be ashes under the soles of your feet, on the day when I act, says the Lord of hosts.

> (Malachi 4:1-3)

Politically oppressed by overbearing Samaritan officialdom and slowly disintegrating from within, the Jewish community in Palestine was slipping toward oblivion. In the year 445 B.C. (or perhaps 440) the process was arrested, even reversed by the appearance of Nehemiah. Nehemiah, a Jew, had attained high office at the Persian court. He was cupbearer to Artaxerxes I and as such had immediate access to the royal person. He was, moreover, orthodox in his religious views and deeply devoted to his people's cause. When his brother, Hanani, returned from a visit to Jerusalem and told him of conditions among the Jewish community there, Nehemiah decided to take action personally. Using his position and influence with Artaxerxes, he secured a reversal of former Persian policy, which forbade the refortification of Jerusalem. Furthermore, Nehemiah was able to convince his royal master to make Yahud a separate province, divorcing it from its hated Samaritan overlords. As a final stroke Nehemiah secured appointment as governor of the newly constituted province.

The chronology of Nehemiah's governorships is somewhat confused. But there is little question about his energy or his character. Once having arrived in Jerusalem he immediately assessed the community's needs and set about meeting them with directness — and without tact. He knew before he arrived that whatever he undertook would meet with powerful opposition. Sanballat of Samaria was, needless to say, displeased with losing control over Jerusalem. He would in no way aid in strengthening the place which it had been his policy and that of his predecessors to keep as weak as possible. But there were other powerful foes. Tobiah, governor of Ammon across the Jordan, had married into important families in Jerusalem and he, like Sanballat and often in conjunction with him, sought to bring influence to bear on the affairs of Jerusalem. In the south, Geshem, a chieftain who had extended his rule from northwestern Arabia right across Edom and into southern Judah, did not wish to see a strong government which could contest his newly won gains.

Surrounded fore and aft Nehemiah moved with caution. One of Jerusalem's major problems was its lack of security. Without defensive walls—which had been specifically forbidden by Persian imperial decree until now—its people and all those who looked to the Holy City were liable to hit-and-run attacks, which came periodically. By night Nehemiah toured the devastated walls of the city, determining firsthand the extent of the damage and the requirements for restoration. At the end of this famous nocturnal walk he called the leaders of the Jewish community together and presented them with a plan for fortifying the city, thus providing the first requisite for stability; namely, security. There was to be a levy of men from the various administrative districts of the province; each would be assigned one section of the wall to rebuild (Nehemiah 3). Almost at once Sanballat and Tobiah found out what was afoot. Perhaps their relatives within the city, those who constituted something of a "fifth column" in Nehemiah's province, told them. But their efforts to undermine the new governor's authority with the people and their threats to seek to undermine it with the king availed nothing. Nehemiah stood up to his enemies as he urged his friends on in their masonry efforts. When there was violence, he divided his work force. Half worked while half stood guard. Within fifty-two days (Nehemiah 6:15) there was at least a skeletal defensive system. From all parts of the tiny province the people came, led by their Levites, to celebrate the reconstruction of the walls with thanksgiving and singing, with cymbals, harps and lyres (Nehemiah 12:27). Extra-Biblical sources tell us that it took another twenty-eight months to finish the strengthening of this skeletal breastwork, reinforcing it with revetments and battlements and securing strong gates. To defend these walls Nehemiah moved families from the countryside and provincial towns into Jerusalem.

Amazingly, within two months of his arrival Nehemiah had been able to provide a secure haven for his people. Now he set about to meet other needs. Although we know very little about his first governorship, it would appear he set himself to deal with the difficult economic situation. Heavy-handed Samaritan tax agents as well as drought had played havoc. It had also played into the hands of usurious moneylenders who preyed upon the poor. Enraged at this violation of covenant responsibility, Nehemiah ordered the offenders before him and using appeal as well as veiled threat got them to agree to make restitution and to take an oath not to repeat their former practices. How successful he was in seeing that these professions were carried out we do not know.

In his first term as governor, a rule lasting twelve years, his energy, conviction and sheer determination gave safety and economic stability to the

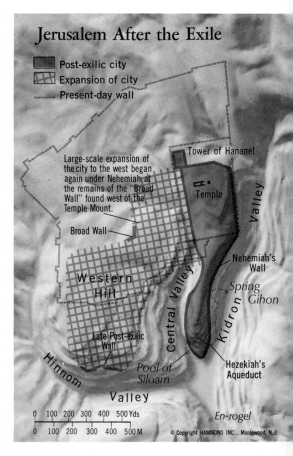

Jerusalem After the Exile

- Post-exilic city
- Expansion of city
- Present-day wall

Large-scale expansion of the city to the west began again under Nehemiah at the remains of the "Broad Wall" found west of the Temple Mount.

Tower of Hananel

Temple

Broad Wall

Nehemiah's Wall

Western Hill

Central Valley

Spring Gihon

Kidron Valley

Late Post-exilic Wall

Hinnom Valley

Pool of Siloam

Hezekiah's Aqueduct

En-rogel

0 100 200 300 400 500 Yds
0 100 200 300 400 500 M

© Copyright HAMMOND INC., Maplewood, N.J.

Building debris dates from the fall of Jerusalem in 587/6 B.C. The wall to the left may be Nehemiah's rebuilt with Maccabean additions.

145

Preparing the Torah, a scroll upon which the Five Books of Moses are carefully inscribed, is an important Jewish task. Only a special copyist or scribe, one who is pious and learned, can prepare a Torah.

Jewish community. But to what extent was he successful in removing or ameliorating religious and social abuses? While hard facts are lacking, it seems that he made little headway with these, especially with religious abuses. One of his problems was the deep involvement of the high priestly family with outside interests such as those in Samaria or Ammon. As Nehemiah journeyed northward once again to take his place at the side of his king, his mind was uneasy. Many things had been accomplished in Jerusalem. But many more remained to be done. Yet he had overstayed his leave from court and must not presume upon Artaxerxes' generosity. Further reform in Jerusalem would have to be left to others.

Within two years Nehemiah was back, having persuaded the king to reappoint him as governor. This time he was determined to deal with religious matters. He strove mightily, raised much havoc, accomplished few things. Notably, however, he decided that Jewish life was being eroded by mixed marriages and sought to take various measures against them. But something was lacking in his attempt at reform. He had his authority as governor, his strict upbringing, his love for his people and their traditions and his fierce anger. But these were not enough and sometimes produced just the opposite of what he desired.

At this juncture, perhaps late in Nehemiah's second administration, Ezra appeared in Jerusalem, provided the missing ingredient in the reforms and gave Judaism a foundation from which it has not departed unto this day. The Bible suggests that Ezra's work preceded that of Nehemiah. At the same time there are no sure dates for Ezra, and scholars are deeply divided on the relationship of his work to that of Nehemiah. The view taken here has received wide, but by no means universal acceptance. It assumes that Ezra came to Jerusalem while Nehemiah was still governor. Perhaps Nehemiah had arranged for this during the interim in which he had returned to court. At any rate, Ezra came with royal authority to regulate the religious life and practice of all those in the satrapy west of the Euphrates who professed to be Jews. His instrument for doing this was the law. Whether this was the Law of Moses (that is, the first five books of the Bible), or some law code taken from that larger section, or something else we do not know for certain. Whatever it was, Ezra and those who had come with him from Babylonia read it aloud in one of the public squares at the Feast of Tabernacles. This Great Assembly, as it has come to be called in Jewish history, was a turning point not only in the history of that local community but in the very life of Judaism. It was an emotional scene. People wept and vowed to renew their loyalty to God by keeping the commandments of the law.

But reform is not so easily accomplished. Social abuses and diluted religious practices were deeply ingrained by habit, greed and design and, moreover, had strong support in high places. It was now Ezra's turn to weep. Again the issue was mixed marriages and their danger to the purity of the Jewish people and to Judaism. In front of the Temple Ezra prostrated himself, weeping loudly and lamenting with bold confession the sins of the people. A crowd gathered, a large crowd. His infectious emotion spread. Then a man named Shecaniah cried out, saying:

> We have broken faith with our God and have married foreign women from the peoples of the lands, but even now there is hope for Israel in spite of this. Therefore let us make a covenant with our God to put away all these wives and their children, according to the counsel of my lord and of those who tremble at the commandment of our God; and let it be done according to the law. Arise, for it is your task, and we are with you; be strong and do it.

> (Ezra 10:2-4)

Ezra bound the religious leaders by solemn oath to do this thing. Then the males of the province were commanded upon pain of confiscation of property and banishment to present themselves in Jerusalem. In a driving rain Ezra announced the new policy to them (such marriages were not actually forbidden before), and with but few protests most agreed. Committees were set up to see that all returned exiles put away their foreign wives as well as children born to mixed unions.

Whatever we may think at this distance of the morality of this phase of the reforms of Nehemiah and Ezra, it appeared to them in that day and under those conditions to be an essential first step in any meaningful religious reform. There could be no purity, in their view, so long as non-Jewish women ran the households. This having been established and regulated, Ezra could proceed to the rest of his reforms. These included a solemn covenant in which the purged community swore to live by the law; specifically, to refrain from mixed marriages, to tax themselves to maintain the Temple and its functionaries, to follow the regulations of the Sabbatical year, including allowing the ground to lie fallow in the seventh year. Regulations regarding the Sabbath day were to be strictly enforced.

Ezra and Nehemiah, whose strong personalities may well have clashed, nonetheless saw eye to eye on the needs of the Jewish community. Neither could do the work of the other. Together they provided what the situation called for. Nehemiah provided safety and stability. Ezra provided the inner structure for reform. In later years the rabbis would say "Ezra gave us the law." This statement contains profound truth. When the Hebrews were foundering, having lost both that political designation and the nationalistic hope by which they could identify themselves in antiquity, Ezra provided a new means for Jewish self-understanding. Henceforth and forever more a Jew could identify himself and would be identified as one who adhered to the Law of Moses. No other designation was necessary. With the work of Ezra the restoration of Israel was completed. There would be difficult even dangerous days ahead, but never again would the fate of the Jewish people be tied to those things which could be destroyed by the hands of man.

Silver coin circa fourth century B.C. is from the Persian period. The obverse has a falcon with wings spread and is inscribed "Yahud." This is the first coin used in the Holy Land.

Top: Double shekel of Sidon c. 342 B.C. Obverse: a Phoenician galley, reverse: a Persian king in a war chariot.

Bottom: Silver tetradrachm struck during reign of Ptolemy I shows Alexander the Great wearing an elephant's skin headdress. Reverse: the goddess Athena.

(coins enlarged about 3:1)

12 WARS AND RUMORS OF WAR

From that day in the fifteenth century B.C. when Thutmoses III, of Egypt, first forced the pass at Megiddo until well into this present century, alien armies have marched back and forth across the land bridge joining Africa and Asia. In the three centuries between the collapse of the Persian Empire and that time when the Romans once again established world order in the *pax Romana,* Palestine played its historic role with bloodied regularity. As never before the land and its afflicted peoples were swept up in the ebb and flow of great power ambitions. In those ill-starred years no less than six empires and kingdoms ruled the land: Persian, Macedonian, Egyptian Ptolemaic, Syrian Seleucid, Hasmonean Jewish and Roman. Each in turn replaced the other in bitter struggles, and apart from the first each unleashed havoc on the countryside and in the towns and cities.

The centuries between the Exile and Jesus are what Christians call The Intertestamental Period; to Jews it is The Post-Biblical Period. It was the formative time of Judaism and provides the background for the New Testament. For the first half of this time down to the eve of the outbreak of the Maccabean War, the Jewish community in Jerusalem passes under a cloud. There are few trustworthy guides, literary or archaeological. Toward the end of the fifth century Persians replace Jews as governors. High priests exercised considerable local authority over the lives of the people, and the Persian policy of regularizing Jewish practice continued. There is also a suggestion that the community was not always treated with kindness by the Persian governors.

Archaeological evidence from this period is skimpy. Two examples will suffice. Lachish, the same that repeatedly fell before conquerors in the days of the Hebrew kings, contains ruins from this time. Among these is a large structure which is thought to have been a public building. Was Lachish an administrative center for the area? Nearby at Tell el-Hesi, whose ancient identification has yet to be firmly established, there are also ruins from this period. They consist mainly of large pits, which, the excavators have demonstrated, were used for storing grain. Hesi is located on the edge of the coastal plain, near the area which Mesopotamian armies used as a staging area for assaults on Egypt. Do the Hesi pits represent an effort by Persian armies to supply themselves before their successful onslaughts along the Nile? Perhaps the pits are nothing more than depots for farmers, places to which buyers could come. Beyond the fact that this was a grain center in the Persian period we really know little else. It is typical of our knowledge of Palestine at the time.

We are almost entirely dependent upon weak evidence and even inference to know what was going on. But of this much we can be sure; momentous events were afoot. Relations between Jews and Samaritans, ever poor, got worse. Those who dwelled in Samaria could neither forgive the insults which the returning Jews had heaped upon them, nor as descendants of the ancient kingdom of Israel acknowledge that the remnant of Judah was the true Israel. The Jews, for their part, regarded the Samaritans as unpure in race and religion and as oppressors who had taken advantage of the postexilic

Samaritan priests carrying the Torah which is covered with an embroidered mantle. Today a small group of Samaritans living near Mount Gerizim continue their ancient traditions.

situation to make life as miserable as possible for the Jerusalem community. At some point a complete break came. As a part of this, the Samaritans withdrew entirely from worship in Jerusalem, or any pretense at such worship, and built their own temple on the summit of Mount Gerizim in the heart of Samaria. It was within sight of this holy house that Jesus spoke with the woman of Samaria (John 4), and it was against this background of hatred that Jesus shocked his Jewish hearers by speaking of a "good Samaritan" (Luke 10:29 f.).

Hebrew was also dying out as the language of the people. Nehemiah had been at great pains to encourage Hebrew language instruction as a means to community solidarity. But it was a losing cause from the beginning. Aramaic was the official language of the empire, and if the Jewish community was to prosper economically Aramaic must be spoken, at least as a second language. During this period it replaced Hebrew as the language of the common man. Aramaic was the tongue Jesus spoke and, although by his day Greek had displaced Aramaic as a commercial language, it did not penetrate to the grass roots. From perhaps as early as the second or third centuries B.C. to the end of Biblical times Aramaic was the common language in Palestine.

And elements of Greek culture were penetrating the Near East at a steadily increasing pace. Ideas from Greece had crossed the seas and come down the trade routes long before Alexander the Great landed his army in Asia. Palestine as a land bridge served not merely as an avenue for imperial ambitions, but equally as a road for commerce. With the prerogatives of petty states now fallen away and empires reaching ever more widely, local ways, tenacious in the countryside, tended more and more to disappear in the increasingly cosmopolitan cities.

As before in their history Jewish groups formed around given responses to social, cultural and religious matters. These groups, sometimes overlapping, sometimes poles apart, were often in conflict. While not all took definite shape in these obscure years, the outlines of Pharisees, Sadducees, monastics, Zealots and other groups were already in evidence. Once more the people were being shaped by external forces, and as before the seeds of internecine conflict took root.

While all these things were fermenting within the Jewish community, ever forming new combinations, the Persian Empire seemed to have weathered its bad days, emerging stronger than ever. Appearances were, however, deceiving. Beneath the surface there was rebellion. Persia staggered into the fourth century with the empire aflame, particularly in the west. Total collapse was averted only by a coup in Egypt which crippled the rebel army. Artaxerxes III, a vicious man, managed to restore order. But the ruling family literally wiped itself out in a series of extraordinarily bloody palace revolts. At this same time Philip II, a Macedonian, was extending his rule over all the Greeks except those in Asia Minor, who were under Persian control. In 336 Darius III came to the Persian throne, momentarily arresting the downward spiral resulting from almost continuous regicide. Persia appeared to have been saved just in the nick of time. But in that same year—336 B.C.—a nineteen-year-old boy named Alexander succeeded his father in Macedonia. Within five years he would be master of the Persian Empire.

As is the case with truly remarkable figures in history Alexander is the subject of much controversy and always has been. Some suggest that he was a visionary genius, conceiving of one great world brotherhood united on the basis of a common culture, a mixture of east and west in which Greek language, manners and custom would erase differences between men. Others assign baser motives to him, suggesting that he was mad with power and, like militarists before and after, had an insatiable appetite which was only whetted by success. Wherever the truth lies, there are few who will deny that he, perhaps above all others, deserves to be designated "the Great."

In 334 Alexander crossed the Hellespont and invaded Asia Minor intent upon freeing the Greeks there from what he—but not apparently they!—thought was Persian tyranny. With him and his army went also scientists, literary men, historians as well as engineers, surveyors and other technicians. Unlike the Persian hordes who had crossed in the other direction only to be smashed at Marathon in 490 B.C., Alexander's men were eager for combat. At Marathon Persian officers had driven their men into battle using whips, while the Greeks had run forward gladly with songs on their lips. It was little different now, and the outcome would be the same. But no one realized it at first. Indeed, the Persians hardly took Alexander seriously.

To underrate one's enemy is a danger of the first order, sometimes, as it proved to be in this case, a fatal danger. Within the year not only were the Greek cities along the coast free, but all of Asia Minor had been conquered. Now it was time to take this matter seriously. Darius moved his massive and unwieldy army westward. Alexander's experienced, eager and brilliantly led veterans probed eastward. At Issus they collided. This momentous conflict in October 333 was one of the turning points in history. The Persians counted on masses of humanity to wear down and finally to overrun their enemy. The Macedonian Greeks, on the other hand, countered with the phalanx, mobile squares of highly disciplined men who could hit and withdraw, moving over the field as one man. And the phalanx was able to withstand the Persian assault waves again and again.

Macedonian forces under Alexander

Persian forces under Darius

Actually Darius had forced Alexander to fight by cutting his lines of communications near the Gulf of Issus. Alexander turned northward to meet the Persian threat to his rear. To his surprise Darius offered battle on terrain that was unsuited to cavalry, the main strength of the Persians aside from numbers. Darius had positioned his forces in deep formations along the Pinarus River on the narrow coastal plain between the Amanus Mountains and the sea.

Darius established his command post in the middle of his army, and this is precisely where Alexander concentrated his attack. Yet he was careful to do so only after he had secured his flanks. The battle began with a preliminary action to clear the foothills on Alexander's right. Once he was sure strong Persian covering forces were driven back, Alexander ordered his main line forward. In the center the phalanx wavered as it sought to cross the river. Then it began to fall back. Darius threw his Greek mercenaries into the struggle at the center, and they continued to drive forward as the phalanx withdrew. It was a dangerous moment for the twenty-two-year-old Macedonian. If the center broke, a tidal wave of Persian humanity would flow in. But the disciplined men in the phalanx were in good order and were bathing every inch of surrendered ground in Persian and Greek mercenary blood. Alexander committed his own cavalry against the flank of the overextended Persian center. Again experienced men, brilliant tactics and lightning swift execution of orders turned the tide of battle. The Persian center reeled under devastating blows; slowly the whole line began to crumble. Darius fled the field in panic with his army and indeed his empire in shambles. He was to face Alexander again — at Gaugamela in 331 — with the same result.

151

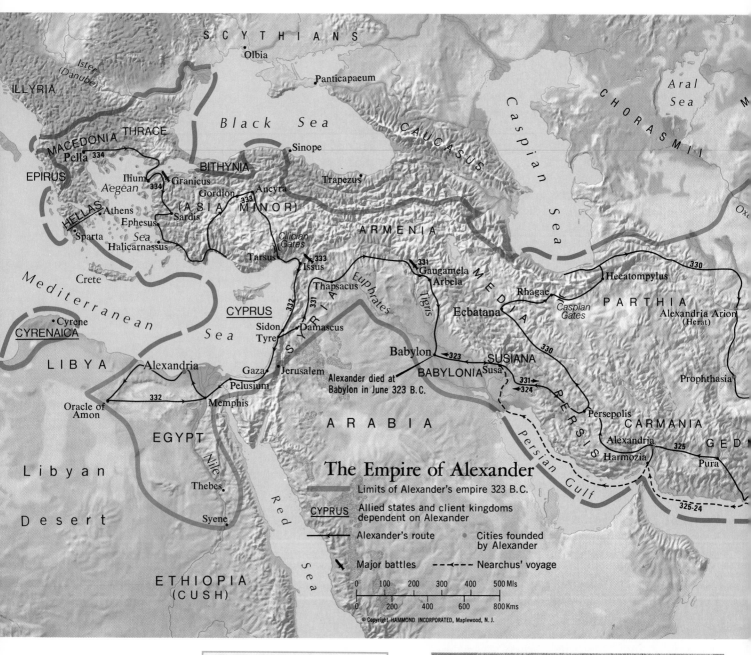

S C Y T H I A N S

• Olbia

• Panticapaeum

Black Sea

ILLYRIA

Ister (Danube)

MACEDONIA THRACE
Pella 334

EPIRUS

Ilium •Granicus
334

Aegean Gordion Ancyra
333

HELLAS (ASIA MINOR)
•Athens Sardis
Ephesus
•Sparta *Sea*
Halicarnassus

Crete

Mediterranean

CYRENAICA CYPRUS
•Cyrene

LIBYA Alexandria

Gaza •Jerusalem
•Pelusium
Oracle of 332
Amon Memphis

EGYPT

Libyan •Thebes

Desert •Syene

ETHIOPIA
(CUSH)

Sinope

CAUCASUS

BITHYNIA

Cilician Gates

Tarsus
Issus 333

Thapsacus
332 331 *Euphrates*

Sidon Damascus
Tyre

SYRIA

Red Sea

ARABIA

Sea

ARMENIA

Gaugamela 331
•Arbela

Tigris

Babylon 323
BABYLONIA Susa
Alexander died at SUSIANA
Babylon in June 323 B.C.

Caspian Sea

Hecatompylus 330
Rhagae
Caspian PARTHIA
Ecbatana *Gates* Alexandria Arion
MEDIA (Herat)

330

PERSIS Prophthasia

331→
324→

Persepolis CARMANIA
Alexandria 325 GED
Harmozia Pura

325-24

CHORASMII

Aral
Sea

Oxus

The Empire of Alexander

⎯⎯ Limits of Alexander's empire 323 B.C.

CYPRUS Allied states and client kingdoms
dependent on Alexander

⎯→ Alexander's route • Cities founded
by Alexander

⚔ Major battles - - -→ Nearchus' voyage

0 100 200 300 400 500 Mls
0 200 400 600 800 Kms

© Copyright HAMMOND INCORPORATED, Maplewood, N.J.

152

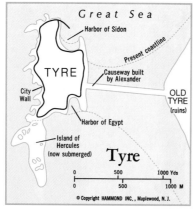

Great Sea

Harbor of Sidon

Present coastline

TYRE

Causeway built
by Alexander

OLD
TYRE
(ruins)

City
Wall

Harbor of Egypt

Island of
Hercules
(now submerged)

Tyre

0 500 1000 Yds
0 500 1000 M

© Copyright HAMMOND INC., Maplewood, N.J.

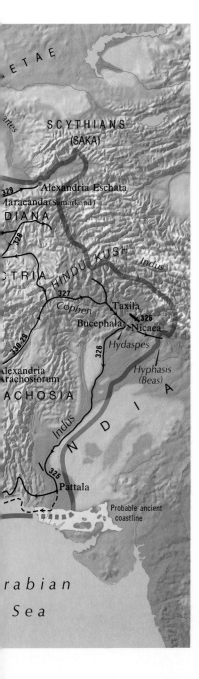

The ancient historians, Diodorus and Plutarch, tell us that Persian losses at Issus included 110,000 slaughtered on the plain between the sea and the hills. According to these writers the Macedonian Greeks lost 450 men. Both figures may be questioned, but there is no questioning the magnitude of the battle and the even greater significance of its aftermath. Alexander captured Darius' wife, his family, baggage and booty at Issus. He had, in effect and in fact, captured the Persian Empire. Many battles lay ahead; there would be more armies to rally and victories won, but it was for the most part piece-meal. Persia and Persia alone had been the major obstacle to Alexander's ambitions. And Persia bled to death at Issus. In the next few years Alexander would force the Khyber Pass and swim in the Hydaspes River in India, rule Greece as "first among equals" and be worshiped as a god in Egypt. When he died at Babylon at the age of thirty-three on June 13, 323, he ruled an empire larger than any before him — larger by far.

Palestine, as one might expect, was not untouched by Alexander. Following Issus he swept down the Mediterranean coast toward Egypt. Fame and fear preceded him. Tyre held out seven months, Gaza two. Tyre's strength lay partly in the fact that it was on an island. In typical direct fashion Alexander simply had the area between the shore and the island filled in, converting the island into a peninsula, which it still is. Egypt had had more than its fill of Persians; it hailed Alexander as pharaoh, descendant of the gods, even as a god incarnate and legitimate ruler of all Egypt. Of the actual conquest of the Palestinian cities we know almost nothing except that they passed effectively into Macedonian hands. Samaria, long a place of strength and independence of mind, opposed Alexander's will. Although details are lacking, there is no reason to suspect that he dealt with this city any differently from other such recalcitrants. It was taken swiftly, the population sold into slavery and then turned into a Hellenistic center peopled by retired veterans. The huge round towers with which Alexander's military engineers fortified this ancient site were set into the walls of Omri and Ahab and were later incorporated into the Roman city. Today they are among the most prominent features of Samaria.

Of even greater importance than the rebuilding, beautification and Hellenization of one city was the massive influx of Hellenistic thought, customs and practices into this conservative, distinctly uncosmopolitan land. For a people who for the most part clung precariously to the traditions of their fathers the new ways would be resisted. In time Greek universalism and Jewish particularism, fundamentally incompatible, would collide, producing the Maccabean War.

Hardly was Alexander dead than his generals, equally young, some exceptionally talented and all ambitious, went about the deadly serious business of dividing up his vast holdings. It was a complex time with peoples, tribes, nations and clans breaking loose to claim their independence, sometimes successfully. After Alexander's generals had calmly divided up the world among themselves they set about seeking to take away each other's portion. The details of all this need not detain us. Only Ptolemy, said to be the ablest of Alexander's officers, and Seleucus, said most nearly to have shared the young genius' vision of a world united by Hellenism, are important to our story. The former seized Egypt and built a brilliant new capital, Alexandria. The latter took Syria (which extended to India in those days!) and also built a brilliant new capital—two of them in fact—Antioch on the Orontes and Seleucia on the Tigris.

Left:
Alexander the Great at the Battle of Issus from a mosaic at Pompeii.

Seleucus I, "Nicator," the only one of Alexander's generals to continue his Hellenizing policies.

Ptolemy I, "Soter," who turned Egypt into his personal domain.

These two joined forces against other rivals and prevailed. By agreement Seleucus was to have both Palestine and the Phoenician coast. But Ptolemy managed to outmaneuver his friend, ally and rival. Palestine and Phoenicia were his. After 301 B.C. Seleucus did not even contest the new Egyptian's claim. But he never forgot, nor did his successors.

We know less about this period of Jewish history in Palestine than almost any other. What evidence there is suggests that the Ptolemies sought to maintain the old Persian administrative system, to confirm the administrative districts and to preserve the old political structures. For example, coins recently found bear the portrait of Ptolemy I Soter with the Hebrew (not Aramaic) inscription "Yehudah," or Judah. That Hebrew had replaced Aramaic on coins may indicate a degree of autonomy for Judah under the Ptolemies that was not available under the Persians.

Of the Jews of the Diaspora we know a good deal more, particularly of the Jewish community in Egypt. Alexandria was rapidly becoming the foremost city of the world, architecturally magnificent, a major center of commerce by land and sea and with a library unrivaled in the ancient world. It drew scholars from far-flung lands, and the brilliance of their thought, if not their creativity, was renowned. One-fifth of the population of this splendid city was Jewish. The synagogue there was wondrous to behold, and the Jewish community as a whole was distinguished, eventually producing no less than Philo, one of the leading philosophers of the Roman era. Like others of of the Alexandrian school he was brilliant without being particularly creative.

It was also in Alexandria during this time that the Hebrew Scriptures were rendered into Greek. The necessity of this is seen in the Alexandrian Jews' loss of Hebrew as a native language. Of course they all spoke Greek. The Jewish community unable to read Hebrew texts was losing touch with the Scriptures. Until in the third century, over a period of years, the Bible of that day was put into their common tongue. The significance of this was far-reaching. It opened the way for Gentiles to participate more and more in the worship and ways of the synagogue, which they did in significant numbers throughout the Greco-Roman period until the two Jewish revolts. The *Septuagint,* as this translation was called, was also the Bible of the early Christian missionaries as they spread out across the Greek-speaking eastern Roman Empire.

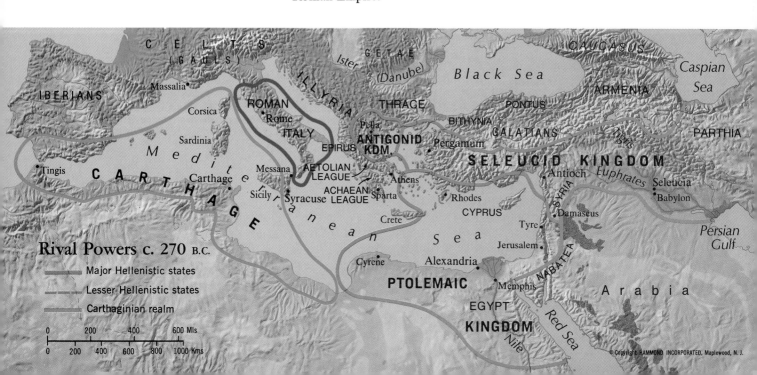

Rival Powers c. 270 B.C.

Major Hellenistic states
Lesser Hellenistic states
Carthaginian realm

0   200   400   600 Mls
0 200 400 600 800 1,000 Kms

© Copyright HAMMOND INCORPORATED, Maplewood, N.J.

Throughout this century the Seleucids in Antioch had not forgotten that the Ptolemies had cheated them in the division of the land. By 198 B.C. with Antiochus III, "Antiochus the Great," on the throne they were ready to settle old scores. Antiochus had exerted his power over Asia Minor and had fought several battles with Ptolemaic Egyptian forces. In 198 at Paneas (modern Baniyas) in the lovely country near the headwaters of the Jordan River, the Seleucids crushed an Egyptian army and marching south were able to annex Palestine and with it Phoenicia.

For reasons which escape us the Jews of Jerusalem rose in revolt against the Ptolemies before Antiochus' army arrived. They attained success, delivering the city to the Seleucid monarch whom they welcomed amid scenes of great public joy. Antiochus responded by relieving taxes for three years or longer in order that the country, which had suffered in the war, might recover. Refugees were to be aided in their return to their homes. Jews who had fought against Antiochus or in some way been arrested for opposition to his aims were to be released. Not only were the Jews to be allowed to continue their traditional ways of life without interference from the state, but monies for the repair and continuing support of the Temple were to be paid out of imperial funds. Moreover priests as well as other cultic functionaries were to be entirely tax exempt. Who could doubt that the Jews of Jerusalem had acted with wisdom in supporting Seleucid ambitions?

As we can see from all this it was not Seleucid policy to repress native cults but rather to encourage them. At the same time the Seleucids, more than any of the other successors of Alexander the Great, carried forward an active, even aggressive program of Hellenization.

In this syncretistic undertaking religion played a large role. Those gods of the polytheistic cults which had the same function were identified one with another. Quite naturally one high god was understood as but a manifestation of all others. To the mind of that day this was not merely unobjectionable, but a positive step in removing countless cultural and national barriers which had so long served to divide peoples. It was, moreover, but one part of a larger policy providing a common culture compounded of east and west and built on the foundation of Greek languages, manners and customs. Thus could divergent peoples find unity. The major vehicle for this was to be the Greek city-state model. Alexander had shown the way in founding cities throughout

Antiochus III, "The Great," who took Palestine from the Ptolemies.

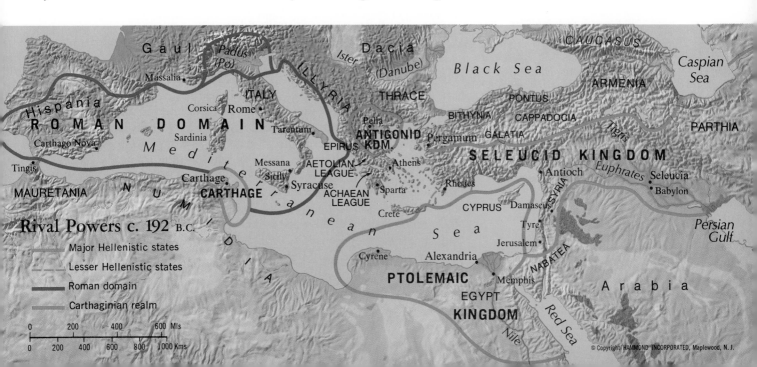

Rival Powers c. 192 B.C.

Major Hellenistic states

Lesser Hellenistic states

Roman domain

Carthaginian realm

© Copyright HAMMOND INCORPORATED, Maplewood, N.J.

Massive round towers such as the one shown here were set in the older walls of Samaria by Alexander's military engineers. Samaria was but one of the strongly Hellenized cities in Palestine.

Terracotta statuette of a war elephant with driver and "tower" on its back.

his empire, either new ones rising from army bases or old ones converted into Hellenistic centers. He had taken Asiatics into full partnership with himself and setting a personal example had taken a foreign wife. His veterans who were settled in these cities were married to native women in mass ceremonies. Greeks and Macedonians, finding their homeland overcrowded and economically depressed, flocked to these new cities.

The Seleucids continued these policies. Everywhere in their vast empire new cities appeared and rapidly became Greek islands in the midst of an enormous Asiatic sea. Palestine was not immune to these developments. Development of the Decapolis, "ten cities" east and northeast of Palestine, had begun under Alexander. Philadelphia (Amman), Gerasa (Jerash), Damascus and the others matured under the Seleucids. In Palestine proper Samaria, already a Greek city, received added impetus. Ancient Beth-shan became Scythopolis, from which Hellenistic life radiated. On the north shore of what is now Haifa Bay Ptolemais (modern Acre) rose. At the southern end of the Sea of Galilee its waters lapped at Philoteria, and deep in the heart of Judea, just west of Hebron, there was Marisa.

Just at the moment when the ancient empires of the east had spent their monumental and long-lived energies, new life from Europe was injected and flowed through the tired veins bringing new life. The countryside began to revive. Cities prospered, particularly Hellenistic cities with their political prerogatives, burgeoning economies and avant-garde manners and customs.

A new era was indeed dawning in the east. Would the Jews be left out of it? Certainly those in the Diaspora were susceptible to the changes, and as evidence from Egypt shows they fell into the spirit of the times in varying degrees, wholly succumbing as at Elephantine, and partially seduced as at Alexandria. The story was the same throughout the Diaspora. In Palestine the community was deeply divided between liberals, who said it was possible to maintain ancient ways in spite of, and perhaps partly because of, what was going on in the larger sphere of culture and government, and conservatives, who saw the entire process as a potentially fatal threat to Jewish life and religion. This was not an academic debate, but involved bribery, premeditated murder and numerous corruptions of Jewish institutions, including the high priesthood itself.

Meanwhile, as so often in the past, events on the international level were developing in such a way as profoundly to affect the debate within the Jewish community. Antiochus III, "the Great," had extended his control over all of Asia Minor. Like his Persian predecessors he cast his eye across the Hellespont. Rome was at the time occupied with Carthage and its interests in the western Mediterranean. Hannibal, the great Carthaginian general, had just been defeated by the Romans at Zama and had fled to Antiochus for protection. As if Antiochus' ambitions needed encouragement, Hannibal urged him to invade Greece. When he did so in 192 Rome immediately declared war on the Seleucid and just as promptly dispatched an army to Greece. Antiochus was sent reeling back into Asia Minor only to find the Roman armies still at his heels. They caught up with him at Magnesia in 190, dealing him a disastrous defeat which was followed by even more humiliating peace terms. Magnesia was really the beginning of the end for the Seleucid Empire. The Peace of Apamea which followed required Antiochus to surrender all of Asia Minor with the single exception of Cilicia, the area around Tarsus. The Seleucid navy was to be joined to the Roman fleet. All war elephants (of which the Romans had seen quite enough in the Carthaginian wars!) were likewise to be surrendered. Those enemies of Rome who had fled to Antioch were to be turned over. This included Hannibal, who, incidentally, escaped. Worst of all, a crippling indemnity was to be paid annually. So massive was this amount that—as the Romans had intended—it seriously restricted Seleucid abilities, particularly their ability to make war. To insure that all these things were faithfully carried out, twenty hostages would be taken to Rome, including Antiochus' own son.

In prospect this was fathomless disgrace and unmitigated disaster. The Romans saw to it that it was carried out to the letter. Henceforth Seleucid rulers were ever scrambling to raise money to pay off the Romans. The many temples in the empire, each with its own treasury and each with its lavish decorations, were at least one source of revenue. Indeed, Antiochus himself was killed while robbing the temple at Elam in 187 B.C.

Seleucus IV inherited not only the throne, but also the Roman burden. Although he confirmed the decree of his father regarding the privileges of the Jews (2 Maccabees 3:3), he cast covetous eyes on the Temple at Jerusalem. Now ensued one of the least worthy pages in Jewish history. Onias, the high priest, journeyed northward to Antioch to plead the cause of his people, seeking to persuade Seleucus to leave the Temple alone. Behind him in Jerusalem he left a quarrelsome faction which had been actively involved with the king to seize the sacred funds. Onias' enemies slandered him to the king, but Onias spoke against no man, pleading only that the Temple be kept inviolate and public peace, which was being endangered, be restored. All arguments came to nothing. While all this was going on Seleucus fell under the assassin's blade. His brother Antiochus, who does not seem to have had an active hand in the plot, was even then journeying homeward from Rome where he had been hostage. He ascended the throne as Antiochus IV and took the further title *Epiphanes* ("god manifest") since he viewed himself as the incarnation of Zeus.

A brother of Onias took the occasion to offer the new king a bribe if he would depose Onias and name him as high priest. Furthermore, promised Joshua or better Jason, for he called himself by the Greek form, he would be done with the conservative policies of his brother and cooperate entirely with the king, fostering the Hellenistic desires of this Epiphanes. Only too pleased to find someone who would solve a potentially knotty problem and who would, moreover, pay for what the king wanted done anyway, Antiochus readily agreed. Jason would pay 440 talents of silver for the high priesthood. Another 150 were promised if the king would allow a gymnasium to be built in Jerusalem and would grant its members citizenship of Antioch.

Antiochus IV, "Epiphanes," attempted to Hellenize Judah. His brutal measures against the Jews led to the Maccabean War.

> When the king assented and Jason came to office, he at once shifted his countrymen over to the Greek way of life. He set aside the existing royal concessions to the Jews, . . . and he destroyed the lawful ways of living and introduced new customs contrary to the law. For with alacrity he founded a gymnasium right under the citadel, and he induced the noblest of the young men to wear the Greek hat. There was such an extreme of Hellenization and increase in the adoption of foreign ways because of the surpassing wickedness of Jason, who was ungodly and no high priest.
>
> (2 Maccabees 4:10-13)

The bitter objections of the more traditional Jews to the establishment of a gymnasium in Jerusalem ought to lead us to realize that it was more than

157

merely an athletic club. Indeed, it was in the nature of a sophisticated and highly class-conscious boys' high school. Its curriculum consisted entirely of Greek learning, doubtless highlighting Greek classical literature and certainly emphasizing the Greek love for sports. This latter was particularly offensive to traditional Jews. As in Greece, so in the gymnasium in Jerusalem, races were popular and were run in the nude. This had long been normal practice among the Greeks. The Olympics were so run, and the Letter to the Hebrews in the New Testament reflects this practice when it says: ". . . let us lay aside every weight, . . . , and let us run with perseverance the race that is set before us" (Hebrews 12:1). Many of the Jerusalem Jews were thoroughly shocked.

Greek manners, dress and customs flourished. And the "Greek hat" mentioned in Maccabees was proudly worn by the boys of the gymnasium as a sign of emancipation from their own tradition and adherence to what must have then appeared as the wave of the future. To others, however, it was little less than a sign of apostasy and a symbol of the growing threat which hung heavy over the land.

There can be little doubt that the gymnasium was dedicated to Hermes, the patron god of athletic contests. Second Maccabees 4:18 says as much when it tells the story of the team from the Jerusalem gymnasium which went to Tyre to participate in games dedicated to Hercules. But interestingly enough, those who took offerings to Tyre to dedicate to this god had second thoughts and gave them instead for the construction of Seleucid warships. So even the best of the athletes from the gymnasium were uneasy.

Then Jason was beaten at his own game. A man named Menelaus, who proved more unscrupulous than even Jason, offered Antiochus another bribe for the high priesthood. Apparently Jason's earlier 440 talents only insured the office for three years. At the end of this time Menelaus was able to outbid him by 300 talents. The price was going up, and so undoubtedly was Antiochus' pleasure at finding that so potentially difficult a problem was in fact a source of considerable revenues. Onias, still in Antioch, protested this continuing skullduggery. For his efforts he was murdered in the gardens of Daphne at the instigation of Menelaus (2 Maccabees 4:33-38). Even Antiochus was outraged at this and took action against those immediately responsible. Antiochus wept for Onias, who seems to have been about the only honorable leader in this sorry episode in Jewish history.

Antiochus had a few imperial ambitions of his own. Having grown up in Rome he had gained a healthy respect for Roman power and Roman determination to use it in self-interest. Greece would be left alone. But there was always Egypt. In 169 he successfully invaded the land of the Nile. In high spirits on his way back home he plundered the Temple at Jerusalem, even stripping the gold leaf from its front. He took everything, including the hidden treasures which were betrayed to him, probably by Menelaus. ". . . taking them all, he departed to his own land, after he had shed much blood."

Naked Greek youths participating in athletic contests are pictured on this 6th century B.C. Greek vase. The introduction of such Hellenizing practices into Jerusalem scandalized many pious Jews.

Greek statue of Hermes, patron god of athletic contests and travelers.

> Israel mourned deeply in every community,
>> rulers and elders groaned,
> maidens and young men became faint,
>> the beauty of the women faded.
> Every bridegroom took up the lament;
>> she who sat in the bridal chamber was mourning.
> Even the land shook for its inhabitants,
>> and all the house of Jacob was clothed with shame.
>> (1 Maccabees 1:24-28)

The reason for this may not have been entirely whim on the king's part. Perhaps he sensed sedition in Jerusalem. Rumors of his death in Egypt had drifted back and spread like wildfire once they reached the Jewish city. Jason seized the opportunity, besieging his rival, Menelaus, in the citadel. But in the process he committed barbaric acts against the population and was driven from the city. Whatever provocation Antiochus saw, he was satisfied that he had taught the city a lesson by sacking the Temple and reestablishing Menelaus in power.

But the lesson the people learned was hardly what Antiochus desired. They, or at least the more religiously conservative among them, were convinced by all this that Antiochus was a monster intent on nothing less than stamping out their religion and their ancestral ways. Unrest, until now more or less below the surface, came into the open.

In 167 B.C. Antiochus was back in Egypt and received an unparalleled, stinging insult. Moving almost at will with his army he drove toward Alexandria, having already sacked Memphis. He was met by one man who stopped his campaign dead in its tracks. Popilius Laenas was the Roman ambassador. Rome, Popilius said, had had enough of Antiochus' Egyptian ambitions. He was to leave the country at once, taking his army with him. Antiochus, so the story goes, asked for time to consider, whereupon Popilius drew a circle around Antiochus in the sand. He was not to step out of that circle until he had made his decision, otherwise he was at war with Rome! Antiochus knew the Romans well. This was no empty threat; the Roman fleet had suddenly appeared at the mouth of the Nile. To disobey Popilius was to invite the legions. He went home taking his army with him.

Passing through Palestine he heard of the difficulties his new royal commissioner and his kept high priest were having maintaining order. He did not break his journey, but he resolved to do something about Jerusalem. Sometime in the year 167 he sent a general named Apollonius to Jerusalem with a large force of soldiers. Apollonius had orders to deal harshly with a population that was getting out of hand. He beguiled the people of the city into thinking that his mission was a peaceful one. They opened the gates to welcome him. At once his carefully instructed soldiers fell upon the civilian population; unspeakable scenes of butchery and rapine followed. Looting was widespread; fires began. Much of the city was destroyed. Then, the soldiers having had their fill, the walls were demolished. With its stones a formidable Syrian fortress was built, the Acra, just south of the Temple Mount. The stamped handles of Rhodian wine jars found on the floors of its storage rooms indicate a flourishing trade with the island kingdom. This fortress stood, garrisoned with Macedonians, Syrians and Hellenized Jews, as a symbol of all that the Jews hated in the Syrian Greeks until it was demolished by Simon the Hasmonean about twenty-five years later.

The Temple was not damaged. Antiochus had something else in mind for it, something that fitted his future plans for the area and its people. The Temple had now passed out of Jewish hands and was to be the shrine of a new city dominated by colonists and Hellenized Jews. The Hebrew God, insofar as he was to be acknowledged at all, was to be identified with Zeus. In December of 167 a new cult was initiated in the Temple, a cult to the Olympian Zeus, complete with an image of the divinity and an altar for animal sacrifice. The meat that was burned there was the flesh of swine. First Maccabees calls this "a desolating sacrilege" (1:54), and the Book of Daniel, in more famous language, refers to it as "the abomination that makes desolate" (9:

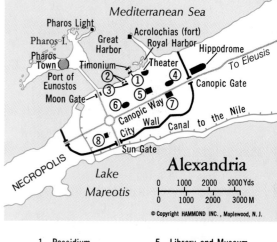

1 Poseidium
2 Obelisks
3 Caesarium
4 Stadium
5 Library and Museum
6 Amphitheater
7 Sports Grounds
8 Serapeion

159

A Jewish "slipper lamp" from the Hellenistic period in Palestine.

Jerusalem of the Maccabees

- ☐ Maximum extent of Maccabean city
- ■ ■ ■ Wall alignment uncertain
- ─── Present-day wall

The Baris

Bridge

Temple

Hasmonean Palace

Market Place

UPPER CITY

Tyropoeon Valley

Gate

LOWER CITY

Kidron Valley

Tombs

ACRA

Tower

Spring Gihon

Aqueduct

Pool of Siloam

Hinnom Valley

En-rogel

0 100 200 300 400 500 Yds
0 100 200 300 400 500 M

© Copyright HAMMOND INC., Maplewood, N.J.

27, 11:31, 12:11). Like so many other cities in the east in the past two centuries, Jerusalem was to be turned into a center of Hellenistic life.

More—the tolerant policy of the Seleucids with regard to local cults could no longer be applied to these people. Judaism was not like the other cults which readily fell into the scheme. It was intransigent, serving the people as a rallying point for political purposes, for sedition, for outright defiance of imperial aims and orders implementing them. It must be banned and the prohibition ruthlessly carried out until this ungrateful people fell in line. Specific orders were issued. The decree giving Jews freedom of religion, a decree reaffirmed by one Seleucid king after another, including Antiochus IV, was revoked. Jewish practices were forbidden. These included a prohibition against the celebration of feasts, performing sacrifices, observing the Sabbath, circumcising children. The religious writings of Judaism were to be destroyed. Jews were to perform the rituals of the Hellenistic cults and were to eat the meat used there, including the flesh of pigs. Those who refused were tortured before they were put to death (2 Maccabees 6:18-20).

These brutal measures and a few people killed as examples would take care of the situation. Antiochus could turn his energies elsewhere. Such measures were regrettable but occasionally necessary in this business of empire. There were, after all, many Jews in Jerusalem only too willing to cooperate with his agents (1 Maccabees 1:43, 52). They would work with the army and other loyal forces in reshaping the area. Yes, everything would be well.

Antiochus never understood that he had driven these people beyond the limits of desperation. When one of his agents trying to enforce the new orders was murdered by an old man named Mattathias in the village of Modein, the king would scarcely have taken notice. And when this farmer-priest patriarch and his five exceptional boys began a hit-and-run guerrilla war in the Gophna Hills north of Jerusalem it was no reason for concern. Antiochus had dealt with the situation in Jerusalem and now was occupied with matters of moment elsewhere in the empire. Ineffective measures were taken against the family of rebels later to be known as the Maccabees.

Even though the cities remained relatively passive the countryside was rising as one man, joining forces with the men from the hills, now brilliantly led by one of the sons, Judas. At Beth-horon, where long ago Jonathan had smitten the Philistines, Judas scored an impressive victory in open warfare, which given his increasing strength had now become his policy. The pass at Beth-horon being denied to the enemy, Judas could move in relative safety on Jerusalem. He captured Mizpah, traditional site of the tomb of Samuel. From this commanding height north of the city he could look down on Jerusalem in the distance. The year was 165 B.C. Antiochus was campaigning against the Parthians in the northeast. Judas massed his forces for a major assault, which carried them right into the city. Apart from the Syrian citadel these farmer-warriors found themselves in possession of their holy city. Reverently and with awe they approached the Temple. Following cleansing, the Temple was rededicated in 164. This event is still celebrated in the Festival of Hanukkah, the feast of the relighting of the lamps in the Temple.

Years of war lay ahead. What had begun as backlash of the tormented turned into a full-scale war for religious freedom and then into a political struggle. The advantage which the Maccabees had been allowed to seize at the outset was never relinquished. They went from victory to victory, pushing to the sea and across the Jordan. But the price was high. One by one the Mac-

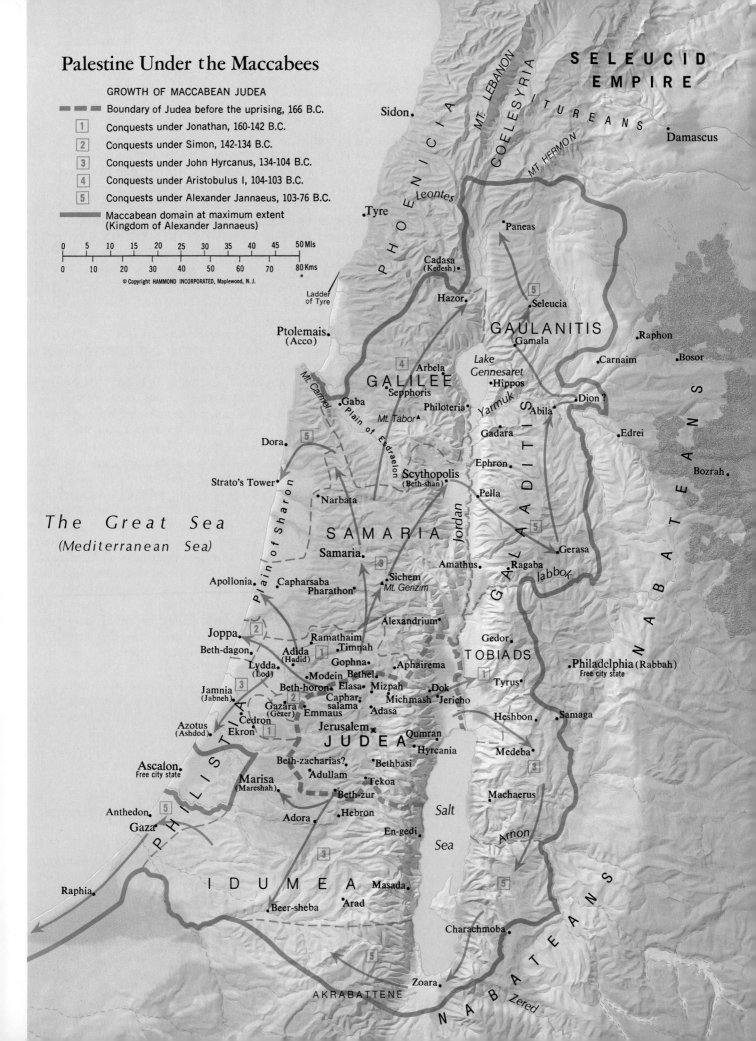

Palestine Under the Maccabees

GROWTH OF MACCABEAN JUDEA

- – – – Boundary of Judea before the uprising, 166 B.C.
- 1 Conquests under Jonathan, 160-142 B.C.
- 2 Conquests under Simon, 142-134 B.C.
- 3 Conquests under John Hyrcanus, 134-104 B.C.
- 4 Conquests under Aristobulus I, 104-103 B.C.
- 5 Conquests under Alexander Jannaeus, 103-76 B.C.
- ─── Maccabean domain at maximum extent
  (Kingdom of Alexander Jannaeus)

0 5 10 15 20 25 30 35 40 45 50 Mls
0 10 20 30 40 50 60 70 80 Kms
© Copyright HAMMOND INCORPORATED, Maplewood, N.J.

SELEUCID EMPIRE

MT. LEBANON
COELESYRIA
ITUREANS
MT. HERMON

Sidon

Damascus

PHOENICIA
Leontes

Tyre

Paneas

Cadasa
(Kedesh)

Hazor

5 Seleucia

Ptolemais
(Acco)

GAULANITIS
Gamala
Raphon
Carnaim
Bosor

4 Arbela
GALILEE
Sepphoris

Lake
Gennesaret
Hippos
Dion?
Edrei

Mt. Carmel
Gaba

Mt. Tabor
Philoteria
Yarmuk
Abila

Bozrah

Dora

5

Gadara
GALAADITIS
Ephron

Strato's Tower

Narbata

Scythopolis
(Beth-shan)

Pella

5

The Great Sea
(Mediterranean Sea)

SAMARIA

Samaria

Jordan

Amathus
Ragaba
Gerasa

NABATEANS

3

Sichem
Mt. Gerizim

Jabbok

Apollonia
Capharsaba
Pharathon

Alexandrium

Gedor

TOBIADS

Philadelphia (Rabbah)
Free city state

Joppa
2
Beth-dagon
Adida
(Hadid)
1

Ramathaim
Timnah
Gophna

Aphairema

1 Tyrus

Lydda
(Lod)
Jamnia
(Jabneh)
3
Gazara
(Gezer)
2
Cedron
Ekron
1

Modein Bethel
Beth-horon Elasa Mizpah
Caphar-
salama
Emmaus Adasa
Jerusalem

Michmash
Dok
Jericho

Heshbon
Samaga

Azotus
(Ashdod)

Qumran
Hyrcania

Medeba
3

Ascalon
Free city state

Beth-zacharias?
Adullam

Bethbasi
Tekoa

JUDEA

Marisa
(Mareshah)

Beth-zur

Salt
Sea

Machaerus

Anthedon
Gaza
5
PHILISTIA

Adora
Hebron

En-gedi

Arnon
5

Raphia

IDUMEA
Beer-sheba
Arad

Masada

3

5

Charachmoba

AKRABATTENE
Zoara
Zered
NABATEANS

The House of Maccabees
and Hasmoneans

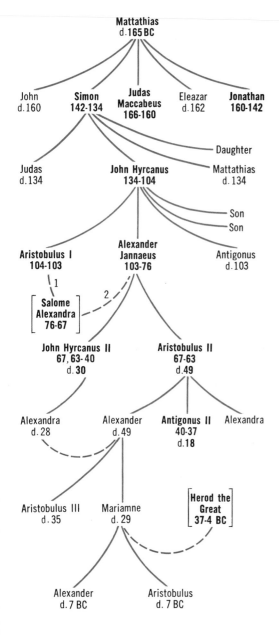

Married - - - -

1. First marriage of Salome Alexandra.
2. Second marriage of Salome Alexandra.

cabee brothers fell in battle, Judas falling at Elasa not far from his beloved hills where the revolt had begun. At the last, when final success was theirs, the Jewish forces were commanded by John Hyrcanus, son of Simon Maccabee. Simon had finally been able to dislodge the Syrians from their citadel in Jerusalem, leaving John the task of enlarging the lands which were coming under Maccabean—or as it now came to be called, *Hasmonean*—domination.

The Romans had denied Egypt to Antiochus. Now through his own folly he had goaded an entire population into taking away the rest of his southern empire. For the first time in over four centuries the Jews of Palestine were free to determine their own political destiny. For the moment no external force threatened, and while there were serious internal stresses they at least could be reasonably contained. There was a Jewish king. He was secure in his rule over his people and was expanding the borders.

No dynasty began more auspiciously or came to a sorrier end than that of the Hasmoneans. John took the Negeb in the south and pushed as far north as southern Galilee. His son, Aristobulus, reigned only one year (104-103 B.C.) but secured the rest of Galilee, settling Jews as quickly as possible in this Gentile area. Sepphoris became a major center of Jewish life. When Alexander Jannaeus, Aristobulus' brother, came to the Hasmonean throne in 103 his kingdom extended from "Dan to Beer-sheba." Much of Transjordan was also under his control, and along the coasts at least three ports had been opened to trade. It was the high-water mark of this dynasty. And, as at other such times in the more ancient history of Israel, internal dissension was reaching the boiling point. Indeed, during Alexander's reign there was something of a civil war involving Pharisees and Sadducees. It was not until after his death in 76 B.C. that his wife and heir, Salome Alexandra, was able to bring it to an end. She was a strong figure and by sheer force of will was able to hold the state together. But when she died in 67 the contending sides each found a champion. These were brothers, Hyrcanus and Aristobulus. Hyrcanus was heir and did reign as Hyrcanus II, but Aristobulus was the stronger of the brothers and indeed seems to have been involved in plots against his mother even before her death. Aristobulus defeated his brother's forces at Jericho, claimed the throne and moved into the palace in Jerusalem. There he reigned for three years until Hyrcanus, strengthened by forces of King Aretas III of the Nabateans and by a strong advisor named Antipater, laid siege to Jerusalem, shutting up Aristobulus, at first behind fifteen-foot-thick city walls recently unearthed, then in the fortified Temple itself. The power struggle between Hyrcanus II and Aristobulus II was not ended, however, by local forces.

There was campaigning in the east at this time a certain Roman general named Pompey. Both sides appealed to him. Aristobulus had already sent to Damascus, seeking Roman aid for lifting of the siege. Pompey reduced the number of interested parties by threatening to invade the kingdom of the Nabateans. Aretas withdrew from Jerusalem and the Romans prepared to march on the Holy City.

The conflict within the Jewish state was not a power confrontation in the usual sense. It was a deep-seated struggle between social classes and religious philosophies. Antipater, Hyrcanus' advisor, saw this. He was the most able man on either side of the conflict. When Pompey decided between the two brothers he choose Hyrcanus, partly perhaps because the throne was rightly his, but more likely because Antipater supported him. Did Antipater support him because he was the weaker and the one on whom he could more easily work his own will?

Antipater's family was not Jewish by descent. It was forcibly converted upon pain of death during the time of John Hyrcanus. Yet this man and his family were to play a major role in shaping Jewish history. One of his sons was named Herod. We know him better as Herod the Great.

From the outbreak of the Maccabean War to Pompey's ending of effective Hasmonean rule was 101 years. It is one of the most curious centuries in the history of the Jews. On the surface it would appear that the messianic age had come. There were capable Jewish monarchs on the throne, religious freedom (at least for Jews) brought its blessings and the country was economically prosperous. Peace, prayers and prosperity—what else was there to ask for? Yet these were not really good times. Reasons for this are controversial. But the change from a struggle for religious freedom to one of political aggrandizement caused severe internal dissension. As early as 145 B.C. Demetrius II of Syria had adopted a policy of noninterference with religion in Judea. By 142 Jews were exempt from heavy Seleucid taxes. Of course, these measures were granted under the gun, so to speak. Simon Maccabee, leader in those days, had taken upon himself the duties of a temporal ruler, striking coinage, levying taxes and maintaining a standing army. The army was a major problem. Not because he maintained an army, but because he maintained a mercenary army made up of soldiers of fortune who carelessly offended the religious sensibilities of the population for whom they were fighting. Moreover, Simon, having gained religious freedom for himself and those who thought as he did, ruthlessly suppressed freedom of religion for everyone else. Captured people had to convert to Judaism on pain of death. This became standard Hasmonean policy and we have already noted that Antipater's family was converted in this manner. Cities were forcibly Judaized and residents terrorized.

There were many Jews who openly opposed such things. To fight for freedom only to deny it to others was wrong in their view. Those who had been tormented ought not to become the tormentors. Hasmonean imperial policy was a major source of division and a prominent factor in bringing a potentially strong dynasty to its knees. Likewise, the callous use of religious office for secular purposes alienated many. Specifically, the kings usurped the high priesthood and were anything but exemplars of the Levitical model. It was during this time that at least one group broke away entirely, went into the wilderness and built a monastery there to await the coming of Messiah. These people were the writers of the Dead Sea Scrolls.

Finally, there was perhaps the greatest curiosity of all. The Maccabean War had been fought because of Hellenization. But the Hasmoneans were themselves Hellenizers. They embodied a strange contradiction involving their apparent desire to suppress alien cults and preserve traditional Jewish ways while at the same time adopting Hellenistic culture and employing mercenary armies. Needless to say, this did not encourage religious conservatives to be strong supporters of this dynasty.

So the Hasmoneans fell, as much a victim of their own folly and imperial greed as of anything else. In power they had proved to be as base as other peoples of the region. As this revival of Jewish monarchy crumbled under the press of its own suicidal policies, something else was also crumbling. It was the Roman Republic. The last years of the Intertestamental Period were played out against the background of the Roman civil war.

Coin of Alexander Jannaeus. This bronze lepton is referred to as the widow's mite or copper in the New Testament (Luke 21:2).

Bronze coin with the earliest known representation of the Jewish menorah. It was minted in the time of the Hasmonean king, Antigonus II, 40-37 B.C.

This aqueduct built by Herod the Great brought water from Mount Carmel to the new port of Caesarea. Hadrian doubled its capacity a century and a half after Herod originally built it.

13 THE ROMAN EAST
AND HEROD THE GREAT

The Romans were seldom taken unaware. A conservative, cautious people, they moved carefully from traditionally known strengths into new endeavors. It was precisely this quality, which paid off handsomely in so many instances, that led them into one of the greatest crises in their history. The Roman Empire had grown like Topsy, without plan and without adequate thought to how the multiplying dominions should be governed. At first, when their rule extended to other parts of Italy and into Sicily, they did well with the aristocratic idea that the "right men" of the state could and should rule the farther reaches as well as at home. To them "right men" meant, of course, those from the aristocratic class. Specifically, only ex-consuls were to be provincial governors. In time the number of provinces increased faster than the supply of ex-consuls, so others of the upper class who had held high offices were sent out. By the middle of the first century B.C. the empire surrounded the Mediterranean and the old system was rapidly breaking down. In effect, ultimate responsibility for provincial administration was lodged with the Senate and its committees. Not only was this structure now too slow-moving to respond to the needs of empire, but "old school" mentality, bribery and corruption brought the entire republican system to a crisis stage.

Opinion was sharply divided. Reformers such as Julius Caesar believed the remedy for decay in government was strong centralized power concentrated in the hands of one man able and willing to act. Cicero and his more traditionally minded allies, on the other hand, were not so sure that this crisis had not been manufactured out of ambition. They opposed the imperial designs of the reformers. It is not our purpose here to discuss in detail this fascinating clash of ideas and able men. Our concern is with its impact upon the Roman East, where this great drama was finally played out, and where it strongly influenced the land in which Jesus was born.

We have seen how the struggle between rival claimants to the throne of the kingdom of Judea brought in Pompey. He championed the cause of Hyrcanus II against his brother Aristobulus and quickly moved to take over. His soldiers ended resistance by Aristobulus' supporters by storming the Temple enclosure. Pompey stripped Hyrcanus of most of his territory and even of his title as king, allowing him to retain only the high priestly dignity. Hyrcanus was thus to be an ecclesiastic, not a political figure. The whole of the former Hasmonean kingdom was annexed to the Roman province of Syria, which had just been organized. Hellenism was encouraged to safeguard Western interests against reassertion of Asiatic power from Pontus, Armenia or Parthia.

Palestine was strategically important to the Romans since it funneled the grain of Egypt to the eastern front in Mesopotamia. To an ever increasing degree Jews were made to feel aliens in their own land.

In 61 B.C. Pompey left the east and returned to Rome. The next year he entered of necessity into a coalition with his bitter adversary, Julius Caesar. Actually, it was a triumvirate, with Pompey and Crassus representing the interest of the aristocrats and merchants and Caesar those of the reformers

Julius Caesar, who conferred many
privileges on the Jews for their services
to him in the East.

Marc Antony, the ablest Roman after
Caesar, gambled everything on an
eastern empire — and lost.

who were bent on social change quite as much as fundamental government reorganization. This First Triumvirate, as it was called, lasted seven years, until 53. During this time Palestine was drawn ever nearer the center of the conflict. Aristobulus and his sons, who had been exiled to Rome, escaped and twice fomented rebellion against Hyrcanus. The high priest was, as usual, ineffective against his brother, and on both occasions a dashing cavalry officer and protégé of Caesar, Marc Antony, intervened to suppress the uprising. After the first attempted revolt of Aristobulus, the Roman grip on the land was strengthened by reconstruction of certain Hellenistic cities of Palestine and founding of others. After the second uprising, Hyrcanus' authority was further restricted. Finally, in the year 55 the Romans sought out the most capable local leader they could find and made him prefect (governor). This man was Antipater, who until now had managed as best he could to manipulate Hyrcanus from the wings. It was now center stage for this consummate politician.

In the same year that Antipater was placed in charge of Judea a new Roman governor of Syria was named. So important had the east become in the thinking of the rival parties in Rome that no less than Crassus himself received the critical post at Antioch. This enormously rich man, one of the wealthiest in Rome, took the treasure from the Temple in Jerusalem to provide funds for a campaign against the Parthians. Caesar had scored a smashing success of arms in Gaul, and with military fame came popular acclaim. Crassus felt that he must offset this by scoring heavily against Rome's most intransigent eastern foe. The difference was that Caesar returned in triumph from Gaul, while Crassus did not return at all from Parthia. His failure momentarily endangered the whole of the Roman East. Cassius, who was later to bury his dagger in Caesar's back, rushed to Syria and in a series of decisive moves managed to shore up the frontier.

Meanwhile Caesar was ever gaining strength in Gaul and coming to the resolve that it was now or never. In 49 B.C. he crossed the Rubicon, a small stream marking the northernmost frontier of Rome proper. It was forbidden for a Roman general to bring an army into Roman territory without the Senate's permission. Knowing that such permission would never come from a body dominated by his enemies, Caesar marched on Rome. The die was cast. The Senate panicked and called upon Pompey to save Rome. But Pompey fled with his followers to Greece, there to establish a base for opposition to Caesar.

With his republican enemies firmly in control of the east—Syria, Greece and Egypt, where the thirteen-year-old pharaoh, Ptolemy XIII, served at Pompey's behest—Caesar hit upon the idea of sending Aristobulus and his two sons to their native haunts to stir up trouble for Pompey. It did not work. Pompey's soldiers killed both Aristobulus and his older son, Alexander. Antigonus, the younger son, escaped to contend later with Herod for Judea.

Although Caesar's hopes for Aristobulus had gone awry, success came his way the next year, in 48. Pompey was defeated in a battle in Thessaly and forced to flee Greece. He sailed for Egypt, expecting to be welcomed royally by the young Ptolemy. But this striking lad wanted to rule without interference. He had just deposed his twenty-one-year-old sister and coregent, Cleopatra. When Pompey landed in Egypt Ptolemy's emissaries were on hand to greet him. They promptly struck him dead! This was the chance Caesar had been waiting for. The east was vulnerable. He rushed to Egypt and placed Ptolemy under house arrest. Then he became involved in a love affair with Cleopatra and soon found himself besieged in the Greek quarter of Alexandria by a native Egyptian army. The siege dragged on from the late autumn of 48 until well into the spring of the following year. Increasingly desperate, Caesar sought aid wherever he could find it. Among others who finally marched to Caesar's rescue were Palestinian Jewish troops sent by Antipater. Caesar, already grateful for Jewish support of his imperial cause against the republicans, now had a personal reason for gratitude in addition to a political one. Journeying northward toward Asia Minor, Caesar granted a number of privileges to the Jews. Moreover, while dictator in Rome he continued to issue decrees favorable to these people. This proved to be important in the years ahead, since both Antony and Octavian reaffirmed these privileges.

Among those things which Caesar did for the Jews after Alexandria was to restore Hyrcanus to political standing by naming him ethnarch of Judea. Upon Antipater was conferred citizenship of the city of Rome, a rare thing for a provincial, and his stewardship of the Jewish state was confirmed. Moreover, his two older sons, Phasael and Herod, were made military governors of Judea and Galilee respectively. Taxes on Jewish cities were reduced, except for Jerusalem which had "bought" the privilege of rebuilding its walls. Jewish priests were allowed to levy heavier taxes for their support and for support of Jewish shrines. Certain of the Jewish territories were excused from the requirement of furnishing auxiliary troops for the Roman army, always an offensive thing for Jews since the Roman army carried images. Most important of all, the ban against private assemblies, passed in 55 to stem potential unrest, was lifted in the case of Jews, who were to be allowed to meet privately and regularly. That this strengthened the synagogue in all parts of the empire and also facilitated its work is certain. This was, of course, a matter of first importance in the spread of early Christianity.

On March 15, 44, the Ides of March, Caesar was struck down in Pompey's Theater where the Senate was to meet that day, falling dead, so we are told, at the foot of Pompey's statue. Antipater, by now fully identified with Caesar's cause, was also marked for elimination. A year later he was poisoned. The struggle for power in Rome, from which so far the Jews had profited much, had come to Palestine with a vengeance. The murder of Caesar touched off flames all over the empire; nowhere with more deadly results than in Jerusalem.

Phasael and Herod, military commanders, gave every indication of intending to succeed their father in the political realm. The priests, who were reaping enormous profits from Caesar's tax scheme, and other aristocrats opposed Antipater's sons. Herod looked around for allies, important allies. Cassius was again in Syria. Herod linked himself with Caesar's murderer and paid large sums for Roman aid.

Then at Philippi in 42 B.C. Antony and Octavian avenged Caesar's murder with a singular victory ending republican hopes. Antony, hero of Philippi, marched east to purge former enemies. Herod's adversaries did not need to slander him. Had he not openly curried favor with Cassius? But here, not for the last time, Herod's charm and diplomacy won the day. Antony reaffirmed Caesar's decrees, including the offices held by Herod and Phasael.

In Rome in the year 40 Herod, flanked by Antony and Octavian, heard himself proclaimed king of Judea. As strange as it might seem, it was a low moment in Herod's life. Earlier in that year Antigonus, Aristobulus' younger son, had taken the occasion of a Parthian invasion of Syria to invite Parthian

The attempts of Pompey the Great to overthrow Caesar came to a bitter end when he died ignominiously on an Egyptian beach.

Through skill, patience and the mistakes of his enemies, Octavian (Caesar Augustus) emerged from the Roman civil wars as undisputed master of an empire.

167

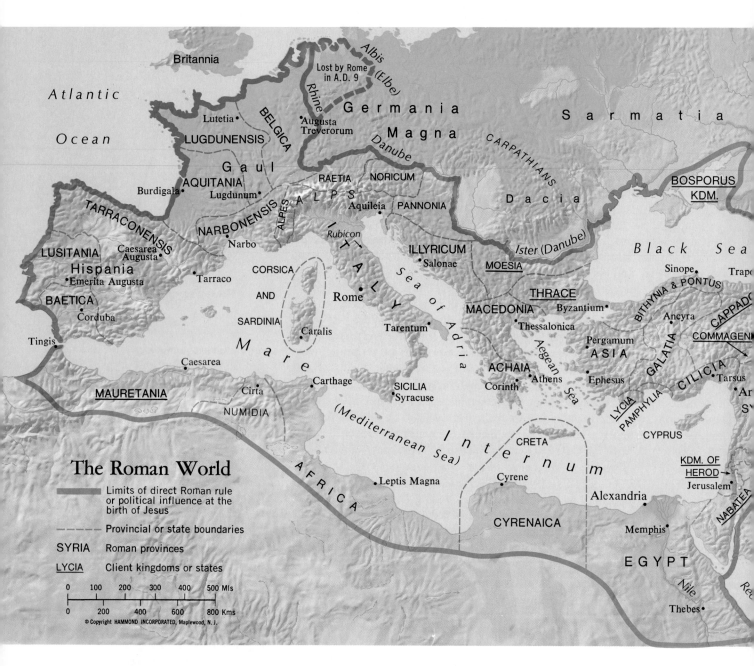

Atlantic

Ocean

Britannia

Lost by Rome
in A.D. 9

Albis
(Elbe)

Germania

Magna

Sarmatia

Rhine

Lutetia

BELGICA

Augusta
Treverorum

Danube

LUGDUNENSIS

CARPATHIANS

Gaul

RAETIA

NORICUM

Dacia

BOSPORUS
KDM.

AQUITANIA

Burdigala

Lugdunum

ALPS

Aquileia

PANNONIA

Narbo

ALPES

Black   Sea

Sinope

Trape

TARRACONENSIS

NARBONENSIS

Rubicon

ITALY

ILLYRICUM

Ister (Danube)

LUSITANIA

Caesarea
Augusta

Salonae

MOESIA

Hispania

Emerita Augusta

Tarraco

CORSICA

AND

Rome

Sea
of
Adria

THRACE

Byzantium

BITHYNIA & PONTUS

Ancyra

CAPPADO

BAETICA

Corduba

SARDINIA

Caralis

MACEDONIA

Thessalonica

ASIA

Pergamum

GALATIA

COMMAGEN

Tingis

Caesarea

Mare

Tarentum

Aegean
Sea

Ephesus

CILICIA

Tarsus

Ar

Caesarea

MAURETANIA

Cirta

NUMIDIA

Carthage

Internum

ACHAIA

Corinth

Athens

LYCIA

PAMPHYLIA

S

CYPRUS

SICILIA

Syracuse

(Mediterranean Sea)

CRETA

KDM. OF
HEROD

The Roman World

Leptis Magna

Cyrene

Alexandria

Jerusalem

NABATEA

Limits of direct Roman rule
or political influence at the
birth of Jesus

CYRENAICA

Memphis

Provincial or state boundaries

AFRICA

EGYPT

SYRIA   Roman provinces

LYCIA   Client kingdoms or states

Nile

Re

| 0 | 100 | 200 | 300 | 400 | 500 Mls |

| 0 | 200 | 400 | 600 | 800 Kms |

Thebes

© Copyright HAMMOND INCORPORATED, Maplewood, N.J.

Senate House in the Imperial Forum, Rome.

Ancient coin showing Romulus, Remus
and the she-wolf, who figure in the legend
of the founding of Rome.

168

aid in an assault on Jerusalem. The attack carried the city. Antigonus took Hyrcanus and Phasael prisoners and proclaimed himself king in a restoration of the Hasmonean line. He was to rule for three years as Antigonus II. Herod was forced to flee southward. Rebuffed in an appeal to the Nabateans for aid, he made his way to Egypt. Cleopatra was helpful to Herod and saw him safely embarked for Rome, something she would live to regret.

Thus the proclamation of Herod as king of Judea by the Roman Senate was a move by the Second Triumvirate—Antony, Octavian and Lepidus—to establish a rival to Antigonus and his Parthian allies. Herod had been elevated to the loftiest of titles, but he was a king without a kingdom. He had, in fact, only his abilities and his friends. They were enough.

Herod returned at once to his contested realm and sought to possess it in fact as well as name. This proved a tough task. Not only was Antigonus a worthy opponent, but the Sadducees and other monied interests financed the stubborn resistance. At length Antony, *imperator* at Rome, and Octavian (now become Antony's brother-in-law in a move to heal a widening breach between them), sent legions under the Roman general, Sosius, to Herod's support. Against his wishes Herod was forced to support a Roman attack on Jerusalem. But Herod wanted to rule here. It was not wise to alienate his subjects by unnecessary brutality even before he began to rule them. For this reason he sent sacrificial offerings and food into the sealed city. If he intended by this means to undermine the determination of its defenders, he failed and resistance stiffened. The city had to be stormed. Antigonus' supporters fell back upon the fortified Temple. It too was immediately attacked, but the defenders managed to hold out for months. Hand-to-hand fighting was ferocious, but one by one the Jews fell until, for the second but not the last time, Roman arms were victorious in David's city. Sosius, as was the Roman custom, claimed the conquered city for himself and his soldiers. Loot and rapine were to be their pay. Herod pleaded with Sosius and finally by heavy payment convinced the Roman to withdraw his soldiers from the prostrate city. Striding into the Temple, Sosius offered a golden crown to the Jewish God, saluted Herod and left. Herod had his kingdom. The year was 37 B.C. Herod was thirty-six. He would reign for thirty-three years, justly earning both his designation as "the Great" and a lasting reputation for cruelty.

Curiously, while Herod is remembered in Christian tradition only for his cruelty, Jews recall him as an alien, a convert by accident of family history, who pandered to Rome in order to further his own ambition. Neither memory is wholly false, yet neither comes near the truth. Herod is a historical figure of truly monumental proportions, the only non-Roman other than Cleopatra to emerge from this period as an individual of extraordinary character. Herod owes his place, not to the stories about him in the Gospels, nor to his place in Jewish tradition, but to his own abilities and the fact that in a turbulent period he was a foundation of Roman stability in the east. He was too valuable to punish for his political indiscretions. This is why he was able to shift from one side to another in the Roman civil wars as suited his purpose. In desperation he allied himself with the republicans, whose hopes died at Philippi. Yet Antony welcomed him after Philippi, as did Octavian later. And to whomever he was pledged he was a faithful and welcome ally.

For the first ten years of his reign, roughly down to the year 27, Herod labored to consolidate his rule and establish a firm financial foundation for his future ventures in statecraft, which included posing, often quite effectively, as the defender of Jews and Judaism throughout the Empire. As the

169

Cleopatra VII, the last of the Hellenistic rulers of Egypt. The queen's almost forbidding visage on this coin belies the popular idea of her beauty but it is probably more accurate.

Coin of Herod the Great shows anchor and double cornucopia.

dust of Sosius' departing army settled into the silence of the Palestinian roads, the tasks which faced Herod would have broken a lesser man. There was, of course, the residual bitterness of the local civil war, a bitterness compounded by extraordinary factionalism among the Jews and by the fact that Herod was not racially Jewish. The opposition to Herod soon took the form of active intrigue. Among the intriguers the Hasmoneans, whom Herod unsuccessfully attempted to conciliate, found a willing ally in Cleopatra of Egypt.

Cleopatra, the seventh of her name to rule in Egypt, had used Caesar's bed as a means to further her ambitions. She wished to rekindle the past glories of Egypt and reestablish the Ptolemaic Empire, including Syria and Palestine. Nothing could have suited her desires better than overtures from Hasmonean sympathizers. In the year 41, Cleopatra, casting around for a Roman replacement for the fallen Caesar, used her seductive charms on Marc Antony in an unparalleled scene at Tarsus. Sailing up the River Cyanus on a golden barge, she was attired as Aphrodite, to whom the willing Antony played Dionysus. From that time forward their fortunes were inseparably intertwined despite Antony's occasional abandonment of her and his various attempts to defend Roman interests in the east. In the end he and Cleopatra sought to establish an empire in the east in opposition to Octavian's in the west. It was Alexandria against Rome. Although in valor and ability Antony may well have been superior to Octavian, his association with Cleopatra allowed Octavian to win the propaganda struggle. Antony, ever a popular figure in Rome, with influential friends in high places, was portrayed by his enemies as being under the sway of Rome's enemy, Cleopatra. He was accused of recklessly giving away Roman provinces to foreign potentates. When the Senate finally declared war on the two Alexandrian lovers, Octavian was careful to see that only Cleopatra's name was mentioned. Moreover, at Actium, the decisive battle, Cleopatra's presence demoralized Antony's soldiers and sailors. Herod was caught in the middle of all this.

Antony's attempts to defend Herod against Cleopatra's imperial designs were not altogether successful. She succeeded in annexing the entire coastline of Herod's kingdom, joining it with her lands at Syria and taking over the lucrative bitumen industry at the Dead Sea. She even managed to get title to the rich plantations at Jericho fifteen miles from Herod's palace in Jerusalem. Slowly she was surrounding him. Once, in what must have been a memorable scene, she came to Jerusalem, pressing her further claims. Herod later said that he intended to kill her on this occasion but was dissuaded by advisers. He also says she tried to seduce him. At the end of the visit he personally escorted her back to Egypt, to Pelusium. If subsequently Cleopatra tried to discredit his behavior to Antony, she failed in that too. She really had met her match in Herod. And anyway, Antony knew his woman. Moreover, Herod and his kingdom were vital to imperial defenses. Antony the military commander was not so love-sick as to forget that.

Despite all his difficulties with political intrigue within his family and outside his borders, one problem which Herod did not have was a lack of money. Unlike most monarchs he seems to have had enough funds for his purposes. Furthermore there never was another ruler of the country, with the possible exception of Solomon, who built so much so well. Where did he get the money to do so much and still bequeath fantastic sums?

A satisfactory answer really defies us. But there are several indications. First of all, he inherited enormous real estate holdings from his family. His father and grandfather had used their positions to accumulate land not only in Judea, but also in Idumea and across the Jordan in Arab areas. Furthermore, Herod followed the family habit, and one scholar suggests that before the end of his reign he personally owned half or perhaps as much as two-thirds of the land of Judea. Land, at any rate, was the basis of his fortune. Then he appears to have run an extremely efficient government. Taxes were high, but not oppressive, and he carefully tailored certain taxes to specific requirements. He also was involved in business in various parts of the Roman Empire, once scoring a major financial coup by entering into an agreement with Caesar Augustus for half of the profits of the copper mines of Cyprus. He also saw to it that Judea was prosperous. The land was never a major asset. Its unpredictable rainfall and rocky hillsides afforded few opportunities. Yet Herod not only made it a source of substantial taxes, but an exporter of oils, fruits and, when he got his lands back after Cleopatra's death, of bitumen. In addition his marvelous port at Caesarea allowed him to enter more fully into maritime trade, and while its revenues are not known to us, Caesarea paid handsomely in the last years of Herod's rule.

In the last two-thirds of his reign, from about 27 until his death in 4 B.C., he pretty much had things his own way. The beginning of this period was tricky and its end—his end—was miserable. In between there were, or should have been, halcyon days.

After the Battle of Actium in 31 B.C. Herod was summoned to the island of Rhodes to give an account of himself to the victor, Octavian, now ruler of the Roman world. The losers, Antony and Cleopatra, were holed up in Alexandria awaiting the inevitable onslaught by Octavian. The situation for Herod was fraught with danger. He had been a faithful ally of Antony almost to the last. Only a stroke of luck had kept him and his soldiers from actually being at Actium. Just to ensure that there would not be a repetition of Hasmonean plots, Herod at this time ordered the death of ill-starred Hyrcanus II. Hyrcanus, a mild-mannered old man of over seventy, had been pushed around by everyone since his unfortunate ascension of the Hasmonean throne. If Octavian should depose Herod, Herod wished the throne to pass to his brother, Pheroras. He made the necessary arrangements and sailed for Rhodes.

Before Octavian, whom he had not seen since those days in Rome when he sat between him and Antony, Herod plead a two-fold defense. First, he had been faithful to Antony. As he had been loyal to Antony, so he would now give unswerving allegiance to Octavian. Octavian admired him for this even if he did not much care for the man himself. Second, said Herod, he had always opposed Cleopatra, taking action where he could (where was that?) and urging Antony to get rid of her (when was that?). But he was the implacable foe of this foreign woman, and Octavian bought this too.

Herod's journey to Rhodes ended with a success he could hardly have imagined. Not only was he reconfirmed in power, but territories were restored to him. Those that Cleopatra received through Antony were given back, and so were those which Pompey had detached from Judea! In the end Herod ruled over a land almost as large as the Hasmonean kingdom in its heyday.

After Rhodes, Herod's story follows two concurrent and fairly consistent tracks: success in his statesmanship, brilliant success; unutterable tragedy in his personal and family life; a plot worthy of Kafka. The squalid intrigues which debauched the Herodian royal family involved irreconcilable ambitions of its two sides, the Hasmonean and the Idumean. Early in his reign Herod had attempted to gain Hasmonean support by taking as his second wife the beautiful Mariamne, granddaughter of Hyrcanus. But the marriage

Jericho's luxuriant plantations were given by Antony to Cleopatra, from whom a furious Herod had to rent them.

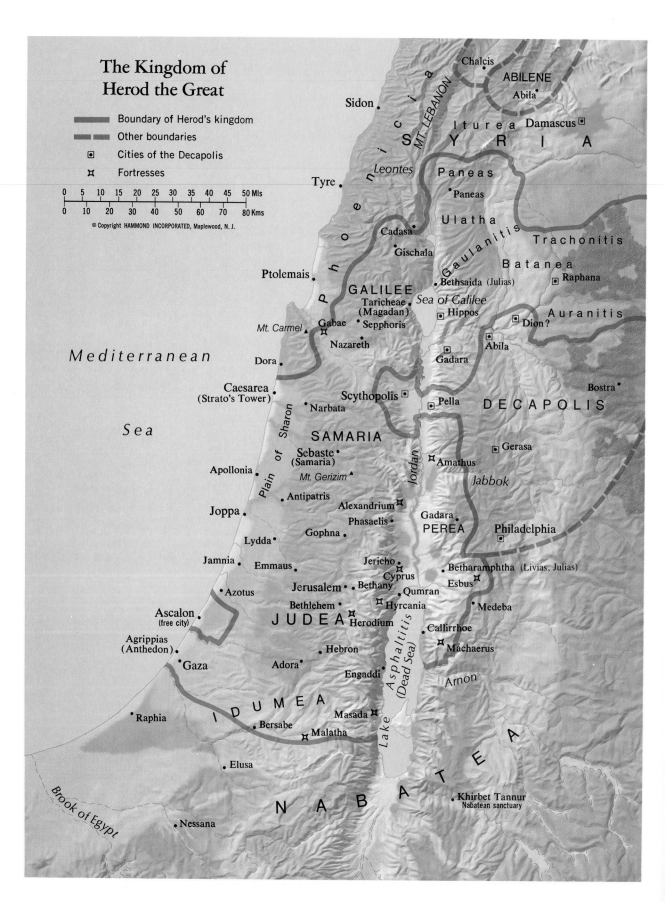

The Kingdom of Herod the Great

- ▬▬ Boundary of Herod's kingdom
- ▬ ▬ Other boundaries
- ⊡ Cities of the Decapolis
- ⋈ Fortresses

0 5 10 15 20 25 30 35 40 45 50 Mls
0 10 20 30 40 50 60 70 80 Kms

© Copyright HAMMOND INCORPORATED, Maplewood, N.J.

Chalcis

ABILENE

Abila

Sidon

SYRIA

MT. LEBANON

Iturea Damascus ⊡

P h o e n i c i a

Leontes

Paneas

•Paneas

Tyre

U l a t h a

Cadasa

Gaulanitis

Trachonitis

Gischala

B a t a n e a

Ptolemais

GALILEE

•Bethsaida (Julias)

⊡ •Raphana

Taricheae
(Magadan)•

Sea of Galilee

A u r a n i t i s

Mt. Carmel

Gabae ⋈

•Sepphoris

⊡ Hippos

⊡ •Dion?

Nazareth

⊡ Abila

Dora•

⊡ Gadara

Caesarea
(Strato's Tower)

Scythopolis ⊡

⊡ Pella

D E C A P O L I S

Bostra•

•Narbata

M e d i t e r r a n e a n

S e a

Plain of Sharon

S A M A R I A

Sebaste•
(Samaria)

Jordan

⊡ Gerasa

Apollonia•

Mt. Gerizim▲

⋈ Amathus

Jabbok

•Antipatris

Alexandrium⋈

Gadara•

Joppa

Phasaelis•

P E R E A

⊡ Philadelphia

•Gophna

Lydda•

Jericho•

Jamnia•

Emmaus•

⋈ Cyprus

Betharamphtha (Livias, Julias)

Azotus•

Jerusalem• •Bethany

Qumran•

Esbus ⋈

•Medeba

Ascalon
(free city)

Bethlehem•

⋈ Hyrcania

J U D E A

⋈ Herodium

Asphaltitis
(Dead Sea)

•Callirrhoe

Agrippias
(Anthedon)•

•Hebron

⋈ Machaerus

•Gaza

Adora•

Engaddi•

Lake

Arnon

I D U M E A

Masada ⋈

•Raphia

Bersabe•

⋈ Malatha

N A B A T E A

•Elusa

•Khirbet Tannur
Nabatean sanctuary

Brook of Egypt

•Nessana

172

to the Hasmonean princess had failed to dampen the enmity between the two factions. Each side had its sinister genius. Alexandra, mother of Mariamne who despised Herod, her son-in-law, was deep in Hasmonean plots with Cleopatra, while Salome, Herod's ever faithful sister, a tireless talebearer, was also tireless in her efforts on behalf of the Idumeans. Under Salome's urging, Herod put his wife Mariamne to death because of her amorous affairs and because she was the center for Hasmonean intrigues. This did not, however, end the matter. It only focused more clearly upon her two sons, Alexander and Aristobulous. The Idumean cause was equally, if not more strongly, represented by another of Herod's sons. Antipater was, in fact, the oldest son and heir apparent. He was the son of Herod and Doris, Herod's Idumean first wife. In the end Herod killed all three of these sons and publicly stated his willingness to kill every one of his children if they plotted against him.

Herod's domestic troubles were widely known. In 7 B.C. Eurycles of Sparta, a thoroughly unattractive character in need of money, came to Jerusalem and collected "gifts" from all sides by carrying stories of the others. It was this in part that prompted Herod to bring formal charges of sedition against Alexander and Aristobulus. Salome and the always scheming Antipater played their parts as well. On the order of Octavian, who now ruled Rome as the Emperor Augustus, Herod brought the two boys to trial before a jury of 150 distinguished men in Berytus (Beirut), which was outside his kingdom. But efforts to secure a fair trial were hopeless. Herod was not only the leading client king of the east, but had also richly endowed various cities of the area such as Berytus and Sidon with colonnaded streets, theaters and marketplaces. It was from these that the jury came. Further, Herod took care to see that men with whom the two half-Hasmonean princes had been in contact were excluded from the proceedings.

The boys claimed that they had only made contingent plans to flee Herod's reach if their lives should be endangered. Needless to say, they were convicted of planning regicide. They were taken to Caesarea and there strangled on Herod's orders. Their bodies were fittingly buried in the Hasmonean royal tombs at the Alexandrium.

With the Hasmonean princes dead and his younger non-Hasmonean half brothers in Rome for their education, Antipater was now in a very strong position. But his past indiscretions had come to the attention of Salome. Among other things, there was some misconduct and intrigue with his uncle, Pheroras. Pheroras, Herod's brother, had a touch of the family stubbornness and did not easily bend to Herod's will. He is indeed the only one who consistently defied Herod and got away with it. Herod finally banished him to Perea, where he had been absentee governor for some years.

It would appear that Antipater had the inside track to the throne, but events were soon to prove otherwise. He went to Rome in 5 B.C. to carry a new will establishing the new line of succession. Meanwhile Pheroras died and evidence came to light that there had been, and indeed *was*, a plot against Herod's life. It appeared that almost everyone was involved — Pheroras, Herod's wife Doris and Herod's son Antipater. Returning home to Jerusalem, Antipater was confronted by his ailing father in the company of Varus, the Roman governor of Syria. Herod announced to his horror-stricken son that he would stand trial the next day before Varus.

As was the custom in those days, the plaintiff served as prosecutor for his own case. Herod opened the attack with a tirade against this ingrate who now raised his hand against his royal father. But quickly the monarch's

The Alexandrium, a desert fortress built by Hasmoneans, is haunted by memories of Herod's cruelty to his sons.

173

strength left him, and Nicolas, his faithful and usually mild-mannered secretary, pressed the case with shocking severity. There was also unimpeachable proof that special poison had been secured from Egypt. It was firmly linked to Antipater. The documentation was secure. It even reached into the household of the Roman Empress Livia. All Antipater offered in his defense was a plea that God send a sign indicating his innocence. Varus suggested rather that the poison should be tested. If it were harmless then surely Antipater was innocent. A condemned criminal was brought before the court and ordered to drink the potion. He collapsed, dying on the spot. Varus was satisfied and departed for Rome to give Augustus his judgment. *Guilty.*

On Herod's orders Antipater was taken from Jerusalem and imprisoned at Jericho, where Herod himself, desperately ill and in excruciating pain, was soon carried. There, in his marvelous palace beside the Wadi Qelt, the traditional "valley of the shadow of death" of the 23rd Psalm, Herod languished, inching nearer to death from arteriosclerosis and/or advanced syphilis.

And the end seemed as though it would never come. Then there were rumors of Herod's death. Antipater, in prison, sought to bribe his jailer to release him so that the throne might come to the rightful heir. The jailer told his superiors and word went at once to Herod, who at that moment was reading a letter from Augustus confirming Varus' verdict. Antipater was released from jail—by death. His body was unceremoniously dumped into a grave at Fortress Hyrcania in the Judean wilderness. Even in English Augustus' bitter pun has its point: "I had rather be Herod's pig than his son."

For the fourth and last time Herod redrew his will. It divided his kingdom among his remaining sons: Archelaus, Antipas and Philip, names familiar to readers of the New Testament. Five days after the execution of his eldest son, Herod died. The year was 4 B.C.

If you should go to the Holy Land today you will literally be surrounded by the ruins of Herod's monuments. The most striking of all Herod's buildings must have been the Temple in Jerusalem. The makeshift affair erected by the returned exiles under the urging of Zechariah and Haggai had lasted almost five centuries. Everyone recognized its shortcomings, and in 22 B.C. Herod announced his intention to replace it with a splendid structure recalling the glories of Solomon. Work did not begin until two years later. The vast conception was not entirely realized until A.D. 63, but when it was completed it far outshone Solomon's fabled shrine.

Certain restrictions were placed upon the size of the sanctuary itself, since it must conform as nearly as possible to the traditional dimensions of more ancient sacred buildings which had occupied the site. All the same it was a very tall structure faced with polished white stone and trimmed in gold leaf. The platform on which it was to stand, however, had no such restrictions. Limitations were purely physical. But even these did not hamper Herod's imagination. The platform was extended over valleys and into rock scarpes until the once pear-shaped hill was crowned with a rectangular enclosure embracing thirty-five acres. Today this platform is still the single most striking feature of the Old City of Jerusalem; a portion of its retaining wall near the southwest corner is revered by Jews as their holiest site, the Western Wall.

At the edges of this platform were colonnades of Corinthian columns. The colonnade which stretched along the eastern side overlooking the Mount of Olives was called Solomon's Porch. It was here, according to John 10: 22f., that Jesus was questioned about the Messiah one winter day during the Feast of Dedication and replied that his sheep knew his voice and followed

Jerusalem in Herod's Time

— Ancient city walls
--- Wall alignment uncertain
— Present-day wall

Pool of Bethzatha (Bethesda)

Fortress Antonia

WALL

Golden Gate

SECOND QUARTER

THE TEMPLE

Solomon's Porch

Valley

Tunnel

FIRST WALL Bridge

Royal Portico

Towers & Palace of Herod Staircase

Market Place

Huldah Gates

UPPER

Theater?

Hippodrome?

CITY

Spring Gihon

Tyropoeon Valley

LOWER CITY

Kidron

Hinnom

FIRST WALL

Valley

Pool of Siloam

0 100 200 300 400 500 Yds
0 100 200 300 400 500 M

© Copyright HAMMOND INC., Maplewood, N.J.

174

him even unto eternal life. The more famous of the colonnades was on the south. Here was the Royal Portico, a triple colonnade 800 feet long; a veritable forest of columns resembling a basilica with a soaring central aisle covered by yet another colonnade superimposed on those below. Where the Royal Portico joined Solomon's Porch on the southeastern corner the platform stood 450 feet above the floor of the Kidron Valley below. This is "the pinnacle of the Temple" and figures prominently in the story of the Temptation of Jesus (Matthew 4:5; Luke 4:9).

On the platform was a series of courts, the largest of which was the Court of the Gentiles. This was entered through several gates, the number of which is now disputed. Remnants of several of these remain. The most famous is the Golden Gate which pierced the walls from the east and is said to be the one entered by Jesus on Palm Sunday. In the southern wall there were two gates still visible today: the Triple Gate, nearer the eastern end, and the Double Gate, still in good condition below the Al Aqsa Mosque. Entering these, travelers found themleves in large courts with huge columns in the center. There were then steps leading to ramps which disgorged into the Court of the Gentiles. On the west one of two gates led to a bridge which spanned the Tyropoeon Valley and joined the western hill, now being developed by Herod, with the Temple. Underneath this bridge, which can still be seen at the northern end of the Western Wall, there was a secret tunnel which led from Herod's new western palace to the Temple itself. This could be used either to escape from the sanctuary or to bring soldiers into the sacred area to quell rioting. After Herod's death it was used for both these purposes. The southernmost gate in the Western Wall seems to have led to a grand staircase descending into the valley, where in Herod's day there was a park. It was on the well-made walks of this area that archaeologists working in the early 1970s found debris from the destruction of the Temple in A.D. 70.

The Court of the Gentiles was the center of life in Herod's Jerusalem, and much trade was carried on here, including the changing of money for use within the sacred precincts and the selling of animal sacrifices to pilgrims. All four Gospels tell of Jesus' efforts to cleanse this area and put an end to what he considered a sacrilegious use of God's House.

The next court was the Court of the Women of Israel and beyond that the Court of Israel, which could be entered only by male Jews. It was from remains of the fence around this court that stones have been found warning Gentiles that they enter only at the risk of death. Within this court was still another and smaller one, The Court of the Priests. Beyond that was the sanctuary itself. It was divided into three parts, the porch or vestibule, the Holy Place or nave, and the Holy of Holies or inner shrine. Into the latter only the high priest could enter once a year, on the Day of Atonement. The holiest of all places was divided from the rest of the sanctuary by a large veil which, according to Mark 15:38 (see also Matthew 27:51 and Luke 23:45), was torn in two at the moment of Jesus' death.

This monumental sacred complex gleaming in the warm-hued limestone of the Judean hills was surely one of the most magnificent buildings of the Greco-Roman era. The sanctuary was finished in eighteen months and dedicated amid splendid celebrations in 18 B.C. The adjacent courtyards took another ten years to finish, and work on the Temple platform and other portions of the site including the gates went on for eighty-three years. The entire structure in its finished state stood only seven years before its destruction by Titus' soldiers in A.D. 70.

Herod's steps, which lead to the Double Gate and then up a ramp into the Court of the Gentiles, have been excavated.

Temple of Herod

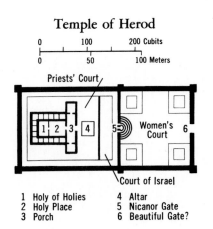

1 Holy of Holies	4 Altar
2 Holy Place	5 Nicanor Gate
3 Porch	6 Beautiful Gate?

175

Phasael Tower, originally a part of Herod's new western palace in Jerusalem, was left by Titus as a monument to his victory in A.D. 70. Today it forms a part of the Citadel.

Lower Aqueduct
Cisterns
Three-tiered Northern Palace
Upper Aqueduct
Water Gate
Large Bathhouse
Admin. Bldg.
Storerooms
Cisterns
Synagogue
Snake Path
Roman Siege Ramp
Large Dwelling
Gate
Western Gate
Western Palace
Masada Valley
Small Palaces
Ritual Bath
Fortress Wall
Cistern
Southern Water Gate
Southern Bastion
Masada

© Copyright HAMMOND INC., Maplewood, N.J.

0   50   100   150 Yds
0   50   100   150 M

Among the other monuments to Herod's genius in Jerusalem was the Fortress Antonia. He tore down the old fortress which stood by the temple site on the northwest, and replaced it with a massive fortified castle with four broad towers which Josephus says was like a "small city." The Fortress Antonia sprawled on two high ridges above the Pool of Bethesda, which in those days was outside the walls of Jerusalem. The huge courtyard of the Antonia, parts of which are visible today beneath the Convent of the Sisters of Zion of the Via Dolorosa, was of such size as to be known as "*the* pavement." Some scholars believe that it was here that Jesus was tried before Pilate (see John 19:13); *gabbatha* in Hebrew means "ridge" (or "height").

Just after that sordid scene when Herod put to death his Hasmonean Mariamne, he undertook to build a palace on the western hill. It was another fortress, but with three towers: the military tower, which he named for his fallen brother Phasael; the water tower, which he named for a friend, Hippicus; and the royal tower, which he called Mariamne. His third wife, also named Mariamne, may have felt flattered, but one wonders if it were named for her or the previous Mariamne. When Titus destroyed Jerusalem he left the stump of Phasael tower as a monument to his victory. It is still to be seen in Jerusalem today. Its beautifully cut, massive stones bespeak Herod, as do the stones in the Western Wall.

Elsewhere in his kingdom Herod also erected the outward symbols of Greco-Roman culture: massive buildings, squares, colonnades, marketplaces. Some, such as at Ascalon, were in honor of his family, which came from that city. Others, such as the beautiful Herodian building which is today called the "Mosque of the Friend" at Hebron, honored Jewish holy places, in this case the traditional tomb of Abraham, Sarah and Jacob. To our knowledge this is the only Herodian structure to survive to its full height. Sebaste he turned into a model Greco-Roman city, adding his distinctive masonry to that of Omri, Ahab and Alexander the Great. He capped it with a temple dedicated to Caesar Augustus, a temple whose silent ruins still grace the fields of Sebaste. Josephus says this temple could be seen gleaming white over twenty miles away at sea. Herod also built model agricultural settlements in areas where crop production had greatest promise. The most famous of these was Antipatris, on the Biblical site of Aphek.

This man, who began his career as military governor of Galilee, was ever mindful of safety, both the security of his realm and of his person. Mention has already been made of the Hasmonean fortresses of the Alexandrium and of Hyrcania, whose names reflect their foundation. The Romans had destroyed both of these refuges, but Herod rebuilt them and built the fortress and supporting village of Herodium near Bethlehem. He also undertook to fortify another site, the most secure place of all, the final refuge — Masada.

Halfway down the western side of the Dead Sea, in one of its more desolate reaches, an enormous singular hill juts up from the barrenness. On its western or desert side it is almost perpendicular for much of its height. The face it shows to the languid waters of the Dead Sea displays an angle of approximately 40 degrees in places. Up this eastern side there was the narrow and dangerous "snake path." To strengthen its natural military gifts, Herod built a casemate wall with towers around the entire summit. From below, according to Josephus, the sight was extraordinarily impressive; the gleaming white wall seemed to float against the blue sky. A system of very large cisterns was devised to capture the winter rains, and extensive storerooms for food and weapons ensured that Masada could hold out against a lengthy siege. Various administrative structures and even a superb western palace were there to house guests, soldiers and civil servants, who saw to the business of the state while the king took his ease, drinking in some of the world's most spectacular scenery and entertaining friends in the privacy of the northern palace. This structure, Herod's own private villa, was built on three rock terraces extending over the edge of the northern slope and requiring considerable underpinning. Although not large, it contained a miniature Roman bath (the main Roman baths were on top of the plateau), royal chambers and a circular terrace. The whole of this structure, as Yigael Yadin excavated it in 1963-65, all richly decorated in mosaics and painted plaster, was joined by concealed stairways. There was nothing else like this in the Roman world.

Yet Caesarea may have been even more spectacular. Herod had maritime ambitions, and he also wanted a fine harbor to integrate Judea more fully into the economy of the empire. But there simply is no good natural harbor south of Mount Carmel. At Strato's Tower, twenty-four miles northwest of Sebaste and convenient to that "safe city," there was a minor port known from more ancient days. Here Herod built a first class port by sinking enormous stones and forms filled with stones and Roman cement into the sea until he had formed a mole with an opening on the north to facilitate easy entry of ships. On top of this man-made breakwater, which extended twenty fathoms before anchoring in the sand, there was a pier, and on either side of the entrance were three gigantic statues. Once in the harbor sailors looked landward to a seawall which gave way to a promenade 200 feet wide. Its backdrop was furnished by warehouses, mercantile establishments and lodgings for sailors and others who had business in this new center of commerce. Fresh water was brought by a high-level aqueduct — still standing — from springs eight miles away on the southern slopes of Mount Carmel. Above the harbor the city itself was no less grand. Laid out on a grid after the example of Alexandria, its streets were built over a vast drainage system. Among its structures were an amphitheater, a hippodrome, a magnificent forum and a theater whose location was superb. It was here in the year 10 B.C., twelve years after construction had begun at Caesarea, that Herod dedicated the city to the emperor. The central, raised temple was dedicated to Augustus, and when Herod presided over the Caesarean games, Empress Livia sent furniture from the royal apartments in Rome to be used in Herod's box.

Almost everywhere you turn in the Holy Land today you see Herod's impress upon the land. Even now the faded grandeur still inspires the same awe and appreciation felt by Jesus' Galilean companions who, beholding Jerusalem, exclaimed, "Look, Teacher, what wonderful stones and what wonderful buildings!" (Mark 13:1) It is more difficult to get a feeling for the impression Herod made upon the people of that land. His conception and execution of the Temple and his crucially important contributions to Judaism in the empire were and still are largely ignored. This may well be because he had serious trouble with the Pharisees and they, in the long run, preserved Jewish tradition. The Sadducees who had bitterly opposed him in his struggles with Antigonus were, by sheer force of mutual interest, won over to his side.

Not all religious opinion was identified with the Sadducees and Pharisees, of course. During Herod's time messianic speculation, which had been growing since the Maccabean War, reached something of a high point. A number of sects patiently awaiting the Messiah flourished during Herod's reign. The most famous of these was the Qumran community, the group which produced the Dead Sea Scrolls.

Masada from the North showing the excavated fortress of Herod. Behind the imperial palace (foreground) is a bathhouse surrounded by storerooms.

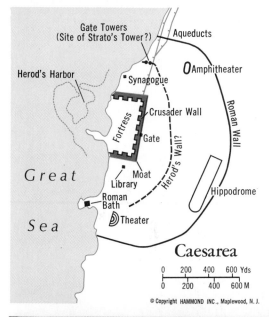

Caesarea

0   200   400   600 Yds
0   200   400   600 M

© Copyright HAMMOND INC., Maplewood, N. J.

The theater by the sea at Caesarea where in 10 B.C. Herod dedicated his splendid new city. Now restored, it is used for concerts.

177

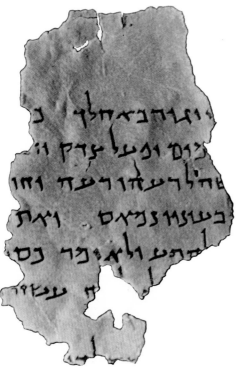

Top:
The ruins of the Qumran community on the western shore of the Dead Sea. The large structure (left) was a defensive tower.

Above:
Fragment of Psalms 15 and 16 from the Cave of the Letters in Nahal Hever.

Right:
Inside Muhammed's Cave (Cave One) where the first Dead Sea Scrolls were found.

14 SCROLLS FROM
THE WILDERNESS OF JUDEA

The most sensational archaeological discovery of the last half century was made entirely by accident. On a morning in the winter of 1946-1947 three shepherds of the Ta'amireh tribe of Bedouin watched their nimble-footed goats skip across the cliffs just north of an old ruin on the northwest shore of the Dead Sea. The ruin, known as the City of Salt, is mentioned in the Old Testament (Joshua 15:62), and from time to time archaeologists had shown interest. But from the middle of the nineteenth century, when they first worked in the area, until those days in winter they had said that there was not much at that desolate site. Possibly it was a minor Roman fort. Perhaps, some of the more fanciful said, it was even Gomorrah!

About a mile to the south of the ruin is one of the larger of the numerous freshwater springs that surround the Dead Sea. This place, known as Ain Feshkha, is where these three Bedouin watered their animals. Then it was up the cliffs and into the forbidding wilderness where shepherds, like David, let their flocks wander in search of food. And so on that fateful day the immemorial scene was repeated, with black beasts defying gravity on steep inclines, leaping, stopping to nibble here and there. A seemingly disinterested shepherd moved leisurely below, but his eye missed nothing. Some of the goats were climbing too high up. It was getting late and time to get them down. Jum'a Muhammed—that was the name of the fellow—now showed his own nimbleness in getting up the cliff face. As he climbed something caught his attention. There were two small openings in the rock. They were caves, or maybe two openings into the same cave. But they were so small. A man could not get through the lower one but might just squeeze through the upper one. He threw a rock into the lower opening. What Jum'a heard caused him to scramble up to the opening and peer in. The rock had broken pottery, and what else would be in these remote caves but treasure? Maybe his days of following the sheep were over. He peered into the black depths of the cave but nothing could be made out. He yelled down to his two cousins. Khalil Musa was older. Muhammed Ahmed el-Hamed was younger, a teenager. They came up and heard the excited tale. But it was now getting very late and the goats had to be gathered. Tomorrow would take them to Ain Feshkha. In the afternoon they would return for another look at this intriguing cave.

But they did not visit the cave the next afternoon, returning somewhat later than planned from Ain Feshkha. At dawn of the next morning Muhammed Ahmed el-Hamed, who was nicknamed "The Wolf" (edh-Dhib), woke first. Leaving his two cousins sleeping on the ground, he scaled the 350 or so feet up to the cave Jum'a had found two days before. With effort the slender young man was able to lower himself in feet first into the cave. The floor was covered with debris including broken pottery. But along the wall stood a number of narrow jars, some with their bowl-shaped covers still in place. Edh-Dhib scrambled over the floor of the cave and plunged his hand into one of the jars. Nothing. Frantically he tore the cover from another, eagerly exploring the smooth inside of the empty container. Another and yet another with the same result. The ninth was full of dirt. The increasingly

179

Cave Four at Qumran (center) in which a wealth of precious scrolls were found.

Interior of a modern Bedouin tent.

desperate young Bedouin at last closed his hand around something wrapped in cloth. He extracted two such bundles and then a third, which had a leather covering but not cloth wrapping. The cloth and the leather were greenish with age. These were all edh-Dhib took from the cave that morning.

He wiggled himself out of the opening and half-ran, half-fell down the hillside to show his sleepy cousins what he had found. Treasure indeed! Scholars who later interviewed edh-Dhib think that what this boy had in his hands on that winter morning was nothing less than the great *Isaiah Scroll,* the *Habakkuk Commentary* and *The Manual of Discipline!*

Khalil and Jum'a could not have been less interested in these scrolls edh-Dhib showed them. Where was the treasure? Had he hidden it for himself? Relentless questions. A little roughing-up. But in the end edh-Dhib was able to convince the other two that there was nothing but these worthless rolls. Had he looked carefully? Maybe there were other jars. Maybe one of the broken ones had spilled its valuable contents on the floor of the cave and it was in the debris.

Once more the three made their way up the hill to the cave. Edh-Dhib passed a number of jars out of the opening, but these were left in front of the cave when they proved to be empty, just as he had said. Downcast, the shepherds zigzagged their way down to the makeshift camp. Jum'a crammed the rolls into a bag. When later they returned to the Ta'amireh center near Bethlehem he took them with him. The bag with its "treasure"—so much more vast than the disappointed men ever dreamed!—was hung on a tentpole. How long it was there we do not know for certain. Occasionally its contents were removed and passed around among more curious members of the tribe. The *Isaiah Scroll* was damaged, but only its cover. The precious text was unhurt. When *The Manual of Discipline* reached St. Mark's Monastery in Jerusalem some months later it was in two pieces. But no one is sure if this was the fault of the Ta'amireh. The break is such that it could have occurred in ancient times.

A few weeks after the initial discovery of this cave—an orifice that came to be known to scholars as Qumran Cave One, the cave of the great scrolls—Jum'a returned with other Bedouin and removed several other scrolls which they found there. As nearly as it is possible to reconstruct the story now, they removed seven major manuscripts altogether, the four that ended up at St. Mark's and the three that came into the possession of Hebrew University.

Such was the discovery of the Dead Sea Scrolls, manuscripts a thousand years older than the then oldest known Hebrew texts of the Bible, manuscripts many of which were written a hundred years before the birth of Jesus and at least one of which may have been written almost three hundred years before the journey of Mary and Joseph to Bethlehem.

How these manuscripts got from a Bedouin tentpole into the scholar's study is as fascinating as their chance discovery. The setting for this part of the story was the last days of the British Mandate in Palestine. His Majesty's Foreign Office had somewhat irresponsibly decided that since the problem of Palestine could not be solved by reason they would withdraw, leaving the two sides to decide the issue by blood. Jewish and Arab families which had lived side by side for generations were being wrenched apart by fear and distrust. Barbed wire appeared in the most unlikely places. Immigrants, legal and illegal, added impetus to the worsening situation. The British were literally besieged by both sides, but particularly by the Jewish underground army. Murders were growing in number. The King David Hotel in Jerusalem was blown up with severe loss of life. In such times the Bedouin youths wondered if they could find a buyer for their greenish rolls.

In early April 1947 Jum'a and Khalil took them to Bethlehem, principal market town of the Ta'amireh. They took three scrolls and two jars to the carpenter shop of Ibrahim 'Ijha who dabbled in antiquities. Faidi Salahi, another dealer in antiquities, was there. He was later to play a large role in the story of the scrolls but on this occasion he cautioned 'Ijha to be careful. These things might be stolen. There might be serious trouble. The two shepherds moved on carrying their jars and their scrolls.

In the marketplace Jum'a, with the scrolls, ran into George Ishaya Shamoun, who was often in Bethlehem on Saturdays selling cloaks to Bedouin. Jum'a imparted the tale of these worthless scrolls to his friend. Someone suggested that they go to the cobbler's shop of Khalil Iskander Shahin— better known as Kando. Kando was Syrian Orthodox Christian. He was also serious about the scrolls. For one-third of whatever the sale price might be, Kando and George would handle the disposal of the scrolls. Agreed. Jum'a and Khalil were given £5 ($14.00) and the scrolls were left in the little shop in Bethlehem.

During Holy Week, George, also Syrian Orthodox, mentioned the manuscripts to Athanasius Yeshue Samuel, Syrian Orthodox Metropolitan of Jerusalem. He told the priest they were written in Syriac, wrapped "like mummies," and were from the wilderness near the Dead Sea. Samuel knew that they would have to be very old, if genuine, because that region had not been inhabited since early Christian times. He expressed an interest in the scrolls and urged Kando to bring them to St. Mark's.

Bethlehem market square where Bedouin brought ancient scrolls to sell.

Within the week Kando and George were at the monastery with one manuscript, *The Manual of Discipline*. It was, the Metropolitan saw at once, not written in Syriac but in Hebrew. Then to the astonishment of his visitors he broke off a piece of the margin and burned it. By this somewhat crude but effective means he determined it was animal skin. Yes, Samuel would buy this scroll and any others the Bedouin might have. Kando, with the manuscript securely in hand, departed but promised to get in touch with his friends from the desert. For several days anxious calls went from St. Mark's to Kando's shop near Manger Square in Bethlehem. The conversations were fruitless. Weeks went by. Samuel's frustration turned to resignation.

On the first Saturday in July Kando called. Two Bedouin had brought some scrolls to Bethlehem. Would they risk bringing them to Jerusalem? asked Samuel. Yes. The tide of violence between Jew, Arab and Briton was swelling. Jewish terrorism, mostly directed against the British, was beginning to be heavily felt in certain Arab areas. The worst was yet to come, but it was already a difficult and dangerous time in and around Jerusalem. In this atmosphere Samuel became anxious when the Bedouin and their scrolls had not appeared by noon. Yet he had not mentioned his appointment to anyone since he was not entirely sure that the whole affair was not some kind of hoax. Hungry, agitated, Samuel sat down to eat. In the idle lunchtime conversation the Metropolitan heard one of the fathers mention that he had turned away some Bedouin from the door earlier in the morning. When questioned he affirmed that they were carrying scrolls. The Syrian monk had even ascertained that they were written in Hebrew. Probably old Torahs from somewhere, but filthy and covered with pitch or something else which smelled equally bad. These he steadfastly refused to allow within the monastery walls, still less into His Grace's presence as the bearers demanded.

181

Samuel returned to his office to call Kando. As he reached for the telephone, it rang. It was none other than the Bethlehem parishioner himself, deeply offended at the treatment given his friends. Explanations were offered, apologies made. Where were the scrolls now? Thanks entirely to George, said Kando, they were safely back in Bethlehem.

It seems that when the Bedouin along with George, who was the man closest to the shepherds in all this, had been turned away from the monastery they went to the Jaffa Gate to catch the bus back to Bethlehem. There in discussion with a Jewish merchant an offer was made to buy them. George, however, had correctly guessed what the trouble had been at the door of St. Mark's. He was, furthermore, committed to the Metropolitan. He argued with his friends and finally prevailed. The three boarded the bus for Bethlehem with the manuscripts. Kando reached for his telephone when he heard what had happened. This reported incident at the Jaffa Gate, it should be pointed out, is not well authenticated and may be a part of the considerable legend that has grown up around the Dead Sea Scrolls.

It was two weeks before Kando could make his way to Jerusalem. He was graciously received by the Syrian fathers. Samuel heard the story of the discovery of the cave and its contents. Of greater interest five scrolls, including the one which had been brought previously, were produced from a bag. Two documents were in a delicate state. Two others looked similar and later proved to be the two halves of *The Manual of Discipline*. The fifth, the largest, was superbly preserved. It could be easily unrolled, revealing graceful Hebrew characters. A deal was quickly made. The Metropolitan gave Kando £24 ($97.00), of which two-thirds went to Jum'a and Khalil.

Three months after Samuel had first heard of the existence of the scrolls they were in his possession. Now doubts began to creep in. Were they genuine? Was there such a cave as had been described to him? With George's help Father Yusef, one of the monks from St. Mark's visited the site and reported to his superior that there was such a cave and indeed it contained scraps of other scrolls as well as a large jar suitable for storing much water.

With his faith in the authenticity of the scrolls revived, the Metropolitan set about to determine their contents and to sustain or destroy his view that they were from early Christian times. One would think that in a city such as Jerusalem, with its multiplicity of religious communities and prestigious scholarly institutions, this would have been a relatively simple matter. But few things are simple in Jerusalem, still less in a time of violence and when the question at hand is so patently improbable as authenticating scrolls 2,000 years old. It was fully six months before Samuel's dreams were confirmed.

His first contact was the Palestine Department of Antiquities in the person of Stephen Hanna Stephen, a member of the Syrian Orthodox Church and thus well known to Samuel. There had been reports in Byzantine and earlier times of scrolls having been found near Jericho (Qumran is seven and a half miles south). From the second, third and fourth Christian centuries came reports of Greek and Hebrew books found in jars in the area. Origen, an early church father, is said to have used some of these in compiling his famous *Hexapla*. In the late eighth century Patriarch Timothy I reported a similar find, noting that the manuscripts were found in caves. These things, common knowledge among scholars, were apparently not known to Stephen. But he did know of numerous incidents of hoaxes involving antiquities. He responded to the Metropolitan by suggesting the embarrassment that might come should his manuscripts turn out to be fake. Would Stephen, asked

Scroll jar from Cave One.

The complete Isaiah Scroll from Cave One. It consists of 17 pieces of leather sewn together to make a roll over 24 feet long. The text column averages 10 inches.

Samuel, call the documents to the attention of those in the Department of Antiquities who might be able to render proper judgment? Stephen had rather not lest he, too, be held up to ridicule before his colleagues.

The Syrian priest, undaunted by this rebuke, now found his way to the famous École Biblique, the Dominican monastery of St. Stephen and home of the French Biblical and Archaeological School. There he was received by Father Marmardji, a fellow Syrian and friend of long standing, who heard the story of the finding of the scrolls with some interest. Some days later Father Marmardji came to St. Mark's accompanied by a young Dutch Dominican, Father J. Van der Ploeg. Together they examined the materials. Neither thought the writings were as old as claimed. The Dutchman did, however, immediately recognize the largest scroll as the Book of Isaiah. He was the first to do so. When he returned to the École, Van der Ploeg spoke with some enthusiasm of the documents he had just seen. L. H. Vincent, the distinguished Dominican scholar and a fixture at the French monastery for forty years, noting that this was the Dutch monk's first visit to Jerusalem, suggested he should not be taken in so easily. Perhaps, thought the learned Vincent, if Samuel could produce pottery from the alleged context where the writings had been found it might help to sustain his claims. When no pottery was forthcoming Van der Ploeg did not pursue the matter further.

Samuel continued to make attempts to find scholarly help with the scrolls and even attempted to learn Hebrew. At one point a chance business contact resulted in the inspection of the scrolls by two men from the library of Hebrew University. According to Samuel they said they wished to photograph a few parts for further study. The monastery was placed at their disposal for such purposes, but they never returned, perhaps because of the increasing danger to a Jew in the Old City. A little later an antiquities dealer suggested sending the manuscripts to Europe or America where they could be evaluated. But with postal services breaking down under the weight of civil conflict Samuel thought it not a good idea to place his materials in the mails.

In late January 1948 the St. Mark's manuscripts came temporarily into the hands of E. L. Sukenik, the distinguished archaeologist of Hebrew University. Unknown to all but a very few, Sukenik had obtained three other scrolls from the Bedouin discovery the previous November. They were *The War Scroll, The Thanksgiving Scroll* and a second, but fragmentary, copy of *Isaiah*. Anton Kiraz now enters the story. Kiraz was a parishioner at St. Mark's. He was, in addition, extremely close to Samuel. In 1945 Sukenik excavated on some of Kiraz' property and was also personally known to him. Kiraz was thus admirably situated to act as contact between the priest and the professor.

Kiraz arranged for Sukenik to see the scrolls at the YMCA, which was at that time in neutral territory. As soon as he saw them Sukenik made an offer of £100 for the materials, as Kiraz recalled. Sukenik, in his written recollection of the event, did not mention an offer. However that may have been, Kiraz allowed one scroll to be removed to Hebrew University for further study. The other documents remained in a drawer at the YMCA. The magnificent *Isaiah Scroll* stayed for about a week at the university, during which time a portion (chapters 42 and 43) was hastily and somewhat incorrectly copied. When it was returned Sukenik spoke of the university's interest in purchasing all of the scrolls.

According to Kiraz the figure of £500 ($2,025) was mentioned. But Kiraz said he would have to talk with Samuel. Sukenik is said to have increased the offer to £1000—750 for Kiraz, 250 for Samuel. Kiraz insisted on talking with the Metropolitan. He would contact Sukenik once he had had a chance to discuss the offer. There the matter was left.

At this juncture, in early February and fully a year since edh-Dhib had first slithered into the cave, Samuel's lifelong friend and fellow monk, Butros Sowmy, returned to St. Mark's after an absence. He was a learned man and one of good judgment. With increasing concern he heard of Sukenik's offer and of Samuel's apparent readiness to accept it. If Sukenik were so anxious to secure these documents perhaps, reasoned Sowmy, it would be well to get another opinion before selling. Kiraz wrote to the distraught professor saying they were not going to sell just now, but would wait until the local situation settled a bit and they could perhaps get some international judgments and perhaps overseas offers.

Meantime, Sowmy recalled his cordial dealings with the American Schools of Oriental Research just north of the Old City, quite near the École Biblique. He telephoned and the call was turned over to John Trever, a fellow of the school, who had been left in temporary charge during the absence of Millar Burrows, the director. Sowmy asked if Trever would help date some old manuscripts that had been lying about St. Mark's library for some years. As a precaution the Americans had not gone into the Old City for some time. It was now dangerous in the extreme. Could the materials be brought to the school? In response Sowmy agreed to present himself and the scrolls the next day at 2:30 P.M.

With mounting excitement Trever examined the manuscripts. The writing on the *Isaiah Scroll*, although clearly Hebrew, was nonetheless strange to his eyes. Yet he had seen a similar script somewhere. A superb and inveterate photographer, Trever was never one to be far away from cameras and their products. On his desk was a series of slides dealing with the background of the English Bible. He extracted a picture of the ninth-century A.D. British Museum Codex. The writing on the scrolls brought by Sowmy was older. Next Trever removed a slide of the Nash Papyrus, a second-century fragment and the then oldest known Biblical Hebrew. The script was similar, but not exactly the same. It was hard to be sure; the slide was much too small for de-

Nash Papyrus, until the discoveries near Qumran the oldest known Biblical fragment.

tailed comparison in the hand viewer. His cameras unfortunately at the moment at the Museum of the Department of Antiquities, Trever copied by hand that portion of the manuscript open before him. He then proposed to Sowmy that a complete photographic record be made of all the scrolls. The monk was agreeable but would have to discuss it with his superior.

Sowmy left. Trever soon determined that what he had copied was a portion of the sixty-fifth chapter of Isaiah. Was the rest of Isaiah on that scroll? Could it be as old as the Nash Papyrus? Early the next morning, after an almost sleepless night, Trever determined to go to St. Mark's in spite of the danger. With the aid of the Arab secretary of the school he secured the necessary permissions and risking life and limb was taken by Miss Faris through the narrow, hazardous streets to the Syrian monastery. There he met the Metropolitan, who was at length convinced the manuscripts should again be brought to the school where there were photographic equipment and better conditions for obtaining good results than in St. Mark's dim library.

For the rest of the day Trever and William Brownlee culled from the library of the American Schools all the material they could find about ancient manuscripts. Unfortunately fighting and sabotage interrupted Jerusalem's electric service in the afternoon. After working by kerosene lamps late into the night the two men were convinced that the form of the script on the *Isaiah Scroll* was as old as or older than the Nash Papyrus.

The next day, a Saturday, dawned bright—on the outside, that is. The lights were still out inside the school. By 9:30 the Metropolitan and Father Sowmy were there with the materials to be photographed. Just as Trever was about to use natural light from a window, the electric lights came on. With Brownlee's help two scrolls, *Isaiah* and the *Habakkuk Commentary,* were unrolled and photographed. By late afternoon the task was not complete. Three scrolls remained. But by this time the two young Americans had won the confidence of the Syrian, who gladly left the unrecorded scrolls and a fragment behind as he returned to St. Mark's. Among the many happenstances surrounding the scrolls none was more felicitous than the presence of so fine a photographer as Trever. His record of the contents of the four Dead Sea Scrolls from the Syrian monastery (a fifth was too delicate to be opened then) now constitute the finest material available for study of these documents. This is especially so since the originals have faded from exposure despite the best of care under controlled conditions.

Subsequent excavations at the caves indicated the scrolls had been damaged when they were removed from their jars and unwrapped. Fragments from the manuscripts were on the floor of the cave. The documents had also been stripped of their linen protection and carried about in sacks, paper and otherwise. But at last the precious scrolls were in loving hands. Before returning them to St. Mark's they were carefully wrapped. The seriously deteriorated leather scroll was placed in a specially constructed box. While this was going on, Trever sent photographic copies to the *doyen* of Palestinian archaeologists and the leading expert on ancient forms of writing, W. F. Albright.

In the following days Trever, sometimes accompanied by Burrows, now returned, made numerous trips to St. Mark's, each journey fraught with its own several perils. Often guards were provided by the monastery to insure safety. At least once the scrolls were returned to the American School. Trever was not pleased with all of his initial pictures. Ever a perfectionist in matters photographic he wished to retake the *Isaiah Scroll.* This involved a difficult search of the shops of the city for proper film. Only outdated portrait film was located. But Trever rejoiced to find even this.

On March 15 a letter from the United States reached the school:

> My heartiest congratulations on the greatest manuscript discovery of modern times! There is no doubt in my mind that the script is more archaic than that of the Nash Papyrus. . . . I should prefer a date around 100 B.C.! . . . What an absolutely incredible find! And there can happily not be the slightest doubt in the world about the genuineness of the manuscript.

Albright's practiced eyes had confirmed the Metropolitan's hopes and the scholarly judgment of Trever and Brownlee.

Two weeks later steadily increasing violence forced the abandonment of the American School. Trever was the last to go. He left on April 5th. Samuel, under various urgings, sought a safe place for his scrolls. St. Mark's was a particularly vulnerable location. Sowmy suggested a bank vault in Beirut as a safer place (shortly thereafter Sowmy was killed by bomb fragments as he stood in the courtyard at St. Mark's).

Still the story was not over. Mar Samuel, the Metropolitan, tried to sell the scrolls from St. Mark's Monastery in the United States, actually taking a display ad in *The Wall Street Journal*. He consummated a sale on July 1, 1954, for $300,000 with a certain "Mr. Esteridge," only discovering later to his consternation that they had been bought by the State of Israel. The four scrolls thus rejoined the other three scrolls from Cave One that were obtained in 1948 by E. L. Sukenik at Hebrew University. All seven scrolls are now on display at the Shrine of the Book in Jerusalem.

What are these scrolls, so innocently found, so doggedly pursued, immediately capturing the attention of a fascinated world public, still studied and debated among scholars? They are a part of the library of a sectarian, monastic Jewish group who lived off and on at the City of Salt—now better known as Qumran—from the middle of the second century B.C. to A.D. 69, when the Romans destroyed the monastery. The group, which many think were Essenes, had withdrawn from worship in the Temple in Jerusalem during the reign of Alexander Jannaeus because of Hasmonean usurpation of the high priesthood and, in the view of these people, the subsequent defilement of worship in the sanctuary. At Qumran they established a community house and with constant prayer, study of the Scriptures and attention to the godly life awaited the coming of the messianic kingdom. The writings of Isaiah were particularly important to them as to Jews elsewhere at the time, and in their own community they saw the fulfillment of the prophet's words: "In the wilderness prepare the way of the Lord, make straight in the desert a highway for our God" (Isaiah 40:3).

In the late 1940s and until 1958 scholars from many nations scoured the hills around Qumran searching for more scrolls. At about the same time others were investigating the source of the scrolls, Qumran itself. A team of French and Belgian archaeologists excavated the ruins in four campaigns from 1951 to 1956.

The excavators discovered a self-contained community that had flourished in the desert under the most difficult conditions. Settlers first came to the site in the eighth century B.C., or perhaps during the reign of King Uzziah.

Shrine of the Book at the Israel Museum, Jerusalem, houses most of the scrolls from the Wilderness of Judea. Its roof is shaped like one of the jar lids from Qumran Cave One.

After all, it was Uzziah who "built towers in the wilderness, and hewed out many cisterns" (2 Chronicles 26:10). These first inhabitants practiced desert farming in this inhospitable environment for a generation before abandoning their courtyard building with its timber-and-reed roofs. This was a forced departure, for the living quarters and storerooms were burned and destroyed, perhaps by the armies of Sargon II of Assyria in 722 B.C.

But it was the second period of the community at Qumran that concerns us most directly. At some time about 100 B.C. settlers made a fresh beginning on this site. They dug out the 600-year-old round cistern to collect life-sustaining water. They reestablished the walls and reset the roof beams so as to cover the rooms and shield themselves from the burning desert sun. They built two potter's kilns side by side to produce their own ceramics. Perhaps most importantly for understanding who they were, they crafted two baths next to the cistern for their sacred, ritual washings, evidence that they were Jews who observed the demand of the law for ritual cleanliness.

This period may have lasted less than a generation before they set to work to double the size of their settlement, to attend to their needs for security, and to provide for a whole new series of industries that busied them six days a week.

An enormous tower with an internal staircase reared up to mark a new entrance on the north and to provide for the common defense. Two other entrances pierced the walls to allow alternative exit or entry. Next a whole series of rooms was built on the west and east sides. Here archaeologists found evidence for a carpenter's shop, a washing and dyeing establishment, a potter's shop, a stable, a kitchen, several other workshops, and a common room for gathering and eating.

One of the more interesting discoveries was the pantry, or perhaps more accurately, the storeroom for their crockery. Here, to the delight of the archaeologists, were found smashed on the floor of the room 1,080 vessels of several kinds, many of them still stacked as though drying after being washed! For example, 708 bowls crushed by a fallen ceiling stood in 59 stacks of twelve each in a rough rectangle. Between the bowls and the door lay the remains of 75 drinking cups. On the wall to the left of the entrance lay what was left of 21 small jars, 38 dishes and 11 jugs. This was everything needed for their common meals.

The archaeologists also discovered remains unique to this ruin. The people who lived here, presumably the Essenes mentioned in Josephus and elsewhere in the first century, buried here and there between the buildings the remains of certain meals — complete with dishes and bones!

Yet probably that which is the most interesting is the system of no less than eight large, interconnected cisterns and ritual baths that the occupants took immense trouble to build. The precious water was brought in by an aqueduct wending its way over the surface of the ground from the Wadi Qumran just to the west. This water channel continued through and among the buildings to feed all the cisterns and their decantation basins. Naturally the inhabitants of Qumran covered the cisterns to control evaporation. Six of the eight water basins were equipped with elaborate staircases that allowed one to walk directly into the water. These were clearly ritual baths rather than basins, more evidence that these were pious Jews who followed the Biblical laws of clean and unclean.

An abrupt end to this period of occupation at Qumran comes in the spring of 31 B.C., the seventh year in the reign of Herod the Great. A huge earth-

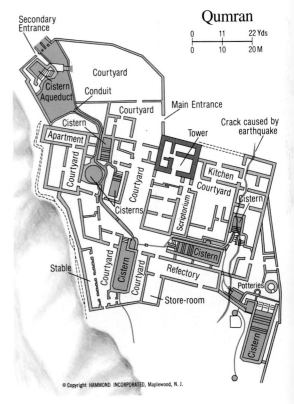

Qumran

quake shattered the relative calm and quiet of the northern shores of the Dead Sea. The steps and floor of the eastern ritual bath suddenly split, and the east side of the rupture dropped 21 inches. In the twinkling of an eye the water system was damaged, and the life-giving fluid spilled over the terraces of Qumran. The massive tower cracked and was rendered a useless heap of ruined walls. Burning lamps and glowing hearths provided the sparks that set fire to stores of oil and linens, and soon the reed-and-wood roofs were ablaze.

Only ten miles to the north King Herod was encamped with his army in the plain of Jericho, making ready to attack the kingdom of the Nabatteans to the south. His troops were terrified by the earthquake and scattered, and it took a splendid speech by Herod to restore order.

But no leader could restore order at Qumran. The survivors sadly packed what they could salvage from the ashes and mud and left, perhaps first burying their dead in the cemetery that would eventually be discovered to the east. The smoking ruin drifted into a generation of obscurity. Yet the water system continued to bring down water from the Wadi Qumran, but not into carefully maintained cisterns. Now water coursed across the ruin, leaving silt everywhere as it slowed to soak into the earth.

In 4 B.C. Herod the Great died and his mantle fell on his three sons. Herod Archelaus ruled Judaea until he was exiled to Gaul by the Romans in A.D. 6. It was sometime early in his reign that the inhabitants of Qumran or their descendants, rejecting the relatively easy life of village and town, returned to the austere desert.

The inhabitants of this small settlement cleaned out some rooms for reuse, but others they abandoned. Their energy was enormous. The tower had to be shored up by a strong buttress on all four sides. The room with the smashed crockery was not cleaned out; a new floor was simply laid over the potsherds and silt, and the walls were strengthened. The settlers abandoned the easternmost ritual bath and cut off the water flowing to it. They strengthened various walls in the buildings, including the rear walls of the annex to the room for assembly and dining. Other spaces they divided into two or combined. They also added a room in the northeast and simply roofed over one courtyard in the west.

Determined as ever to ensure their self-sufficiency, they continued some of the crafts that had been practiced here earlier. Others they added. Again we can locate the kitchen, and also the potter's shop. They milled their own flour, forged their own iron and bronze and washed and dyed their own clothes.

Among these mundane activities, one stands out. In the collapse of a second-story room just west of the main courtyard, archaeologists found the remains of a long, narrow table made of plaster. It was fully 15 feet long, but only 16 inches across and only 25 inches high. There were also fragments of two other smaller tables. Further, two inkwells were found which attested to the room's use; it presumably was used by scribes who labored to copy scrolls either by eye or by dictation, although no manuscripts or parchments were discovered on the site.

Many coins were found in the ruin, all of which aid us in determining how long the group stayed. For example, someone or some group buried here a treasure of 561 silver coins in three pots. The latest coins are of the year 9-8 B.C. Some two dozen other coins tell us that the settlement was refounded at the death of Herod the Great, as mentioned above. Nearly three hundred coins from the period of the destruction of this miniature village tell us that it was destroyed in the third year of the First Revolt against Rome, or in A.D. 69.

Thus for nearly four generations a group lived at Qumran in relative self-sufficiency. From other explorations we know that at least two other identical groups, but much smaller in size lived south of Qumran, but also on the shores of the Dead Sea. People from all these communities secreted many of their sacred writings in caves in the jagged hills west of Qumran before they abandoned their villages. Now we turn our attention to these writings.

Biblical writings from Qumran are very interesting, showing as they do the state of the text before the rabbis of Jamnia moved toward a standard text at the end of the first century A.D. Previous to the sensational finds near the shores of the Dead Sea the oldest known Hebrew text of the Bible was from the tenth Christian century. At one stroke the scrolls pushed our knowledge of the Hebrew Bible back a thousand years into a time before the entire Old Testament had been canonized and locked into its present form. Some of these Biblical writings were on scrolls by themselves, while others were recovered from commentaries the Qumranites had written. This was the case with Micah, Nahum, Habakkuk, Zephaniah and, as one might expect, Isaiah. There were among this collection what scholars call *testimonia*, collections of verses offering proof-texts of distinctive beliefs. One of these collections contains Deuteronomy 5:28-29, Numbers 24:15-17 and Deuteronomy 33:8-11 supporting the community's messianic hope. The use of such testimonia is also known among early Christian writings, especially Matthew. There were other Biblical writings and also Hebrew apocryphal and pseudepigraphical works which had been previously known only in Latin, Greek, Syriac or Ethiopic versions.

In addition to scriptural texts, commentaries and other specifically Biblical materials, there are large numbers of sectarian writings, a few represented by major scrolls. Some of these contain histories of the sect based upon Old Testament prophecies; others are collections of psalms and prayers; still others are speculative exegeses of Biblical texts giving highly idealized pictures of ancient Israelite worthies such as Abraham, Enoch and Sarah.

Papyrus fragments of prayers.

The largest scrolls among the sectarian writings are *The War Scroll, The Manual of Discipline* and *The Temple Scroll. The War Scroll,* more popularly known as "The War of the Sons of Light with the Sons of Darkness," contains infinitely detailed plans for the final holy war between a purified righteous remnant in Israel and the profane enemies of God. Specifically, the Sons of Light are identified as "the Sons of Levi, the Sons of Judah and the Sons of Benjamin, the exiles of the wilderness." The last named are clearly those who have withdrawn to the Wilderness of Judea, who have gathered themselves in purity and prayer beside the Dead Sea. Why no other tribes other than the southern two and the priestly tribe are mentioned among these holy warriors is not known. Those whom they opposed are "the Sons of Darkness, the army of Belial, the troops of Edom and Moab and the Sons of Ammon and the army of the dwellers of Philistia and the troops of the Kittim of Asshur, and in league with them the Offenders against the Covenant." Here are the ancient enemies of Israel with the very interesting addition of "the Offenders against the Covenant." These seem clearly to be other Jews, those who do not agree with the Qumranites, those whom these people living in their messianic community in the desert see as unfaithful to the heritage of Israel and therefore to be numbered among the Sons of Darkness. It is fairly common among sectarians to find them expressing hatred for those within their own tradition who do not agree with them. So it was at Qumran, whose covenanters envisioned themselves fighting against God's enemies.

And this as to be no casual or short struggle. It was a holy war and was to be entered into with all due military and religious preparation. *The War Scroll* is unique among contemporary religious writings, as it lays out with exact care and in great detail the preparation of this sacred army, its weapons, formations, support units, banners, trumpets and its attack plans. There are 28,000 infantry supported by light and heavy cavalry; 4,500 of the former, 1,400 of the latter. These large numbers, when compared with the small number of people actually in the community, show the ideal character of this struggle. And as this godly band moves into battle it is a colorful sight. Above it flutter numerous banners bearing names such as Battle of God and Vengeance of God. Their armor was to be polished mirror-bright and their horses had to be chosen specially. In particular the men who composed this great army of God were to be ritually and morally pure, cleansed and kept sanctified by an accompanying array of priests who blew the sacred trumpets, trumpets which not only called to prayer but gave signals on the battlefield.

While the final outcome of this titanic struggle with evil is a certain victory for God and the Sons of Light, the warfare will not always go well; there will be setbacks, even defeats. Then in the seventh and decisive battle, the Sons of Light will emerge completely triumphant. This fluctuating nature of the struggle reflects the community's belief that persecution and even defeat must be borne with the unshakable faith that in the end God will triumph. In this sense this writing, although vastly different in design and imagery, is much like the last book of the New Testament, Revelation, which in the midst of persecution also envisions the final victory of God over his enemies. This aspect of *The War Scroll* may be a clue to the date of its writing, but it is at best an ambiguous clue. The community seems to be living in a time when the Sons of Darkness are ascendant. Does that mean, as some think, that this was the Maccabean period when the Qumranites were under pressure from their fellow Jews? This certainly appears to be the thrust of the *Habakkuk Commentary.* But it is also possible that *The War Scroll* points to Roman times and to a low point in the fortunes of the people. Of this much we can be sure: they believed in the providence of God and that in the end he would accomplish his purposes, which would include the overthrow of the wicked.

The Manual of Discipline may well be the most important document among the sectarian writings. Without this we would have to make many guesses about the nature of the group that produced the Dead Sea Scrolls. The *Manual* is not unlike the rules by which Christian monasteries were governed in the Middle Ages. It gives specifics about life in the community, the requirements for full entrance, statements on doctrine, the holy life and different ceremonies. There is also a lengthy section dealing with behavior within the community, including punishments for everything from speaking ill of a fellow member of the group to spitting in public.

While most of this scroll is in good condition, the first part seems to be missing. Moreover, there is evidence that it was in use for a long time; there are numerous corrections and additions including a change from six months to a year as the period of punishment for anyone who slanders another without cause. It was a fellowship which walked by those laws of God which had been given through Moses and the prophets. As a matter of fact, the rules which are set down for members sound very much like ethical injunctions of one of the great prophets of Israel: "to love what God has chosen," "to do truth and righteousness and justice in the land," "to cease from walking in

The Manual of Discipline contains the rules by which the Qumran community lived.

stubbornness. . . . " Initiates are declared and are called upon to hate all Sons of Darkness. This call to hate has been noted by many who contrast this sectarian hatred for outsiders with Jesus' words: "You have heard that it was said, 'You shall love your neighbor and hate your enemy.' But I say to you, Love your enemies" (Matthew 5:43). Is it possible that Jesus knew of this burden of hatred which was laid upon the initiates of Qumran?

Another point at which the Qumran community can be compared and contrasted with the early Church is in the matter of common property. According to the *Manual* all members of the Qumran fellowship were required to contribute all their wealth to the community. But the scroll makes clear that this requirement includes more than property. Each must give his knowledge and his strength as well as his property. Sharing is thus understood to be in various modes: study, devotion and physical labor as well as such less permanent things as silver and gold. Severe punishments are invoked upon those who fail to live up to this requirement. Anyone found guilty is excluded from coming into the purified community house for a year or from meeting in public with the fellowship. He would also lose one-fourth of his food ration for the year. According to Acts 4:32ff. the early Church in Jerusalem likewise "had everything in common." When two members of the group, a man and his wife, lied about their contribution the man "fell down and died." The passage in Acts does not indicate, as some have suggested, that giving up all property to the community was a condition for entrance into the Church. It seems to indicate an ideal, not a requirement. The death of Ananias and his wife occurred because they had lied, not because they had withheld funds from the sale of land (Acts 5:1-10).

Baptism was a part of the rite of initiation into both Qumran and the early Church. But at Qumran, in contrast to the Church, it seems to have been a continuing rite. We cannot be sure, but ritual cleansing in water seems to have been an annual if not a daily event at Qumran. Yet the *Manual* leaves no doubt that if the inner heart is not pure all of the water in the world will not suffice to make a person clean. True purity depends on obedience, obedience to the Torah and to the life of the community which is drawn from it.

The Temple Scroll was not a part of the original find. Although its existence had been known for several years it did not come under scholarly scrutiny until after the Six-Day War in 1967, when it came into possession of Hebrew University. The longest of the scrolls yet found—at 28 feet it is 4 feet longer than the great *Isaiah Scroll*—its outer portions are damaged and indeed the beginning of the text seems to be missing. But almost all of the writing is there, and it is a remarkable document indeed. Its subject matter is divided into four parts. The first is a general collection of religious rules, many of which are concerned with ritual purity, a subject treated throughout the scroll. The second has to do with the sacred calendar used at Qumran and dates of various festivals as well as proper offerings. In this regard *The Temple Scroll* throws more light on a subject known previously from *The Manual of Discipline,* which indicates that the Qumran community used a special religious calendar which further set them apart from the rest of Palestinian Jewish society. In sectarian Judaism of the predestruction era there was great debate over dates of festivals and over acceptable practices. As we should expect, these two scrolls show the Qumranites greatly concerned with these matters and with purity laws associated with festivals.

The third section of *The Temple Scroll* is by far the longest, occupying about half of the document. It contains a description of a temple (hence the

General view of the Qumran site looking over the ruins toward the south where the cliffs meet the Dead Sea.

name of the scroll), but this is not any known sanctuary. On the other hand, it does not seem to be an idealized temple in the sense that it is projected into a future kingdom of God. The writers of this scroll looked forward to an actual temple. But this seems very curious when we recall that when this writing was made, perhaps sometime around the end of the first century B.C., there was a temple standing in Jerusalem. The answer may lie in the fact that the Qumranites had rejected the Temple in Jerusalem as impure and looked forward to another and purified sanctuary. Those who argue for a slightly later date for this scroll note that these sectarians may have rejected Herod's monumental construction as being out of harmony with the dictates of Scripture. But what exact Scripture is in mind? Much of this writing seems to owe something to Exodus 35 and its description of the Tabernacle. But it may owe even more to I Chronicles 28:11, David's instruction to Solomon concerning the building of the first Hebrew temple. First Chronicles notes that David gave plans for that structure to his son. But it does not give a detailed description. It would seem the people of the Qumran community undertook to supply those missing plans; *The Temple Scroll* is written in the first person, as though it were God speaking directly to Moses. The writing presents itself, then, as a sort of second Torah, divine words delivered to Moses. And among those words are detailed descriptions for the building of God's house.

The fourth and final section of this large scroll concerns another holy war. Unlike *The War Scroll*, however, *The Temple Scroll* furnishes instructions for a purely defensive struggle, one in which the ritually pure army of Israel will defend the king, the temple and the land. "Men of truth, God-fearing, hating unjust gain" will keep Israel from falling into profane hands. With an eye to detail, battle plans are given for various contingencies. In all these plans are clear statements that it is the land itself which is to command the largest number of defenders and is to be protected at all costs, the idea being that if the borders can be held the king and the temple will not be defiled by impure Gentiles. This aspect is curious, unlike anything previously known from contemporary Jewish literature. That it does not fit into a Roman context, at which time the scroll may have been written, is obvious, but it does appear to reflect the situation toward the end of the Hasmonean dynasty. Yet could the Qumranites have idealized this house against which they had rebelled and withdrawn? It is possible that other scrolls may come to light which will give answers to these questions and probably raise new ones.

The Dead Sea Scrolls were an absolutely sensational find, and the stories and legends that have grown up around them are fitting, if sometimes confusing. So far as we now know, the most significant find of all was the very first, in Cave One in the jagged cliffs west of Qumran. But Qumran, it is now abundantly clear, had not been a singular discovery. What other treasures did these oppressively quiet and rugged hills hide? Since that day in the winter of 1946-1947 when the seven scrolls were found by the Ta'amireh tribesmen, shepherds, scholars and archaeologists have peered into every dim cave and crevasse in search of new scrolls. The searches were rewarded, for a total of eleven caves in the Wilderness of Judea were found to contain writings. The first of these appeared in December of 1951 while documents were still emerging from caves around Qumran. It was then that some Bedouin made another find in caves in a large valley twelve miles south of Qumran.

In the spring of 1952 several caves in the Wadi Murabba'at were excavated and many others explored. Among the materials recovered were a number of docmments left by followers of Bar-Kochba, who had rebelled against Rome

The copper scroll as found in 1952 in Cave Three at Qumran. To read the brittle scroll it was necessary to carefully saw the copper into strips.

in A.D. 132-135. A few Biblical works were represented, but in very fragmentary form. Most were legal documents, some in Hebrew, others in Greek and Aramaic, but there were two letters bearing the name of Bar-Kochba. The most interesting find from Murabba'at is the earliest Hebrew papyrus yet discovered. It is from the seventh century B.C. Earlier writings in Hebrew exist, but not on papyrus.

Only a few months later, in the summer of 1952 still more ancient writings began to appear for sale in Jerusalem. Once more it was the Bedouin who had them. There was another letter by Bar-Kochba and more legal documents, this time in Aramaic, Nabatean and Greek. A few Biblical fragments were offered. Among these was a first century A.D. copy of a lost recension of a Greek text of the Minor Prophets. The shepherds who had these said that they came from "south of Ein Gedi" (En-gedi), but it was some time before scholars found out exactly where. It was not until 1960 that a systematic search was made of the Nahal Hever, which proved to be the source of these writings and others.

That same summer, while archaeologists were working on structures in the Wadi Qumran, Cave Four was discovered. This may well have been the main deposit of the Qumran community's library; altogether there were some four hundred documents. Most of these, unfortunately, were in poor condition and scholars have not yet been able to study many of them in detail. Yet it is known that the find contains the books of Hebrew Scriptures (except Esther) as well as large numbers of apocryphal writings and various sectarian writings.

Also in the summer of 1952 shepherds found documents in a ruined Byzantine monastery at Khirbet Mird — the infamous Hyrcania of the Hasmoneans. The monastery, *Castellion* ("fortress"), was founded in A.D. 492 by Saint Sabas, and it flourished until the ninth century. From this monastic site came portions of *codices* (books of unbound sheets) containing part of the Gospels of Mark and John as well as sections of the Acts of the Apostles. These were in Greek. Of greater interest were parts of Joshua, Matthew, Luke, Acts and Colossians written in a form of Aramaic called Syro-Palestinian, or sometimes Christo-Palestinian, because it was used by Byzantine Christians in Palestine until the coming of Islam and classical Arabic in the seventh century.

In February of 1953 a Belgian team undertook a thorough excavation of the ruins. In a grotto these scholars found what seems to have been the library, or perhaps a storage place for scrolls. Whatever its use in antiquity, this subterranean chamber yielded large fragments of writings all dating from the late Byzantine and early Arabic periods. In addition to Biblical materials (some of these were also in Syro-Palestinian) and a number of Arabic papyri there was a portion of Euripides' *Andromache*. Among the holy fathers who had withdrawn to the stillness of the Judean wilderness there was at least one who had more worldly tastes.

In 1955 new finds were made in the Wadi Murabba'at. Explorers noted a small cleft in the rock that gave an appearance of having been artificially closed. When opened it proved to be a burial cave which also contained a scroll of the Twelve Prophets in very good condition. One of the striking things about this is its close similarity to the traditional Hebrew text which was, before these discoveries, known only in its tenth century A.D. form. In this regard the Murabba'at scroll differs from similar manuscripts from Qumran, which show considerable variation from the traditional text. A year later still another Qumran cave was found.

This one, known as Cave Eleven, is less than a half mile from Cave One. It was a hermit's shelter and shows three distinct periods of occupation, the earliest going back to Chalcolithic times, the latest in Roman times. Although most of the finds from this cave were mere fragments, there are important texts from Leviticus, Ezekiel, Psalms and an Aramaic translation of Job. Such a translation is called a Targum. Other finds include fragments of some non-canonical psalms, of Jubilees and a text dealing with a messianic Melchizedek. It appears that the *Temple Scroll* was originally from Cave 11.

Discoveries continued, and again it was the indefatigable Bedouin who led the way. Late in 1959 they were back in Jerusalem with still more documents for sale. These were written on papyrus and were from the time of the Second Revolt (ca. A.D. 132-135). It was in the Jordanian part of Jerusalem that these documents were being sold, but they were discovered to have come from Nahal Hever, a great valley on the Israeli side of the line, between En-gedi and Masada. The consternation of the Israeli defense forces can be imagined! When the exact location of the source of this material was discovered, however, consternation turned to amazement. In the Nahal Se'elim as well as in the Nahal Hever the Bedouin had managed to get into caves high up on sheer cliff faces, caves which scholars were able to enter with difficulty even when employing helicopters. From Se'elim archaeologists were able to recover a few scraps, mostly inscribed leather and papyrus, which the earlier visitors had left behind.

But the "Cave of Letters" in Hever produced something quite different in several ways. We now know that this was the final hiding place of some of Bar-Kochba's followers. Apparently using rope ladders they had lowered themselves to a treacherous ledge leading to the cave and had then managed somehow to destroy or block this means of access. The Romans found them and built a small camp on the cliff above. There those who had followed the eagle from the banks of the Tiber kept watch, while below them in the cave, a self-made prison, the tough rebels preferred the horrors of starvation rather than surrender. Among numerous skeletons scholars using mine detectors found a buried treasure. At least it is a treasure to us. It was a woven basket containing perfectly preserved Roman cult objects which the Jewish fighters who had captured them had defaced by removing the human images. There were also skeins of wool and colored cloth looking as though it had just come from the loom. Woven mats in superb condition were there, as were some fifty letters and other documents ranging in date from the end of the first century A.D. to the time of the Second Revolt. Among these are fifteen military dispatches from "Simon Bar-Kochba, Prince over Israel." A number of these, including one written on wood, are actually signed by him. From these it would appear that En-gedi was a supply base for the rebels who were operating in the wilderness south of Jerusalem. The documents, some in Hebrew, some in Aramaic, a number in Greek and a few in Nabatean, are all dated. The earliest was written in A.D. 88 and the latest in A.D. 132, the eve of the revolt. In this collection are records of a family from En-gedi, including marriage contracts, deeds, wills and one document specifying who was to be guardian of an orphaned grandson.

Work in these desert caves south of En-gedi was very difficult. The years 1960 and 1961 saw some of Israel's finest scholars occupied in this work. The spring of 1962 found other scholars probing in a different but equally difficult area. Word was heard in the Jordanian section of Jerusalem that the Bedouin had made important discoveries, this time about eleven miles north of Jericho in the rugged and all but inaccessible cliffs of the Jordan fault. The rumors were true. From the Wadi Daliyeh the Bedouin brought a magnificent collec-

Nahal Hever. Caves in the cliff face (center right) could be reached only by rope from above. The Roman siege camp is visible at the top.

Objects found at Nahal Hever include household utensils, knives, baskets and even textiles, all in a remarkable state of preservation.

194

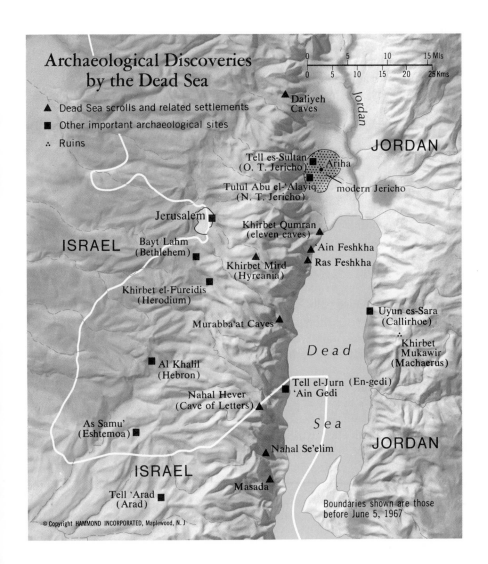

Archaeological Discoveries by the Dead Sea

▲ Dead Sea scrolls and related settlements
■ Other important archaeological sites
∴ Ruins

JORDAN

Daliyeh Caves

Tell es-Sultan (O. T. Jericho)
Ariha
Tulul Abu el-'Alayiq (N. T. Jericho)
modern Jericho

Jerusalem

Khirbet Qumran (eleven caves)

ISRAEL

Bayt Lahm (Bethlehem)

'Ain Feshkha
Ras Feshkha

Khirbet Mird (Hyrcania)

Khirbet el-Fureidis (Herodium)

Murabba'at Caves

Dead

Uyun es-Sara (Callirhoe)

Khirbet Mukawir (Machaerus)

Al Khalil (Hebron)

Tell el-Jurn (En-gedi) 'Ain Gedi

Nahal Hever (Cave of Letters)

Sea

As Samu' (Eshtemoa)

JORDAN

ISRAEL

Nahal Se'elim

Tell 'Arad (Arad)

Masada

Boundaries shown are those before June 5, 1967

© Copyright HAMMOND INCORPORATED, Maplewood, N.J

tion of papyri. Two scholarly campaigns were mounted, one in January of 1963 and the other in February 1964. Using pack donkeys to get his staff and supplies to the spot, Paul Lapp, Professor of Archaeology at the American School, excavated with his usual care under almost impossible conditions. He found a number of fragments but also discovered that the Bedouin had been exceedingly thorough in their explorations. Some one hundred twenty-eight separate documents seem to be represented in the Wadi Daliyeh materials; forty of the more important ones had to be purchased from the original finders of the cache. And what a cache it is—the largest early collection of papyri yet uncovered.

The contents of the Wadi Daliyeh materials showed them to have been brought to this desolate spot by people fleeing from Samaria, possibly as a result of the revenge which Alexander the Great took on that city in 331 B.C. The earliest papyrus is from about 375 B.C. while the latest was written on March 18, 335 B.C. All but two of the documents are in Aramaic and all are legal in character.

Another major find took place at Masada. In the first season of excavation, 1963-1964, while laying bare a building which later was found to be a

195

synagogue, a pit was discovered in the floor near the rear cell. At the bottom of the pit was a scroll containing the last two chapters of Deuteronomy. A little later yet another pit was found in the floor, this time with a document in very poor condition. It was a part of the Book of Ezekiel; namely the thirty-seventh chapter telling of the Valley of Dry Bones that would some day come together and live again. What we have here in the Masada synagogue is an early practice of burying worn sacred writings beneath the floor of the sanctuary. The *Genizeh,* a special room provided for this purpose, later became a feature of synagogues.

Before the end of the Masada excavations in the 1964-1965 season fourteen scrolls or fragments had been found in addition to a number of ostraca. One of the ostraca is from a jar of Roman wine which was marked for "Herod, King of Judea." One of the more intriguing scrolls contains a writing previously known only from Qumran Cave Four. This has raised the question of what, if any, relation the defenders of Masada had with the monks of Qumran. In 1973 John Trever, having carefully studied the handwriting on the documents from Masada and those from Qumran, has suggested that the same scribe may have copied both. Where they were written is not known.

The importance of these various writings from the Wilderness of Judea is immense, and not without considerable controversy. Many questions have been answered, but many others have been posed. Yet why all the excitement? Is it merely antiquity? Yes, partly that. But these are not the oldest writings ever found. Far from it. They are not even the oldest writings discovered in Palestine. However, these writings found since 1946-1947 are the oldest to survive on leather and some even on wood. Yet not even this points to their real value. Their inestimable worth lies in the light they shed on an extremely complex and vastly important period in the history of Judaism and the background of Christianity. The date of the Dead Sea Scrolls is mid-third century B.C. to A.D. 69. This is the time of the Hasmonean dynasty, of the coming of the Romans, of some of the greatest rabbis and of the ministry of Jesus. The writings from Nahal Hever, Nahal Se'elim, Murabba'at and Masada turn in another direction and speak of events prior to and during the Second Revolt. Khirbet Mird pushes our knowledge from contemporary documents into the Byzantine period. And from the Wadi Daliyeh has come firsthand information on family and legal affairs for a dim period in Palestinian history, one about which we know precious little. Thus a vast and extremely important period—from early fourth century B.C. down to ninth century A.D.—has begun to reveal its own secrets; it speaks in its own terms and in its own colors, moods and feeling.

It is difficult to exaggerate the importance of these finds. Yet, as always, there are a few who do so. Indeed, some extraordinary claims have been made for these wilderness writings. They completely destroy the foundations of Christianity, some discordant voices insist. They establish without question the claims of the Christian religion, certain pious minds suggest. In fact, they do neither. The scrolls and other writings are extremely important for our knowledge of (1) the text of the Hebrew Scriptures, (2) Judaism in those turbulent years before the First Revolt and the resurgence of nationalism in the Second Revolt, and (3) the background of early Christianity. When one recalls that before 1947 our earliest Hebrew manuscripts came from a thousand years after the Qumran materials the importance of these writings for our understanding of the Biblical text becomes clear. Among other things, they show the faithfulness with which the text was preserved over the cen-

The synagogue at Masada, one of the earliest yet discovered. Under its floor were found scrolls containing portions of Deuteronomy and Ezekiel.

turies. For the history of Judaism we are given an insight into a sectarian group with strong messianic concerns; a monastic group which had been strongly penetrated by various ideas and intellectual currents from outside Judaism. Many of these, such as ethical dualism, may well have come from Babylonia and Persia, the land of the Exiles. Christianity, in its inception, was also a Jewish sectarian movement. It had many beliefs similar to those held at Qumran: both held the Scriptures in esteem and devoted themselves to prayer; both used testimonia as messianic proof-texts; both saw themselves living in the last days; both believed strongly in the coming of Messiah and the establishment of the Kingdom of God. Yet here the differences emerge strongly. Qumran was an anticipatory community. In the silence of the wilderness the monks could hear the footsteps of the Messiah coming. The Christians were a fulfilled community. They confessed that in the dust of the roads of Galilee and Judea they had followed the Messiah who had come. Moreover, while Qumran saw itself as a "highway in the desert," preparing the way for the Lord and as the final defense of Israel, the Church emphasized another part of Isaiah and saw itself as "a light to the nations." The community by the Dead Sea was never anything other than a Jewish sect and for all intents and purposes it was a victim of the First Revolt against Rome. Christianity meanwhile leaped across human barriers, confessing that in Christ there was "neither Jew nor Greek, slave nor free."

For what they are and what they can do for historians and theologians, the scrolls are of inestimable value. Yet we need not claim too much for them. They supply an important and previously missing part of the vast, vibrant mosaic that was Judaism before the First Revolt, a Judaism which survived in the form of Rabbinic Judaism and a Judaism which was the context for earliest Christianity.

15 JESUS

The world into which Jesus was born was Roman—at least politically. Everywhere the eagle was ascendant. Octavian sat enthroned as Caesar Augustus, undisputed ruler of all the shores lapped by the Mediterranean and far inland as well. Republican hopes, to which Cicero had given voice and Brutus action, were dead. The empire was a fact and *pax Romana,* "the Roman peace," had begun. Along the Tiber the functional brick city of the Late Republic was rapidly being transformed into a splendid, colonnaded marble marvel, befitting the capital of empire under Augustus' aegis.

Meanwhile in Jerusalem Herod's temple was resplendent in the Judean sun, which beat down upon hundreds of workmen laboring daily to complete the grand scheme of walls and colonnades for the rest of the sacred enclosure. Outward signs of prosperity were in abundance. Fruits from the luxuriant orchards of Jericho were plentiful. Mineral deposits of the Dead Sea brought revenues to the land. And the port of Caesarea, so recently little more than sand dunes, was beginning to realize the promise which Herod held for it. Galilee was tranquil; the hills of Samaria echoed to the seemingly ageless ways of its shepherds; Judea, on the surface at least, appeared to have no greater worries than those ever present taxes.

But this was facade. Herod's kingdom was seething. The squalid and never ending intrigues within the royal family were but the kingdom in miniature. The Jews of Herod's realm, divided among themselves, hated the Romans only slightly less than they despised their own king. Sectarian groups of every stripe and hue were multiplying. The Pharisees, sickened of Hasmonean politics, eschewed the desire for temporal power and sought to realize a godly life by applying the Law to every possible human situation. Along the northwestern shore of the Dead Sea another group, the monks of Qumran, were in even stronger revolt against the ceaseless political bickering of the past century and had withdrawn themselves from society, looking rather to the coming of the Messiah and his kingdom. Others strained less to hear the footsteps of Messiah and worked more fervently to bring about their idea of how things should be. Hasmonean sympathizers were watchful for an opening which would restore that line. As Herod's health declined these people took heart and waited with growing impatience for his death. Still others could say to both Hasmonean and Herod, "a plague on both your houses." These people, the Zealots, schemed to bring about the violent overthrow of the entire system. The Romans and those who collaborated with them were their targets, but so were all in authority. Out of the ashes these people would build their ideal state. Only if you were a Sadducee, born to wealth and position, did you already enjoy the ideal state. The Sadducees controlled the high priesthood and revenues of the Temple, the largest single industry in the land. But for the vast majority of people religious dreams and political schemes mattered little. They, like other peasants of antiquity, sought mainly to hold mind and body together, scratching the soil, urging it to provide a little food and following their sheep and goats through the monotonous hills of Palestine.

Opposite:
In the Wilderness of Judea flat stones shaped like loaves of bread recall one of the temptations of Jesus. When the devil asked that he turn a stone into bread Jesus answered him, "It is written, 'Man shall not live by bread alone'" (Luke 4:3-4).

A woman from an agricultural village weighing grapes in a fashion well known in Jesus' day.

Judea was not to share in the Roman peace. It was to live in tension and finally to be torn and shattered in two suicidal wars, wars which were at the same time struggles against Rome and civil wars among sectarian groups. So long as Herod lived things remained relatively under control. But when he died the fabric of his kingdom began to unravel. Archelaus, his son and heir in Judea, sailed off to Capri, seeking to have Augustus confirm him in office. This was the atmosphere into which Jesus was born and these were some of the events which took place shortly after his birth, for Jesus seems to have been born in the same year in which Herod died—4 B.C.

The reader might ask why Jesus was born in 4 B.C. and not A.D. 1 as one would expect. The reason lies in an error in the Julian method of calculating years. With the advice and help of Sosigenes, Julius Caesar abolished use of the lunar year and regulated the Roman civil year solely by the sun. While this proved to be a convenient method, it also contained an error which accumulated over the centuries and displaced the usual position of the seasons. In the sixteenth century the distinguished astronomer of Naples, Aloysius Lilius, devised a new calendar which corrected the error the Julian calendar had accumulated over the years and prevented its recurrence. In March 1582, Pope Gregory XIII abolished the Julian calendar in the west (it continued to be used in eastern Christendom) and instituted that of Lilius. Reckoning by this Gregorian calendar, Jesus' birth year is a B.C. date.

The story of Jesus' birth as told in Scripture is one of haunting beauty enhanced by remarkable simplicity. The themes of exaltation and humility are intertwined throughout, producing a rare fabric. The way had been carefully prepared for the birth of this holy child. An angel had appeared to Zechariah, an aging priest with a barren wife, Elizabeth. To the astonishment of this man the angel announced that his wife would give birth to a son, a special child who "will turn many of the sons of Israel to the Lord their God." This long-desired child would become the messenger who would go forth in the spirit and power of Elijah to declare that the Kingdom of God was at hand. This child was to be named John, *Johanan*—"gift of God."

And the angel appeared also to Mary, Elizabeth's younger cousin living in the hill country of Galilee, saying:

> "Hail, O favored one, the Lord is with you! . . . Do not be afraid, Mary, for you have found favor with God. And behold, you will conceive in your womb and bear a son, and you shall call his name Jesus.
>
> > He will be great, and will be called
> > > the Son of the Most High;
> > and the Lord God will give to him
> > > the throne of his father David,
> > and he will reign over the house of Jacob for ever;
> > and of his kingdom there will be no end."
> > > > (Luke 1:28, 30-33)

The beautiful narration of the nativity in Luke weaves together the stories of the births of John and Jesus, punctuating the account with hymns and poetry based upon Old Testament models and reflecting both the antiquity of the hope which Christians saw fulfilled in these children, and the deep piety with which Christians came to hallow the birth of Jesus. When Mary, the maid betrothed to Joseph, carpenter of Nazareth, visits her cousin Elizabeth, Luke chooses to describe the spirit of the women and the character of their meeting by noting only Elizabeth's greeting and Mary's response. "Blessed are you among women," said Elizabeth, "and blessed is the fruit of your womb!" Mary's response is captured in the now familiar words of the *Magnificat*, the opening of which is:

> My soul magnifies the Lord,
> and my spirit rejoices in God my Savior,
> for he has regarded the low estate of his handmaiden.
>
> (Luke 1:46-48)

When John the Baptist is born it is hymn and poetry again which Luke uses to convey the solemnity and joy of the event and its portents for the future. In the mouth of John's father, Zechariah, are set the exalted strains of the *Benedictus*:

> Blessed be the Lord God of Israel,
> for he has visited and redeemed his people,
> and has raised up a horn of salvation for us
> in the house of his servant David,
> as he spoke by the mouth of his
>   holy prophets from of old,
> that we should be saved from our enemies,
> and from the hand of all who hate us;
> to perform the mercy promised to our fathers, . . .
>
> (Luke 1:68-72)

The birth of Jesus is told by Luke in chapter two of his Gospel. It is a literary masterpiece of the first order in the original Greek, and this character survives in several of the English translations, notably the King James Version and the Revised Standard Version, the two which not surprisingly seek to be most faithful to the original rendering. Luke, the ever careful historian, pins down the time of Jesus' birth to a decree which went forth from Augustus that there should be a census of the empire, a census which would doubtless determine for the first time just what capabilities, financial and military, might reside within that vast complex. Moreover, says Luke, this was done when Quirinius was governor of Syria. It is quite natural that anyone in that part of the Roman East would date an event to the rule of the legate of Syria, the most powerful Roman official in that part of the world. But Luke has done something else, too. By placing the birth of Jesus firmly within the orbit of known historical events and figures he has removed it forever from the realm of those dying and rising gods which were well known to the Ancient Near East. This Jesus, proclaims the Gospel, was born into history and not into myth. The Apostles' Creed proclaims the same thing when it declares that he was "crucified under Pontius Pilate." From the very outset the Christians believed that God, revealing himself in this Jesus of Nazareth, was acting in a new and decisive manner. This participation was not out of harmony with God's known character as a God who had revealed himself in concrete historical persons and situations to his people over the centuries. This emphasis, which is in the nativity stories and elsewhere, forever sets the story of the life, death and resurrection of Jesus over against the mythical gods of the East, whose place and time could not be determined.

Further to underline the point, Luke notes that Joseph and Mary journey southward (by what way we are not told) into the Judean hills south of Jerusalem, to the City of David, Bethlehem, there to be enrolled in the census.

City of Bethlehem viewed from bell tower of the Church of the Nativity.

And there is a homey touch: Bethlehem is crowded and Joseph can find no room at the inn for the pregnant Mary, so he takes the weary woman to a stable. There Jesus is born in utter humility, surrounded not by kings and potentates but by beasts which daily bear the burden of the fields. Yet the theme of exaltation is not wholly absent as the tiny child, the hope of the world, lies in a manger wrapped in swaddling clothes. In fields to the east of the town, quite near the Herodium, which was so soon to be the resting place for Herod's mortal remains, shepherds watching their flocks were summoned to the manger by angels who intoned:

> Glory to God in the highest,
> and on earth peace among men with whom he is pleased!

This account of the shepherds and the angels in Luke 2:8ff. may give a clue to the time of year in which Jesus was born. It may well have been in the spring, perhaps during lambing season. But of this we cannot be sure. What is certain is that Jesus was not born in the dead of winter. While Christmas may be validly hallowed by piety, it is not a correct historical memory. The celebration of the birth of Christ was shifted to the end of December displacing pagan festivals.

It is difficult today when visiting the Church of the Nativity in Bethlehem to reconstruct in the mind's eye those humble events of so many years ago. The ancient basilica now marking the traditional spot over the cave in which Jesus is said to have been born has been much ravaged by time and the enemies of Christianity, yet its pleasing proportions and magnificent columns give it a stateliness, an aura of grandeur. The multitude of lamps hung by Greek Orthodox Christians and the massive silver chandelier given by a Russian czar near the end of the last century seem oddly out of place. And the church is shabby, yet this may be its most compelling feature as one tries to recover the poverty in which Jesus was born. In the cave under the central altar one struggles amid Crusader crosses carved into the rock, asbestos trappings, hanging lamps, pious pilgrims and incense to catch however fleetingly the smell of hay which was present on that first Christmas. It eludes. In the end one's private thoughts become a refuge. It is so often thus today in the sacred places of the Holy Land.

Luke tells us that Jesus was circumcised on the eighth day according to the Law of Moses and on that day received his name: Jesus—"Joshua," "he will save his people." It is also Luke who tells us that shortly afterward Jesus was presented before the Lord in the Temple in Jerusalem. There an old man, Simeon, a righteous and devout soul who earnestly looked for the redemption of Israel, took the young child into his arms saying:

> Lord, now lettest thou thy servant depart in peace,
> according to thy word;
> for mine eyes have seen thy salvation
> which thou hast prepared in the presence of all peoples,
> a light for revelation to the Gentiles,
> and for glory to thy people Israel.
> (Luke 2:29-32, the *Nunc Dimittis*)

It is Matthew who tells us that now Joseph and Mary were forced to take the infant Jesus into Egypt. Further weakening under the onset of his final illness, the paranoid Herod (according to Matthew 2:7-18) became furious upon hearing of the birth of a rival "king." When the Wise Men did

The Church of the Nativity, Bethlehem; traditional birthplace of Jesus. The exterior reveals a much-ravaged facade flanked by monasteries. The interior of the basilica (below) contains columns from Justinian's time.

not return to identify this child to him the depraved monarch ordered the death of all of the male children of the region, all of the boys under two. Although this story of the slaying of the innocents has become a fixture in the lore surrounding Herod and a favorite theme in art, historians have been unable to confirm it. In Matthew however it is the context of Jesus' flight into Egypt from which, like Moses, he is called.

While Jesus was in Egypt Herod died. Joseph gathered the young child and his mother and journeyed northward, far northward past Bethlehem and Jerusalem, across the Samaritan hills and the vast northern valley to Nazareth, a village huddled in the Galilean hills. Modern Nazareth has spread well beyond its ancient limits, with the bustling lower city populated mostly by Christian Arabs and the cement new city — Upper Nazareth — populated entirely by Israeli Jews. Dominating the older portion of Nazareth is a huge church, the Church of the Annunciation. In its crypt are the remains of a Byzantine church built in turn over a cave, the traditional site of the home of Mary and Joseph. Here according to ancient legend Jesus grew up, learning his father's profession and from his mother the traditions of his people. If this is the site of the angel's visit to Mary and of Jesus' childhood home, the sounds which are heard in the streets are vastly different from those that echoed from the stones in bygone days. Now one's path to the door of this truly extraordinary modern sanctuary is lined by tourist trinkets for sale at whatever price the wary may bargain for and by vendors who prey on the praying faithful.

Excavations beneath the Church of the Annunciation at Nazareth have confirmed that it was an agricultural village during Jesus' day. It was occupied as early as about 1850 B.C., judging from the contents of some of its ancient tombs. However, it reached its peak in the Roman period. By locating the first century tombs it is possible to determine its approximate boundaries and therefore its approximate size. Nazareth covered about 60 acres at its maximum, or about 900 yards by 200 yards. If the space needs of the ancient population of Nazareth were like those of Palestinian agricultural villages in the area prior to 1918, Nazareth could have housed and fed around 800 souls in this fertile 60 acres.

Nazareth, in Jesus' day a small village in the hills of Galilee.

Another thing about Nazareth: it was Jewish. This may not seem very remarkable until we realize that in this period Galilee was predominantly Gentile. There were Jewish enclaves such as Nazareth, Cana, Capernaum and other places well known to the Gospels. Thus Jesus grew up in a Jewish village, but would likely from earliest memory have had contacts with Gentiles or at least known that he was in a mixed area. One of the perplexing issues in Biblical study is why Jesus did not minister among the Gentiles of Galilee but seems rather to have taken some care to restrict himself to Jews and Jewish areas. While this may be explained in terms of historical situation, it nonetheless appears strange in light of the early and pervasive universalism which Christians felt to be inherent in the life and teaching of Jesus.

Whatever abrasions there may have been between Jews and Gentiles in those northern hills, it did not break into open hostility until perhaps the First Revolt against Rome, when conditions had altered radically. Furthermore, Galilee is a garden spot when compared with Samaria and Judea. The pleasant uplands have an attractive climate year-round, as anyone who has traveled from the Galilean hills down to the shores of the Sea of Galilee will readily testify. The landscape is one of flowing hills and fertile valleys producing

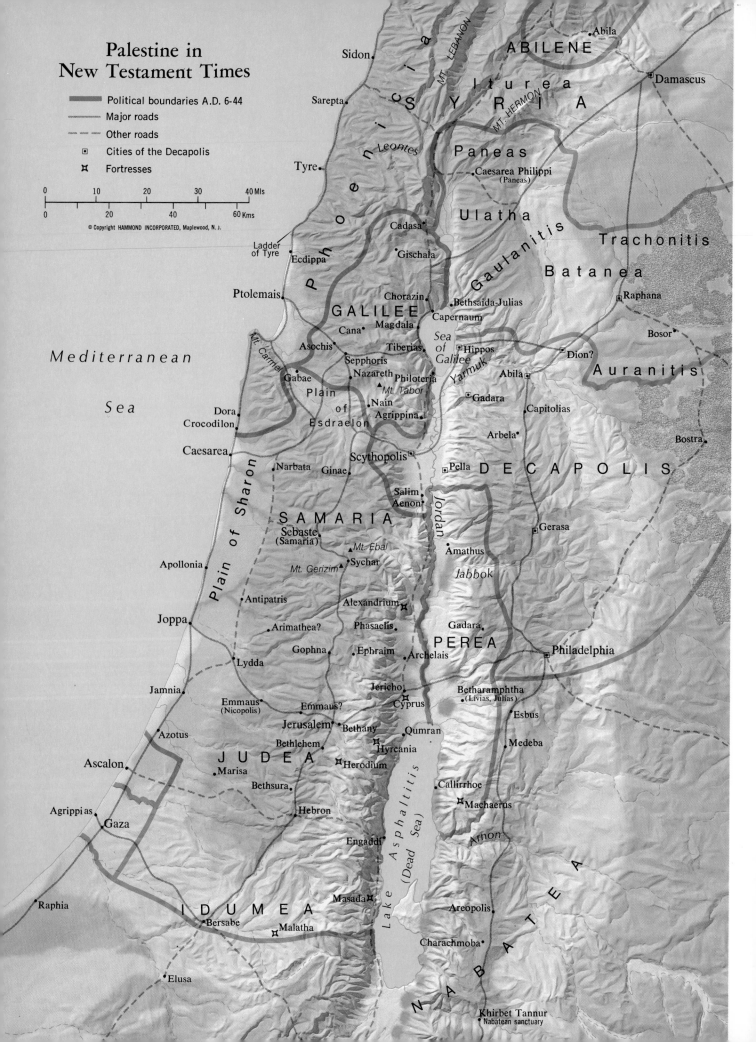

Palestine in New Testament Times

Political boundaries A.D. 6-44
Major roads
Other roads
□ Cities of the Decapolis
⬥ Fortresses

0   10   20   30   40 Mls
0   20   40   60 Kms
© Copyright HAMMOND INCORPORATED, Maplewood, N.J.

Mediterranean

Sea

ABILENE

Abila

Sidon

MT. LEBANON

Iturea

□ Damascus

Sarepta

SYRIA

MT. HERMON

Paneas

Tyre

Leontes

Caesarea Philippi
(Paneas)

Ulatha

Trachonitis

Ladder
of Tyre

Cadasa

Gaulanitis

Batanea

Ecdippa

Gischala

□ Raphana

Ptolemais

GALILEE

Chorazin

Bethsaida-Julias

Capernaum

Bosor

Cana

Magdala

Sea
of
Galilee

Asochis

Tiberias

□ Hippos

Dion?

Auranitis

Mt. Carmel

Sepphoris

Nazareth

Philoteria

Yarmuk

Abila

Gabae

Plain
of
Esdraelon

Mt. Tabor

Gadara

Capitolias

Dora
Crocodilon

Nain

Agrippina

Arbela

Bostra

Caesarea

Scythopolis

DECAPOLIS

Narbata

Ginae

□ Pella

Plain of Sharon

Salim
Aenon

SAMARIA

Jordan

Sebaste
(Samaria)

Mt. Ebal

Amathus

Gerasa

Apollonia

Mt. Gerizim

Sychar

Jabbok

Antipatris

Alexandrium

Phasaelis

Gadara

Joppa

Arimathea?

Ephraim

PEREA

Philadelphia

Gophna

Lydda

Archelais

Jamnia

Jericho

Betharamphtha
(Livias, Julias)

Emmaus
(Nicopolis)

Emmaus?

Cyprus

Esbus

Jerusalem

Bethany

Qumran

Azotus

Bethlehem

Hyrcania

Medeba

Ascalon

Marisa

Herodium

Lake
Asphaltitis
(Dead Sea)

Callirrhoe

Agrippias

Bethsura

Machaerus

Gaza

Hebron

Engaddi

Arnon

Raphia

IDUMEA

Masada

Areopolis

Bersabe

Malatha

NABATEA

Charachmoba

Elusa

Khirbet Tannur
Nabatean sanctuary

two crops a year. There are striking geographical features, not merely the breathtaking blue bowl that is the Sea of Galilee, but mountains such as Tabor, that rounded height which juts up from the plain, and the Horns of Hattin, an extinct volcano whose double peaks witnessed a decisive defeat of the Crusaders by Saladin in 1187. The Roman road from Capernaum to Nazareth, whose route is followed by the modern highway, is a succession of spectacular sights and views as it climbs from the heat of the Jordan rift to the pleasant highlands. Here Jesus grew up among friends and family, among pomegranates and peppers, with the Torah of the synagogue and the toil of the carpenter's shop. Most, maybe all, of his disciples were Galileans, and it was here that he worked for the greater part of his ministry among men.

Hard by Nazareth, scarcely an hour's walk away, loomed a large, walled city that must be reckoned as one of the formative factors in the background of the early life of Jesus. The city was Sepphoris, "the ornament of all Galilee," according to Josephus, and a sprawling economic and intellectual center. Here Herod Antipas built his castle for his comfort, and here he built a theater to entertain his friends and the leading citizens of the city. Within its walls two markets teemed with hawkers and shoppers as the city sought to handle the produce from the lush fields of its dependent villages, including Nazareth. But sophisticates from the towns and cities of the broad province of Syria were also to be found busy at work in an archive building, an old fortress, and in various government buildings, or buying the linens for which Sepphoris was famous. Others would be at prayer in numerous synagogues. Its fields stretched fully seventeen miles to the north and seven miles to the south or to the Nazareth fault, the cliff that drops off to the Plain of Jezreel. The city territory of Sepphoris extended to Mount Tabor nearly ten miles to the southeast and insured that Sepphoris would remain a wealthy city for generations. Is it possible that the Nazareth family of Joseph the carpenter built forms, scaffolds and other aids for the masons in the great building program that Herod Antipas instituted here? Probably we will never know for sure, but it is an arresting thought that in Matthew 6:16 Jesus refers to actors ("hypocrites") and seemingly mimes (painted faces) that he might have seen in Herod's theater.

Of Jesus' early life we are told only one incident. At the age of twelve he made a pilgrimage with his family and some of their friends from Galilee to Jerusalem. Luke 2:41-51 tells us that when Joseph, Mary and their friends left Jerusalem, making their way northward along the road to Samaria, they went about a day's journey when Jesus was discovered not to be among the company. Returning to Jerusalem his parents searched in vain for three days until finally they found him in the Temple with the learned doctors of the Law astonishing them with his knowledge. To his worried mother's justifiable rebuke for his having treated his family thus, Jesus replied with the enigmatic words, "How is it that you sought me? Did you not know that I must be in my Father's house?"

The River Jordan near the Dead Sea, traditional site of Jesus' baptism.

This is all we know of Jesus' life until that fateful day when as a young man he appeared on the shore of the Jordan River just north of the Dead Sea and asked his cousin John to baptize him. When he was about thirty years old, perhaps in A.D. 26 or 27, he came south to the edge of the Jordan River just north of the Dead Sea. By his own desire Jesus submitted to John's baptism for reasons which are not now clear. The Gospels tell us that this event was accompanied by heavenly signs and wonders designating Jesus, not John, as God's anointed, the Messiah, or in Greek, *Christos*.

Ruins of the Pool of Bethzatha (Bethesda)
in Jerusalem where Jesus healed
a cripple according to John 5: 2-9.

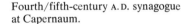

Fourth/fifth-century A.D. synagogue
at Capernaum.

This was the beginning of Jesus' ministry, a ministry which according to Fourth Gospel lasted three years. From among the circle of John's followers Jesus chose his first disciples. But before he set out with them to declare to all who had ears to hear and eyes to see that God's "good news," his "gospel" had come; that in his person and words God was acting decisively to create humanity anew — before all this Jesus was driven up into the wilderness, there to wrestle inwardly with the meaning, implications and methods of his ministry. The literary descriptions of these classic "temptations of Christ" are drawn from the very fabric of the land. From heights in the wilderness of Judea the view can be striking as one gazes for miles and miles over the blue Dead Sea and the hills of Moab and in other directions down the Arabah as it disappears in the purple haze to the south and the wilderness itself undulating, ever changing. Viewing this vastness Jesus is tempted to become a temporal ruler, "master of all he surveys." Around his feet lie the endless flat stones of the desert, many, if not most, small and round and resembling the bread which in antiquity as today has been the staple food of the Near East. "If you are the Son of God," a voice whispers to him, "command this stone to become bread." "Man shall not live by bread alone," says Jesus rejecting the temptation to dazzle men into following him. In Jerusalem, as we have seen, the southeast corner of the platform of Herod's temple soared over 400 feet above the floor of the Kidron Valley. This was known as the "pinnacle of the temple." Here, according to the first three Gospels, the devil tempted Jesus to throw himself down to see if the angels of God would catch him. "You shall not tempt the Lord your God," Jesus replied, and the devil departed from him.

Shortly after Jesus returned to his native Galilee he went with his mother and some of his disciples to Cana, a small Jewish village eight miles north of Nazareth, there to attend a wedding. In the course of the festivities he quietly turned water into wine, thus performing his first miracle. After this he did not return directly to Nazareth, but went along the Roman road through the pass in the hills down to the shore of the Sea of Galilee, to Capernaum. The western shore of the lake was ringed by towns and villages, some of ancient foundation; others such as Tiberias are of later origin. Jesus taught in most of the synagogues of the Jewish villages of Galilee, but Capernaum seems to have been his favorite. It was a small, unwalled fishing village extending nearly a mile along the shore and occupying perhaps not more than 750 feet inland to the point where the hills begin to rise away from the lake. In short, Capernaum in Jesus' day was a long, narrow border town. He came to live in Capernaum, as Matthew 4:13 tells us, and Matthew 9:1 calls it Jesus' "own city." From this village or its immediate vicinity Jesus chose several of his disciples: Matthew, who was a tax collector (Mark 2:14), Simon Peter and his brother Andrew, fishermen who owned a house in Capernaum (Mark 1:16, 29), and those two firebrands John and James, the sons of Zebedee (Mark 1:19), likewise fishermen.

Much of Jesus' healing ministry in Galilee was centered in Capernaum. In the synagogue he healed a man with an unclean spirit (Mark 1:21-28), and in the village he healed the servant of the Roman officer who had been instrumental in building the synagogue (Luke 7:1-10). And he also healed the daughter of Jarius, a ruler of the synagogue (Luke 8:40-46). It was here that he helped Peter's mother-in-law (Mark 1:29-31), and it was here that needy crowds pressed upon him seeking healing and solace (Mark 1:32-34). On one occasion the crush was so great that Jesus who was indoors

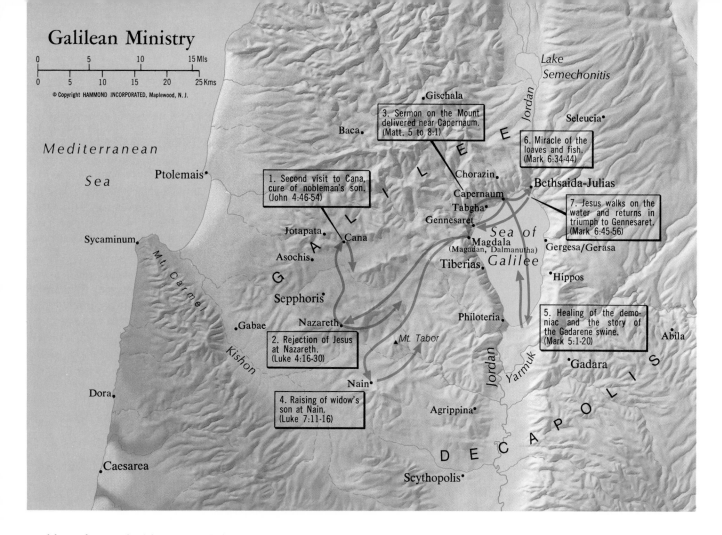

Galilean Ministry

0   5   10   15 MIs
0   5   10   15   20   25 Kms
© Copyright HAMMOND INCORPORATED, Maplewood, N.J.

Mediterranean
Sea

Lake
Semechonitis

3. Sermon on the Mount
delivered near Capernaum.
(Matt. 5 to 8:1)

6. Miracle of the
loaves and fish.
(Mark 6:34-44)

Gischala

Baca.

Seleucia.

Ptolemais.

Chorazin.

Capernaum

1. Second visit to Cana,
cure of nobleman's son.
(John 4:46-54)

Tabgha.

Bethsaida-Julias

7. Jesus walks on the
water and returns in
triumph to Gennesaret.
(Mark 6:45-56)

Gennesaret.

Sycaminum.

Jotapata.

Cana

Sea of

Magdala
(Magadan, Dalmanutha)

Gergesa/Gerasa

Asochis.

Tiberias.   Galilee

.Hippos

Sepphoris.

.Gabae

Nazareth.

Philoteria.

5. Healing of the demo-
niac and the story of
the Gadarene swine.
(Mark 5:1-20)

Abila.

2. Rejection of Jesus
at Nazareth.
(Luke 4:16-30)

.Mt. Tabor

.Gadara

Dora.

Nain.

4. Raising of widow's
son at Nain.
(Luke 7:11-16)

Agrippina.

Scythopolis.

could not be reached by some of the more severe cases. This was the setting for the four men who removed part of the roof of the house, letting down their paralytic friend into the presence of an astonished Jesus. "My son," said Jesus, "your sins are forgiven. . . .I say to you rise, take up your pallet and go home" (Mark 2:5, 11). This plunged Jesus into controversy with the scribes, whose legalistic bent of mind plagued Jesus throughout his ministry.

Capernaum was also the scene of Jesus' famous discourse on the "bread of life" recorded in John 6:22-40, which says in part:

> I am the bread of life; he who comes to me shall not hunger, and
> he who believes in me shall never thirst. But I said to you that you
> have seen me and yet do not believe. All that the Father gives me
> will come to me; and him who comes to me I will not cast out.
>
> (John 6:35-37)

Capernaum in Jesus' day was an active fishing village surrounded by forests and orchards. Since it stood on the border with the territory of Gaulanitis and the city of Bethsaida-Julias, it was important enough to the Roman authorities to have its own tax collector. Its narrow streets once rang with the laughter of chldren and with the shouts and conversation of fishermen and travelers. Today, Capernaum's chief feature is silence. In a grove of trees beside the blue lake stand two modern buildings: a Franciscan monastery and a Greek Orthodox church. Excavators have opened up the earth and its history in the vicinity of both buildings, including within and around the magnificent white limestone synagogue building of the fourth century A.D. Guides used to say that Jesus himself preached in this gem of building, so beautifully decorated, but now we know it is more likely that he taught in the simpler black basalt synagogue that has been discovered directly beneath it. Furthermore, scarcely 90 feet to the south stand the black basalt remains of a first century house almost completely concealed beneath ruins of fourth and fifth century Christian churches. It seems clear that early Christians believed that the house first belonged to the apostle Peter, and they built their churches above and around the house to preserve it. They honored the memory of Jesus in the pious graffiti written on its walls and on the walls of the later churches. Whether they were right to identify this as Peter's house we cannot now say, but the house they honored so long ago is in fact a first century A.D. home.

In the immediate vicinity of Capernaum there are other sites sacred to the memory of Jesus. Between Tiberias and Capernaum there is Magdala (Magadan), home of Mary Magdalene, with its recently uncovered first century A.D. synagogue. Farther north on the lakeshore there lies Tabgha, which from early Christian times has marked the traditional site where the resurrected Jesus ate fish with his disciples in the dim light of approaching day. Here stands the completely reconstructed fifth century church that commemorates that event. Inland a commanding hill is crowned by a relatively recent Italian convent and a beautiful octagonal church built in 1937. This hill is called the Mount of the Beatitudes and is the traditional place of the Sermon on the Mount, which begins:

The Church of the Beatitudes dominates the hill above the Sea of Galilee where tradition says Jesus preached the Sermon on the Mount.

> Blessed are the poor in spirit, for
> theirs is the kingdom of heaven.
> Blessed are those who mourn,
> for they shall be comforted.
> Blessed are the meek, for they
> shall inherit the earth.
> Blessed are those who hunger
> and thirst for righteousness, for they
> shall be satisfied.
> Blessed are the merciful, for they
> shall obtain mercy.
> Blessed are the pure in heart, for
> they shall see God.
> Blessed are the peacemakers, for
> they shall be called sons of God.
> Blessed are those who are persecuted for
> righteousness' sake, for theirs is the kingdom
> of heaven.
>
> (Matthew 5:3-10)

But Jesus was not always welcomed elsewhere in Galilee and its synagogues as he was in Capernaum. In the synagogue of his hometown, Nazareth, he barely escaped death at the hands of a mob (Luke 4:16-30), and he pronounced a curse upon the villages of Chorazin and Bethsaida for their lack of response (Matthew 11:21; Luke 10:13). But if he was not heard gladly in all of the synagogues, the common people flocked to him, sometimes even forcing him into a boat to teach them as they stood upon the shore (Mark 4:1; Matthew 13:2). But the multitudes too had their ideas of what a messiah should be, and when he rejected their notions that he be a nationalistic, military leader to drive out the Romans the crowds left him. When he fed 5,000 with a few loaves and fishes, they adored him. But when he disappointed their hopes, they scorned him. As his popularity waned he turned more and more in the journeys of his later Galilean ministry to instructing his few faithful disciples who went about with him. He spoke to them of the nature of discipleship, warning them of its rigors and costs, telling them that "he who finds his life will lose it, and he who loses his life for my sake will find it." (Matthew 10:39) He disdained what he considered to be meaningless purity laws, reminding his followers that among other things the Sabbath was made for man and not man for the Sabbath. What is important, he said echoing Amos, is "mercy, not sacrifice" (Matthew 12:7). All the while he had compassion on those in need and went about doing good. Yet religious leaders took counsel how they might destroy him. Any man who was not careful about laws of ritual purity and who, being rejected in the synagogues, claimed to take God's word to laborers in the fields and to those who farmed the sea must be dangerous or crazy or both.

But not all the more traditionally religious opposed him. On one occasion some Pharisees came to him, warning him to flee Galilee because Herod Antipas meant to kill him. Jesus, already determined to go to Jerusalem, doubtless also recalled that this same son of Herod the Great had put his cousin, John the Baptist, to death in a squalid scene involving incest and lust —fully worthy of the Herodian name which this monarch bore. So Jesus left Galilee and, in the words of Luke, knowing that "the days drew near for him to be received up, he set his face to go to Jerusalem" (Luke 9:51).

On this dedication stone found at Caesarea is the only known inscriptional reference to Pontius Pilate.

The impression given by the first three Gospels is that Jesus' ministry in Jerusalem lasted only one week — Passion Week. The Gospel of John, on the other hand, suggests a longer ministry, one of six months, lasting from the Feast of Tabernacles in late fall to Passover in early spring. John 10:23 gives a striking picture of Jesus walking on Solomon's Porch in the Temple (one of the colonnades) at the Feast of Dedication; that is, at Hannukah. He disputes with those who have gathered around him. They are so outraged at his words that they take up stones to kill him. He eludes them and those who have come to arrest him on this occasion. It would seem that Jerusalem's opposition to Jesus was building for some time. Yet, for all of the weeks that Jesus may have been in and around Jerusalem, everything focuses upon that fateful week before Passover — the events of Passion Week.

The first day, Sunday, followed the Jewish Sabbath; the tempo of Jerusalem could pick up once more. The day of rest and worship and study was over; commerce revived and the pace of everyday activities quickened. With Passover almost at hand, Jerusalem was swelling with pilgrims. Soon the Roman governor, Pontius Pilate, would come from Caesarea with some soldiers to keep an eye on things in this busy and occasionally volatile season.

Thus as the warm spring sun bathed Jerusalem and the surrounding Judean hills on this particular day, noisy crowds elbowed their way through the narrow streets, some rushing to the holy places, others complaining to merchants about suddenly increased prices, still others gawking at Herod's magnificent buildings. And over on the Mount of Olives there was shouting; shouting which continued and indeed grew louder as a throng of people came nearer and nearer to the city. Many were waving branches which they had cut or torn from palm trees. They were beginning to throw these branches in the path of a man riding on a donkey. The path down the hillside and leading to the Golden Gate was rapidly becoming a green highway strewn with palm leaves. Some of the people were even taking off their cloaks and laying these in the way of the man on the donkey! The shouts were becoming increasingly audible. "Hosanna! Blessed is he who comes in the name of the

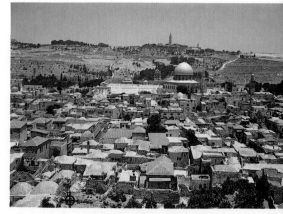

View of the Old City of Jerusalem looking towards the Mount of Olives.

Lord, even the King of Israel. Hosanna! Blessed be the kingdom of our father David that is coming! Hosanna in the highest!"

The man on the donkey stopped. There was an argument. Some of the Pharisees present were angry. "Teacher," they said, "rebuke your disciples." "I tell you," said the man, "if these were silent, the very stones would cry out." And the donkey moved on, somehow majestically. The shouts rose again. But once more the man stopped as the city came into sight. He wept for Jerusalem:

> Would that even today you knew the things that make for peace! But now they are hid from your eyes. For the days shall come upon you, when your enemies will cast up a bank about you and surround you, and hem you in on every side, and dash you to the ground, you and your children within you, and they will not leave one stone upon another in you; because you did not know the time of your visitation.
>
> (Luke 19:42-44)

Curious visitors and concerned residents swelled the crowd as Jesus of Nazareth entered Jerusalem, riding on a lowly donkey yet in regal splendor. Later some of his followers recalled the words of Zechariah:

> Fear not, daughter of Zion;
> behold your king is coming,
> sitting on an ass's colt!

But just now they did not quite understand what was going on. Some people from among the spectators were being caught up in the joyous spirit of the occasion; others were scornful. This man, this religious fanatic from Galilee, could only bring trouble. Did he not understand the situation in Jerusalem?

The procession rode through the Golden Gate and was within the Temple precincts, in the vast Court of the Gentiles. Jesus gazed around him. People were everywhere. The lengthening shadows of the late afternoon formed an almost eerie backdrop for the brisk business of the money-changers and those who were hawking sacrifices. Evening was now fast approaching as it seems to do with a peculiar suddenness in Jerusalem. Jesus stored these familiar but increasingly irritating scenes in his mind. His twelve disciples with him, he withdrew from the Temple and made his way over the Mount of Olives, retracing his steps to Bethany and the warm home of Mary, Martha and Lazarus.

Bethany was full of memories for Jesus; memories now foreboding in their rhythm of life and death. Here Jesus wept with the grieving Mary and Martha. Here he had spoken deathless words: "I am the resurrection and the life; he who believes in me, though he die, yet shall he live, and whoever lives and believes in me shall never die" (John 11:25). Here he had commanded the lifeless Lazarus to come forth from the sepulcher. Here, only days before, while at dinner with Mary, Martha and Lazarus, he had been anointed. Anointing in those days was a rite reserved for a king or a corpse. Here in Bethany he now rested.

The next morning Jesus seemed angry, even peevish. On his way back into the city he cursed a fig tree that offered him no fruit to quench his hunger. "May no one ever eat fruit from you again," he said. Once more in the Court of the Gentiles, Jesus' eyes fell upon the numerous tables and booths that dotted the area. Already the merchants were at their trade, selling sac-

The town of Bethany was less than an hour's walk (some two miles) from Jerusalem.

rifices, mostly pigeons, to pilgrims and other worshipers. And since the sacrifices must be undefiled to be acceptable they could not be purchased with profane common money. Thus money-changers were also much in evidence, each more eager than the other to exchange coin from any part of the empire for special Temple currency which could be used to buy sacrifices. It was, needless to say, an extraordinarily profitable business and one which the Sadducees kept tightly under control. But on this day Jesus could not keep his indignation under control. It boiled over. He flew at the money-changers, overturning their tables, coins scattering. The purveyors of sacrifices were to him but peddlers of sacrilege. They too were an object of his wrath. "It is written," he cried out as he made a wide path among the scampering merchants, "'My house shall be called a house of prayer'; but you make it a den of robbers."

There were also harsh words for Temple officials who were affronted by what they considered an outrage in this holiest of places. But the needy who came to him found solace and healing and, while the authorities began to take counsel together how they might rid themselves of this nuisance-become-threat, people in ever increasing numbers flocked to hear him.

Pilgrims continued to pour into Jerusalem for Passover season. Romans glared down from the heights of Fortress Antonia into the Temple, ever watchful for serious trouble. And daily Jesus was there, locked in a battle of wits with those who were seeking to trap him in some indiscretion, some wrong word—something that would allow the authorities to move against him. With mounting tension they watched unfolding events, events seemingly

Bronze lepton of Pontius Pilate (top). Silver denarius of Tiberius (center) is "tribute money" of Luke 20: 21-25. Silver shekel of Tyre (bottom). Judas' 30 pieces of silver may have been of this type.

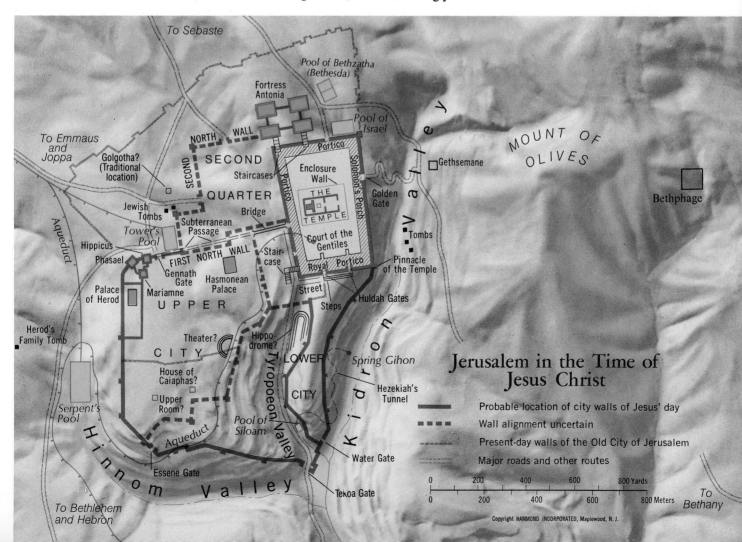

Jerusalem in the Time of Jesus Christ

——	Probable location of city walls of Jesus' day
- - -	Wall alignment uncertain
———	Present-day walls of the Old City of Jerusalem
· · · ·	Major roads and other routes

beyond their control. If this goes on, they told one another, there will be an outburst triggering a Roman reaction, bringing them down upon us and our holy place. But Caiaphas, the high priest, saw a solution. "You know nothing at all," he told them, "you do not understand that it is expedient for you that one man should die for the people, and that the whole nation should not perish" (John 11:49). Jesus must die!

As these authorities sought a way to implement this seemingly simple solution, an unexpected opportunity was just dropped into their laps. One of Jesus' most trusted followers offered to betray his master. He would show how Jesus could be taken in the dead of night, away from the crowds which thronged him in the day. Even so, it was risky business. But they would do it. When could Judas make the arrangements?

Jesus was not unaware of danger closing around him. His disciples likewise sensed that things might not be well. When on Thursday evening they gathered in an upper room to celebrate the Passover meal, tension split the air and troubled the surrounding darkness. Now, during supper, Jesus did a strange thing. He rose, laid aside his garments and, having girded himself with a towel, took a basin of water and began to wash his friends' feet. Simon Peter, in particular, objected to Jesus' taking upon himself this servant's role. But Jesus explained that unless he was permitted to be a servant to his followers they could have no part with him.

Again at the table Jesus took bread, blessed it and broke it saying, "Take, this is my body." Then he took a cup and having given thanks he gave this to his friends and they all drank from it. Then he said to them:

> This is my blood of the covenant, which is poured out for many.
> Truly, I say to you, I shall not drink again of the fruit of the vine
> until that day when I drink it new in the kingdom of God.
>
> (Mark 14:24-25)

Jesus' words and his strange behavior in reversing roles between master and servant must have deeply troubled those with him that night. The tiny flickering lamps seemed less effective against the night as deep gloom settled upon the room. Jesus, obviously struggling with his emotions, spoke words which sent a chill to the heart of each man: "Truly, truly, I say to you, one of you will betray me." It was as though a wholly unexpected lightning bolt had with suddenness crashed into their midst. These men, who had been together for three years and who had shared so much, might under other conditions have reacted differently. But now on this night in this place with such forebodings at every hand, accusing glances flashed around the room.

At last Peter motioned to the person nearest Jesus. Quietly Jesus was asked, "Lord, who is it?" "It is he to whom I shall give this morsel when I have dipped it," replied Jesus. When he had dipped the food in wine he passed it to Judas Iscariot, saying, "What you are going to do, do quickly." For some reason the others missed the signal, or else it was completely unthinkable that Judas, the only one of them to hold a more or less official position (he was treasurer of the group), would betray Jesus. Since Judas normally handled the affairs of the group, Jesus was doubtless telling him to get on with the arrangements he had made for the rest of Passover. And Judas went out into the night.

After Judas left, Jesus talked for a long time with his friends teaching them many things, explaining that he must go away in order that the will of God be fulfilled. He promised them that God would send them the Com-

Chalice of Antioch shows Christ and apostles. It dates from fourth or fifth century A.D.

212

forter, the very Spirit of God who would draw near to them and guide them. He also promised that he would come again and take them to his Father's house where he was going to prepare a place for them. And he gave them the only commandment that he was to give those who followed him:

> A new commandment I give to you, that you love one another; even as I have loved you, that you also love one another. By this all men will know that you are my disciples, if you have love for one another.

(John 13:34-35)

In a very troubled conversation one after another of Jesus' disciples tried to fathom what was being said to them. It was all so difficult; this talk of going away. Where was he going? Why could they not come? The webs in his mind drawing slightly aside, Peter sensed that Jesus was talking about his own death. "Lord," this impetuous fisherman blurted out, "why cannot I follow you now? I will lay down my life for you." Jesus' reply was hardly what Peter or any of the others expected: "Will you lay down your life for me? Truly, truly, I say to you, the cock will not crow, till you have denied me three times."

Sometime later, after more difficult dialogue and a multitude of misunderstandings, the meal was ended in the traditional Jewish manner. They sang a hymn and went out. As the tiny, troubled band made its way over the rough cobbles of the narrow streets they were puzzled and worried. Now they were descending into the Kidron Valley and in a few minutes would be on the slope of the Mount of Olives. There, near the Garden of Gethsemane, they would take a much-needed night's rest. Sleep would help.

When they reached the spot Jesus took three of his closest friends and moved deeper into the garden. Then he drew apart from them, asking only that they watch while he prayed. In agony Jesus saw clearly the fate which was before him. "Abba, Father," he prayed, "all things are possible to thee; remove this cup from me; yet not what I will, but what thou wilt."

Jesus rose and came to his three disciples only to find them fast asleep. "Could you not watch with me one hour," he asked sadly of the still figures. And once more he withdrew to pray, saying the same thing about the terrible cup and his willingness to drink it. Again he came to the sleeping men, again returning to prayer. The third time he waked them, pointing out that Judas was coming. With a kiss and the words "Hail, master," Judas identified Jesus to the Temple police who accompanied him. And although some of his disciples wished to resist and made a short-lived abortive attempt to do so, Jesus went willingly.

The course of events which now ensued is not entirely clear. That there was some sort of hearing before a fairly large group of religious authorities seems certain. Whether there was also a private hearing before Annas, the father-in-law of the high priest and the real power behind the throne, is less sure. Not all of the Sanhedrin, the politico-religious ruling body, was in agreement with this course of action, as the stories of Nicodemus and Joseph of Arimathea make clear. Likely this was a Sadducean business, although some Pharisees may well have been involved. In any event, Jesus was now in the hands of his bitterest enemies. They had taken a desperate gamble seizing him and were now resolved to pursue the high stakes to the end. They had, moreover, been able to secure the support if not the enthusiasm of Pilate, the Roman governor. Had they not cooperated with him when he wanted to use

Olive tree in the Garden of Gethsemane.

Temple funds to build an aqueduct for Jerusalem? He owed them a few favors. It was time to collect.

In the courtyard of the house of the high priest, to which Jesus had been taken, a number of people were around a fire warming themselves against the chill of the Judean night. One of these was Peter. His accent gave him away as a Galilean. One of the housemaids asked if he were not a follower of Jesus. Three times he denied it. And from the Fortress Antonia the first trumpet call of the Roman morning — "Cockcrow" — sounded. The Romans, as was their habit, were ready for business at dawn.

Pilate's role in Jesus' death is much debated. Was he in on it from the beginning or was he duped? Was it some sort of political trade-off? Likely it was something of the latter. Roman governors throughout the empire cared little for local religious squabbles and made it a point to stay out of them. It is hardly likely that Pilate would have insinuated himself into this one. Nor would he have entertained a case against Jesus on a religious charge. In the hearing before the religious authorities Jesus was condemned for blasphemy. A Roman official would have been unconcerned with such things. So when Jesus is brought to Pilate he is cited on a political charge: he wants to make himself a king. To this charge Pilate will listen, and on this matter he will question this strange fellow from Galilee. Three times—as was necessary in a Roman provincial trial involving a capital crime—Pilate puts the question to Jesus: "Do you realize what you are charged with?" Three times Jesus makes no defense. Pilate then offers to extend clemency to Jesus, but the crowd demands instead the release of Barabbas, a man imprisoned on a charge of insurrection and murder. Pilate reluctantly orders Jesus to be beaten and crucified. So horrible was crucifixion that the Romans considered it an act of mercy to scourge a person, thus to weaken him and perhaps to bring on death all the more quickly. During the night, however, while Jesus was being held prisoner, he had already been abused by both police and soldiers. They had spit on his face, given him a crown of thorns and a mock royal robe and struck him, laughing and saying, "Hail, King!"

Now, about eight in the morning, a piteous procession made its painful, bleeding way through the streets of Jerusalem. Pilgrims, come to this holy place in a joyous spirit, stood appalled. Women of Jerusalem wept as the sorrowful spectacle passed. But Jesus, faltering under his cross, paused and told the women to weep for themselves and for their children. Terrible days were coming, he said, days in which people would cry out for the mountains to fall on them and the hills to cover them.

Finally, Jesus, with the help of a man from the crowd, perhaps one of the pilgrims, struggled his way out of the northwest gate of Jerusalem, onto the road that leads toward Emmaus. There, just outside the city wall, there was a small hill, *Golgotha*, "the place of the skull." Here, between two criminals who had come through the streets with him, Jesus was crucified.

One of the more remarkable things about the Gospels is the restraint with which they describe the crucifixion of Jesus. No appeal is made to popular passion. It was left for later generations of Christians to emphasize his suffering. For those in Roman times the mere mention of crucifixion conjured up all of the tortures man can inflict upon man: physical pain, impotence, degradation. Flies swarming in the wounds earlier opened by the whip. Forced immobility, whether the victim was tied or nailed to the cross. Nakedness, thirst, the sense of being a living body, whose vital force is being distilled drop by drop, and the insults and jeers of those who take a sickening

"The pavement" of the Fortress Antonia was perhaps the site of Jesus' trial before Pilate.

pleasure at the suffering of others; these are but a few things suggested in the first century by the image of the cross. It is extraordinary that for Christians this cross, this symbol of all the worst tortures combined into one, should become a symbol of joy and hope and life itself.

By nine in the morning Jesus hung from a Roman cross, nails piercing his hands and feet. It was not unusual for victims to take two or three days to die when crucified. Some were known to have gone raving mad and to have torn themselves loose, only to die writhing at the foot of their crosses. Throughout the morning and into the afternoon Jesus cried out several times from his cross. He spoke to one of the criminals being executed with him. He showed concern for his mother, who was present and whose sorrow at this moment can hardly be imagined. He cried out in anguish. He thirsted and was given vinegar and herbs which were used in these situations. At three in the afternoon — just when the high priest was preparing the Passover sacrifice in the Temple — Jesus cried out with a loud voice and died.

It was normal Roman practice to leave bodies of crucified criminals to rot as a warning to others. The crime for which they had been killed was posted above their heads. Anyone coming along the road would have unmistakable indication of how the Romans felt about certain matters. But Jesus' body was not left on the cross. The religious authorities asked that his and those of the two others be removed before sundown so as not to defile the High Holy Day. Orders were given. The soldiers went up to break the legs of the men so that death would come quickly. But when they came to Jesus he seemed to be dead already. Just to be sure, one of the soldiers took his spear and slammed it into Jesus' side. He was dead all right. Who was going to take him down and what were they going to do with his body? Sundown was fast approaching. The soldiers did not intend to do everything. This was unpleasant duty anyway, and the extra pay was hardly worth considering. They got the belongings of the criminals. And this man from Galilee had only a cloak. It was seamless. No use tearing it up and dividing. The men decided to cast lots to see who got it.

Some of Jesus' friends, along with his mother, lovingly took down his body. Among them was Joseph of Arimathea, a member of the Sanhedrin who had not agreed in the moves against Jesus, to whom Pilate had given permission to take the body of Jesus and dispose of it. He, with the others, took the body, wrapping it in a linen shroud. They laid it in a rock-cut tomb which had never been used before. Mary Magdalene was among them and they intended to prepare the tomb for the burial. But, as the day was near an end and sundown signaled the beginning of the Sabbath of Passover, they did not treat the body with spices and ointments as was the custom of the day. They would return when Passover was over and do that.

At the very first light of dawn on Sunday, the first day of the week, Passover being past, Mary Magdalene and some of the other women came to the tomb where Jesus had been laid. They wondered whom they would get to roll away the round stone that blocked the door. But when they got to the tomb the stone was rolled back. Entering they discovered the body was gone! They did not know what to make of this. Two angels then appeared to them, saying:

> Why do you seek the living among the dead? Remember how he told you, while he was still in Galilee, that the Son of man must be delivered into the hands of sinful men, and be crucified, and on the third day rise.

(Luke 24:5-7)

The Garden Tomb, a second-century A.D. rock-cut tomb of the type in which Jesus was buried.

Queen Helena's tomb, Jerusalem, has rolling stone closure similar to that mentioned in burial of Jesus.

Early Christian figure with orb and
scepter, from fifth century A.D. Egypt.
As is common in Coptic art the symbolism
is mixed. The figure may be an archangel.

16 THE FIRST CENTURY AS CHRISTIAN HISTORY

He is risen! The incredible message quickly spread among Jesus' disheartened friends. Their hopes, dreams and deepest beliefs so recently and cruelly shattered began to revive. Could it be possible that, as he had said he would, he had risen on the third day? Nothing is more certain than that the followers of Jesus believed that after being crucified, dead and buried he did indeed rise on the third day and in the course of the next few weeks appeared to numerous people. The New Testament reports that on the very day of the resurrection Jesus appeared no less than five times to different individuals or groups (Matthew 28:8-10; Luke 24:34; 1 Corinthians 15:5; John 20:11-18, 19-23; Mark 16:12-13, 14-18). A week later he appeared to the eleven apostles while they were securely behind the doors of a room (John 20:26-29). Still later by the Sea of Galilee he appeared to a number of men, including four of the apostles (John 21:1-23), and again to five hundred people at once (1 Corinthians 15:6). First Corinthians 15:7 also says that the risen Jesus appeared to James, his brother. Luke 24:50-52 and Mark 16:19 (see also Acts 1:3-9) tell of Jesus being with the apostles in Jerusalem on the day of his ascension.

There are many difficulties associated with the resurrection narratives of the New Testament, not the least the fact that there are two focal points for the appearances: Jerusalem and Galilee. Yet, for all the problems in any attempt to reconstruct the course of events in those first extraordinary days of the Christian movement there are few, if any, who will deny that belief in the resurrection galvanized the scattered and shattered followers of Jesus. From the moment news reached them on the first Easter their strength began to revive, vastly greater than ever before, and they went forth to proclaim that God had vindicated Jesus. In his life, words and in the greatest of his deeds, the overcoming of death, he had ushered in a new age. The simple fishermen of Galilee who had faithfully followed Jesus along the dusty roads of Palestine, half understanding what he did and said, did not now claim to understand fully all that had been done nor all of what was being said. Yet with their imperfect knowledge they boldly challenged the religious authorities in Jerusalem, authorities who saw them as uneducated, common men. When commanded by the learned and powerful men of the council to cease their preaching, they replied with clear conviction and not a little impertinence: "Whether it is right in the sight of God to listen to you rather than to God, you must judge; for we cannot but speak of what we have seen and heard" (Acts 4:19-20). If nothing else is clear from those earliest days of Christianity, the transformation wrought in these followers of Jesus is unmistakable. He that was dead is alive, they said, and the power that is in him is in us. First Corinthians 15:3-4, which Paul says was handed down to him from earlier tradition, sounds very much like a creed: ". . . that Christ died for our sins in accordance with the scriptures, that he was buried, that he was raised on the third day in accordance with the scriptures . . ." This is the unshakable conviction on which the Church rests, and it is the beginning of the history of the Christian community.

The small twelfth-century crusader chapel on the Mount of Olives stands at the traditional site of the Ascension.

"Church" in this context may be misleading. That earliest group in Jerusalem did not consider themselves to be something separate from the larger body of Judaism. On the contrary, they saw themselves as "the New Israel"; as the fulfillment of the promises of God given through the prophets of old. From the point of view of historical study they were sectarians, and like all sectarians they saw themselves as the true community, the possessors of the right understanding, the children of the promise. The early Christians remained faithful to worship in the Temple and to services in the synagogues. They would not have understood themselves as other than good Jews, and it was only with great rending that many of these people came to give up the laws of ritual purity for what they saw as a greater necessity, the necessity of preaching the gospel to all men.

Yet it would be wrong to think that the early Christian community in Jerusalem was a casual affair. Acts 1:15 speaks of Peter standing up "in the midst of the brethren," and 1 Thessalonians 1:1 (probably the earliest of the New Testament documents in extant form) uses the term *ecclesia*, "church." Both references are to some sort of recognized community. Furthermore, from the very beginning there is acknowledged authority (Acts 1:25). There is also a sense of common worship as these people as a group devote themselves to prayer and have common meals (Acts 2:42, 46). These things are taking place in their homes, for their houses of worship are the Temple and the synagogues.

During this time these people are called "the company of those who believed" (Acts 4:32) or more simply "the Way" (Acts 9:2). It was not until later, in Antioch, that the name Christian came to be associated with this group (Acts 11:26).

From the very first the Christian community began to spread remarkably, both numerically and geographically. Some fifty days after the resurrection at the Feast of Pentecost there was a large response to a sermon by Peter, and many were added to the company of believers. Of this number some were from the Diaspora, and it may have been this very early impetus which caused Christianity to move out into the larger Roman world. By the time Paul began his missionary journeys the new faith was already established in many of the major centers of the empire, including Rome. But for a while the church in Jerusalem was the center of Christian activity and the nucleus from which radiated a vibrant and appealing message.

But almost from the very first there was present a considerable tension within the fellowship. There was among these people an overwhelming compulsion to give away, as it were, what they confessed they had received as a free gift. They were to the last degree a missionizing group. The question naturally arose: to whom are we to go and under what conditions, if any, are they to be admitted to our fellowship? The obvious answer for a sectarian Jewish group would seem to be that they would go to the rest of Israel, proclaiming the good news that the Messiah had come. This answer was an important factor in the early church. Yet somehow those people had the gnawing feeling that it was not enough. We have already seen that the touchstone of this community was belief in the resurrection of Jesus of Nazareth, an unmerited action by God which had opened up new possibilities for a faith relationship with God himself. So the question kept presenting itself: is it also necessary to fulfill the ritual laws of Judaism including circumcision of converts and their adherence to purity laws? Is this required before one can enter into the power of the resurrection? Today the answer may seem clear to

Christians, but it was by no means an easy matter for those people, who were sectarian Jews faithful to the Temple. They were deeply involved in the synagogues and devoted to the traditions of their fathers, without which they could not understand Jesus, whom they said was the Christ, the Messiah promised by priest and prophet of old.

The issue simmered unresolved and various practices proliferated as the new faith spread beyond the confines of Jerusalem, beyond the boundaries of Palestine, across seas and into scores of regions and hundreds of cities, towns and villages. It would be brought to a head by a growing community in Antioch, which would come to rival and then to surpass Jerusalem, and by an ambitious young Diaspora Pharisee named Saul.

Saul of Tarsus (later known as Paul) was an extremely gifted person. Reared in a famous university town, capital of the Roman province of Cilicia, he apparently benefited greatly from the best of both Greek and Jewish education. He could, moreover, speak Aramaic, the tongue of Judea, with fluency. His family were Roman citizens and they may well have possessed wealth, although this cannot be established for certain. There is no doubt that he early showed himself an exceptional student, for he was sent to Jerusalem to study and was there accepted as a student by Gamaliel, one of the greatest of all the rabbis. Yet Gamaliel's common sense and balanced liberality did not take seed in his brilliant student's mind and heart. Saul was ambitious, and he was zealous for the religion of his fathers. He first appears in the New Testament as a willing witness to the murder of Stephen, who was dragged out of a synagogue and stoned to death by an angry mob when he proclaimed that Jesus of Nazareth whom they had killed was the Messiah (Acts 6:8-8:1). This was the spark for a general persecution of Christians in Jerusalem and many fled the city. Saul, ever watchful for the main chance, saw an opportunity to advance his own cause. An outspoken extremist, he now went to the high priest and received from him letters of authority to bring from Damascus all "belonging to the Way." They were to be dragged back to Jerusalem for trial.

So Saul set off on the road to Damascus. His exact route is not known, but by whatever way he went he was haunted by Biblical memories. They lay all about him and whispered to him from the soil of the great deeds God had done. Here a memory of Abraham, there of Jacob. Here Deborah strove against mighty odds in the name of her God and prevailed. And here Saul, his own namesake, fell in battle. And here Joseph was sold out of a pit to passing merchants. And here Joshua . . . And here . . . What thoughts were going through Saul's mind? The slow pace, the heat, time to think. Was God silent now? Where now were those to do his will as had his servants of old? What was it that Stephen had said as the stones rained down on him? "Lord, do not hold this sin against them." What kind of man would die like that? What else was it that he had said? "Lord Jesus, receive my spirit." What was going on here? ". . .hold not this sin against them."

The roads leading to Damascus from the south come together on the plateau above the Syrian (Golan) Heights. And it was somewhere along here that Saul came to the turning point of his life. Suddenly there was a great light; he and his companions saw it, and there was a voice intelligible only to Saul. "Saul, Saul," it called out, "why do you persecute me?" "Who are you, Lord?" "I am Jesus, whom you are persecuting," said the voice to the astonished zealot, "but rise and enter the city, and you will be told what you are to do" (Acts 9:5-6). Saul rose from the ground, groping about. He was blind.

The Theodotus inscription from a Jerusalem synagogue. This much-debated inscription is thought by some to refer to "the synagogue of the Freedmen" (Acts 6:9).

Lion Gate in Jerusalem's east wall. Medieval Christian tradition locates the martyrdom of Stephen (Acts 7: 58-60) nearby.

219

Chapel of St. Paul, Damascus. This is the traditional site for Paul's escape from the city as told in Acts 9:25.

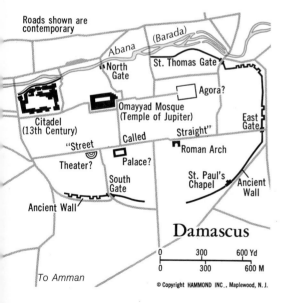

Roads shown are contemporary

Abana (Barada)
North Gate
St. Thomas Gate
Agora?
Omayyad Mosque (Temple of Jupiter)
Citadel (13th Century)
Called
Straight"
East Gate
"Street
Theater?
Palace?
Roman Arch
South Gate
St. Paul's Chapel
Ancient Wall
Ancient Wall
To Amman

Damascus

0   300   600 Yd
0   300   600 M

© Copyright HAMMOND INC., Maplewood, N.J.

Tenderly his friends took him by the hand and led him into Damascus, to which he had come with a writ to lay hands upon the friends of Jesus. He was taken to the house of a man named Judas on a street called Straight. There in his darkness he devoted himself ceaselessly to prayer, disdaining food and drink. On the third day a follower of Jesus, Ananias, came not without fear to Saul, laying his hands on him and saying, "Brother Saul, the Lord Jesus who appeared to you on the road by which you came, has sent me that you may regain your sight and be filled with the Holy Spirit" (Acts 9:17). And Saul saw again. There and then he was baptized. And he took food and was refreshed.

The following days found him among those whom he had come to destroy. Indeed, he became their chief advocate in the synagogue, where he boldly proclaimed that Jesus was the Son of God. At length there was a plot against Saul's life by the Jews of Damascus, who with cause considered him a traitor and not the champion that they had expected. By day and by night the gates of the city were watched lest Saul slip away to safety. But he did escape by being lowered over the wall in a basket.

It was now, according to some reconstructions of Saul's life, that he withdrew into Arabia to meditate upon the momentous events of recent days, to contemplate the past and plan his future course of action. He decided that he must go back to Jerusalem to see the leaders of the Christian community and to gain from them their understanding of the meaning of the life of Jesus. He also wanted to share with them his own experience with the resurrected Christ and to hear more about theirs. So he returned to Jerusalem and sought to join the Christian group there. They were justifiably wary and would have nothing to do with him. Then Barnabas, a man of infinite good sense and compassion, always possessed of the right word of conciliation, brought Saul into the fellowship. So this man, newly converted to the faith he had sworn to exterminate, went about in Jerusalem disputing with his former rabbinic colleagues and friends. Once more there was a plot to kill him, and when his Christian friends discovered it they hurried him off to Caesarea where he took ship for his native city of Tarsus.

Meanwhile the church in Jerusalem prospered, and in Samaria and Galilee as well there were many converts. It was here that the matter of the necessity of the Law and the sufficiency of the Sacrifice of Jesus on the cross attained a new urgency. A large number of Roman and Greek settlers in the land had joined themselves loosely to synagogues and "God-fearers," honoring the ethical teachings but rejecting full membership. In practical terms it was a matter of whether these Gentile converts could be fully admitted to the fellowship if they refused circumcision, the purity and dietary laws and the sacrificial requirements of the Temple. The crisis came at Caesarea and involved Peter, who was apparently staying in Joppa and preaching in towns along the coast. Cornelius, a devoted God-fearer, sent to Joppa for Peter.

About noon the next day, as Cornelius' servants were approaching, Peter went up on the roof of the house of Simon the Tanner to pray and there had a vision. Peter was deeply troubled by the matter of admitting unclean persons into the fellowship and seemingly could agree to no such thing without violating his conscience. But in his vision he saw something like a great sheet descending from heaven and on it were all kinds of animals, reptiles and birds. He was commanded to eat but recoiled, protesting that it was unclean and he strictly observed the laws of purity. "What God has cleansed,

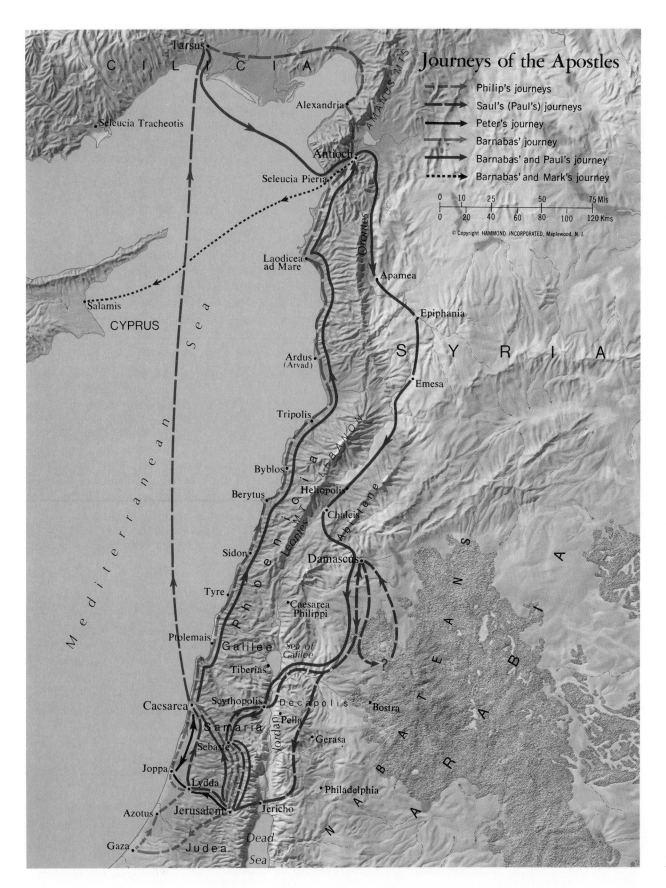

Journeys of the Apostles

- – – – Philip's journeys
- — — Saul's (Paul's) journeys
- —→ Peter's journey
- —→ Barnabas' journey
- —→ Barnabas' and Paul's journey
- ······ Barnabas' and Mark's journey

```
0   10    25         50        75 Mls
0   20   40   60   80   100   120 Kms
```

© Copyright HAMMOND INCORPORATED, Maplewood, N.J.

CILICIA

Tarsus

Seleucia Tracheotis

Alexandria

AMANUS MTS.

Antioch

Seleucia Pieria

Laodicea ad Mare

Apamea

Orontes

Epiphania

SYRIA

Salamis

CYPRUS

Mediterranean Sea

Ardus (Arvad)

Emesa

Tripolis

LEBANON

Byblos

Heliopolis

Berytus

Leontes

Chalcis

Abilene

Sidon

Damascus

Tyre

Caesarea Philippi

Ptolemais

Galilee

Sea of Galilee

Tiberias

Caesarea

Scythopolis

Decapolis

Bostra

Jordan

Pella

Samaria

Sebaste

Gerasa

N A B A T E A N S

A R A B I A

Joppa

Lydda

Philadelphia

Azotus

Jerusalem

Jericho

Gaza

Judea

Dead Sea

221

you must not call common," said the voice. Three times this happened—a not ungentle reminder of the three times he had denied Jesus.

As Peter pondered what this vision meant the emissaries from Cornelius came to the door of the house asking for him. They made their mission known, and the next day Peter and some other Christians from Joppa accompanied them to Caesarea. At that splendid city, surrounded by every possible reminder of Greco-Roman life, the deeply pious Roman officer poured out his heart to the fisherman from Galilee. In the end Cornelius and others with him were baptized upon Peter's order "in the name of Jesus Christ." Thus the Christian tradition ascribes to Peter the conversion of the first Gentile. But wide acceptance of Gentile converts was not immediate, and in the future Peter himself would waver on the issue.

Peter, returned to Jerusalem, was called upon to justify his actions at Caesarea. In Antioch, meanwhile, a number of believers who had been scattered by the persecution following the death of Stephen had formed a virile and growing fellowship. Among the converts were a large number of Gentiles. When this news reached the ears of those in the Jerusalem church there was great concern over the admission of Gentiles who did not strictly observe all things required of a convert to Judaism. Barnabas was sent to investigate.

Barnabas not only approved of what he found in the church at Antioch but, remembering the gifted and energetic young rabbi from Tarsus whom he had earlier brought into the fellowship at Jerusalem, he took ship for Asia Minor to find Saul and came to the ancient city of Tarsus. As early as 2300 B.C. Tarsus was involved in trade with Troy. Tarsus was destroyed by both Hittites and the Sea Peoples and was resettled by Mycenean Greeks, probably early in the Iron Age; from that time on it held a position of importance. Situated at the southern end of the Cilician Gates, that narrow passage that knifes its way through the Taurus Mountains and forms a vital link in the east-west highway crossing Asia Minor, Tarsus was once a part of the Seleucid Empire. Later it became a pawn in the Roman civil war, suffering at the hands of both factions until Antony placed it firmly on the imperial side. Now in that city Barnabas sought out Saul, intent upon taking him back to Antioch to aid in the rapidly expanding work.

When they reached Antioch they heard of a famine which gripped Judea. The church in Antioch wished to send relief to the brethren in Jerusalem; Barnabas and Saul were asked to take relief funds. About this time other terrible events befell the church in Jerusalem. Herod Agrippa, made king of Judea by the Emperor Claudius in A.D. 41, fell with murderous intent upon the church during Passover. The year was perhaps 44. James, the brother of John, was killed. Peter was imprisoned, only miraculously to escape (Acts 12: 3-17). Agrippa's persecution resulted in the further scattering of Jerusalem's Christian community. When Barnabas and Saul returned to Antioch they took with them one of the young men from Jerusalem, John Mark.

In the vast panorama of the history of religions no faith has spread so far so fast as did Christianity with the exception of Islam, but that was spread by the sharp edge of the sword. By the end of the first century Christianity may well have been known in all parts of the Roman Empire and beyond. In India today the Christian church is known as the *Mar Toma* church, "the church of Saint Thomas," preserving a tradition that its founder was none other than the Apostle Thomas, "Doubting Thomas." Acts 8:26-40 contains the story of the conversion of the Ethiopian eunuch by Philip from whom the Coptic Church of Africa traces its origins.

The Taurus Mountains and the Cilician Gates. A natural pass in the mountain wall widened by man made Tarsus, Paul's birthplace, an important city.

The story of the early church as told in the Acts of the Apostles comes quite soon to focus exclusively upon the work of Paul. Paul was not the first nor the only Christian missionary, nor was he always successful. Of the five great cities of the Roman Empire that he visited on his missionary journeys, he succeeded in establishing a church in only one—Ephesus—and to all intents and purposes he was laughed out of Athens. Nonetheless Paul was a zealous missionary and of prime importance in the spread of early Christianity. To follow the early church one must follow Paul.

On his return from Jerusalem Saul had joined the flourishing Antioch church, which was becoming more and more cosmopolitan and outward-looking. Perhaps it was sometime around the year 47 when the Antioch church commissioned Barnabas, Saul and Mark to undertake a missionary journey to Cyprus, Barnabas' home. It was probably from Seleucia Pieria, the port of Antioch and one of the finest harbors on the coast, that the three took ship. After a relatively short sea voyage they landed at Salamis, a shallow but important harbor on the east side of the island. Here, in a pattern which was to become familiar, Saul preached in the synagogue (Acts 13:5). The three crossed the island, going all the way to the southwestern coast to Paphos, where in Roman days the governor had his residence. Here also Saul came into conflict, apparently a bitter conflict, with someone named Bar-Jesus, described in Acts 13:6 as a "false Jewish prophet." Bar-Jesus was momentarily blinded. The Roman governor, impressed, gave Saul a full hearing. It is from this point on that Saul came to be known by his Roman name, Paul.

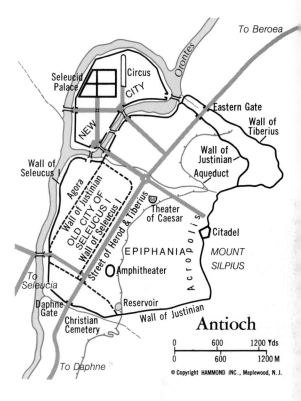

Antioch

No further Cypriot activity is recorded. Soon the three missionaries found themselves on the low-lying littoral of Pamphylia, the southern coast of Asia Minor. They were in Perga, an ancient city with splendid monuments and a central thoroughfare ninety feet wide. They pushed on as quickly as possible, perhaps to escape the stifling heat of summer on the low plain and made their way up into the cooler highlands, ninety miles northward to Pisidian Antioch. "They," however, is now only Paul and Barnabas. At Perga John Mark decided to return to Jerusalem. Why he left is not known and has long been the subject of speculation. Some think he became ill. But it seems more likely that Paul himself became ill in Perga. If so, perhaps it was decided that Barnabas would take him into the highlands to recover, and since the work seemed to be momentarily over Mark left. John Mark may have wished to dissociate himself from this work among the Gentiles of which he increasingly disapproved. Perhaps he and Paul had a serious argument over some other matter. It does seem that the Perga incident resulted in bitterness between Paul and Mark. Later, when Barnabas suggested another missionary journey with John Mark, Paul refused to go.

So Paul and Barnabas found themselves alone in Pisidian Antioch, a brilliant Roman colony whose inhabitants held Italian citizenship. Emperor Augustus had showered monumental buildings upon the site, and more recently it had found favor with Tiberius. It was a truly Hellenized environment, not massive, but grand. It had, moreover, a large Jewish population. Paul made straight for the synagogue, exhorting his fellow Jews to embrace his new faith by acknowledging Jesus as the long-awaited Messiah (Acts 13: 16-41). His appeal was rejected and he himself personally rebuffed. Now, Paul with the help of Barnabas turned his efforts to the non-Jewish citizens of this Greco-Roman town. There was limited success, then greater success. Then some of the stricter adherents of the synagogue, deeply hostile toward Paul and his companion, caused a riot and drove them from the city.

223

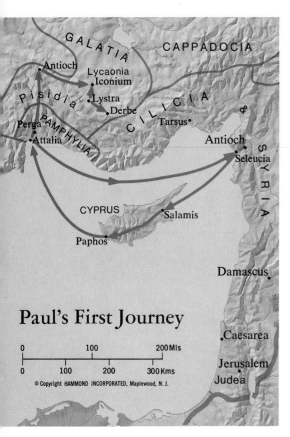

Paul's First Journey

```
0          100        200 Mls
0     100     200     300 Kms
© Copyright HAMMOND INCORPORATED, Maplewood, N. J.
```

Attalia (modern Antalya) was the port from which Paul and Barnabas sailed at the end of their first missionary journey.

Seventy-five miles and many days later the two entered Iconium, capital of Lycaonia. They had crossed fertile fields interlaced by swift streams and doubtless fed themselves on the abundant fruits and rich produce of the area. At Iconium they found themselves in a city whose recent history somewhat paralleled that of Antioch but which had not had royal favor lavished on it. There was also a sizable Jewish population and a synagogue. Events repeated themselves with a slight twist. Within the synagogue fellowship there was a positive response to Paul's message, mostly from God-fearers but also from some Jews. There was a division, then hostility, then an attempt on the lives of the two visitors. Once more they fled but not before a church had been planted in the verdant Lycaonian plain.

Fleeing southeast along the road that ran toward Lystra and Derbe, the two found themselves in new surroundings. The countryside was harsh and its inhabitants rustic and for the most part ignorant people virtually untouched by the Hellenistic and Roman sophistication in such evidence at Antioch and Iconium. Even the language of the people was not the usual Koine Greek. The local dialect was tenacious, perhaps indicating a stubborn resistance by these people to the general tenor of Greco-Roman life. Here Paul and Barnabas encountered something else they had never seen before. At Lystra, where they caused a cripple to walk, they found themselves surrounded by a crowd bowing down and worshiping them as Hermes and Zeus. The local priests wished to sacrifice oxen in their honor. This was at least different from the previous treatment, but in many ways it was worse. How could they convince these people that the unseen God had sent his Son for their salvation while the people proclaimed them as gods? With difficulty Paul prevented the sacrifices being made and was able to work in a calm atmosphere for some time. Eventually, however, word of these activities reached opponents in Antioch and Iconium and Paul would again find himself an object of controversy. A more immediate problem arose in Lystra where he was actually taken by some of the people under the urging of his enemies, beaten, stoned and left for dead on the outskirts of the city. Barnabas and other Christians came to him and gently carried him back into the town. When Paul had recovered sufficient strength on the next day, they went on to Derbe. Of the work of Paul in Derbe we are told only that he preached, made converts and left (Acts 14:21).

It would seem that the effective work of the First Missionary Journey was over. The apostles were at the southeastern boundary of the province and they decided to retrace their steps. At Attalia, the port near Perga, Paul and Barnabas found a ship bound for Seleucia Pieria. One can only wonder what thoughts went through Paul's mind as the blue waters of the Mediterranean turned white under the ship's bow. The highlands of southern Asia Minor had seen momentous things in the past months, and they had given much of value and of harm to this man. Some think that Paul may have contracted malaria for the first time in Perga. At any rate, the bruises and cuts of the Lystrian stones remained. The synagogues had been open to him, but his words had found few open ears and fewer willing hearts. Animosity plagued him. Was this the pattern of the future? How could one measure success in these ventures? At least he had one extraordinary thing to report to the church at Antioch: many Gentiles had received the word gladly and had formed churches. The gospel had leapt across human barriers.

At Antioch, however, there was trouble. Peter, ever vacillating on the issue of Gentiles in the fellowship, first sided with Paul and then, when some people from Jerusalem appeared, withdrew himself from table fellowship with Gentiles in the church at Antioch. Paul confronted Peter and apparently carried the day. But all was not over. The church in Jerusalem sent a rebuke to Antioch and along with it a demand: no Gentiles were to be admitted to the church unless they had fully complied with the requirements of conversion to Judaism, including adherence to the ritual law, circumcision and the dietary regulations. Clearly something had to be worked out.

A conference was held in Jerusalem. The year seems to have been A.D. 49. Paul and Barnabas went with others from Antioch and with joy reported the results of their missionary journey. But the joy was not shared. How dare they admit impure Gentiles! Both sides held firm. Stalemate. Then, James, leader of the Jerusalem church, suggested a compromise. Gentiles who were to be admitted to the church must agree to abstain from meat which had been offered to idols. They were to refrain from unchastity and they must agree not to eat meat of animals which had been strangled. Blood also must not be eaten. Apart from this the church at Antioch was free to admit Gentiles on any other terms it wished. These were minor concessions for Paul and his people, and word of the compromise was received with rejoicing in Antioch. Henceforth, for all practical purposes Antioch and Jerusalem would follow diverging paths, with the faithful orthodox in Jerusalem slipping ever further away from burgeoning and increasingly Gentile Christianity.

When they had been back in Antioch for some time Barnabas suggested to Paul that they undertake another missionary journey. Barnabas proposed, moreover, that they take John Mark with them again, but Paul would have none of it, citing the failure of the young man to complete their previous journey. Nevertheless, Barnabas insisted that Mark be given a second chance, even if it meant that he and Paul had to follow separate paths. And this is what they did. Barnabas and Mark returned to Cyprus, while Paul in the company of Silas set out along the main road toward Tarsus (Acts 15:36-41).

As far as we know Paul did not tarry long if at all in his hometown, but passed with haste through the Cilician Gates, coming as quickly as possible to Derbe and Lystra to bring news of the council's decision. At Lystra he met a young man, son of a Greek father and a Jewish mother. The man's name was Timothy. His mother, Eunice, and his grandmother, Lois, had instructed Timothy carefully in the new faith. Yet he had never been circumcised and this Paul now caused him to do. It was apparently a desire to avoid giving offense to the "Judaizers," his more strict Jewish-Christian opponents, that prompted Paul to see that his half-Jewish new traveling companion was acceptable to the more orthodox party.

The missionaries, now three in number—Paul, Silas and Timothy—followed the main Roman road westward. Almost exactly one hundred years earlier Cicero, on his way to become governor in Tarsus, had traveled the route in the opposite direction. Judging from Cicero's information it was slow going, requiring almost a month from Iconium to Tarsus. We may safely assume that Paul's trip took at least two months before he reached Troas, perhaps as many as three. The normally slow pace of walking was compounded by the heat and the dust. More than once Atticus, Cicero's financial advisor, complained of the "hot and dusty" roads. But Atticus at least had a wagon in which to ride and tells us that on a good day he could make twenty-five miles. All was not choking clouds of dust however. The scenery could change within a few miles from near desert to cultivated fields, lofty mountain peaks, forests and swift streams.

Paul traveled by foot through Asia Minor over roads traveled by Cicero, one hundred years earlier.

So Paul and his friends pressed forward, going, as we are told in the Book of Acts, "on their way through the cities." Unfortunately, we are not told which cities. Very likely they went to Iconium and also to Pisidian Antioch. But where else? We do not know. At some point they left the main road to Ephesus and went north, intending to enter Bithynia, the region along the southern coast of the Black Sea. They turned back, however, when "the spirit of Jesus did not allow them" to enter this new area of work (Acts 16:7). In northern Asia Minor they went west once more, west from Dorylaeum toward Troas and a fateful decision.

Troas, on the Aegean coast only ten miles south of fabled Troy, had earlier received attention from both Julius Caesar and Augustus, each considering, as Constantine was later to do, that Troas might make an ideal site to replace Rome as capital of the empire. Although the visible ruins today are mostly from a time after Paul, the six-mile circuit of the more ancient walls is still there to be seen. And Strabo speaks of it as a renowned city. In Paul's day it was no doubt splendid in every sense of the word. To this place Paul now came, and he was to return twice more. Here in Troas Paul met a Greek, by tradition a physician who was to become one of the more important historian-theologians of early Christianity, writing not only an account of the story so far rehearsed here, but also one of the Four Gospels. His name was Luke. It was also in Troas that Paul had a night vision in which a Macedonian appealed to him saying, "Come over to Macedonia and help us" (Acts 16:9).

Paul and his three friends left Asia Minor, crossing to Europe and landing at Neapolis after a stop at Samothrace. Neapolis, one of the many "new towns" of the Romans was an important port. Before the battle of Philippi (42 B.C.) Brutus and Cassius had sheltered their triremes here. Neapolis stood at the eastern end of the *Via Egnatia,* the Egnatian Way, the major highway which joined the Roman East with the home provinces. From Neapolis this road ran across northern Greece to Dyrrhachium and Apollonia, ports on the Adriatic just across from southern Italy. A branch of the Egnatian Way turned north from the Adriatic ports through what is today Albania and Yugoslavia, reaching the northern end of the Adriatic where it joined three other Roman roads. It was one of the longest and most important of the Roman roads and if again we may depend upon Cicero's correspondence, provided means of swift movement between the two halves of the empire.

Inland along the Egnatian Way the road passes through rugged landscape. But in a few hours Paul and his companions came to *Colonia Augusta Julia Philippensis,* better known to readers of the New Testament simply as Philippi. It was here in 42 B.C. that Antony and Octavian had avenged Caesar's murder, totally crushing the republican armies and thus changing the direction of the Roman civil war. While Philippi was under Roman domination it had the status of a *colonia,* and many honored veterans retired to lands given them there. Money and privileges were lavished on the city. French excavations, begun in 1914 and continuing for twenty-eight years, uncovered the remains of a small but remarkably beautiful Greco-Roman city. It was to this place and to the descendants of Antony and Octavian's hardened veterans that Paul now came.

His first contacts came on the Sabbath, when Paul and the other three went to a place of prayer outside the gate by the riverside. There some Jewish women were gathered. Paul preached to them, and Lydia, "a seller of purple goods," was converted and baptized along with her household.

The port city of Neapolis (modern Kavalla) was Paul's first stop in Europe.

The first efforts of the missionaries in Philippi met with unexpected success, but difficulties lay ahead. There was a slave girl thought to have powers of divination who followed the travelers through the city streets, crying aloud, "These men are servants of the Most High God, who proclaim to you the way of salvation." Either in irritation or compassion Paul turned on the girl, exorcising the strange spirit that held her. But this same spirit had been seen by her owners as a gift and as a source of revenue. They seized Paul and Silas, dragging them before the public authorities, charging them with disturbing the peace. Paul and Silas were stripped, beaten and thrown into jail. During the night as they were praying and singing an earthquake occurred, shattering the jail. The keeper, certain his prisoners had escaped and just as certain that this would cost him his life, was distraught. Paul called out to him assuring him that all was well and that his prisoners were still there. The jailer wished to know more of these strange people, and when he had heard of their faith and the salvation offered to him he was baptized and his family with him (Acts 16:33).

The next morning the magistrates discovered that they had made a terrible mistake. Paul and Silas, both Roman citizens, had been beaten and thrown into jail without charge or trial. Apologies were given and accepted. But Paul was asked to leave the city, doubtless in the interest of public order. He obliged, but not until he had visited Lydia and the other converts, the nucleus of what was to be a church perhaps the closest of all to Paul's heart. His later letter to these people, the New Testament book of Philippians, is sometimes called Paul's love letter.

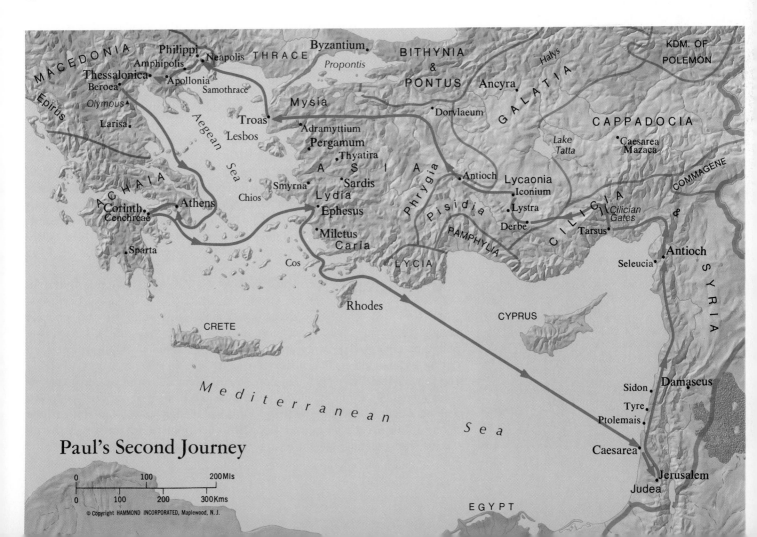

Paul's Second Journey

0   100   200MIs
0   100   200   300Kms
© Copyright HAMMOND INCORPORATED, Maplewood, N.J.

The Parthenon dedicated to Athena with its majestic Doric columns dominated Athens. Paul suffered a sharp rebuke on the nearby Areopagus (bottom photo, left).

Leaving Luke behind in Philippi (perhaps this Gentile could continue to nurture the church there without opposition) Paul, Silas and Timothy walked westward along the Egnatian Way, through the cities of Amphipolis and Apollonia until, after seventy-five miles, they came to Thessalonica, capital of the Roman province of Macedonia. Founded in 315 B.C. by Cassander, Alexander the Great's brother-in-law, Thessalonica had enjoyed uninterrupted prosperity, owing in large part to its natural setting at the head of a large gulf on the Aegean, and also owing to the fact that in ancient times as today the Egnatian Way formed the main street.

Here Paul stayed for a long time, working at his tentmaker's trade to support himself while preaching the gospel with considerable success. The church in Philippi, already well established, twice sent gifts to support the growing work in Thessalonica. As before opposition from Jewish groups began to plague Paul, but in Thessalonica it took the form of accusations against Paul's host, Jason. This friend of the apostle faced charges brought against him, in particular that he was disloyal to Rome because he harbored a man who said that Jesus was king. For the sake of his friend, Paul decided to leave and go to Beroea, fifty miles away. But this was not far enough. Enemies from Thessalonica were once more upon him, preventing any effective ministry. Again Paul moved on but left Silas and Timothy behind to continue to nurse the fledgling churches.

From Beroea, or perhaps some smaller port farther south, Paul took a ship bound for Piraeus, port of Athens. As he sailed along the coast Paul would have had a clear view of Olympus, mythic home of Zeus, and the magnificent temple of Poseidon which crowned the headland at Sounion.

In many, perhaps most ways, Athens was a disaster for Paul. It was a time of decision of sorts for him and determined the focus and content of his subsequent missionary message. At the time of Paul's visit Athens was well past its prime, living on bygone glories, rich in monuments but an intellectual desert compared to what once had been. While waiting for Silas and Timothy, Paul wandered the streets. Looking down on the city from the Acropolis stood the beautiful temple to the dominant goddess, Athena. Here Paul also found an abundance of statues and temples to other gods, including an altar to an "unknown god." The crafty Athenians were taking no chances. On the Sabbath Paul, as was his habit, went to the synagogue, where he argued both with Jews and God-fearers. On other days he went to the marketplace, the Agora, to proclaim his faith to all who would listen and to debate with any who would offer him the chance. On one such day at the Agora a group of Epicurean and Stoic philosophers engaged in dialogue with Paul. They decided to invite him to the Areopagus, better known to us as Mars Hill, to hear more of this new faith.

The Areopagus is a small hill between the Acropolis and the Agora. In other days the high council of Athens had sat in session in this conspicuous place. Now it had lost its political power and was more or less an honorific group of older men who spent most of their time listening to and discussing philosophic ideas. The philosophers who brought Paul to this learned group did so because they understood him to be speaking about a new divinity. Faced with these men and this opportunity, Paul delivered an eloquent address (Acts 17:22) in which he undertook to tell them about the "unknown god" to whom Athens in pantheistic spirit had already erected an altar. In the course of his speech he quoted from two poets, one of whom was native to Tarsus, and generally sought to argue from a philosophic position which the

Council of the Areopagus might find compatible. When he went beyond that position and spoke about the resurrection, some began to make fun of him, but others wishing to end the talk politely suggested it would be interesting to hear more, but perhaps at some other time. Paul withdrew, finding some little solace in the company of a few converts. Disconsolate, he left Athens determined henceforth "to preach Christ and him crucified" (1 Corinthians 1:23, 2:2). He had had enough of philosophic arguments.

Just west of Athens on the isthmus of Corinth is the city of Corinth itself, then a brawling seaport. By sea it is a long and dangerous way around the Peloponnesus, that massive peninsula constituting southern Greece. But at Corinth the land narrows. It was easier and more profitable to bring goods into the Saronic Gulf on the Aegean and carry them overland by cart, reloading on ships at the Gulf of Corinth on the Adriatic side. The Emperor Nero unsuccessfully sought to cut a canal here, but it was not until 1893 that such a waterway became a reality. For centuries Corinth had been renowned for its wealth as well as being notorious for its blatant immorality. Much of its population was transitory — sailors, freebooters, adventurers, swindlers of every sort. Most of the rest of the population saw these people as an opportunity to make money. The hunter was hunted; those who preyed upon others were themselves preyed upon.

In antiquity Corinth was twice destroyed by earthquakes, but the worst disaster was man-made. In 146 B.C. the Romans leveled the city, keeping it in ruins for more than a hundred years, until in 44 B.C. Julius Caesar resettled the site with colonists from Italy mixed with some citizens from the eastern portion of the empire, including a large number of Jews. There were, of course, numerous Greeks in the new Corinth, a city which bore the proud title *Colonia Laus Julia Corinthiensis.* The Athenians looked scornfully upon this new foundation with its mixed population, but Corinth was on any reading a remarkable place. And it was here that Paul had one of his greatest successes.

In the year 49 the Emperor Claudius expelled Jews from Rome. The Roman author, Seutonius, suggests that this was because of rioting in the Jewish quarter of the city, rioting that had to do with *"Chrestus."* Perhaps this was an argument turned to violence over whether or not Jesus was the Christ, the Messiah. At any rate, the emperor did expel these people and many fled eastward, some coming to Corinth. Among these was Aquila, a Diaspora Jew from Pontus, and his wife Priscilla. They were tentmakers, as was Paul. They became friends. Aquila and Priscilla were converted, and when Paul later left Corinth they went with him.

When Silas and Timothy came from Macedonia they found Paul's work well underway in Corinth. He was fully occupied testifying among the Jews of the city that Jesus was the Christ. In the synagogue and outside he pursued his mission with obvious success but with growing opposition. At length Paul's relation with some of the more orthodox Jews seems to have become bitter, consumed in strife until Paul left the synagogue vowing to go to the Gentiles. He did, in fact, move the center of his activities to a house next door to the synagogue, the home of a God-fearer named Titius Justus. For eighteen months the words of these missionaries found fertile ground in the hearts of the people of Corinth. A church took shape and grew. It was to prove a strong church but a contentious one which would be a source of difficulties not only during Paul's lifetime but long after.

In the year A.D. 51 Annaeus Novatus Gallio, older brother of the Roman poet, Seneca, was proconsul in Corinth. This date is one of the few

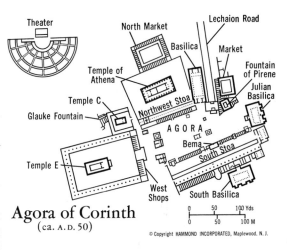

Agora of Corinth
(ca. A.D. 50)

Theater
North Market
Lechaion Road
Basilica
Market
Temple of Athena
Fountain of Pirene
Temple C
Northwest Stoa
Julian Basilica
Glauke Fountain
AGORA
Bema
Temple E
South Stoa
West Shops
South Basilica

0   50   100 Yds
0   50   100 M
© Copyright HAMMOND INCORPORATED, Maplewood, N.J.

Cornice stones from a building in the Agora of Corinth. In Paul's day the city had been rebuilt by the Romans and it served as capital of the province of Achaia.

dates we have in the chronology of Paul's life, for it was before this Roman governor that certain of the Jews of Corinth now brought Paul. They charged him with various religious offenses in which the Roman official had no interest. If these were criminal matters, particularly if they had political overtones, then the governor would be interested. But Roman governors consistently sought to avoid entanglements in local religious affairs. "Since it is a matter of questions about words and names and your own law, see to it yourselves; I refuse to be a judge of these things," said Gallio in throwing the case out of court. Then Sosthenes, ruler of the synagogue and apparently the one who brought the charges, was seized and beaten right in front of the tribunal on which Gallio was seated. But the Roman took no notice of it, perhaps thinking that Sosthenes deserved as much.

Paul returned to his work in Corinth but at length decided it was time to return to Antioch. In the company of his friends, Aquila and Priscilla, he set sail for the east. At Cenchreae, the port of Corinth, he shaved his head in compliance with a Nazirite vow which he had taken. When they came to Ephesus he went to the synagogue, where he received a sympathetic hearing, but declined an invitation to stay longer. Aquila and Priscilla stayed in Ephesus but Paul pressed on toward Caesarea and from there by land to Antioch.

It is possible that Timothy had been sent back to his native area and from there now brought disturbing news to Paul in Antioch. Judaizers had been active and influential in the churches of central Asia Minor, teaching that circumcision and the rest of the Law was, if not essential to salvation, necessary to perfection. In response to this Paul wrote to these churches restating

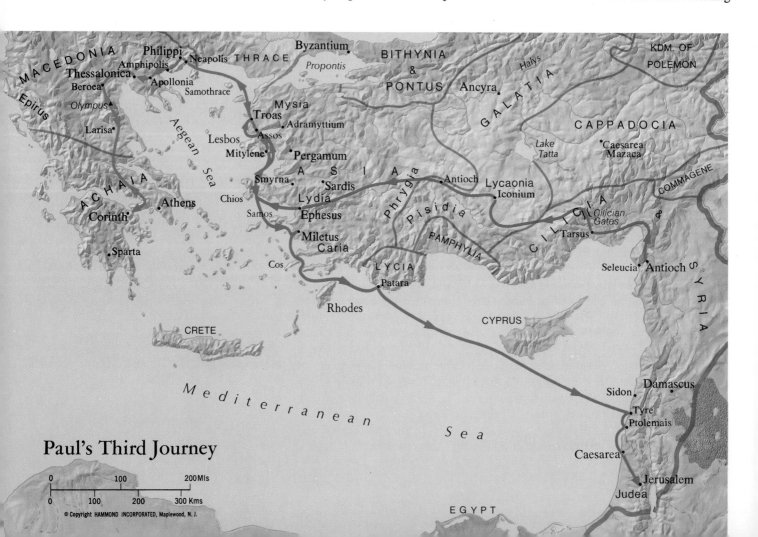

Paul's Third Journey

0   100   200Mls
0 100 200 300 Kms
© Copyright HAMMOND INCORPORATED, Maplewood, N. J.

his position that Christ died for all men and that it was necessary only to have faith in Christ in order to receive salvation. This letter of Paul, sent by Timothy's hand to the Christians of Galatia, was later spoken of by theologians as the charter of freedom for the Christian man.

After some time in Antioch Paul decided that he must personally go to these Galatian churches and set out to do so along the main road, passing through the Cilician Gates, thus retracing his earlier steps. We are told little about what he did on this visit to these churches. We know that he came to Ephesus by the northern route and not through the Lycus Valley, the more direct east-west route and the location of so many churches with which he would later be concerned. At Ephesus were his friends, Aquila and Priscilla, and also the synagogue elders, who were anxious to hear more of his message. He stayed in Ephesus for over two years, perhaps as long as twenty-eight months. Great success attended him there, and he was able to establish a center from which other missionaries went to cities and towns in the area, especially those in the Lycus Valley, such as Magnesia, Colossae, Laodicea and Hierapolis. Whether Paul caused churches to be founded in these cities or merely strengthened those already there is difficult to say.

Paul's greatest successes were in Ephesus, and the effects of his work were being felt far beyond the limits of that great city. But news reaching him from other churches which he had founded on his previous missionary journeys was not good. Difficulties of all sorts had arisen, not least in the church at Corinth, which was split into factions in a civil court case. Worse, there was another scandal in that contentious fellowship, one involving incest. When the Corinthians wrote to Paul asking guidance on the question of marriage he took the occasion to answer them on a broad range of topics, including the specific matters which he had heard were rending the fellowship at Corinth. This letter, known to us as 1 Corinthians, also announced Paul's intention to come personally to Corinth by way of Macedonia (1 Corinthians 16:5-6). At the same time he indicated that he did not know where he would go after that. Several things seemed to have been in his mind: to return to Jerusalem, or perhaps to go in the other direction to Rome. But Rome seems never to have been a prime target of Paul's, not at least as a place where he intended to work. There was already a flourishing church in Rome. However perhaps the Romans would serve as a base for work in Spain. In the midst of success at Ephesus, where there was, to use his phrase, "a wide door for effective work," he considered Spain for future work. But first there were the matters of the present. His dear new churches, how like children they were, not ready for meat but having to be fed milk and tenderly nursed. He had sent Timothy to Corinth by way of Macedonia. The letter would perhaps clear things up so that when Timothy got there he would be able to send back an encouraging and cheerful report. If not, then Timothy himself would have to deal with the situation until Paul arrived. Titus also seems to have been sent to help deal with these churches; perhaps he was already in Corinth.

In writing to the Corinthians Paul had said that he planned to stay in Ephesus until Pentecost because of the "wide door." But now something happened that slammed that door shut. In order to understand what happened it is necessary to see what kind of city Ephesus was in Paul's day.

Ephesus was one of the greatest cities of the Roman Empire, ranking fourth perhaps to Rome, Alexandria and Antioch. By Paul's time it may even have surpassed Antioch. It was the chief city of Aisa Minor, the center of proconsular government, at the head of the trade route that ran down the Lycus

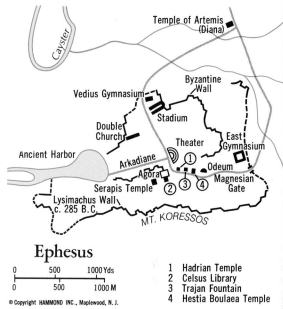

Ephesus

| 0 | 500 | 1000 Yds |
| 0 | 500 | 1000 M |

© Copyright HAMMOND INC., Maplewood, N. J.

1 Hadrian Temple
2 Celsus Library
3 Trajan Fountain
4 Hestia Boulaea Temple

231

Artemis of Ephesus was a fertility goddess worshiped in Asia Minor long before the rise of Greek culture. The statue shown here was discovered in 1956 at Ephesus.

The marble street (Arkadiane) from the harbor to the great theater at Ephesus dates from a time later than Paul but it follows an earlier conception.

Valley, and a major port directly across from Athens. Long before the coming of the Romans it had been the focus of the worship of Artemis of Ephesus. This Artemis (Diana to the Romans) is different from the chaste maiden and patroness of the hunt known to us from classical mythology. The Ephesian Artemis was a fertility goddess of Asia Minor worshiped long before the rise of Greek culture. She was portrayed in statues with rows of many breasts (or eggs?) and wearing a high crown depicting the seasons. The Artemision, one of the seven wonders of the ancient world, was the great temple dedicated to Artemis of Ephesus. It had burned in 356 B.C. but had been rebuilt along even more magnificent lines. The platform for this sanctuary was 220 feet wide and 425 feet long and was reached by thirteen steps. The temple proper was about 180 feet by 378 feet. There were 127 columns, each more than six feet in diameter and twenty of these sculptured to a height of sixty feet. The central focus of worship was a "sacred stone that fell from the sky" (Acts 19:35), doubtless a meteorite. The temple that Paul saw was destroyed by the Goths in A.D. 262. Archaeologists working at the site over the past fifty years have recovered some beautifully painted fragments of carefully cut stone. There are also indications that much of the structure was decorated with beaten gold.

The rest of the city was in keeping with its crowning glory, the Artemision. A mile from the temple was the heart of the city, nestled between two hills and running down to the harbor's edge. There was a splendid theater, a stadium, a marketplace resplendent with marble as well as many other public and private buildings in harmony with the whole. The main street, which ran between the harbor and the theater, was rebuilt by the Emperor Arcadius toward the end of the fourth century. It was the most splendid street of the Roman Empire and took its name, the *Arkadiane,* from its builder. It was thirty-five feet wide, with another fifteen feet on either side devoted to colonnading and statues. Quite likely the lines of this more recent construction followed ancient conceptions, and from it we can get an idea of what it was like when Paul traversed it.

The silversmiths of Ephesus made the larger part of their living from votive images sold to the many pilgrims and other tourists who came to the Artemision. Paul, as is well known, cared little for "temples made with hands," and the success of his two-and-a-half-year ministry in Ephesus was having a devastating effect on the silversmiths' trade. One of them, Demetrius, organized some of his colleagues, and they were able to convince many of the citizens of the city that Paul and his friends endangered not merely the silversmith industry but the very worship of Artemis, for which Ephesus had been justly famous for many centuries. A mob gathered. "Great is Artemis of Ephesus" began to ring through the streets, growing in intensity as the mass of humanity moved toward the great theater. Set against a hill in the Greek fashion, this marble-faced structure held 24,000 people. Two of Paul's friends were seized and dragged along. Paul wanted to go to their aid and also to make a defense of his views. But such a course of action would have been foolish and his friends restrained him while the shouting continued. "Great is Artemis of the Ephesians." For over two hours the words hung in waves over the city. The pandemonium in the theater was spilling over into the nearby streets. The town officials finally took action, convincing the crowd that should they continue the Roman garrison would soon be upon them and even more unhappy consequences might ensue. So the tumult died and the crowd melted away. And very soon Paul also went away.

He went to Macedonia and "to Greece," the latter likely a reference to Corinth. There a plot against his life was discovered. Apparently he was to be murdered on board the ship he planned to take to Asia Minor. It was for this reason that he returned to Macedonia and eventually crossed the Aegean from Neapolis to Troas. It was on this visit that Eutychus, a lad sitting in a window, tired of Paul's overlong sermon and fell asleep, tumbling out of the building and knocking himself unconscious (Acts 20:7-12).

From Troas Paul traveled overland to Assos while his companions went by ship. At Assos Paul rejoined his companions and together took ship again. After a stop at Mitylene on the island of Lesbos and a brief stop at Samos, they reached Miletus where Paul had an emotional meeting with the elders of the Ephesian church. Among other things he told them that he would not see them again and encouraged them to carry on the good work in Ephesus. He ended by quoting words of Jesus not recorded in the Gospels: "It is more blessed to give than to receive" (Acts 20:35).

Once more on board ship he touched first one island and then another until he reached Patara where he found a ship bound for Phoenicia. He landed at Tyre and once the ship's cargo was unloaded continued down the coast to Ptolemais. The last leg of the journey was made on foot by way of Caesarea, where his friends begged him not to go to Jerusalem. In the Holy City the church received his report with joy, telling him that they had sent letters to various churches informing them of the decision of the council. They also told Paul that others in Jerusalem had heard of his work and that they were saying that he had abandoned the Law of Moses. To show that this was not so Paul went to the Temple with four men under Nazirite vows and paid their expenses for the final fulfillment of their vows. Thus this strictest of all Jewish vows was openly honored by this man who had been accused of laying aside the faith of his fathers. But some Jews from Asia Minor saw Paul in the Temple and stirred up a mob against him. There was a riot in the Court of the Gentiles. The Romans feared just this kind of scene and had laid plans for swift intervention. The doors of the sanctuary proper swung shut at once to prevent the mob from entering and looting. Within minutes Roman soldiers from the Antonia were racing down the monumental stairs that joined the garrison with the sacred courts. Paul was being beaten and would likely have died there and then had not a Roman officer dashed to the center of the tumult. Paul was placed in chains and led off toward the Antonia. As they pushed through the hostile crowd Paul sought to persuade the officer that he should be allowed to address the milling people. On the steps he got his chance, and from that high vantage point he began to speak. But angry shouts and the clear possibility of renewed violence caused the Roman officer to hustle his prisoner into the fortress.

Paul had already asserted his Roman citizenship. This probably is one reason the officer had relented and let him attempt to speak to the mob. This also saved him from baser forms of punishment. Various hearings were held to try to determine what to do with this man. The Romans allowed the Sanhedrin to question Paul, but it was an unruly session in which the apostle skillfully played one faction off against another (Acts 23:1-10). The session also seems to have convinced Roman authorities that Paul's life would not be worth anything if they turned him over to the local religious authorities. Thus, when Paul's nephew reported that there was a plot afoot in Jerusalem to kill Paul, the officer had him removed to Caesarea and delivered into the jurisdiction and care of the governor, Antonius Felix. Tacitus, the Roman his-

Inscription to Antonius Felix.

torian, tells us that Felix ruled Judea "with the powers of a king and the soul of a slave." His treatment of Paul supports Tacitus' judgment. He had several conversations with the apostle, even giving indications of interest in his new faith. But his real interest was in money. When none was forthcoming from Paul's friends, Felix simply let him languish in prison for perhaps two years, uncharged with any crime and unable to appeal to any higher authority.

When Porcius Festus came to Caesarea to assume the governorship he found Paul, probably among others, in the cells. Festus was a different cut from Felix. He was proper in every regard. Among the first things he did was go to Jerusalem to confer with local authorities there. He found them exceptionally interested in that prisoner back there in Caesarea. They would like to have him brought down to Jerusalem to be tried. But Festus realized that Paul would never reach Jerusalem alive. In the situation he acted properly. The authorities from Jerusalem could come to Caesarea if they had charges to press against Paul. And they came. In the governor's court at Caesarea Paul denied all accusations. Festus was in a difficult situation. He hardly wished to offend leaders of the area he had just been sent to govern. On the other hand, perhaps Paul was innocent. Would Paul like to go to Jerusalem to be judged by his own people? Paul would not. Indeed, he invoked his right as a Roman citizen and appealed directly to the emperor in Rome. "You have appealed to Caesar," said the relieved Festus, "and to Caesar you shall go." Paul had been delivered from the Sanhedrin.

Paul was no ordinary prisoner. He was an imperial prisoner, a Roman citizen being sent from a governor to the emperor. It was also a curious case. He was not charged with high crimes and treason. As a matter of fact it is not clear what, if any, charges had been lodged. Now Paul was treated with the utmost courtesy, being allowed, among other things, to have two companions accompany him. Luke and Aristarchus were chosen and at the quayside at Caesarea went on board ship with Paul. The man charged with delivering them to the proper authorities in Rome was an important officer, a centurion of the Augustan Cohort. His name was Julius. So the four sailed the normal sea route, which followed the coast northward until it could safely venture into the open sea under the lee of Cyprus. Their original vessel apparently having completed its circuit at Myra, Julius took his charges aboard another ship, a government grain ship on its way from Egypt to Italy. They crossed with difficulty to Crete, sheltering in the harbor at Fair Havens. It was now late in the summer season, and storms at sea were increasingly possible. But they would risk it. The odds were, after all, in their favor.

No sooner had they left Fair Havens than a terrific storm struck, driving their helpless vessel westward. Then the steering mechanism failed. Attempts to reach the island of Cauda (modern Gavhos) were unavailing and the ship was driven past that wisp of land. Endlessly the ship rolled and tossed before the wind in the darkness and in the day that was night. Paul alone seems to have kept up courage, all the others abandoning hope. He had had a vision strengthening him and he said to the others, "so take heart men, for I have faith in God that it will be exactly as I have been told."

On the fourteenth night of their terror the sailors began to suspect that they were nearing land. They sounded and then sounded again. The water was getting shallower. In the darkness their straining eyes could not make out a coastline. Four anchors were put out the stern, and they all longed anxiously for dawn. Some sought to jump overboard, hoping to make shore safely, but Paul urged them to stay with the ship. At the first light of dawn

Roman ship of a type on which Paul journeyed.

Paul's Voyage to Rome

—— Boundary of the Roman Empire
—— Provincial boundary

they spotted an inlet with a good beach. Anchors were cut away and ropes holding the rudder sliced. A sail was lofted and the battered craft swung around toward the sands of this island that none recognized. There was a crash and then grinding. The bow was rammed on a shoal, and the waves, still high, began to batter the stern to pieces. Mindful of their duty the soldiers moved to kill their prisoners lest they escape, but Julius intervened in order to save Paul. Those who could swim flung themselves into the boiling sea, while others clung desperately to wood floating free from the disintegrating vessel. One way or another all came safely to shore.

The land which felt so stable, so marvelous under their feet was Malta and the inhabitants showed great kindness. Because he showed no ill effects from a snakebite, Paul was taken to be a god, and when he cured the chief man of the island, Publius (Acts 28:1-10), his stature was increased. What else he did on Malta we are not told. But he stayed there for three months, and the tradition that traces the Christian faith on the island back to this time may well be correct.

235

Early Christian mosaic beneath St. Peter's Cathedral, Rome, near the traditional tomb of Peter. The mosaic combines Christian and pagan motifs in portraying Christ as a sun-god.

In the harbor at Malta was another ship from Alexandria, a ship which had taken shelter from the winter storms. As soon as the major danger period was passed, perhaps in February, its captain decided to make for Italy by way of Sicily. Julius secured passage for his group, and soon they all set foot on Italian soil at Puteoli (modern Pozzuoli) on the Bay of Naples. For a week the kind Julius allowed Paul to stay with local Christians, then they set out along the Appian Way toward Rome. Thirty-three miles south of the imperial capital, Paul was met at the Forum of Appius by Christians from Rome who knew him from his letter to them and who had heard of his coming. Ten miles nearer Rome, at Three Taverns, a second group greeted him.

Thus Paul entered Rome technically a prisoner but in truth a completely free man, for his spirit was unshackled. And he was surrounded by Christian friends. Things looked good in Rome. Since his days in Ephesus, Paul had looked forward to getting to Rome as a base for work in Spain. For this purpose he had written to the Roman church from Asia Minor, introducing himself and his ideas and asking their help. Now perhaps he would soon be free of the charges against him and could pursue his plans.

But for the most part the promise seems to have remained only prospect. He was placed under house arrest, and, while this was infinitely preferable to any of the ancient prisons whose grim remains can be seen in Rome today, it did not allow Paul the freedom of movement for which he had hoped. His extant writings from those days (Colossians, Philippians, Philemon, Ephesians [?], 1 and 2 Timothy [?] and Titus [?]) contain references to the ease with which companions came and went. Others also came, including the leaders of the Jewish community in Rome, who spent a day discussing matters with the apostle.

Here our sure knowledge of Paul and his activities ends. Seemingly the church at Rome did not provide the support he had sought. There are even suggestions that when some of Paul's friends came seeking him the church did not even know where he was. The larger question concerns his death. Was he tried, condemned and put to death at this time? We have noted his desire

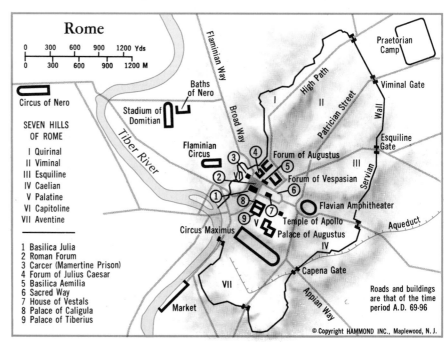

Rome

| 0 | 300 | 600 | 900 | 1200 Yds |
| 0 | 300 | 600 | 900 | 1200 M |

Circus of Nero

SEVEN HILLS OF ROME

I Quirinal
II Viminal
III Esquiline
IV Caelian
V Palatine
VI Capitoline
VII Aventine

1 Basilica Julia
2 Roman Forum
3 Carcer (Mamertine Prison)
4 Forum of Julius Caesar
5 Basilica Aemilia
6 Sacred Way
7 House of Vestals
8 Palace of Caligula
9 Palace of Tiberius

Flaminian Way
Praetorian Camp
Baths of Nero
High Path
Viminal Gate
Stadium of Domitian
Patrician Street
Broad Way
Wall
Flaminian Circus
Forum of Augustus
Esquiline Gate
Tiber River
Forum of Vespasian
Servian
Flavian Amphitheater
Temple of Apollo
Circus Maximus
Palace of Augustus
Aqueduct
Capena Gate
Market
Appian Way

Roads and buildings are that of the time period A.D. 69-96

© Copyright HAMMOND INC., Maplewood, N.J.

to go to Spain, and there is a writing from the end of the first century which says, "He taught righteousness to the whole world, having traveled to the limits of the west; and when he had borne his witness before the rulers, he departed from the world. . . . " (1 Clement 5:7). Does "to the limits of the west" refer to Spain? Was Paul released and did he go to Spain, only later returning to Rome where he died? We do not know. Rome today is alive with memories of Paul, and one can be shown a dungeon near the Imperial Forum where he is said to have been confined, the Church of St. Paul of Three Fountains indicating the spot where he is said to have been beheaded (a Roman citizen would not have been crucified) and finally the splendid basilica St. Paul's-Outside-the-Walls on the *Via Ostiense* which marks the traditional site of his grave. PAULO, says the stone beneath the altar, and since the fourth century piety has hallowed the spot.

St. Paul's-Outside-the-Walls, Rome, traditional site of the tomb of Paul.

So Paul leaves the scene, this passionate rabbi who endured the dust of thousands of miles, the beatings and ridicule of various enemies, shipwrecks, cold, hunger—all for the surpassing knowledge of knowing Christ and seeking with his whole heart to share that knowledge with others. Paul was not the first Christian, nor the first missionary, nor the first theologian. But surely no one has ever been more devoted than he, more faithful to his missionary task. He was by all odds the greatest theologian of the Church. He was zealot and genius, fearless before men and humble before God. He was—in the last analysis—uniquely Paul.

But there were others, many others, and their numbers were rapidly multiplying. No less devoted than Paul, no less willing than he to lay down his life for his belief, many of these did earn the martyr's crown. Roman hostility was being added to that of the Christians' religious opponents. The first and in some ways the most famous of the persecutions of Christians by the Roman state occurred when Nero was emperor. Peter is said to have been crucified upside down during the Neronian persecution in A.D. 64. It may well have been in the same year and under the same circumstances that Paul fell before the blade. In the heat of an Italian summer on July 18, 64, fire broke out in the Circus Maximus in Rome. When it finally subsided nine days later, two-thirds of the ancient city beside the Tiber, the center of empire and foremost city of the world lay in smoldering ruins. The Forum and the Capitol escaped; almost everything else was lost, including the Palatine Hill palaces and Nero's new additions to them. At Antium when the fire started, the emperor raced to Rome, and rumors began to spread that he was watching the fire from the tower of Maecenas with great relish while strumming his lyre and singing of the sack of Troy. There is no proof that he did this nor even that he had the fire set in order to rebuild the city along new lines. He is accused of this by almost all Roman historians of the time and later, yet they may only be repeating the gossip that spread through the terrified city with the speed of the wind-whipped flames. Nero stood accused, and his immediate and vigorous attempts to house and feed the thousands upon thousands of homeless did little to quiet the rumor. According to the historian Tacitus, Nero found a scapegoat in a group of people who had talked about a fiery end of the world. These people were *Chrestiani*, followers of "*Chrestus* who, in the reign of Tiberius, suffered under Pontius Pilate, Procurator of Judea." Relentlessly Nero tracked down Christians in and around Rome, making a public spectacle of them to distract the populace and shift suspicion from himself. Ingenious ways of killing these people were found, including soaking them in flammable fluid, putting them on crosses and igniting them

Coin of Nero showing the emperor and the port of Ostia.

237

The Seven Churches
of Asia Minor

Samothrace
Imbros
Byzantium
Chalcedon
Propontis
Nicaea
Cyzicus
Prusa
Abydos
Ilium
Mysia
Troas (Alexandria)
Assos
Adramyttium
Mitylene
Pergamum
Lesbos
Aegean
ASIA
Thyatria
Smyrna
Sardis
Chios
Philadelphia
Sea
Metropolis
Lydia
Claros
Ephesus
Hierapolis
Samos
Panionium
Tralles
Magnesia
Laodicea
Priene
Aphrodisias
Colossae
Trogyllium
Miletus
Delos
Patmos
Didyma
Caria
Naxos
Halicarnassus
Cos
LYCIA
Cnidus
Xanthus
Patara
Rhodes

The Seven Churches
of Asia   (Rev. 1-3)
Principal roads

0   50   100 Mls
0   100 Kms

© Copyright HAMMOND INC., Maplewood, N. J.

Patmos Island, where John the Divine
had his revelation.

238

to light the emperor's gardens. "At length," say Tacitus, "the brutality of these measures filled every breast with pity. Humanity relented in favor of the Christians."

The Neronian persecution ended, but other momentous events were afoot. While Nero was in Greece entering athletic and drama contests (he won them all to no one's surprise), rebellion broke out in Judea. For the Christians it meant that it was now in their interest to disassociate themselves from Jews who had become suspect all over the empire and who, in city after city around the Mediterranean, had been engaged in riots. Judaism had been sanctioned by the Senate, but Christianity had no such status, and as it emerged as an increasingly separate group it was illegal.

Another and perhaps more serious crisis faced Christianity as it entered the second generation. Eyewitnesses were dying and the expected end of the world, fervently looked for, had not occurred. In the 60s and 70s of the first century this crisis was met by the drawing together of various oral and written traditions into a new form of writing—the Gospel. Mark was perhaps the first. Certainly of those we have today Mark was first. It is thought to have come from the church in Rome and is generally dated in the early 60s. Some think that it was a response to the Neronian persecution. Others appeared in the 70s; Matthew perhaps in Antioch and Luke seemingly from Asia Minor. Both disciples knew and used the Gospel of Mark. Toward the end of the first century after the death of Christ another Gospel appears, this one from a very different tradition from the other three. This is John's Gospel, thought by some to have originated in Ephesus and by others to have come from Alexandria. There were, of course, other Christian writings of the time, as the preface to Luke's Gospel tells us and as the existence of Paul's letters shows. Among the literature of the second generation of Christians are various types of writings, some attributed to the apostles and others not, which deal with different internal problems and external pressures which were bearing upon the churches. First Peter offered encouragement to Christians of northern Asia Minor in the midst of a persecution; the letter to the Hebrews is a sustained argument emphasizing Jesus as both high priest and perfect sacrifice; the letter of James notes the importance of expressing faith through good works; 1 John was written to counter a growing heresy regarding the person of Jesus. So the literature grew in response to the diverse situations in which the Church found itself.

Toward the end of the century two remarkable documents came from the Church; one, found in the New Testament, is the Revelation to John, and the other, not in the Scriptures, is 1 Clement. The Revelation is an apocalypse depicting the coming end of time in poetic and enigmatic imagery. In form it is related to parts of Ezekiel and to Daniel in the Old Testament and to a vast body of noncanonical Jewish literature from Maccabean times and later. Apparently during the persecution of Domitian (A.D. 96) earlier materials were woven together into a whole in the form of a great cosmic vision. It is a persecution document whose central message is that to which Handel gave such magnificent voice: "Halielujah! For the Lord our God omnipotent reigneth" (Revelation 19:6 b, KJV).

The temper of 1 Clement is very different. It is a pragmatic document from the church at Rome addressed to the still troublesome Corinthian church. A younger faction in the church has deposed the older one previously in authority. Clement takes a dim view of this, urging upon the Corinthians a proper respect for orders in the church. We thus have in 1 Clement at the

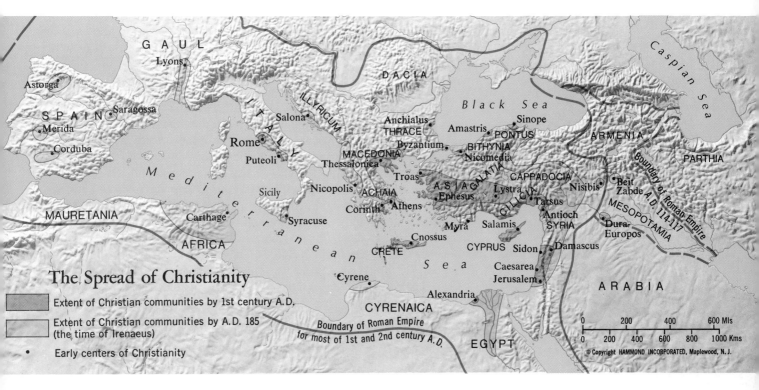

The Spread of Christianity

Extent of Christian communities by 1st century A.D.

Extent of Christian communities by A.D. 185 (the time of Irenaeus)

• Early centers of Christianity

Boundary of Roman Empire for most of 1st and 2nd century A.D.

© Copyright HAMMOND INCORPORATED, Maplewood, N.J.

end of the century a clear indication of the movement in the early Christian church toward hierarchy. This was not to be fully developed for another century, but the tendencies are already present. Clement also takes the occasion to extol Christian virtues in practical terms, speaking of faith, compassion, humility, hospitality and what was doubtless quite hard for the Corinthians—self-control. Factiousness and those things which support it; namely, pride, envy and jealousy are to be avoided. But it is mostly respect for constituted order that concerns this writer. Bishops, elders and deacons are to be obeyed. Further, the goodly example of recent martyrs is to be remembered with thanksgiving and the Corinthian church is also reminded of the "good apostles," Peter and Paul.

Thus, as the first Christian century draws to a close, we see various tendencies present in response to rapid growth, internal strife and to external pressure from persecution. Prominent among these tendencies are self-definition over against Judaism, a movement toward specifically Christian literature, and thus toward a Christian canon, and the growth of a hierarchy. Along with this went the necessity to define belief. Authority either in the person of hierarchy or present in tradition from the apostles was used to keep the faith undiluted by the multitude of competing religions and cults in the polyglot early empire. Thus the Church on the threshold of the second century while still spreading rapidly is under increasing internal and external pressure to define its belief, its practices and its structures. The Church moving into the second century was not without many problems but it was still characterized by the compulsion to tell the world that there was "good news:" God had acted on man's behalf in and through Jesus Christ.

Papyrus fragment of the Gospel of Matthew from Oxyrhynchus, Egypt, third century A.D.

239

17 THE LATER HERODS AND BEGINNINGS OF REVOLT

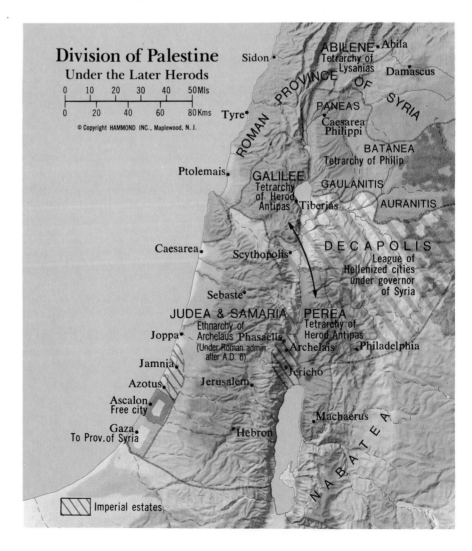

Roman eagle on an altar in Jerusalem.

The first century of the new era dawned with deep forebodings for the Jews of Judea. The kingdom which Herod the Great had carefully welded together through wars, intrigues and good management was broken up. Knowing that Augustus was hardly likely to allow any of his heirs to wield the power that he had held in the Roman East, Herod had left a fourth and final will dividing his kingdom between his remaining sons and his sister. Archelaus, the oldest still living, was to be ruler of Judea and Samaria. Archelaus, we should note, was the son of Herod and Malthace, a Samaritan woman. However much this may have helped him with Samaritans it did little to endear him to his Jewish subjects. Galilee and Perea were to go to Herod Antipas, full brother to Archelaus. This is the Herod who put John the Baptist to death and who apparently also had designs on the life of Jesus (Luke 13:31). Herod Philip, son of Herod and a Jerusalem Jewess named Cleo-

Division of Palestine Under the Later Herods

0 10 20 30 40 50 Mis
0 20 40 60 80 Kms
© Copyright HAMMOND INC., Maplewood, N. J.

Sidon
ABILENE · Abila
Tetrarchy of Lysanias
Damascus
ROMAN PROVINCE OF SYRIA
Tyre
PANEAS
Caesarea Philippi
BATANEA
Tetrarchy of Philip
Ptolemais
GALILEE Tetrarchy of Herod Antipas
Tiberias
GAULANITIS
AURANITIS
Caesarea
Scythopolis
DECAPOLIS League of Hellenized cities under governor of Syria
Sebaste
JUDEA & SAMARIA Ethnarchy of Archelaus (Under Roman admin. after A.D. 6)
PEREA Tetrarchy of Herod Antipas
Joppa
Phasaelis
Archelais
Philadelphia
Jamnia
Jericho
Azotus
Jerusalem
Ascalon Free city
Machaerus
Gaza To Prov. of Syria
Hebron
NABATEA

Imperial estates

240

patra, was to receive the northeastern portions of his father's domains: Gaulanitis, Batanea, Trachonitis and Paneas. Herod's sister, Salome, who had been ruthlessly loyal to her royal brother, was not forgotten. Jamnia and Azotus on the southern coast as well as Phasaelis, an extremely rich plantation near Jericho, were to be hers. Nor in his last days did Herod forget whose vassal he was. He left enormous sums to Emperor Augustus and to his wife, Livia, and to other members of that family. After all, Herod's settlement was subject to Augustus' approval. Finally, Herod bade Archelaus take his ring to Rome along with state papers for approval of his last wishes.

A few days before his death Herod had given donatives to the army, urging them to be loyal to his designated successor, particularly in strategically important Judea. The soldiers, most of whom were mercenaries anyway, carried out Herod's commands in death as in life. Yet not much else remained as it had been. From the time of the Maccabean War in the middle of the second century B.C. Judaism in Palestine had been in ferment, with occasional outbreaks of violence among the factions. Herod's death released the pent-up anger and ambitions of individuals, groups and interests. Over the next half century they tore at each other, until in a senseless fury they threw themselves upon their Roman overlords.

For the first few days after Herod's death all seemed well. Archelaus was duly proclaimed by the army. Herod was buried with befitting pomp on the Herodium and the court went into mourning in accordance with Jewish law. Then everything went wrong. It was triggered by a serious miscalculation on the part of the teenaged monarch. Archelaus, Idumean-Samaritan by birth, Roman by education (he had spent most of his life in Rome), knew little of the temperament of his Judean subjects. He went to the Temple clad in a plain white robe and from a raised golden throne addressed his subjects in a conciliatory mood. He admitted that Caesar Augustus had not yet accepted him as Herod's successor. He said further that he would seek to be a better king than his father, who, he knew, had mistreated his subjects.

The boy did not know what he was doing. He believed he was ingratiating himself as the epitome of reason and good sense. The mob, for such it had become, saw him simply as a weakling. They had respected his father because they had to. Demands were shouted. Certain taxes were to be reduced, others abolished altogether. Political prisoners were to be released from dark and stinking dungeons in Antonia, Alexandrium, Hyrcania and other prisons. Archelaus, intimidated, agreed to the demands and then withdrew.

The crowd continued to mill about. Some among them seized on an incident which had occurred in the last days of Herod's reign. Embittered Pharisee students had torn down the eagle adorning the Beautiful Gate in the Temple enclosure in a demonstration against Herod. Herod had shown clemency to many, but two teachers and several students were put to death. These were now proclaimed as "martyrs." Into the late afternoon and evening funereal dirges for these people mingled with cries for revenge. All of Jerusalem was being engulfed by rising hysteria.

Archelaus responded with appeasement. He sent a Temple official to reason with some of the mob there. He was stoned. The king sent others who met the same fate. It was clear that the Temple area had become a focus of the crisis. The Court of the Gentiles was full of people; many were pilgrims who had come for Passover, which was fast approaching, but others were agitators now become organizers. Their immediate cause was to claim the life of the high priest, Joazar, as revenge for the "martyrs."

The Herodium, fortress and burial site of Herod the Great. His tomb has never been found. It may have been in the round tower at the top of the picture.

Herod and His Descendants

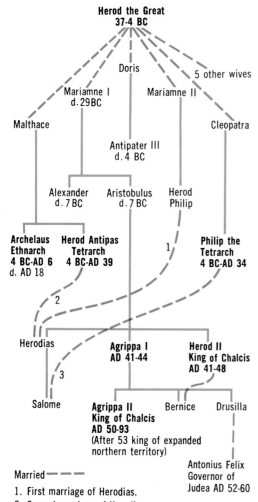

Herod the Great
37-4 BC

Doris

5 other wives

Mariamne I
d. 29 BC

Mariamne II

Malthace

Cleopatra

Antipater III
d. 4 BC

Alexander
d. 7 BC

Aristobulus
d. 7 BC

Herod
Philip

**Archelaus
Ethnarch
4 BC-AD 6
d. AD 18**

**Herod Antipas
Tetrarch
4 BC-AD 39**

1

**Philip the
Tetrarch
4 BC-AD 34**

2

Herodias

**Agrippa I
AD 41-44**

**Herod II
King of Chalcis
AD 41-48**

3

Salome

**Agrippa II
King of Chalcis
AD 50-93**
(After 53 king of expanded
northern territory)

Bernice

Drusilla

Antonius Felix
Governor of
Judea AD 52-60

Married – – –

1. First marriage of Herodias.
2. Second marriage of Herodias.
3. Salome, daughter of Herodias and Herod (sometimes referred to as Philip), danced before Herod Antipas for John the Baptist's head. She married her great-uncle Philip the Tetrarch.

d. died

Archelaus decided to arrest the leaders. But the soldiers sent for this purpose were killed! The mob had turned to violence. Archelaus now mobilized the entire Jerusalem garrison and dispatched them in full battle dress to the Temple. Swords in hand, they poured over the splendid bridge spanning the Tyropoeon Valley and into the sacred area. The dying and their blood were all over, even at the altar. Between the cavalry outside the walls and the infantry inside some 3,000 people were slain. Archelaus held Jerusalem. He would do so for ten more years, but the cost was staggering. Things in Judea were never to be the same.

And now Archelaus prepared to go to Rome as quickly as possible. The will must be confirmed. Others would be contesting it. Antipas had been named sole heir in Herod's third will. You can imagine his shock when a fourth will appeared, one which literally shoved him into the northern hills and the eastern desert. Furthermore, almost all of Herod's contentious family were either in Rome or on their way, including Salome, past master at the intriguer's art and friend of Empress Livia. Salome was supporting the claims of Antipas.

While Archelaus was at Caesarea waiting to take ship for Rome, another — and as events were later to prove — serious matter arose. Sabinus, a Roman financial officer, arrived saying that he intended to impound all of Herod's vast fortune! Archelaus sent to Antioch for Quintilius Varus, legate of Syria, who came down to Caesarea and vetoed Sabinus' plans. All must wait for the emperor's pleasure regarding the will. Varus went back to Syria, and Archelaus set sail for Rome. But Sabinus, contrary to Varus' orders, went to Jerusalem and moved into the palace.

Meanwhile in Rome the emperor was distressed at the scene now forming. Rival kings were one thing, but all of Herod's horrendous family at one time was something else again. But there they were, Salome in the lead. When the day came she put forth her son, Antipater, to speak on behalf of Antipas' claims. Archelaus was unfit. He had been drunk when he should have been mourning his father. He had already arrogated to himself the powers of a king. And besides, that slaughter in the Temple—statements for a claim had become a harangue.

Archelaus sent in his father's ring and the state papers. He also sent in Nicolas, Herod's chief minister and one of the most capable men of the era. Nicolas argued dispassionately, legally, coldly. The contrast between Antipater's presentation and that of Nicolas was striking. As for the rebels in the Temple, well, what was one to do with the enemies of Rome? At the end of Nicolas' presentation Archelaus came forward and without a word knelt before Augustus, placing his bowed head on the imperial knee. Augustus, sick of the whole matter and disgusted with what he had had to witness this day, lifted up the boy, saying that he was worthy to succeed his father. But the emperor did not say that he *would* succeed his father.

There things stood. Augustus temporized. How often he must have wished for Herod himself, urbane, capable, hail-fellow and above all reliable. Why Augustus hesitated we do not know. He knew Herod's sons. They had all been in Rome. Perhaps he felt that none could really rule. If he selected one what would the others do? Then there was Salome, the sole remaining heir from her generation. If she could manipulate the worldly-wise Herod what could she do to these young and inexperienced boys? What to do?

When Augustus faltered, Sabinus apparently took it as a sign that this might be an auspicious moment for daring. Perhaps none of the Herodians would be back. Perhaps a Roman governor would be on the next ship to touch Caesarea. Perhaps many things. But now Sabinus was in Jerusalem with a legion at his command with all the riches of Herod somewhere about. Why not reach for that fortune or at least part of it? Sabinus sent legionnaires to search out and report on the location and amounts of various caches. He even went so far as to arm locals who professed loyalty to him and sent them into the surrounding country to see what they could find.

It was less than two months since the Passover massacre; as a matter of fact, it was fifty days later, since the Feast of Pentecost was at hand. Imagine Sabinus doing this under the best of conditions still less in the tense, explosive situation then in Jerusalem. Almost at once he found himself shut up in the western palace, Herod's beautiful creation, and cut off from troops in the Antonia. The greedy Sabinus was no military officer. Fearing for his life, he lost his nerve. A stream of messengers went north to Antioch begging Varus to come and save the situation—or at least save Sabinus. Finally he broke under the strain and from the heights of Phasael Tower signaled to the Antonia to disperse the rabble.

The legionnaires went into the Temple with nothing prepared such as occupying the roofs. Objects of all sorts rained down on them from above. Attempts to take the roofs failed. Finally an order was given to set fire to the wooden columns of the portico. These were covered with a gilded waxy substance easily made into bas-reliefs. The whole thing went up like tinder and many people were burned to death. Another slaughter ensued, but nothing to compare with Passover, for the soldiers were interested in the Temple treasury which they now partly looted.

But the siege of the western palace was not lifted. Sabinus was still unable to get out. The Antonia controlled the Temple but little else. Indeed, the whole country was slipping rapidly toward anarchy. Jews everywhere attacked Romans. To add to the turmoil many of the mercenaries rebelled, taking what they could lay their hands on. Self-proclaimed leaders took towns and even cities. Sepphoris, the leading city of Galilee, was one of these. Jericho only just escaped being burned. Sebaste — Herod's ever faithful Sebaste! — alone did not mutiny.

Varus acted. Varus acted swiftly, without mercy and with a military precision which in its best moments made the Roman army the most feared in the ancient world. He swept out of Syria with his two legions and what auxiliaries he could pick up. He took Sepphoris, burned the city, and sold its population into slavery. Towns that had supported insurrection were treated similarly.

Then Varus concentrated his forces and drove on Jerusalem. At their approach the rebels melted into the hills. The people of Jerusalem, either in sincerity or as the better part of discretion, welcomed the Romans as saviors. The besieged legion marched out of the city to meet their oncoming comrades. They were joined by those mercenaries who had remained loyal. Sabinus absented himself from the growing throng and disappeared. Well he might, for Varus wished to see him. The Romans brought forth those who had been leaders in this awful business. The luckier ones filled up the prisons; others, 2,000 of them, were crucified around Jerusalem.

Varus sent news of all this to Rome where Augustus was still trying to make up his mind. Ever a supporter of his old friend Herod, Varus also sent Philip, the other son named in Herod's will, to support Archelaus' claims. But fifty leading men from Jerusalem had also come to the imperial city and, supported by the Jewish community there, expressed their desire for an end to Herodian rule. Augustus heard them all out and considered the choices again.

What Augustus did was essentially to confirm Herod's will, but with a little bit thrown in to sweeten the decision for Archelaus' rivals. The three sons got what the will laid down, except that the Greek cities in the northeast were detached and placed directly under the Syrian legate. Gaza was included in this. Salome could have what her brother had left to her, but these areas were to be administered by Archelaus. That was a bitter pill for Salome. Augustus eased it a bit, however, by giving her the palace at Ascalon, which Herod had left to the emperor. Augustus also sought to quiet the displeasure of certain other members of this factious family by dividing among them the enormous fortune which Herod had left for the imperial family in Rome. The emperor decreed that he himself should receive only a few works of art by which to recall his old friend, now sorely missed. Further, no one was to have the title of king. Archelaus was granted the title *ethnarch,* which was somewhat higher than that of *tetrarch* given to his two brothers. It was clearly understood, however, that should Archelaus prove himself a worthy ruler he might in future be allowed the title formerly held by his father.

The settlement was not a good one, and few if any expected it to last. Archelaus was weak, as Augustus knew, and either Philip or Antipas would have been preferable, as events were to show. Augustus' prime concern was to protect the roads between Egypt and Syria. Palestine was vital. Perhaps the settlement would restore calm and buy time until something better evolved. And that is just what happened. The contending brothers obeyed the emperor, returned to their new realms and for a time there was peace.

Philip, a man of grace, moderation and good sense, was easily the most attractive of the three who shared Herod's realm. His little backwater tetrarchy contained some Jewish subjects, but it was Gentile for the most part. There was little industry in the area and there were no cities of note. Philip was able to remedy the latter at any rate and established two cities which are known to readers of the New Testament. At Paneas, site of one of the springs that feeds the Jordan River, Herod had built a temple to Pan. Philip used this as the center of a new city which he named for his patron, calling it Caesarea. But to distinguish it from the more famous foundation on the coast he added his own name, so that the place is known as Caesarea Philippi. He also enlarged and enhanced the fishing village of Bethsaida at the northeast end of the Sea of Galilee and further honored the emperor by naming this place after his daughter. It is known to history as Bethsaida-Julias. Philip died quietly in A.D. 34, after thirty-eight years of a good and undistinguished reign.

Jesus once called Antipas "that fox" (Luke 13:32). It was an apt description of the ablest of these brothers, the most scheming, the one who most closely resembled his father. Tiring of cold winters in Sepphoris, the capital of Galilee which Herod had once captured in a snowstorm, Antipas went down to the shore of the Sea of Galilee near the hot springs of Ammathus (ancient Hammath), and there built a new city, Tiberias, which he named for the new emperor, Tiberius. This is what his father would have done in the same situation. And like his father Antipas was careful to maintain his personal ties in Rome, particularly with the court. Again in imitation of his father, he had an eye for the women. And this proved to be a source of endless trouble. He fell in love with the wife of another half brother (also named Philip, but not the tetrarch). Herodias, for that was her name, responded to his advances. She was the granddaughter of Herod the Great, and marrying her uncle was permitted by Jewish law. But marrying a brother's wife was not permitted unless the brother was deceased. Divorce was out of the question.

Pan niches carved in rock at Paneas. Herod's son Philip built a new city at this cult center and named it Caesarea Philippi.

No matter; Antipas meant to marry her. And he did. Among those who vehemently denounced the marriage was John the Baptist. Antipas had him shut up in the forbidding fortress of Machaerus east of the Dead Sea.

Antipas' legal wife, the daughter of the king of Petra, returned to her father, and relations between the Nabatean king and his son-in-law soured. Antipas apparently also desired Salome, Herodias' daughter. He promised her anything she wished if she would dance before him. When Salome told her mother, Herodias encouraged Salome to do as Antipas wished and to ask for the head of John the Baptist in reward. The sordid scene ended with the head of John being presented to Herodias. The possible reappearance of this prophet of God whom he had killed was feared by Antipas until the day of his death in the year A.D. 39.

The third brother, Archelaus, after having been confirmed by Caesar, did not prove himself a worthy successor to Herod. He did not understand his people nor after the riots attendant upon his accession did he care to understand them. He took the riots as opportunities to collect heavy taxes. He spent lavishly, expanding some of his father's marvelous palaces, especially the one at Jericho, which had been damaged by riots while he was in Rome before Augustus. He also improved and enlarged the plantations in the area, diverting water from neighboring villages to irrigate his fields. By these and other means he increased his subjects' hatred for him. This feeling was not limited to his Jewish subjects, for in the year A.D. 6 the people of Samaria joined with Jews of Jerusalem in asking Augustus to remove Archelaus, who was summarily ordered to Rome and after investigation of the charges banished to Gaul. He died in A.D. 18.

With Archelaus deposed the old emperor now faced the same problem he had confronted earlier: who was going to rule in Jerusalem? But this time the answer was relatively easy. War was brewing in Dalmatia; legions would have to be sent. It was no time to risk further trouble in the east. Who was going to rule in Jerusalem? A Roman. Judea was to become a province.

Coponius, the first Roman governor of Judea, arrived in Caesarea and there he set up his government. Jerusalem was no longer to be the political capital. Archelaus' huge fortune was confiscated, including his lucrative plantations near Jericho. Moreover, as was normal in a new province, a census was undertaken. For such an important purpose the legate of Syria came personally to Caesarea. Unfortunately for all, there was ancient Jewish tradition forbidding a census. Even David had been punished for seeking to number the people of Israel (Samuel 24). There was trouble as Roman fiscal agents canvased the countryside. For an instant the flames of open rebellion flickered a little, but they died down again, partly because memories of Varus' coldly systematic intervention were still vivid, and partly because certain Jewish leaders labored mightily to avoid a disaster. Among these was Joazar, the high priest, who was also Herod the Great's son-in-law. Another was Hillel, revered leader of the more liberal school of Pharisees. Jewish sectarian politics had played a major role in aiding Roman establishment of the new province, but these same politics were now and for the next sixty years to plague these new overlords. Romans witnessed the ebb and flow of Jewish sectarian politics with increasing bewilderment. At length they were ready to make an end to the whole lot if the chance came. But they themselves were partly responsible for the encroaching chaos that finally engulfed Judea. For example, before he returned to Antioch, Quirinius, the legate, deposed Joazar, not because he was unhappy with him but in order to ap-

Machaerus, desert fortress east of the Dead Sea, where John the Baptist was put to death.

pease the more rigorist school of Pharisees. This school, associated with the name of their master Shammai, rivaled that of Hillel. These people objected to the pro-Roman high priest who had been put into office by Herod the Great. So Quirinius removed him and established Annas in the sacred office; Annas, the one mentioned in the Gospels (Luke 3:2; John 18:13, 24; see also Acts 4:6).

This Roman meddling in the religious affairs of the country had immediate and serious repercussions. One of the strangest and most far-reaching of these was the reaction of some of the very people whom Quirinius sought to pacify. Zaddok, an extremist of the Shammai party of Pharisees, joined with a man called Judas the Galilean (although he was from east of the Sea of Galilee) to form a new group, one dedicated to the violent overthrow of the Romans. This party came to be known as the Zealots. But the origins of this group and of various other Jewish sectarians who were now to play so large a role in the fortunes of their people and land lay further back in history, long before the Romans came to Judea, long before the Romans came to the east. The shape of Jewish sectarianism of the Roman period was determined by the Maccabean War and the Hasmonean dynasty which followed it.

The policies which the Hasmoneans adopted once they were established in power had alienated many of their Jewish subjects and sharply divided the country. Among these policies were: imperial aggrandizement, forceful conversion to Judaism of all inhabitants of captured areas, callous use of religious offices and influence for patently political gains, and lastly a curious contradiction involving an apparent desire to suppress alien cults and religious ideas while adopting Hellenistic culture and employing non-Jewish mercenaries. Underlying these policies was unlimited personal ambition, which beat in the breast of each Hasmonean in turn. The causes of divisions within Judaism and the Jewish community of Judea were thus deep and compounded of religious, cultural, political and economic factors as well as social stratification. In person and in policy the Hasmoneans were entirely too controversial to be healers. They worked to divide, not unite.

Another factor—serious in the extreme—was the lack of criteria for orthodoxy. Judaism has often been said to be a religion defined by practice rather than theology. But what dictates that practice? In Greco-Roman times various Jewish groups both in the Diaspora and in Judea had a tradition in common, but there was hardly agreement about the interpretation and implications of that tradition. There were, moreover, historical, regional and cultural variations. Not only was there no acknowledged body of interpretation, there was not even an agreed-upon collection of scripture. There was, however, one institution which formed the single visible common bond between individual Jews and competing Jewish groups. This was the Temple in Jerusalem and its sacrificial cult. The importance of this can hardly be exaggerated, since the synagogue, that institution which came to symbolize Judaism after the Revolt, was not yet fully developed nor universally accepted. Yet relations to the Temple were by no means uniform and in the case of the Qumranites the Hasmonean usurpation of the high priesthood resulted in their physical withdrawal from the Temple and its services.

The Pharisees also came to prominence during the Maccabean War and seem to have reached their zenith of political power around 140 B.C. No one really knows the origin of this group, but they were certainly related to the *Hasidim,* "the Holy Ones," those most devoted to the hallowing of life by strict adherence to the Law of Moses. During the reigns of John Hyrcanus

(134-104) and Alexander Jannaeus (103-76) the Pharisees came into conflict with the Sadducees in an intermittent and sometimes bloody struggle for political power. The Pharisees lost and indeed were almost totally crushed politically. They emerged again during the reign and with blessings of Queen Salome Alexandra (76-67) but having shifted, as one scholar has put it, "from politics to piety."

By the time the Romans made a province out of Judea the Pharisees, as mentioned, had themselves become deeply split between the more conservative group which followed the great rabbi, Shammai, and the liberals who looked up to the saintly Hillel. There were others at all points on this Pharisaical spectrum. And yet it is still possible to speak of a "Pharisaical position" as over against other sectarians of the time. This position was characterized by a number of things, the most important of which was their insistence upon the authority of the Oral Tradition. While the Sadducees argued for strict interpretation of the letter of the Written Law, Pharisees held that along with the Written Law there was also an Oral Law which had been revealed to Moses. This Oral Law was the proper interpretation of Torah, the Written Law. This meant that the Pharisees were developing a body of authoritative oral tradition alongside the Torah. Even before the Revolt they had developed Oral Law into set procedures and practices known as *Halakha*. Here is the direct ancestor of Midrash and eventually Talmud, for it was Pharisaical Judaism which survived both the First and the Second revolts and eventuated in Talmudic Judaism.

We can see why the great sages of the time were all Pharisees. They were the ones who had a certain amount of creative freedom of interpretation. This should be kept in mind when one reads various accounts of the Pharisees in the literature of that time, particularly in the New Testament, where these people are portrayed as inflexible defenders of a moribund legalistic system. Such a view is hardly adequate. Pharisaism did have its legalistic tendencies and there were inflexible Pharisees, but essentially this group sought to hallow all of life and to do so with an openness which was quite remarkable at the time. They are the ones, for example, who argued for an open canon, seeking to include as holy writings many things which were rejected by such others as the Sadducees and the Samaritans. It is to the Pharisees that we owe the preservation and canonization of the thirty-four books of the Old Testament other than the Pentateuch, the first five. It is the Pharisees who were open to "foreign" ideas such as belief in angels and demons and belief in the resurrection of the body. Such beliefs distinguished Pharisees in the Roman period. All were rejected by the Sadducees as "unscriptural"; that is, not found in the Five Books of Moses.

The Sadducees represented a religious position, as did all of the sectarian groups in first-century Judaism. But, more than any others, they were also defined by economic and social factors. A Pharisee could become such by study of the sacred writings and of the Oral Tradition. He would spend many hours at the feet of the rabbis, memorizing the long succession of ideas and interpretations. A Sadducee, on the other hand, was more likely to be born to his position, a position defined by wealth and social class. These people were also priests, and some think that the name of the group comes from Zadok, high priest under David. In any event, they had long been influential in priestly and political matters and were, until Herod the Great converted them by brutality and common economic interest, staunch Hasmonean supporters. After the fall of the Hasmoneans they were able to seize and

Roman milestones in the Jordan valley.

to hold, with but a few intervals, the high priestly office and control of the Sanhedrin that went with it. Most of all, at least from late Hasmonean times until the First Revolt, they controlled the Temple and its lucrative business. This was the single greatest industry in the country, and it was effectively in Sadducean hands.

The Sadducees were a curious mixture. On the one hand they were religiously conservative, rejecting anything for which they could not find literal warrant in the Five Books of Moses; on the other hand they embraced Greco-Roman culture and collaborated with their Roman overlords almost until the eve of the Revolt. The Sadducees were later to disappear, but in those years before the uprising against Rome they were a powerful force, a very powerful force indeed.

There were many other sectarian groups within the Judaism of that day. A third school of Jewish thought was that voiced by the Essenes. Whether the Essenes were a separate group living in urban centers or are to be identified with the people of Qumran is a lively question. We do know that in peaceful times the Qumranites also lived in the cities. There were also, as one might expect, groups which agitated for the restoration of the Hasmonean dynasty or the reestablishment of the throne of Herod. There was the opposite extreme to these monarchists, and this group was the right wing of the Zealot movement. The Romans called them *sicarii,* "dagger men," from the short curved knife called the *sica* which was easily concealed beneath flowing robes. How they performed their work is obvious, but that they concentrated on Jewish collaborators for many years before turning their blades on the Romans is less well known.

By far the largest group of people was, of course, the peasant population, the toilers on the land. The Pharisees called these people "sinners" because they did not observe ritual laws with care. They might have done so had they had the leisure, but tilling the soil and providing for their families occupied all the time they had. Nonetheless, their sympathies lay with those sectarians who showed the most interest in their plight and compassion for their impoverishment. This meant that they favored the Pharisees and heard the Christians gladly. We ought to remember that Christianity was also a Jewish sectarian movement at this time, although its contributions to the political and social life of pre-Revolt Judea were minimal.

From this brief survey it is clear that there was little in Judaism of the time that could be called normative. Judaism was sectarian, and every sectarian thought that he and he alone was right. Hostility and even violence between these groups was commonplace. Not even hatred of Roman overlords could unite these people. On the contrary, while they did occasionally seek to present a united front against the outsider, they did not slacken for a moment their internecine struggles. Yet there was one brief and glorious moment near the middle of the first century when it looked as though events were going to take a different turn and disaster would be averted. This was the reign of Agrippa I, who assumed the throne in A.D. 41.

On his paternal side Agrippa was the grandson of Herod and Mariamne, the Hasmonean princess. His father was Aristobulus, whom Herod had put to death. Thus he united in his heritage opposing monarchical factions, one with a claim to ancient Jewish rights and one which enjoyed more recent Herodian connections with Rome. And it was the Roman connections that made him king. Born in the year 10 B.C., he took his name from Marcus Vipsanius Agrippa, Augustus' chief minister and friend of Herod. But old Herod was careful about the education of his grandsons, sending them off to

Coin of Herod Agrippa I, ruler over Palestine from A.D. 41 to 44. A human image on a Jewish coin is unusual.

Rome, where they enjoyed imperial patronage. In fact, the young Agrippa became the closest friend of Drusus, son of Tiberius and heir to the imperial throne.

Agrippa was rich, handsome, easygoing, suave and full of good fun. He was a great favorite in Rome, and his popularity was enhanced by his lavish parties and willingness to share his fortune when he wanted favors. But things did not always go well for him, and the career of this improbable king was a series of ups and downs: he was either flat broke or wealthy beyond words, he languished in jail fettered by heavy chains or sat upon a golden throne. His salvation lay in his connections. He was a favorite of Tiberius, Gaius Caligula and Claudius in succession and with typical Herodian savvy knew just when to ease himself out of a losing cause and tie his future to an ascending star. Caligula summoned him from prison to make him king of his dead uncle Philip's territory. The idea of Agrippa as king in Caesarea Philippi was too much for Herodias, Antipas' wife, however, and she agitated through her Roman connections for an audience for herself and her ethnarch husband. The result was that the emperor gave Antipas' dominion to Agrippa and exiled Antipas to Spain!

There now occurred an incident which completely endeared Agrippa to the Jews. Caligula ordered that his statue be set up in the Temple in Jerusalem and that sacrifices be made before it. Petronius, the Syrian legate who had been told to have the statue made and erected, hesitated. He knew that it would trigger a violent reaction, if not a wholesale rebellion. It was Agrippa who saved the day, persuading Caligula as a personal favor to abandon the plan.

As Caligula's madness grew worse, Agrippa almost alone in Rome began to attach himself to Tiberius Claudius Drusus Nero Germanicus, the cripple who, although heir to the throne, had been shunned by the royal family and Roman society alike. Agrippa not only drifted over to Claudius' side, but after Caligula was assassinated it was none other than Agrippa who was intermediary between the Senate, The Praetorian Guard and Claudius. When Claudius took the imperial diadem he owed much to Agrippa and the reward was equal to the debt. Claudius reconstituted the whole of Herod the Great's kingdom and gave it to Agrippa and elevated him to consular rank.

"When in Rome, do as the Romans," and Agrippa certainly did. But when in Jerusalem . . . well, that is a different matter, and in Jerusalem Agrippa was a model Jew, even pious to a fault. He continued this dual pattern of behavior, conducting himself as a Roman in Caesarea, Sebaste, Tiberias and the like, but wholly within the Jewish code of conduct elsewhere in his realm. Coins minted in the Greco-Roman cities of his kingdom bore his image and that of the emperor. Those minted in Jerusalem bore no human image whatever. Both areas, Jewish and Gentile, were ruled with moderation, generosity and grace. Agrippa had inherited all of his grandfather's good traits and none of the bad ones.

He had also inherited his grandfather's passion for building. Herod had built so much, however, that Agrippa often had to go beyond the borders of his realm to satisfy this architectural passion. He did continue work on the still unfinished Temple platform, and he was able to build one massive construction of his own in Jerusalem. This was a monumental wall enclosing the suburb of Bezetha. This "third wall" ran along the lines of the present north wall. According to Josephus, Agrippa's Wall was forty feet high and fifteen feet thick, with ninety square towers. Before it was a moat twenty feet

Tiberius

Gaius Caesar Germanicus "Caligula"

Claudius

249

The Kingdom of Agrippa I

▬▬▬ Boundary of Agrippa I's kingdom
▬ ▬ ▬ Other boundaries
⊡ Cities of the Decapolis
⌘ Fortresses

| 0 | 5 | 10 | 15 | 20 | 25 | 30 | 35 Mls |
| 0 | 10 | 20 | 30 | 40 | 50 | 60 Kms |

© Copyright HAMMOND INCORPORATED, Maplewood, N.J.

S Y R I A
Byblos
Berytus
CHALCIS
Chalcis
ANTI-LEBANON
Abilene
Abila
Damascus
Sidon
MOUNT LEBANON
Leontes
MT. HERMON
P h o e n i c i a
Tyre
Caesarea Philippi (Paneas)

Mediterranean
Sea
Cadasa
Ptolemais
GALILEE
Bethsaida-Julias
Raphana
Taricheae
Sea of Galilee
Tiberias
Hippos
Dion?
Mt. Carmel
Sepphoris
Gabae
Mt. Tabor
Abila
Dora
Gadara
DECAPOLIS
Caesarea
Scythopolis
Pella
SAMARIA
Sebaste
Gerasa
Apollonia
Mt. Gerizim
Sychar
Jordan
Jabbok
Antipatris
Joppa
Phasaelis
Gadara
PEREA
Philadelphia
Lydda
Archelais
Jamnia
Emmaus
Jericho
Esbus
Jerusalem
Qumran
Julias (Livias)
Azotus
Medeba
Ascalon
Bethlehem
J U D E A
Herodium
Asphaltitis (Dead Sea)
Gaza
Hebron
Machaerus
Engaddi
Arnon
Lake
Masada
Bersabe
Malatha
N A B A T E A

Coin of Agrippa I, from the year 42/43.

250

deep and fifty feet wide. When one realizes that the terrain in this area of Jerusalem undulates, mounting rock scarps and sinking into valleys, one marvels that Agrippa's engineers managed to keep the height of the towers the same.

A number of Romans grumbled at this wall, noting how it immeasurably strengthened the defenses of Jerusalem. Others said that the Jews were preparing for war. Agrippa's motives were apparently just Herodian; that is, to build something on a massive scale. But those who saw the military implications of this fortification were right, and twenty years later many a young Roman was to lose his life assaulting it.

Agrippa died suddenly at Caesarea in A.D. 44, the same year in which he sanctioned a persecution of some sectarians we know as Christians. But this violence was out of character with the rest of his reign. He was an able administrator and used his abundant charm in personal diplomacy to defuse potentially explosive situations. Had he reigned more than the three years he sat on the revived throne, history might have been different. As it was, he and his rule were an interlude in a downward spiral to disaster.

Agrippa's death touched off rioting, but not by the Jews, who were in deep mourning. It was the Greeks and the mercenary soldiers who poured through the streets of Caesarea, even looting the palace itself. Disorder spread to Sebaste and to other Greco-Roman centers in the realm. Those who had gone to great lengths to flatter Agrippa while he lived abused his memory now that he was gone.

Agrippa II, only seventeen at the time of his father's death, was not appointed to the throne but remained in the emperor's household. Instead a succession of Roman governors ruled in Judea. Peaceful periods were punctuated by times of trouble. When famine caused great misery, Tiberius Julius, an apostate member of a Jewish family in Egypt who had become governor in 46, organized relief aid as best he could, given the meager resources of the area. And others also helped. Acts 11:27-30 tells about Paul and Barnabas bringing money from Christians in Antioch to the church in Jerusalem. And it was during this terrible time that Helena, Queen of Adiabene and a convert to Judaism, distinguished herself by importing food into Jerusalem from Egypt and Cyprus. She won a lasting place in Jewish memory and her tomb is still to be seen in Jerusalem.

There was also the inevitable political unrest. In the north, at Ginae, Samaritans attacked Jews traveling to Jerusalem. Zealots were crucified for stirring up trouble. In the year 48 when Ventidius Cumanus became governor there was rioting in the Temple precipitated by the contempt shown by Roman troops for the Jews. Repressive measures were taken, including the burning of villages, the crucifixion of Jews found bearing or harboring arms and the beheading of leaders of recent outbreaks. At last a delegation of influential Jews including Annas, the former high priest, and some important Romans were sent to Rome to explain the situation to Claudius and seek relief.

In Rome the arguments raged back and forth. It may well have been that Claudius' expulsion of Jews from Rome in 49 was related to all this. In any case Claudius now listened to the endless complaints of the various Judean groups. His mind made up, Claudius banished the governor, Cumanus. The commander of the troops was publicly executed in Jerusalem, and three of the Samaritan leaders were put to death for their part in the recent troubles.

Agrippa's Wall followed the line of the present-day north wall in Jerusalem.

Tomb of Queen Helena of Adiabene.

251

Each incident, no matter who was at fault, contributed to the growing spirit of malevolence. Jewish extremists such as the Zealots and Sicarii had not been too successful in radicalizing the masses. Indeed, the liberal Pharisees of Hillel's persuasion had been a positive counterbalance. Slowly, almost inexorably, the mercenary soldiery were to do for the Jewish extremists what they could not do for themselves. The antagonism caused by the Roman troops drove increasing numbers of Jews to a more radical position.

Claudius had shown his usual balance and fairness in dealing with an awkward situation in which governor, army commander and others had behaved badly. But in the appointment of a new governor his good judgment abandoned him. He appointed Antonius Felix. Felix was a freedman who had come—by what means we do not know—into enormous riches and by these riches had acquired good family connections. One of his three wives was the granddaughter of Antony and Cleopatra. Felix was "somebody" in Rome and received the appointment to Caesarea because of influence, not qualifications.

When Claudius died in 54, he was succeeded by Nero Claudius Germanicus, son of the first marriage of Claudius' wife, Agrippina. Nero was by heritage and practice a degenerate and his rule was one of unbroken personal debauchery. The baseness with which he decimated the Christian community of Rome following the great fire in 64 was wholly consonant with his character. He and his rule were preserved as long as they were by the frequent use of exile against opponents, judicious murders of friends and foes alike, and Tigellinus. Tigellinus, who was officially urban prefect, became chief minister to Nero. He indulged Nero with one hand and ran the empire with the other. Both were full-time occupations. Other advisors who had kept the empire more or less on an even keel dropped away. Burrus, head of the Praetorian Guard, died; Seneca was dismissed for criticizing the emperor's poetry. Slowly the inner circle of power came to resemble Nero himself.

Felix, governor of Judea, was to bring disaster to the Jews. He set himself at once to eliminate the brigandage which had wracked the country for many years. Using every means—dogged pursuit, informers, torture—he hunted down, tried, shipped off to Rome or crucified many of the leaders of the Zealots and other such groups. The measure of Felix' success is to be seen in the fact that he drove terrorism into the dark.

In the deteriorating situation Felix poured gasoline on the flames. He wanted to be rid of Jonathan, the same who had asked that Felix be appointed to Caesarea. So the governor, in the best traditions of the times, bribed Jonathan's best friend to hire some assassins, some Sicarii, to do the job. They did, but they did not stop with Jonathan. Everywhere Jewish officials who had cooperated with the Romans were marked for elimination. The governor himself had unleashed a virtual reign of terror. To make matters worse various messiahs arose, calling the people to holy war. No one could tell where or when there might be a murder or an abortive uprising. Soldiers and auxiliaries were almost constantly on the road, moving from place to place as mutinous events dictated. The worst incident happened, as we have come to expect, in Jerusalem. A self-proclaimed messiah called "the Egyptian" seized the Mount of Olives and called upon the local population to join him in destroying all the Romans in the city. But the people sided with Felix, who sent his soldiers across the Kidron and up the Mount of Olives. The Egyptian escaped with many of his followers, but he left 400 behind him dead or dying amid the rocks and olive trees.

Nero

In the summer of 60 Porcius Festus replaced Felix who had been recalled to Rome. A greater contrast could hardly be imagined. Festus was correct to the last detail; fair-minded, tough, incorruptible, with a touch of great good sense. It was Festus who sent Paul from his prison in Caesarea to Nero in Rome. Also on the scene at this juncture was Agrippa II, the last in the line of Herodian kings. He had been given territory in the far north, but he involved himself in matters of concern to the Jewish people in all of Palestine. His friendship with Nero had won him additional cities in Galilee and Perea. Agrippa II had nominal control over the Temple in Jerusalem and he enlarged the old Hasmonean palace to use as his residence while in the Holy City. Political authority remained, of course, in the hands of the Roman governor.

In addition to the disposition of Paul's case the new governor Festus was bequeathed another problem which had more far-reaching consequences for the Jews. During Felix' time the Jews of Caesarea, who had parity with Greeks in that city, claimed superior status. They wished to turn this seaport into a second Jerusalem. The claim was based upon the curious view that Herod was a Jew, surely a strange basis for a legal argument, especially considering the way the Jews had viewed and treated Herod. The Greeks became increasingly annoyed with Jewish claims and blood was shed. When Festus came to Caesarea the situation was extremely tense and decision in the matter of the Jewish claim had been referred to Rome.

Jewish tombstone from catacombs along the Appian Way, Rome. Second or third century A.D.

A ruling on this serious matter did not come until the year 62. Nero decided against the Jews. There were several reasons for this, some valid, some not. At base the Jewish claim to supremacy over the Greeks of the city was empty. But Nero seldom settled such matters on their merits, and we must assume that other factors played a larger role. Among these was the influence wielded by Felix' relatives who were close to Nero. For whatever personal or legal reasons Nero handed down his decision. It said that by attempting to usurp rights that they were not entitled to, the Jews of Caesarea had in fact forfeited their status to equality in the city. In short, their claim to superiority had led to its being granted to the Greeks! The Jews were infuriated by the decision and, in spite of Festus' evenhanded policies, bands of Sicarii spread out once more over the land. As in previous times of unrest messiahs arose and the army had to be called out. Order was everywhere breaking down. Could things get worse? Yes. Festus died in office.

In such situations there was a short interval between governors, and these times offered opportunity for those who wished to make mischief. At Festus' death the Syrian legate took no action to insure order. Lucceius Albinus, who seems to have been in Alexandria, was finally appointed governor. But it would be some time before he arrived. In the interim Ananus, son of the high priest, reasserted the high priest's previous rights to political power and turned murderously upon the Christians in Jerusalem. This was part of the internecine sectarian hatred which was rife in the land. James, the brother of Jesus, a saintly man and an ascetic, was thrown from the Temple platform and his broken body pelted with stones until life left him. This was the decree of the Sanhedrin, before whom he had been tried. Many of the Jews of Jerusalem were outraged at this, and later the new governor deposed the high priest.

Yet another disaster occurred about this time. Gamaliel, the third of the great rabbis of the era (Hillel and Shammai being the other two), died. He was a grandson of Hillel and like him had consistently urged moderation. His

253

lineage, learning and saintly life lent him great influence. Just at this critical moment a most influential moderate passed from the scene.

Albinus came to Jerusalem as one of the "new breed" which were important to Nero after the death of Tigellinus. He possessed few good qualities except one which Nero prized highly; he wanted to please his emperor in everything. And Nero wanted money more than anything else just now. The Golden House in Rome and other extravagances had cost a dozen fortunes. The provinces were called upon to refurbish the royal coffers. Albinus as governor of Judea did everything he could to comply. Taxes skyrocketed, and methods of coercing payment became more brutal. Opposition stiffened. Albinus replied by cracking down on extremists. They, in their turn, countered with something new: political kidnapping. The Sicarii seized the son of Ananias, a high official in the Temple hierarchy, and offered to exchange him for ten of their own men held in prison. Ananias was very rich and may have bribed Albinus to release the ten men. Within days kidnappings multiplied, the victims being always friends and followers of Ananias. And always Albinus, after receiving something, released a group of terrorists from the prisons in exchange for the victims. Prisoners who were not ransomed in this way merely began to pay Albinus directly for their freedom. The administration of the province—if one could still speak of such—fell into ruins as this venal man made what he could from an explosive situation.

While Jews and Greeks harassed each other in Caesarea, Albinus got rich and the roads of Palestine became unsafe day or night. The Temple complex in Jerusalem was brought to completion. It had been eighty-three years since Herod had laid the foundations of his most magnificent creation. Now it was finished. But what an inopportune moment; it threw 18,000 men out of work. The Temple authorities, sensing what might well happen with this new disgruntled mass in the city, took steps to avoid trouble. They paid the men promptly and even spoke of a bonus out of the Temple treasury, but wiser heads realized that if that were opened for such a purpose Albinus' hand would undoubtedly find its way in.

All this while Agrippa II was in Jerusalem urging moderation, seeking to conciliate, fearing the worst. He seems to have been the only person who realized what might be the fearful outcome of the play whose characters were assembling and whose last act had already been written. It was he who sought to put the unemployed to work repaving the streets of Jerusalem. It was a desperate measure for difficult times, a sort of WPA ahead of its time. But it worked for a little while, and some of the pavements may still be seen in Jerusalem.

Albinus retired with his fortune and was succeeded by Gessius Florus in 64. Like Felix he was newly arrived in the halls of power. Like Felix he owed his appointment to connections at court. Unlike Felix he had no taste, no tact, no decency. Florus openly sought all the money he could get, by means fair or foul and used his vast powers to assault any and all who opposed him. At this fateful juncture in Jewish history the legate of Syria was Cestius Gallus, an enfeebled old man incapable of making his own decisions or of carrying out another's. Between the two, Florus and Gallus, it was hard to see which one was worse for the Roman East.

It is difficult to know what Florus enjoyed more, stealing or flaunting it in the faces of those from whom he stole. For two years none dared denounce him to the legate, but when Gallus came to Jerusalem for Passover in 66 a delegation waited upon him with a request that he restrain the governor.

These steps near St. Peter in Gallicantu may be remnants of Agrippa II's efforts to employ men in repaving the streets of Jerusalem.

Florus, who was present, merely laughed. Gallus, as Florus knew he would, did nothing whatever other than offer a few consoling words to the beleaguered provincials.

The first real hostilities broke out in Caesarea. The Jews' claim to supremacy and Nero's denial of that claim was the cause. The Greek owner of property near the synagogue had not only refused to sell it to the congregation, but deliberately built on it, renting out the structures as workshops. The synagogue could now be reached only by a very narrow passage. Florus arrested some Jews who tried to stop construction of still more buildings in the area. Foolishly he was offered a bribe if he would release the men and stop the building. He retired to Sebaste with the money to consider the matter. Next day was the Sabbath. As Jews came to the synagogue they saw a Greek sitting before a large overturned jar sacrificing birds on it—right in the doorway of the sanctuary. A fight broke out. Soldiers were called out to stop it. Some members of the congregation took the sacred Torah from the synagogue and fled the city. Still others went off to Sebaste to see Florus. When they mentioned the bribe, he flew into a rage and had them thrown into prison. In this mood he sent to Jerusalem, demanding twice the bribe amount from the Temple treasury. Words of this sacrilege spread through the narrow streets, from shop to shop, house to house. Someone decided to take up a collection of small coins for the "impoverished" governor. When Florus heard of this he came at once to Jerusalem to deal with the insult. In front of Herod's new palace in the Upper City he was met by a delegation who wished to remonstrate with him about looting the Temple treasury, but Florus wanted from them only the names of those involved in the insult and subsequent demonstrations against Rome's governor. When the elders of the people said they did not know, Florus sent his troops into the nearby market, ordering them to loot and kill. It was butchery, and the stones newly laid by Agrippa's semi-unemployed shone deep crimson. Many, including some Roman citizens, were dragged before the crazed Florus, given a rump trial and summarily crucified. Before the day was over some 3,600 people were dead or dying.

Florus had not caused the trouble in Caesarea, but he had done little to resolve it. Responsibility for the latest Jerusalem debacle with its staggering human toll was, however, his and his alone. The date for the beginning of the First Revolt is given as mid-August 66, when rebels holding the Temple brought an end to sacrifices offered for the emperor. This is probably correct, yet the opening stages of the war were really these actions of Florus because there was from this time forward no turning back. Jewish extremists were on the move, and even large numbers of Sadducees were joining the increasingly organized resistance. Florus, moreover, had weakened the garrison in seething Caesarea by bringing still more troops into Jerusalem with orders to use force against any suspicious person. Numerous incidents occurred, including yet another attack on an unarmed crowd. Then he withdrew to Caesarea, thinking he had made his point and angry because he had failed to get his hands on the rest of the Temple treasury. If there had been any hopes of averting a full revolt this rapacious governor murdered them in the streets of the Holy City. Judea was clearly on the brink of full-scale war.

18 JUDAEA CAPTA

To many the breach between the Roman state and the Jews may have been unexpected. For years the Herodian family had had close and important ties with Rome. Since Herod the Great's time the Jewish royal family, as we have seen, had enjoyed an intimacy and occasional influence with Roman emperors that was extraordinary. And the Jewish people had benefited from the edicts and desires of Caesar, Antony and Octavian — however politically motivated. If from time to time there was friction it did not affect the toleration shown the Jews by the Romans. Even the expulsion of the Jews from Rome under Claudius seems to have been more for the purpose of maintaining order than religious persecution. However, the present situation in Judea required a different reaction. An entire province was passing out of control and the Roman East was in jeopardy. If the Jewish Revolt succeeded, Parthia, Rome's enemy in the east, was ready to pick up the pieces. Once the Romans were sufficiently alerted to the danger, past associations and toleration would be quickly forgotten in suppressing the rebellion. The Roman response was inevitable; only the time it took those in authority to react was surprising.

Gallus, legate of Syria, receiving messages from Florus blaming the Jews and also confronted by a Jewish delegation complaining of Florus, acted in his normal way. He sent an officer to investigate. And that was that. Other legates had reacted far stronger to less serious situations. Gallus, however, was enjoying Antioch, and his legions would stay there to enjoy it with him.

Agrippa II, who had worked so hard to prevent hostilities, counseled moderation but his people threw stones at him. Florus had passed the mobs over to the extremists. Roman brutality and greed were to be met measure for measure by Jewish fanaticism and intransigence. There was nothing for it now but war. With sorrow Agrippa withdrew from Judea to his own realm north of the Sea of Galilee, from which he watched his beloved, long-suffering and completely furious people throw themselves before the Roman juggernaut. Only Agrippa seemed to comprehend the intensity of the fury that was about to overwhelm the land. Gallus did not recognize the seriousness of the situation. Florus either did not see or did not care about the implications of his actions.

Strangest of all, the officers of some of the military garrisons in Judea were also caught completely off guard by events. Seemingly impregnable Masada fell to a group of rebels with ease, and with it an enormous armory Herod had prepared for use against Cleopatra more than a century earlier. And the Antonia, that massive monument to military mentality, fell after only two days of siege by a mob. Both fortresses were self-contained and should have held out for years. But the storm broke over the somehow unsuspecting garrisons before they could deploy their potential might. The signs of the times were everywhere and had been clear for a long time. The Romans seemed totally unable to read them.

When word of hostilities in Judea was brought to Nero, he too seemed bored with the whole thing and resented such an intrusion upon other affairs. For over a century Judea had been vital to Roman interests. It is difficult to

Opposite:
Masada, the impregnable rock fortress of Herod the Great, was the last stronghold of the Jews in the revolt against Rome.

see how, when the supreme crisis came, no one in the chain of command took the initial events seriously. All of this, of course, only gave the rebels much needed time to consolidate. Had Gallus moved in the spring of 66 with the speed and determination Varus had shown earlier, the whole thing might have been over in a matter of weeks. As it was, the war went on for seven years.

The Revolt itself falls into four stages: the rebel success, the appearance of Vespasian and his Galilee campaign, the siege and fall of Jerusalem and the mopping-up of the desert fortresses.

The rebel success at Masada surprised everyone. They had induced the garrison there to surrender and then slaughtered the lot in cold blood. Oddly enough, not even this steeled the sinew and strengthened the nerve of other garrisons. Jerusalem was in chaos and shortly the scene at Masada was repeated at the Antonia — a wholesale butchery of the surrendered soldiers. The focus now fell upon troops holding out in Herod's new palace. These men abandoned the royal apartment complex and barricaded themselves in the three towers. Agrippa, who had striven mightily to prevent this war, now sided wholly with the Romans. Some of his forces were sent to reinforce the besieged fortress. But the situation was hopeless, and they too soon found themselves in desperate straits. The "Roman" soldiers who were now shut up in this splendid edifice were not, of course, from Italy. Apart from Agrippa's men they were, like those who fell at the Antonia, from Caesarea and Sebaste, mostly Caesareans. Rebel hatred for these men knew no bounds. They agreed to allow Agrippa's troops to leave the city, but no Caesareans could be allowed to escape. In smart files the reprieved marched away while the doomed watched from the towers. Those left behind may have held the hope that the rebels' lust for blood had been satisfied at the Antonia, but unknown to these men the rebels had been conducting a blood purge of their fellow Jews in the Holy City. All who opposed the uprising or who had counseled moderation were sought out. Ananias, the high priest, was dragged from a tunnel under the Temple and slain. Others followed him. Then it was the turn of the hated Caesareans who unwisely surrendered the virtually impregnable towers. None were assaulted with more senseless brutality than were these men.

There was no need to exaggerate the details of this wanton slaughter of these Gentile soldiers; the truth was horrible enough. The Jews may with some justification have felt that they were merely getting even. But the results were predictable when word of events in Jerusalem reached Caesarea and other predominantly Gentile cities. As one candle passes flame to another in the darkness, so the cities around the eastern Mediterranean blazed one after another with anti-Jewish feelings and actions. Caesarea was first. The whole place literally exploded. In a little over an hour the entire Jewish population was massacred—20,000 people! The few hapless Jewish survivors were chained to galleys, there to end their miserable days.

The reaction in Caesarea produced a counterreaction. Jewish terrorist gangs were organized by extremists and sent to various nearby Gentile cities, especially those of the Decapolis. Both Gaza and Ascalon were attacked and burned, as was magnificent Sebaste, long a focus for Jewish hatred. The Jewish terrorists did their work as far north as Tyre and even sought to infiltrate now watchful Caesarea.

Events at Scythopolis illustrate the awful plight in which some sections of the Jewish community found themselves. When the terrorists struck there, local Jews joined their Gentile neighbors in driving away the rebels. But the action, as we might well expect, had been a confusing one, and the fearful

Gentiles drove 13,000 Jews from their homes lest they have a change of heart and join the rebels. These Jews had nowhere to go and feared for their lives lest the rebels come and take vengeance upon them. They should have looked in the other direction, for it was the Gentiles of their own city who attacked them. These poor Jews, caught in the middle, had not moved far enough away from the city in time to satisfy the security needs of their panicked and terrified former neighbors. Gerasa was the singular example of an entirely different situation. There Jew and Gentile alike realized that it would not long be safe for the Jewish community of Gerasa to remain in this important city on the road to Damascus. With loving care and sorrow Gentiles helped their neighbors pack, supplied them with what they could and bid them Godspeed and safe journey. Later in the course of the war Gerasa paid dearly for "aiding the enemy" in this manner.

Ionic columns from the circular forum in Gerasa still stand as witnesses to the once-elegant Greco-Roman city.

Not even Caesarea Philippi, Agrippa's capital, escaped the madness. Agrippa had dashed north to urge Gallus to move. The troubles were now spreading beyond the borders of Judea. Tyre had been attacked. There was fierce fighting in Egypt. While Agrippa appealed to the incompetent Gallus the Gentiles of his own city turned murderously on the Jews there, eliminating them. Agrippa returned to find himself one of the few Jews left in Caesarea Philippi.

What was Florus doing all this time? The primary duties of a Roman governor were two: to see that his province was not invaded from without and to maintain order within. Florus had not only the authority and the duty to act, but also every possible motivation of self-preservation. He would be held responsible for all this. Yet there is reason to think that he was involved with some of the terrorists. Although he probably did not share their treasonable intent, he did find it possible to make money by dealing with them. It would not have been the first time in Roman provincial history that a corrupt governor schemed to make enough money to bribe the jury that he knew was to try him in Rome. For a certain mentality this was standard practice, and in Neronian Rome it was more or less expected.

Roman soldiers attacking a wall with scaling ladders under cover of a "tortoise" formed by shields.

Perhaps Gallus was waiting for Florus to request intervention by the legions. Gallus, however, had the authority and duty to intervene without such action on the part of the governor. And finally he did. It was not too late, but with the situation, too little. He marched south with only the XIIth Legion (about 4,200 men) plus six cohorts of infantry and four units of cavalry (another 2,520 men) picked from other legions under his command. He also had auxiliaries (some 15,000 men) sent by Rome's client kings. The uprising began to collapse at the sight of the spears and short swords, of the standards and flashing armor. Almost at a stroke and much to his surprise Gallus soon held the coast. In October he moved from Caesarea to retake Jerusalem and proved that he was as incompetent as a field commander as he was as an administrator. Passing through Beth-horon where Jonathan had routed the Philistines so many years before, Gallus, having failed to take the most elementary precautions in unfamiliar hill country, saw his train set upon by swift guerrillas who hit and ran. The lesson was lost on the Roman commander. Gallus temporized before the walls of Jerusalem, apparently not knowing exactly what to do. When he did finally assault Agrippa's wall, its defenders fled almost at the sight of the waves of approaching soldiers. Gallus occupied the New City and burned it. The advantage lay with him. Jerusalem's rebels were in panic and were, moreover, fighting among themselves. Again Gallus hesitated, this time for almost a week. Then he tried to take what remained of the Antonia, which the rebels had partially burned. While a "tortoise" (soldiers

holding shields over their heads) approached the walls, others undermined a large section of the defensive barricade. A path lay open for an attack on the Temple which, we should recall, was also a fortress and the center of rebel operations. But again Gallus did not follow his opportunity, not even one he had made for himself.

Gallus had lost his chance. Winter was almost upon him. He decided to retreat. The defenders of Jerusalem, many of whom thought their days were numbered, could hardly believe it. Yet it was true; the camps were being broken up, supplies that had to be left were in flames, and the road to the northwest had a cloud of dust over it. They were marching toward Beth-horon.

Gallus had learned nothing from his earlier experience on that road. The Jews had counted on this and in the hills around Beth-horon attacked the demoralized column. Gallus withdrew to the town of Beth-horon and fortified it through a sleepless night. By morning he had decided to get out of those hills as quickly as possible, so he ordered the soldiers onto the road once more. They were to leave behind everything that would slow them down. No time to burn it, just go! It was thus that vast amounts of Roman siege machines including catapults fell into Jewish hands. This artillery would prove extremely valuable in the defense of Jerusalem against Vespasian and Titus.

Even without encumbering weight Gallus' army did not make it. The XIIth Legion was cut to pieces between Beth-horon and Antipatris. Over 6,000 lost their lives. It was one of Rome's more ignominious military disasters. In the interval following Gallus' retreat, efforts were being made to prepare for the assault to come. But who would lead it? Certainly not Gallus.

The first phase of the war had come to an end. The rebels held most of Judea and a Jerusalem vastly strengthened by captured Roman equipment. They had even been able to spread the rebellion across the Jordan and had invested Machaerus.

What now was to happen? The Jews knew that the Romans would be back. They set about to organize the country into military districts following, as it turned out, the administrative arrangement by which Albinus had milked the land. At the same time internal strife among Jewish groups continued and in the flush of first success even intensified. When Agrippa had earlier urged upon the Jerusalemites the futility of opposing Roman arms, he had been right. The rebellion was doomed from the beginning. But its character was in large measure determined by a virtual state of war which existed among various Jewish factions. The first split was between those who supported the Revolt and those who did not. As the war dragged on some of those who did not support the cause were able to extract themselves. Large numbers of Pharisees withdrew from Jerusalem to Jamnia, while some Gentile Christians fled across the Jordan Valley to Pella. This did not, however, leave a unified front against the Romans. Some of the most savage fighting of the war took place between Jewish groups supporting the war.

News of Gallus' military affairs came to Nero in Greece. The emperor looked around for someone who could save the situation and make an end to it. Among his party was an old general, Flavius Vespasian, past fifty-eight. His parentage was undistinguished, and indeed his military career was hardly outstanding. But he had fought well in Britain under Claudius and he had served as consul in Rome. He had also been a provincial governor in Africa, where he had shown himself scrupulously honest. He was also bored with this whole Greek trip. Perhaps Nero could get rid of a dampening spirit and also find a competent man to deal with the Judean mess. So Vespasian was appointed military commander of Judea with the rank of legate. In addition

Twelfth Legion stone. The XIIth Roman Legion under Gallus was soundly defeated in the first phase of the Jewish Revolt.

to the four legions under Gallus (the XIIth was being reconstituted), he was given two others, the Vth Macedonians and the famous Xth, *Fretensis,* "the Free Legion." It was also decided that he should have the XVth, *Apollonaris,* which was in Alexandria. Tiberius Julius now had that city under control and the legion could be spared. Titus, Vespasian's son, was dispatched to Egypt to bring that legion into Judea. Furthermore, all of the client kings of the east were required by Nero to supply auxiliary forces to Vespasian.

The Judeans had seen legions before. But they had never seen an entire Roman army with seven legions acting in concert. The mere appearance of this vast array of might had an extraordinary effect, weakening the rebel cause by defections. But there were others who recalled the XIIth bleeding to death in the Judean hills and were willing to see what this new bunch were made of. Gallus had had upwards of 30,000 men, most of them untried auxiliaries. Vespasian commanded something like 60,000 men, most of them battle-hardened veterans. It was going to be different.

If any one quality characterized Vespasian it was prudence. He did everything with care, step by step. Neither impetuosity nor temporizing was in him. He might have temporary setbacks in the field, but the next day his plan just continued to unfold. He was thorough, he was careful; in the end he was successful. His first action was to move against Galilee. He strengthened Sepphoris and made it the nerve center for northern operations. Villages that gave support to the rebels were to be burned and their inhabitants massacred without exception. Horrors and human tragedy of every kind occurred since, if we are to believe Tacitus, the Roman veterans were determined to avenge the dishonor heaped upon Gallus and the XIIth Legion.

The Jewish forces in Galilee were concentrated in Jotapata, a site blessed by nature with natural defenses. To these Josephus, rebel commander in the north, had added massive walls. This is the same Josephus who as a historian recorded many of these events. The siege took forty-seven days, and in his account of the war Josephus gives us an almost moment-by-moment account of the Roman siege operations, the bravery of the defenders, the tenacity of the Romans and the suffering which was endured by the town's inhabitants. In the end, it was Roman rams, ramps and assault towers that brought victory.

During the fighting for Jotapata, other cities and towns, heartened by the gallant Jewish defense, declared for the rebels. The fact that Vespasian could calmly detach units and send them to put down these risings shows both the care with which he had made his plans and the confidence he had in his work.

In Galilee Vespasian showed other qualities which distinguished him when he later became emperor. He did not seem to share the feeling of many of his troops that the defeat of a legion had to be revenged by bloodshed. The reputation of Roman arms did not, in his view, lie in their success or failure on a given occasion. It was the overall plan that mattered. He also wished to avoid harsh measures and bloodshed where possible.

In seeking to avoid unnecessary fighting the Roman general and his son Titus were sometimes taken in by their opponents. Vespasian's treatment of the town of Tiberias was one such case. He had no wish to destroy Tiberias, which after all, belonged to Agrippa. So he sent officers to parley with some of the leaders of the town. While this meeting was going on the officers were attacked and, although they escaped with their lives, they lost their horses and personal weapons. A normal military response would have been to attack the city. But Vespasian restrained himself and his troops and, determining that the treacherous assault had been made by rebels seeking to provoke the

Tenth Legion stone. After the fall of Jerusalem the "Free Legion" was based there, as this second-century inscription shows.

Romans into just such an attack, arranged to have the leaders of Tiberias demolish part of the wall as a sign of good faith. Then he entered without further incident.

At Gischala, the last town in Galilee remaining in rebel hands, the Romans again were deceived. This time it was John of Gischala, the rebel leader, who tricked Vespasian's son Titus into withdrawing from the outskirts of the town so that they could parley without being "under the gun," as it were. As the next day was the Sabbath, John wanted to know if the Roman commander would honor Jewish law and wait until Sunday to talk. Titus agreed. John seized the opportunity and, taking women and children as hostages, fled south toward Jerusalem. By the end of the year 67 all of Galilee was in Roman hands.

Vespasian and Titus had learned a few things in the north. They never again responded to rebel pleas or promises, not even when these ostensibly involved missions of mercy. They also were not prepared to offer quarter once the rebels had rejected their offers. To parley with these people was, on the basis of their Galilean experience, to offer the enemy new opportunities.

In the spring of 68 Vespasian moved east of the Jordan to secure Perea. Suffice it to say that Vespasian was successful, except in the case of Machaerus which he was unable to subdue. A second Roman campaign that year in Judea and western Idumea added to the toll of Jewish losses. As before in Galilee Vespasian sent hordes of slaves to man galleys or cut away at the Isthmus of Corinth in a vain attempt to build Nero's Corinthian canal.

As the second phase of the war moved slowly to completion our focus can shift to Jerusalem and the ever interesting John of Gischala. He is a type known to many ages. Having failed in Galilee and escaped only at the expense of the people he was supposed to be defending, he set himself up in Jerusalem as a hero. If he had not succeeded, he had at least—so he said—done much better than anyone else could have done under the circumstances. John also brought with him a faithful body of brigands. Religious extremists as well as plain bandits and ruffians were being squeezed out of the countryside by the Roman operations and poured into the heights above the Kidron. To say that Jerusalem became lawless is to suggest an order which it did not have. John gathered many of these people to himself. He was just like them, and they shared common purposes. They styled themselves "zealots," and it is from this self-designation that the name was applied to others.

It would be wrong, of course, to say that John and his followers were merely thieves and murderers. It was much more complicated than that. Brigands who had come or been driven into the city strengthened a religious movement which was already present and had existed long before the Revolt, as we have seen. The land must be purified, which meant that the foreigners—Romans, Greeks, Syrians, no matter which—must be driven out. And this could only be done by force, since these defilers of sacred soil obviously had no intention of leaving on their own. Such a religious call to violence suited John and his Zealots admirably. They began with a purge of the priesthood. They accomplished several things at once by their actions. They appeased the religious, who longed for a purified Temple; they satisfied the ultranationalists, who hated the priests, many of whom had either openly cooperated with the Romans or had refused to support the revolt; they rallied the poor, who had been downtrodden partly—so they thought—by these rich Sadducees and last, but by no means least, they helped themselves to the fortunes of their victims.

Silver shekel from "the year two," the second year of the Revolt, A.D. 67.

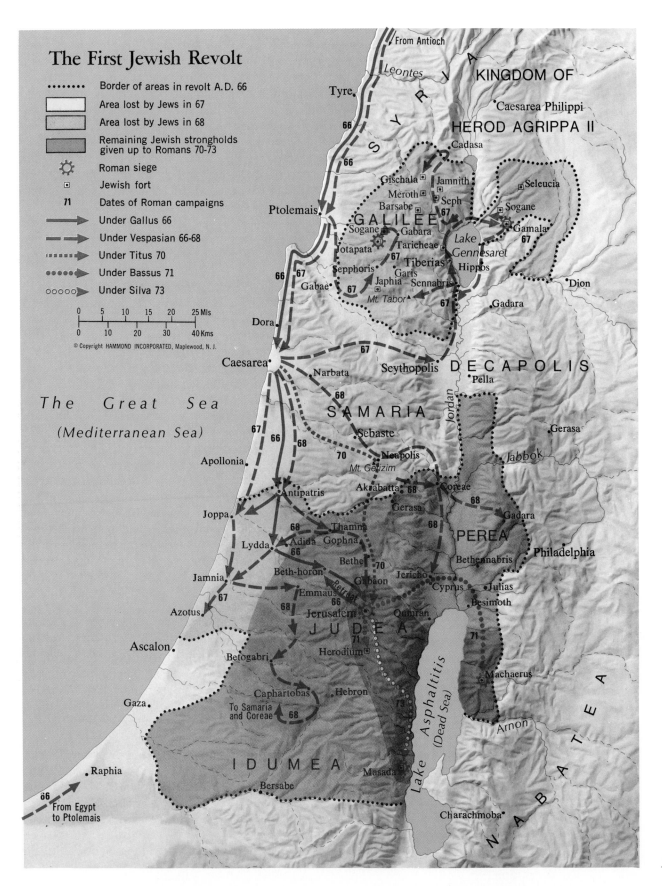

The First Jewish Revolt

- ••••••• Border of areas in revolt A.D. 66
- ▭ Area lost by Jews in 67
- ▭ Area lost by Jews in 68
- ▨ Remaining Jewish strongholds given up to Romans 70-73
- ☼ Roman siege
- ▣ Jewish fort
- **71** Dates of Roman campaigns
- → Under Gallus 66
- ⇢ Under Vespasian 66-68
- ┄► Under Titus 70
- •••► Under Bassus 71
- ∘∘∘► Under Silva 73

| 0 | 5 | 10 | 15 | 20 | 25 Mls |
| 0 | 10 | 20 | 30 | 40 Kms |

© Copyright HAMMOND INCORPORATED, Maplewood, N.J.

The Great Sea

(Mediterranean Sea)

From Antioch

Leontes

KINGDOM OF

Tyre

Caesarea Philippi

HEROD AGRIPPA II

66

Cadasa

66

Gischala
Jamnith
Seleucia
Meroth
Seph
Sogane
Barsabe
67
Gamala
GALILEE
67
Sogane
Gabara
Lake Gennesaret
Jotapata
Taricheae
Ptolemais
67
Sepphoris
67
Tiberias
Hippos
Garis
Dion
Gabae
Japhia
Sennabris
67
Mt. Tabor
67
Gadara

Dora

67

Scythopolis
DECAPOLIS

Caesarea
Narbata
Pella

68

SAMARIA
Jordan
Gerasa

Sebaste
Jabbok

67
66
68
Neapolis
Mt. Gerizim
70

Apollonia
Akrabatta
68
Coreae
68

Antipatris
Gerasa
Gadara

Joppa
68
Thamna
68
Adida
Gophna
PEREA
Lydda
66
Bethe
Bethennabris
Philadelphia
Beth-horon
Gibeon
70
Jericho
Jamnia
Cyprus
Julias
Emmaus
66
Besimoth
67
68
Jerusalem
Qumran
Azotus
71
JUDEA

Ascalon
Herodium
73
Betogabri

Lake Asphaltitis
(Dead Sea)
Caphartobas
Hebron
Gaza
To Samaria
and Coreae
68
Machaerus

Arnon

IDUMEA
Masada
Raphia
Bersabe

Charachmoba

NABATEA

66
From Egypt
to Ptolemais

263

So John brought a new reign of terror to Jerusalem. The Zealots next cast lots to select a new high priest. Phannias Ben Samuel was chosen. He was a provincial stonecutter from a minor priestly family who was now consecrated, adorned in the sacred vestments and quickly told what he was supposed to do. This somewhat bewildered man was the last in the line of Jewish high priests which traced its origin to Aaron, who had stood with his brother Moses defying the pharaoh and had been at sacred Sinai when the Law was given.

Other citizens of Jerusalem did not quietly acquiesce to all this—the bloodshed, looting and mockery of the highest holy office. Many may well have cast anxious eyes upward to the damaged heights of the Antonia, hoping to see Roman helmets, which previously had kept some semblance of order in the city. But they were not there now, and if order there was to be, the more conservative Jews would have to provide it. The Sanhedrin led the people in an attack on the Zealots, who fell back on the Temple and barricaded themselves there.

John of Gischala learned of the plan of the Sanhedrin and spread the word that it was but a ruse to betray the city to the Romans. He schemed to bring a huge force of Idumeans into the city to finish off the population opposing him. But the plan was momentarily thwarted when the gates were shut against the howling mass which had come up from Hebron. Eventually, however, the Zealots managed to open one of the gates and with their newfound allies from the south they murdered, raped and pillaged at will. Nothing was sacred to these people. Even the attendants in the Temple were killed. Jew slashed away at Jew, and the overall slaughter was greater than the Romans had yet inflicted in any single place. Over 8,500 lives were lost. Anyone, rich or noble or suspected of being either, was hunted down. Leading Sadducees including the former high priest, were murdered, their bodies disgraced and left unburied. The Zealots had begun to "democratize" Jerusalem society in a manner not unknown in recent times.

This appalling butchery was ended only when the Idumeans grew tired of killing and had gathered all the loot they could safely haul back to Hebron. Only then did they leave the city. As they withdrew from the moans of the dying and wails of the survivors they cast about, wary lest the Romans attack them. But Vespasian had no intention of attacking them. He and his army were northwest, at Jamnia and Azotus, which they had just reduced. Why should he attack anyone? The Zealots were doing his job for him. All he had to do was wait, or so it seemed at that juncture. There were still a few unfinished tasks in the Jordan Valley. Among these was the destruction of any sites that might prove useful to the rebels when he did mount his attack on Jerusalem. It was in this part of Vespasian's plan that Qumran was overrun by the Xth Legion. Gadara, chief city of Perea, was surrendered to Vespasian by the rich and powerful men of the city without the knowledge of the rebels. Those who were able to flee were overtaken and slain at the Jordan.

Following the destruction of so many of his opponents John of Gischala tried to unite all of the people under his aegis. More than likely the attempt would have failed anyway, but the appearance of a rival leader changed the situation. Simon Bar Gioras, head of the extremist Sicarii who held Masada, made an appearance in Jerusalem challenging John. He was a genuine hero, having led the group that laid waste to the XIIth Legion earlier. It was, incidentally, partly because Simon was from Gerasa and also because Gerasa had been "soft" on the enemy that Vespasian ordered a thousand of its young men killed and the city looted.

Disquieting rumors from across the sea now drifted to Vespasian's ears. It was said that the army in Gaul had revolted against Nero. Further, Rome itself had had enough of this insufferable degenerate. Vespasian could not confirm these rumors, but they had the ring of truth about them. He knew Galba, commanding in the west, and also Nero. The reports just might be true. He had been at this business in Judea for three years. His careful plan may have moved a bit slowly, but it had succeeded brilliantly. Galilee, Perea, Judea had each in turn been subdued. A few desert fortresses held out—Machaerus, Herodium, Masada—but these were of little moment. The problem was Jerusalem. It was time to assault the city. It was time because of the chaos within its walls, and it was time because of those rumors.

The portrait of Vespasian on this silver denarius catches the emperor's cautious yet forceful character.

Having carefully deployed his army Vespasian now began preparations to leave Caesarea for the attack on Jerusalem. On June 9, 69, Vespasian heard officially that Nero was dead. Plans to take Jerusalem were abandoned while Vespasian awaited developments in Rome. Once more in this curious war the rebels, on the verge of self-destruction, were given an interval in which to get hold of themselves and prepare for the coming onslaught.

The year 69 became the year of the four emperors. Galba had indeed revolted against Nero and had been hailed by the army as *imperator*. But he was murdered by a member of his staff, Otho, who in turn lost the crown to Vitellius, a complete bore whose ruffian soldiers found it difficult to distinguish between Italians and enemies. His march to Rome with his troops made it certain that he would never hold the imperial dignity. Rome was learning a bitter lesson: the army could not be trusted with its newfound power.

Vespasian was in the field with almost half of the Roman army. On his staff was Tiberius Julius Alexander, who held sway in Egypt. With this military might plus control over the eastern grain supply he just might become emperor. Vespasian's hand was being forced as officials and military units declared for him. Nevertheless he was as careful as ever. He was, after all, sixty. Was it worth it to throw the empire into another civil war? Vitellius would not last under any circumstances. Then maybe the Senate would restore sanity. But three things turned this old soldier's steps toward the royal diadem. First, he was popular with the army and if the army were to choose an emperor it was increasingly evident that most of it would choose him. Second, Vespasian was superstitious, and as early as the Galilee campaign Josephus had prophesied that he would come out of the war as emperor. Other priests and prophetesses of various cults in the east had said the same thing. It weighed on his mind. Maybe this was the will of the gods. Third, on July 1, 69, Tiberius Julius openly declared for Vespasian and stopped the Egyptian grain ships from sailing.

Vespasian was never indecisive. It just took a long time for him to decide upon the right course. Now he had made up his mind. He would go to Egypt. Titus, his son, would finish the war in Judea. Mucianus, commander of the Syrian legions, would march to Italy and attack Vitellius on native soil in hopes that the offended citizenry would rise up in support of Vespasian. Before Mucianus had a chance to carry out this plan, the seven Danubian legions smashed Vitellius' army and dashed his imperial ambitions. The Danubians moved quickly down the Italian boot and right into Rome, where they did a good deal of damage. They were looking for Vitellius, and when they found him they literally tore him limb from limb. Less than six months after Tiberius Julius' avowal of Vespasian the old soldier was on his way to Rome and triumph.

Titus, conqueror of Jerusalem in A.D. 70.

A Roman assault tower (background) with
its bridge down upon a city wall.
Battering rams were housed in the base
of such towers. Powerful crossbows
(foreground) picked defenders off the walls.

Enter Titus as commander; the decisive phase of the war could begin after almost a year of inactivity. His preparations were as careful as his father's, but Titus had a good deal more personal daring than his sire. He was, after all, barely thirty. Titus thus combined his father's plodding good sense with personal courage, a courage which often placed him in the very front lines of the fight. He now assembled his legions and advanced toward Jerusalem. It was the spring of the year 70.

Basically, Titus followed Vespasian's battle plan. The north and west walls were the most vulnerable, especially the northwest corner, even if it did contain the massive Psephinus Tower. The entire city was surrounded, with the major strength concentrated from the Mount of Olives around the north to Mount Scopus and westward from the Tomb of Queen Helena. Titus decided not to assault the Third Wall, that massive structure which had fallen so easily to Gallus. Agrippa I had died before completing the wall on its western end. Here Titus would mount his attack. He flung the full force of his army into battle.

It may be worth noting some of the Roman siege machines and techniques employed against the walls of Jerusalem. Cumbersome assault towers, some over seventy-five feet high were brought up. These towers were plated outside with armor and/or skins. A battering ram suspended at the base was capable of smashing through heavy masonry. At the critical moment a drawbridge could be let down from the tower so that soldiers could scamper onto the battlements. Sometimes siege machines were used in conjunction with an earthen ramp thrown up before the enemy wall. Before Titus could employ any of these things he had to clear away obstructions and fill up the moat in front of the wall. The moat did not contain water, its purpose being merely to keep the siege machines from making contact. All the while catapults within and without the city kept up a constant fire, filling the air with murderous iron darts and huge stones. The Jewish machines were those taken from Gallus at Beth-horon. From the top of the walls the Jews were throwing down what they could on the Romans working below. At the same time Roman archers tested their marksmanship. Add to this confused scene the work underground. It was common practice in a siege of that day to seek to undermine a section of wall. A large tunnel would be constructed and then the supporting timbers burned away, bringing down the roof and hopefully the foundations of the wall above. Also used in ancient times was the countertunnel. The defenders would hollow a cavern underneath an emerging assault ramp. Just as the siege machines, usually towers, were being drawn up the incline the substructure would collapse toppling the tower. At Jerusalem the defenders used this with great effectiveness. They also organized desperate sallies outside the walls to try to destroy the Roman machines. Once it was Titus himself who led his men in repulsing a Jewish attempt to burn the machines. One of the towers did collapse, either from hostile action or the constant shock of the ram suspended at its base. Another proved ineffective, but the third succeeded in breaching the wall. It happened in the dead of night, and perhaps it was the absence of the constant thud, thud, thud over the Judean hills which awoke the defenders to the danger. It was already too late. Romans were pouring through the breach and it was a matter of little time before the New City was theirs.

At once Titus put this part of the city to the torch and began to tear down Agrippa's Wall. Before him lay the Second Wall, anchored on one end by the Antonia and on the other by Herod's new palace towers. In the middle was a

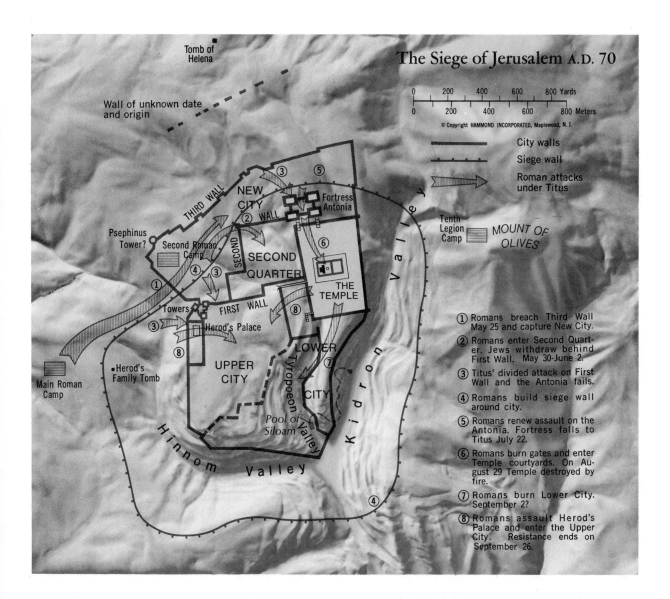

The Siege of Jerusalem A.D. 70

City walls
Siege wall
Roman attacks under Titus

① Romans breach Third Wall May 25 and capture New City.

② Romans enter Second Quarter. Jews withdraw behind First Wall. May 30-June 2.

③ Titus' divided attack on First Wall and the Antonia fails.

④ Romans build siege wall around city.

⑤ Romans renew assault on the Antonia. Fortress falls to Titus July 22.

⑥ Romans burn gates and enter Temple courtyards. On August 29 Temple destroyed by fire.

⑦ Romans burn Lower City. September 2?

⑧ Romans assault Herod's Palace and enter the Upper City. Resistance ends on September 26.

massive tower, only a few remnants of which now remain near the Polish Hospice. Titus planned to hit the wall squarely at this tower and brought his machines into place. Then the defenders of the tower offered to surrender. Titus, suspicious, decided to wait and see. It was, in fact, a trick to allow the Jerusalem defenders time to withdraw behind the First Wall. In street fighting in this part of the city the Romans were thrown back; they were not very good at this sort of thing. But they came on relentlessly, and nine days after they had breached the Third Wall they possessed fully half of the city.

Titus now tried a little ruse of his own. He held a full-scale military review within full sight of the defenders who crowded the remaining walls but remained discreetly out of range of their catapults. Endless scarlet tunics passed before their commander, erect on his horse and clad in white. Polished armor gleamed in the bright June sun, and dust rose drifting slowly over the city. It was an old trick: show the opposition that you have not been hurt by requirements of recent days. Roman losses were, everything considered, minimal. Maybe this display would induce surrender of the remainder of the city.

Roman catapult. Artillery used effectively by both Romans and Jews in the siege of Jerusalem.

267

But the people crowded together in the Temple area and Upper City were carrying on a murderous war between rival groups; anyone who even whispered that it might be a good idea to give up to the clearly superior forces beyond the walls was sure to have his throat cut. The Romans may have thought it was just about over but it had hardly begun.

Now Titus made a fundamental mistake. He assaulted both the wall and the Antonia simultaneously. Countertunneling at the Antonia brought disaster to his efforts just as they seemed to be on the verge of success. At the wall, too, the defenders successfully set fire to some machines. He then recalled one of his father's chief military principles: never divide your strength. Titus paused to study the entire operation. His intelligence units reported that Jerusalem was well watered by the Pool of Siloam, which Hezekiah had built to withstand Sennacherib. Furthermore, food supplies were coming into the city through various means.

Several decisions were made. First, a siege wall was to be thrown up around the city. Only thus could supplies be kept out of the city, and only thus could defenders be kept from escaping through Roman lines. This would require a construction five miles in circumference. Titus also ordered thirteen towers spaced along the circuit, each 200 feet around! There was certainly enough rubble available for such a wall, and there were many captured hands. Within three days Jerusalem was encircled! Traces of the wall are still to be seen at various places in the city.

This wall had a psychological impact on the defenders, many of whom now threw down their weapons. But this was only temporary. The full and long-range psychological effect of Titus' wall may well have been to stiffen the defense of the city, since the people now knew that their choices had narrowed to two: death or slavery. There was from this point forward no escape. Titus may thus have unwittingly increased his difficulties. But from a purely military point of view the wall was the right move. The city began to starve. Those who tried to escape were captured and crucified, about 500 every night. There were so many that the Romans literally had people waiting for an empty cross.

Next, Titus concentrated his forces on the Antonia. This was the key to the Temple area, and that was the key to the city's defense. Much hard fighting lay ahead, and through the heat of summer the unspeakable horror continued, with the stench of rotting bodies offering a nauseating perfume to the crumbling city. The Romans worked away with efficiency on the northern wall. The rams kept up their relentless, sinister pounding. Each night people who would rather brave crucifixion than face starvation slipped out of the city. Word passed that these people were swallowing gold before they came out of the city. Crucifixions lessened as hundreds of people were ripped open by soldiers seeking the precious metal.

On July 22nd the Antonia fell to Titus. He was now faced with assaulting the Temple, that fortress-like structure, stronghold of the Zealots. It is clear that he had no desire to attack this sanctuary. Perhaps on hard military grounds the projected cost in terms of his own men was too great. Perhaps he genuinely wanted to preserve the structure for its sanctity. If so, Bernice, Agrippa II's sister who was now in Titus' camp as his mistress, may have had some influence. Whatever the reason, for once Titus temporized. He kept pressure on the defenders, but he did not move to take the sacred bastion. Meanwhile his engineers were demolishing the Antonia, save for a tower left for him to observe events in the Temple courts.

The Pool of Bethzatha (Bethesda) with the Fortress Antonia in the background, from a model in Jerusalem.

On August 7th Josephus told Titus that the Zealots had allowed the sacred flame to be extinguished in the Temple and that the daily sacrifices had ceased. Titus responded by sending a message to John of Gischala offering to pull back Roman troops if John would abandon the Temple and fight him elsewhere. John's reply was an abortive attempt to break out by Solomon's Porch on the eastern side. Titus' engineers continued to clear, a wide path through the rubble of the Antonia so that the siege machines could be brought into the Court of the Gentiles. Clearly the Temple area was going to be the scene of the decisive struggle.

Now Titus tried something else. He brought forth a number of leading Jews who had gone over to the Romans and bade them plead with their countrymen not to force this terrible issue. This partly accomplished what Titus wanted because previously the Zealot leaders had told of the awful fate of these men in Roman hands and had hailed them as martyrs. Their healthy appearance at this point caused many disillusioned Zealots to abandon their posts and surrender. But the core held fast. The gates of the inner wall were shut tight. Titus ordered the battering rams forward. They had virtually no effect on the solid Herodian masonry. At the same time the fanatical leaders of the Zealots ordered catapults set up on the roof of the Temple and from there began to pelt the assaulting troops. They also burned a portion of the cloisters over the heads of some unfortunate Romans whom they trapped there.

Titus ordered scaling ladders forward. This effort failed. They tried to force open the massive gates by the use of levers. This also failed. Finally the gates were set on fire. Through the night flames licked at the wood and silver reliefs that decorated the entrances. Perhaps taken aback, the defenders made no attempt to extinguish the fires. By morning the entrances to the inner court were open, and Titus ordered a path cleared so that legionnaires could pass through. While a detail was putting out the fires and pushing debris aside the Zealots attacked them from the sanctuary. There was a furious fight as other Romans rushed forward to aid their outnumbered comrades. At the time Titus was resting in preparation for the all-out assault which according to plan would come in a few hours. But his carefully prepared timetable was upset by events. Slowly the legionnaires gained the upper hand. At some point one of the soldiers picked up a still-burning beam and rushed toward the Temple proper. Other soldiers were with him as he dashed across the northern side of the Court of Israel. Above him was a window. Climbing on the back of a comrade, he threw the flaming wood inside. We do not know what was in the storeroom but it immediately went up. Titus, roused from his rest, came running to the scene. Fighting was everywhere. Smoke was beginning to pour from the entire northern side of the sanctuary. More and more Romans were coming into the courtyards. There was hand-to-hand combat at every turn. The roof was burning. Everything was confusion.

It was five days before the Romans completely secured the Temple courts—thirty-five acres! But the morning after fire had ignited the House of the Lord it was completely gutted, a massive smoldering ruin. It was August 29, 70. A heavy pall hung over Zion and drifted with the prevailing breeze out over the Judean wilderness down toward Jericho and the Jordan. At the remnants of the eastern gate of the Temple, Roman soldiers set up their standards and made sacrifices. They hailed Titus as *imperator*. The gold taken by the soldiers later glutted the Syrian market and the price plummeted by a half.

The Wailing Wall. This Herodian masonry on the west side of the Temple platform has been for the Jews a place of prayer and of mourning for the destroyed Temple.

Jewish oil lamp from after the Second Revolt bears temple pillar decoration recalling the lost glory of Israel.

The siege was not over, however. John and Simon, finally united, held the Upper City across the then deep Tyropoeon Valley west of the Temple. They asked Titus for a parley. He agreed and they faced each other at opposite ends of the bridge which Herod had built to join the Temple courts with the Upper City. If recent archaeological work in Jerusalem is correct, the meeting took place at Wilson's Arch, immediately north of the old Wailing Wall. And what a scene it was. At one end of the bridge stood the young, confident Roman, son of the emperor and heir-apparent, flushed with victory. Surrounding him were his victorious legions, eager at that very moment to rush across the bridge and finish the job. Their backdrop was the ruinous mass that once was Herod's Temple, one of the marvels of the Roman world. At the other end of the bridge were the ragged, desperate rebels, tired of this thing they had done so much to bring about, seeking a way out for themselves and their families. Behind them lay the ruins of a city: smoke, stench, rubble.

Titus addressed this ragtag group across the bridge. They, he said, had brought on this disaster by their rebellious nature, which had been in evidence since Pompey's time. He rehearsed the leniencies of the Romans and the perversity of the people of Judea. As to the matter of the burning of the Temple, he blamed the rebels for it.

> When I came near your temple (Titus said), I again departed from the laws of war, and exhorted you to spare your own sanctuary, and to preserve your holy house to yourselves. I allowed you a quiet exit out of it, and security for your preservation; nay, if you had a mind, I gave you leave to fight in another place. Yet have you still despised every one of my proposals, and have set fire to your holy house with your own hands.
>
> (Josephus, *Wars* VI 6:2)

Titus may not have known how the Temple was set alight or may have viewed these people before him as responsible for its destruction. He ended his speech by offering to spare the lives of those who surrendered, but they would be his and he would act "like a mild master of a family." That is, they would be sold or end up in galleys or Egyptian mines. But they and their families would have their lives.

The rebels dismissed the offer out-of-hand, countering with their offer that they would quit the city if they were allowed safe passage into the desert with their families. Titus became furious. Who were these beaten dogs to dictate terms to him? He ordered a proclamation read. Henceforth no prisoners would be taken by the Romans. Any deserters who came forth would be slain. Let those who would dictate to the victor prepare to defend themselves against his entire army.

He ordered further that all of the city in Roman hands be put to the torch, even down Ophel to the Pool of Siloam. This may not have been, as it seems to appear, a spiteful response to the rebels. There were, as Josephus never tires of telling his readers, hundreds of rotting bodies in the ruins. Houses, he says, were crammed full of corpses which had been cleared from the streets. Disease lurked down every alley. It was normal Roman military procedure to burn bodies after a battle. This may well be what Titus now ordered.

Meanwhile he meant what he said about assaulting the Upper City with his whole army. Ramps went up along the western walls by Herod's palace. Within eighteen days the battering rams were relentlessly at work again.

Bas-relief on Arch of Titus shows Roman soldiers carrying sacred vessels from the Jerusalem Temple through the streets of Rome.

Titus also began to pound away at the walls down by the Tyropoeon Valley. Through the day and by moonlight the Romans smashed at the walls. Some rebels, knowing that it was a matter of time before the walls gave way, crowded into the many subterranean passages of the city; others tried to slip away undetected. A few, not many, manned the walls and did what they could to slow the martial work below. The hard core of defenders took refuge in the three towers of Herod's palace. Here they would make a memorable stand, the last act of the drama. Their brave boasts supported each other in a conviction to endure to the death. Titus was more than ready to grant their wish.

Then the rams breached the walls, and assault towers disgorged legionnaires along the ramparts. The eager Romans had expected a hot reception. But the walls were empty, unmanned. They raced along the heights, their red capes floating from their shoulders. Peering down into the streets and alleys they saw thousands of bodies; some torn by knives, others bloated by starvation. Hurrying footsteps dashed down steps from the tops of the walls. The soldiers came across a few people whom they killed at once. But in house after house they found piles of corpses. These hardened veterans, who had seen death so many times and who were even now spoiling for a fight, stood in horror as they gazed upon the carnage.

And now occurred a very strange thing. Those of the defenders who had shut themselves up in Herod's impregnable towers threw open the doors, came running out, abandoning their safety. They ran toward Siloam, perhaps hoping to escape by means of the Kidron Valley into open country. But they, like so many others, fell victim to the encircling wall and the Roman soldiers who awaited them there. From the top of the three western towers Roman standards fluttered.

When Titus had moved his men out of the Upper City he put it to the torch. Josephus tells us that it burned brightly through the night and into the next day. He does not tell us what became of all those people in the subterranean chambers in this holocaust. Doubtless, if we are to believe the figure he gives us of the prisoners taken in the siege (90,000), the Romans found many of them. But probably not all.

It was September 26, 70.

The Arch of Titus commanding the Imperial Forum in Rome celebrated the victory of Vespasian and Titus.

271

The sequel to the siege was as horrible as those awful five months. All the prisoners were herded into the Court of the Women; thousands upon thousands of people. Aged and infirm were separated and slaughtered. The tallest and most handsome of the youth were set aside to be sent to Rome to grace the victor's triumph through the streets of the imperial city. Eleven thousand others died of various causes right there where once the priests had offered sacrifices to the God of Abraham, Isaac and Jacob. Many starved, either because they had offended their guards and then were denied food, or because they refused food, preferring to starve to death rather than live in slavery. And many were destined for slavery, some in the galleys, others in Egyptian mines. And Titus had not forgotten about the masses in the other cities of the east. From Jerusalem men and women were shipped to virtually every large city in the Roman East, there to die in the arenas. Titus himself held games at Caesarea, Beirut and even Caesarea Philippi.

There now remained the final phase of Titus' plan. The first step was to catch the few rebel leaders who had managed to hide in the subterranean passages of Jerusalem. John gave himself up and was spared. Word of the capture of Simon Bar Gioras came to Titus at Caesarea Philippi. He was put to death. No one else of very much importance was at large.

Second, it was necessary to rout the last three pockets of rebels who were holed up in the desert fortresses of Herodium, Machaerus and Masada. The Herodium fell with ease. It was not large, and was in any case more of a signal post than a fortress built to withstand a long siege. The wonder is the Romans allowed it to remain in rebel hands for so long, considering how close it was to Jerusalem. Machaerus proved something of a problem. This natural defense in extremely desolate country east of the Dead Sea could not be taken by direct assault. The Romans settled in for a long siege, and then by a stroke of luck they captured Eleazer, hero of the Machaerus garrison. Feigning the intention to crucify Eleazer in full sight of his friends within the fort, the Roman military governor, Bassus (Titus having long ago started on his way to Rome), gladly accepted an offer to trade Eleazer for the fortress citadel.

That left Masada, where this whole business had started. This extraordinary bastion presented a formidable challenge to Silva, the field commander. He decided to besiege it, since there was no natural way it could be taken by storm. But a siege meant little at Masada. Herod had a century earlier placed quantities of dried food there. It was still edible. There were, moreover, abundant sources of water from the winter rains, which were trapped in mammoth cisterns. And to top it off, it was possible to grow crops on the summit. The Romans could build their camps and their siege walls and stay as long as they wished. There was just one way for the Romans to take Masada; that was to build an enormous earthen assault ramp. The ramp had to span a ravine to reach the fortress wall and when finished was over 200 feet high and some 645 feet long. At the top of the ramp a huge siege tower was placed. From the tower the Romans were able to fire down upon the defenders of the walls while the battering ram was at work in the lower parts of the tower. This wondrous tower, standing such a vast height above the valley floor far below, also had catapults for throwing stones, many of which have been recovered by the archaeologist who worked at Masada in the early 1960s. Excavation has revealed that a portion of the casemate wall directly above the assault ramp is missing, presumably carried away by the ram. The Sicarii who held Masada built a temporary wall in the breach but,

Masada. Rocks used by the defenders to hurl down upon the attacking army.

as it was made of wood and earth, the Romans soon fired it. The final assault was put off for the next day.

Throughout the night the Romans were watchful lest any of the defenders of this citadel escape. But another Eleazer, leader of the rebels at Masada, neither intended to sneak away himself nor allow anyone else to try it. He had in mind something else. He assembled the besieged, reminding them of the fate that awaited them with the coming of day. He warned them of imminent slaughter in the fighting to come and the abuse of their wives and enslavement of their children. It was time to die as they had professed to live: in freedom. Each man was to kill his wife and children and in his turn to be slain. All their belongings were to be burned. The food stores alone were to be left intact to show the Romans that they chose to die this way.

> We were the very first that revolted from them (said Eleazer), and we are the last that fight against them; and I cannot but esteem it as a favor that God hath granted us, that it is still in our power to die bravely, and in a state of freedom, which hath not been the case with others who were conquered unexpectedly.
>
> (Josephus, *Wars* VII 8:6)

This was the burden of Eleazer's speech. It was greeted with mixed reactions. In the end, however, all agreed and each man bid his wife and children farewell with embraces and fond kisses. And the sad deed was done. Then ten were selected by lot to kill the rest. Another lot was cast, and one of the ten dispatched the rest. He then set fire to the palace and ran himself through with a sword.

At dawn on the second day of May in 73 the Romans poured through the wall and spread out over the summit. Fires were still burning. There was a deathly silence. The soldiers gave a great shout; two old women and five children emerged from hiding and told what had transpired. The Romans could hardly believe this tale. They then moved to put out the fire, and when they came within the palace they saw the mass of bodies which had been placed there. Nine hundred and sixty people, including the women and children, lay dead.

The Revolt had come to an end.

(coin enlarged about 3:1)

Throughout the Roman Empire victory coins were struck with the inscription *Judaea Capta*. This one depicts a legionnaire standing in triumph while a woman (Judea) mourns beneath a palm tree.

273

19 · AFTERMATH

The long spiritual journey which had begun in the hoary mists of antiquity — some said with the giving of the Law at Sinai, others insisted with the journey of Abraham and still others claimed it existed since the very dawn of creation — this struggle did not end in the flame, smoke and stench of a dying Jerusalem. Indeed, as is so often the case, death and disaster were impetus to new life and previously unknown vigor. The debacle of A.D. 70 with its calamitous aftermath did not bring an end to the Jewish community of Palestine. Even before the curtain began to ring down on that awful scene Titus had given permission for the founding of a Jewish settlement at Jamnia, west of Jerusalem and not far from the coast. Strange as it may seem, this may well have been Titus' most enduring act. For the most part, those who now came to this place were Pharisaical refugees from Jerusalem who were able to bring their "treasure," that is, their precious scrolls with them. Before long Jamnia was a flourishing center for the study of the Law. Johanan Ben Zakkai was the dominant figure, and it was from his fertile mind and that of his successor, Gamaliel the Younger, that at Sepphoris in Galilee, the tradition of interpretation was continued and expanded by Judah ha-Nasi (Judah the Prince) as the *Mishnah,* that monumental codification of rabbinic interpretation which not only served as the seedbed for *Talmud,* but also continues to play a major role in Jewish life today.

By the end of the first century these rabbis at Jamnia had also taken another significant action whose consequences outran even the far-flung, scattered body of Judaism down through the centuries. They canonized the Scriptures. They settled on thirty-nine books which were to be considered authoritative wherever Jews gathered to worship, to study or to ask about faith and practice. It is these same thirty-nine books which form the basis of the Old Testament.

The codification of tradition and canonization of Scripture represented visible evidences of the triumph of Pharisaical Judaism. From the sectarian confusion of the predestruction era the Pharisees emerged as the dominant force and finally as the only force in Judaism. Of the Sadducees, Herodians, Essenes and many other groups we hear no more. The Zealots did continue, but within sixty-five years their religious fanaticism had once more clashed with the inexorable force of Roman arms. This time it was more of a guerrilla war, fought for the most part in southern Judea which suffered immeasurable damage on the village and town level. It was a terrific struggle, with cruelty freely employed on both sides, as is often a characteristic of this type of fighting. Moreover, it was infused with fanatic and unyielding messianism and no less than the great Rabbi Akiba styled Simon, leader of the revolt, as "Bar-Kochba," "Son of a Star," a messianic title. Hadrian, emperor of Rome at the zenith of its expansion and power, had only recently been in the area. At once he recognized the danger this uprising held for the Roman East and crushed it as quickly and as thoroughly as possible. At the end of the Second Revolt he razed Jerusalem, filling up much of the Tyropoeon Valley with debris from the remnants of the Herodian city (at least half of

Aelia Capitolina as preserved in the sixth-century mosaic map at Medeba near Mount Nebo east of the Dead Sea.

which had survived Titus' fiery destruction). On the spot he erected a new city named for his own clan, the Aelian clan. The city was Aelia Capitolina. It is basically the outline of Hadrian's city which is still preserved in the Old City of Jerusalem today; the Suk, now the chief market street, follows the line of the *Cordo Maximus,* the main north-south street of Aelia Capitolina. Hadrian forbade any Jew to come within sight of the new city on pain of death. The focus of Palestinian Judaism slowly shifted northward, to Galilee, where it was to flourish until the Islamic wave drowned it along with much other life and culture of the area.

As rending as the effects of this second rebellion were, for all the heart ache renewed in another generation, for all the rekindled distrust between Jew and Gentile in city after city in the empire — for all this — Judaism was not basically threatened as it had been in the years after the First Revolt. Those were extremely dangerous and difficult days, with widespread Jewish congregations cut loose from the single visible focus of the Temple with its ritual and as yet without recognized official tradition and canon. The zealots had sought to save Judaism by the sword. But they failed and disappeared after the Second Revolt. Pharisaism endured, and it was the preservation by the Pharisees of the ideal of study of Torah, practice of commandments, and acts of loving-kindness that enabled Judaism to maintain itself through prosperity and through difficulty across the centuries.

As for the mainstream of Christianity, its course had leapt clear of Jerusalem by the year 44, although strong ties were maintained for a few years after that. For the most part, however, the destruction of Jerusalem in 70 passed unnoticed in Christian literature except insofar as it determined a certain character which the writings took in their attempts to dissociate themselves from the rebellious Jews. Those Jerusalem Jewish Christians who fled the city about the same time as the Pharisees returned after the war only to fall victim—as Jews, not Christians—during an outbreak in 109. Eventually Jewish Christianity died out altogether, and a later Christian council condemned these people (who came to be known as *Ebionites,* "Poor") as heretics because they did not place proper emphasis on the divinity of Jesus Christ.

While the Jewish community of Judea and with it its Christian sectarians were suffering two horrible wars within three generations, with all the atten-

275

dant unrest of the intervening years, the Christian faith which radiated from Antioch, Alexandria, Ephesus and other urban centers was crossing all barriers, reaching to the farthest ends of the empire and beyond, offering salvation to any and all who would believe. When internal disharmony and external persecution fell upon the young churches Christians reacted in some of the same ways that Jews had after the First Revolt; that is, they began to identify an authoritative tradition and they moved toward a canon of specifically Christian writings (the New Testament). They did two other things besides. First, they developed a concept of orthodoxy with its corollary, heresy, to safeguard the emergent tradition. This resulted in creeds such as the Nicene Creed and the Apostles' Creed which came near the beginning and near the end of the fourth century respectively. Second, as Christianity grew the lines of authority drew tighter than had those of Judaism, and the emerging structure was again a safeguard for faith and practice. The hierarchy of the Church was to continue to grow in response to the needs of the times.

But Christianity, for all its inward turning (a tightening-up dictated by events and to a certain degree by rapid and widespread expansion), never lost its universal thrust for a moment. Judaism after the revolts, on the other hand, could no longer afford to be as accommodating as it had been in predestruction days, and for its own self-preservation turned inward, emphasizing its developing tradition — the *Talmud*. All the while that Judaism was struggling to define itself over against alien culture, which through assimilation was a deadly threat, Christianity was moving in the opposite direction to overcome the culture and conform it to its own image. In this process they collided as only the closest of relatives can do. Out of that clash came enmity, and from that enmity came a denial of the highest insights and basic human and religious values of each in their dealings with one another. Only in our own time have we begun to throw off those positions of eighteen centuries ago and look with mutual respect upon those two vines sprung from the same soil, upon two of the most sublime religions in the long history of mankind.

Left: Christ fransfigured. Sixth-century Byzantine mosaic at the Monastery of St. Catherine, Mount Sinai.

Right: Jewish gold glass decorated with the Ark of the Law and the menorah. Fourth century, probably from catacombs in Rome.

SELECTED BIBLIOGRAPHY

The following represents a selection of titles for further reading. It includes books of solid worth to the general reader and avoids the more difficult technical treatments. Most of the titles are generally available. (*PB* = also available in paperback, n.d. = no date)

Aharoni, Yohanan, *The Archaeology of the Land of Israel*. Ed. by Miriam Aharoni. Trans. by Anson F. Rainey, Philadelphia: Westminster Press, 1982 (PB).

Aharoni, Yohanan, *Land of the Bible*. Revised and enlarged edition. Trans. by A.F. Rainey, Philadelphia: Westminster Press, 1982 (PB).

Anderson, George W., *The History and Religion of Israel*. London: Oxford University Press, 1966.

Baly, Dennis, *Basic Biblical Geography*. Philadelphia: Fortress Press, 1987 (PB).

Bornkamm, Gunther, *Jesus of Nazareth*. New York: Harper and Row, 1975 (PB).

Bright, John, *A History of Israel*. 3rd Edition, Philadelphia: Westminster Press, 1981.

Burrows, Millar, *Burrows on the Dead Sea Scrolls*. Grand Rapids, Mich.: Baker Book House, 1978 (PB).

Conzelmann, Hans, *History of Primitive Christianity*. Trans. by J.E. Steely, Nashville, Tenn.: Abingdon Press, 1973 (PB).

Davies, J.G., *The Early Christian Church*. Grand Rapids, Mich.: Baker Book House, 1980 (PB).

de Vaux, Roland, *Ancient Israel, Its Life and Institutions*. Trans. by J. McHugh. New York: McGraw-Hill, 1965 (PB, 2 vols).

Finegan, Jack, *The Archaeology of the New Testament: The Life of Jesus and the Beginning of the Early Church*. Princeton, N.J.: Princeton Univ. Press, 1970 (PB).

Finegan, Jack, *Light from the Ancient Past*. Two vols., 2nd edition. Princeton, N.J.: Princeton Univ. Press, 1959 (PB).

Frank, Harry Thomas, *Atlas of the Bible Lands*. Revised edition. Maplewood, N.J.: Hammond, 1984 (PB).

Freedman, D.N. and E.F. Campbell, editors, *The Biblical Archaeologist Reader No. 4*. Winona Lake, Ind. Eisenbrauns, 1983 (PB).

Grant, Michael, *Ancient History Atlas*. Long Island City, N.Y.: S.J. Durst, 1981 (PB).

Grant, Michael, *The History of Ancient Israel*. New York: Scribner, 1984 (PB).

Grant, Michael, *Jesus: An Historian's Review of the Gospels*. New York: Scribner, 1978 (PB).

Hoppe, Leslie, *What Are They Saying About Biblical Archaeology?* Mahwah, N.J.: Paulist Press, 1984 (PB).

Josephus, Flavius, *Complete Works of Josephus*. 4 vols. Grand Rapids, Mich.: Baker Book House, n.d.

Josephus, Flavius, *The Jewish War*. Ed. by E. Mary Smallwood, trans. by G.A. Williamson. Baltimore: Penguin Books, 1984 (PB).

Kenyon, Kathleen M., *The Bible and Recent Archaeology*. Atlanta, Ga.: John Knox Press, 1979 (PB).

Kenyon, Kathleen M., *Archaeology in the Holy Land*. 5th ed. = British 4th edition. Nashville, Tenn.: Thomas Nelson, 1985 (PB).

May, Herbert G., editor, *Oxford Bible Atlas*., Edited and revised by John Day. London: Oxford University Press, 1985 (PB).

Meyers, Eric M. and James F. Strange, *Archaeology, the Rabbis, and Early Christianity*. Nashville, Tenn.: Abingdon Press, 1981 (PB).

Negev, Abraham, editor, *Archaeological Encyclopedia of the Holy Land*. Revised edition, Nashville, Tenn.: Thomas Nelson, 1986.

Nock, Arthur D., *St. Paul*. New York: Harper and Brothers, 1938 (Santa Fe, N.M.: William Gannon, 1970).

Pearlman, Moshe, *Zealots of Masada: The Story of a Dig*. New York: Scribner, 1967 (PB).

Pritchard, James B., *Gibeon, Where the Sun Stood Still*. Princeton, N.J.: Princeton Univ. Press, 1962 (PB).

Ringgren, Helmer, *Religions of the Ancient Near East*. Trans. by J. Sturdy. Philadelphia: Westminster Press, 1973.

Simon, Marcel, *Jewish Sects at the Time of Jesus*. Trans. by J.H. Farley. Philadelphia: Fortress Press, 1980 (PB).

Tarn, William W., *Alexander the Great*. Chicago: Ares Publishers, 1981 Repr. of 1948 edition. Beacon Press, n.d. (PB).

Weiss, Harvey, *Ebla to Damascus: Art and Archaeology of Ancient Syria*. Washington, D.C.: SITES, 1985 (PB).

Wilson, John A., *The Culture of Ancient Egypt*. Chicago: Chicago Univ. Press, 1956 (PB).

Yadin, Yigael, *Masada: Herod's Fortress and the Zealots' Last Stand*. New York: Random House, 1966

Zeitlin, Solomon, *The Rise and Fall of the Judaean State*. 2 vols., Philadelphia: Jewish Publication Society, 1967

TIME CHART OF BIBLE HISTORY

DATE	PALESTINE	EGYPT	MESOPOTAMIA & PERSIA	ANATOLIA & SYRIA	GREECE & ROME
4000 BC	Neolithic culture (Jericho)	— First use of metal: copper and bronze —	Halaf culture		
	Ghassulian culture c.3500	Hieroglyphic writing developed	Cuneiform writing developed		
	The Canaanites, a Semitic people, were ancestral to the Phoenicians	**Archaic Period** Menes unifies Egypt	Sumerian city states c.2800-2360	Early Bronze cities Byblos, Troy, Ugarit	
	Early Bronze urban culture c.3300	**Old Kingdom** The Great Pyramids at Gizeh c.2550	**Akkadian Empire** Sargon I 2360-2305	Ebla culture Syria under Akkadian Empire	Beginning of Minoan civilization on Crete
	Amorite invasions c.2500-2300	Old Kingdom falls	Gutian kings Ur dominance	Hittites enter Anatolia	Greeks invade Balkan peninsula
2000 BC	Egypt controls Canaan	**Middle Kingdom** Hyksos invaders from Asia c.1720-1550	Ur falls c.1950 Isin-Larsa Period **Old Babylonian Empire** Hammurabi 1728-1686	Amorite invasions Hittites intro. Iron Labarnas I c.1600	**Minoan Sea Empire**
	Abraham — oral tradition Israelite sojourn in Egypt	**New Kingdom** Ahmose 1550-1525 Akhenaton 1370-1353	**Kassite Period** Hittites sack Babylon 1531	**Old Hittite Kingdom** Mursilis I c.1540	Mycenae shaft graves Cretan palaces destroyed c.1400
	Battle of Megiddo 1468 Amarna letters c.1370-1353 The Exodus c.1290 Israelite invasion	Tutankhamen 1353-1344 Ramses II 1290-1224 Ramses III defeats Sea Peoples c.1170	Mitanni Kdm. **Rise of Assyria** Shalmaneser I	Suppilullumas **Hittite Empire**	Dorians invade Greece
	Philistine penetration Kdm. of Saul c.1020-1000	**Late Dynastic Period**	Tiglath-pileser I 1115-1078	Battle of Kedesh 1296 Sack of Troy 1192	Trojan War c.1200
1000 BC	**United Kingdom** David c.1000-961 Solomon c.961-922 First Temple completed c.950	Period of decline		Arameans flood into Syria Hiram of Tyre 969-936 Damascus city state	Decline of Aegean Bronze Age civilization
	Divided Kingdom Rehoboam & Jeroboam I Omri dynasty 876-842 Samaria founded c.875 Jehu dynasty 842-745	Shishak c.945-924 Libyan dynasties 945-712	**Assyrian Empire** Asshurnasirpal II 883-859 Shalmaneser III 859-824 Adad-nirari III 807-782	Ben-hadad II Battle of Qarqar 853 Phoenicians found Carthage 814	Latins settle in central Italy
800 BC	Israel resurgence under Jeroboam II 786-746 Amos, Hosea Fall of Samaria and exile of Israel 722/721		Tiglath-pileser III 745-727		First Olympics 776 Legendary founding of Rome 753 Etruscan period
	Hezekiah of Judah 715-687/6	Nubian dynasties 715-663	Sargon II 722-705 Sennacherib 705-681	Phrygian Kdm. Midas c.715	Homer
	Isaiah Micah Judah resurgence under Josiah 640-609 Jeremiah	Egypt under Assyrian rule 671-652 Thebes sacked 663 Neco II 609-593	Asshurbanapal 669-633 Rise of Babylon under Nabopolassar Fall of Nineveh to Medes and Babylonians 612	Lydian Kdm. Gyges of Lydia 680-652	Draco codifies Athenian law 621
600 BC					

DATE	PALESTINE	EGYPT	MESOPOTAMIA & PERSIA	ANATOLIA & SYRIA	GREECE & ROME
600 BC	Destruction of Jerusalem and exile of Judah 587 Ezekiel **Babylonian Captivity** Edict of Cyrus allows return of Jews 538 Zerubbabel Temple rebuilt 520-515 **Persian Period** Ezra's mission 458?? Nehemiah comes to Judah 445 (440?)	Egypt under Persian rule 525-401 Unsuccessful revolt Return to native rule	**New Babylonian Empire** Nebuchadnezzar II 605-562 **Persian Empire** Cyrus 550-530 Babylon falls 539 Cambyses 530-522 Darius I 522-486 Xerxes I 486-465 Artaxerxes I Darius II 433-404	Syria and Anatolia under Persian rule Phoenicians provide fleet for Persian attacks on Greece	Solon's judicial reforms c. 590 Rome ruled by Etruscan kings Roman Republic established 509 Persian Wars 499-479 Thermopylae-Salamis 480 Pericles 461-429 Herodotus
400 BC	Ezra's mission 398? Palestine passes under Alexander's rule and Hellenization begins 332 Ptolemaic Egyptian rule 312	Persian rule 342-332 Alexander conquers Egypt 332 Ptolemy I 323-284 **Ptolemaic Kingdom** Alexandrian Jews translate Pentateuch into Greek Ptolemy V 203-181	Artaxerxes III 358-338 Alexander invades Persia 331 Seleucid rule Parthians and Bactrians gain independence c. 250	Alexander takes Tyre 332 Seleucid rule Seleucus I 312-280 **Seleucid Empire** Antiochus I 280-261 Seleucus II 246-226 Antiochus III (The Great) 223-187	Socrates' death Sack of Rome by Gauls Philip II of Macedon Alexander the Great 336-323 **Alexander's Empire** Wars of the Diodochi 1st and 2nd Punic Wars Hannibal in Italy 218
200 BC	Palestine comes under Seleucid Syrian control 198 **Maccabean Period** Judas Maccabeus leads revolt of Jews 166-160 Temple rededicated 164 Jonathan 160-142 Simon 142-134 John Hyrcanus I 134-104 Aristobulus I 104-103	Ptolemy VI 181-146 Antiochus IV campaigns in Egypt Ptolemy VII 146-116	**Parthian Empire** Mithridates I 171-138 Mithridates II 124-88	Battle of Magnesia 190 Antiochus IV (Epiphanes) 175-163 Antiochus V 163-162 Demetrius I 162-150 Demetrius II 145-139 Tyre independent	Spain annexed by Rome **Empire of the Roman Republic** 3rd Punic War Romans destroy Carthage and Corinth 146 Reforms of the Gracchi
100 BC **50 BC**	Alexander Jannaeus 103-76 Alexandra 76-67 Aristobulus II 67-63 Pompey takes Jerusalem for Rome 63 Hyrcanus II, high priest 63-40 Antipater governor 55	Ptolemy VIII 116-81 Ptolemy XI 80-81 Cleopatra VII 51-30	Tigranes of Armenia Phrates III 70-57 Orodes I 57-38 War with Rome 55-38 Crassus defeated	Mithridatic Wars Antiochus XIII 68-67 Anatolia and Syria under Roman control	Sulla dictator 82-79 1st Triumvirate Pompey's campaigns in Asia 66-63 Caesar's Gallic Wars 58-51

279

DATE	PALESTINE	THE WEST	THE EAST
50 BC	**Roman Rule** Caesar in Judea 47 Parthian invasion 40 Antigonus 40-37 Herod the Great 37-4 BC Herod's Temple begun 18 Birth of Christ c. 4 BC Archelaus 4 BC-AD 6	Death of Pompey 48 Death of Caesar 44 2nd Triumvirate Battle of Philippi 42 Battle of Actium 31 Augustus — First emperor 27 BC-AD 14 **Roman Empire**	**Parthian Empire** Phraates 37-32 Parthians defeat Antony 36
0	Roman governors 6-41 Pontius Pilate 27-37 Death of Christ c. 29 Herod Agrippa I 41-44 Paul's 1st journey, Council at Jerusalem 46/47	Varus defeated in Germany 9 Tiberius 14-37 Gaius (Caligula) 37-41 Claudius 41-54 Conquest of Britain begun 43	Artabanus II 10-40
50 AD	Antonius Felix 52-60 Imprisonment of Paul 58 Porcius Festus 60-62 Paul sent to Rome 60 Gessius Florus 64-66 First Jewish Revolt 66-73 Destruction of Jerusalem 70 Fall of Masada 73 Jewish center at Jamnia	Nero 54-68 1st Persecution of Christians 64 Galba, Otho, Vitellius 68/69 Vespasian 69-79 Titus 79-81 Domitian 81-96 Nerva 96-98 Trajan 98-117	Vologases I 51-80 Parthian War with Rome 53-63 Osroes (Chosroes) 89-128
100 AD 135 AD	Jewish uprisings in Palestine, Egypt, Mesopotamia 116-117 Bar-Kochba Revolt 132-135 Jerusalem razed, Aelia Capitolina built on site	Campaigns in Dacia 101-107 Hadrian 117-138	Conquest of Nabateans by Romans Trajan invades Parthia 114 Territory lost to Romans regained 118

INDEX

ACKNOWLEDGMENTS

The author and the publishers wish to express their thanks and appreciation to the following individuals and institutions for help in obtaining illustrations:

to Dr. Richard Cleave, Director of Pictorial Archive (Near Eastern History), for the generous use of his striking aerial photographs of Holy Land sites;

to the American Schools of Oriental Research for their courtesy in allowing reproduction of various photographs associated with the Dead Sea Scrolls;

to Professor Yigael Yadin for photographs of the Nahal Hever materials;

to B. Phelps Shonnard of the American Numismatic Society, Arnold Jacobson of the Brooklyn Museum and Irene Lewitt of the Israel Museum, Jerusalem.

Picture credits

By Professor H. Thomas Frank: pages 5, 8 (top, center right, bottom right), 9, 17 (both), 19, 20, 21 (both), 25 (bottom), 26 (both), 34, 38, 39, 41, 45, 48 (bottom), 56 (bottom), 57, 63 (bottom), 74 (top), 76 (bottom), 77, 84, 86, 93, 95, 102, 103 (bottom), 112, 121 (top), 156 (top), 163 (top), 164, 171, 173, 175, 176, 177 (bottom), 180, 186, 196, 200, 202 (top), 205, 206 (both), 208, 213, 215 (both), 233, 237 (top), 240, 244, 247, 250, 251 (bottom), 254, 259 (top), 260, 261, 262, 265, 268, 272, 275.

All others. Alinari, Florence: pages 234, 271 (bottom). The American Numismatic Society, New York: pages 148, 154 (both), 157, 168 (right), 170 (both), 211 (all), 237 (bottom), 249 (top, bottom), 273. American Schools of Oriental Research: pages 184, 190. Henry Angelo-Castrillon: page 224. Archaeological Institute, Hebrew University, Jerusalem: pages 163 (bottom), 248. Bruno Barbey (Magnum): page 51. The Bettman Archive, New York: pages 259 (bottom), 266 (both), 267. Roger S. Boraas: pages 66 (bottom), 100, 106 (top), 130 (both), 145, 178 (top, bottom right), 209 (bottom), 222. The Trustees of the British Museum: pages 10, 13, 15, 16, 113, 118, 127 (bottom), 129, 140 (top). The Brooklyn Museum: pages 56 (top), 61 (bottom), 142 (bottom), 216. Rene Burri (Magnum): page 30 (bottom). Capitoline Museum, Rome (Alinari, Florence): page 166 (top). Dr. Richard Cleave: Title page, pages 22, 27, 29 (top), 40, 59 (both), 61 (top), 62, 63 (top), 74 (bottom), 87, 88 (top), 108, 198, 251 (top), 256, 276 (left). Alan Clifton (Black Star): page 97. Bruce Davidson (Magnum): page 25 (top). Ernest J. Dupuy: pages 228 (bottom), 229, 238. N. R. Farbman (Time/Life Picture Agency): page 236. GAF Pana-Vue Slides: pages 24, 168 (left), 191, 210. Greek Nat'l Tourist Office: pages 158 (bottom), 226. From Gressman, *Alt-orientalische Bilder Alten Testament:* page 115. Himmer Verlag, Munich: page 32. Iran Nat'l Tourist Office, New York: pages 133 (left), 140 (bottom), 144 (bottom). Israel Ministry of Tourism, New York: pages 23, 66 (top), 72, 177 (top), 180 (top), 219 (bottom), 241. David Harris, courtesy the Israel Museum, Jerusalem: pages 46 (top), 47, 49, 53, 65, 70 (both), 91, 98. The Israel Museum, Jerusalem: pages 48 (top), 76 (top), 125 (top), 127 (top), 147, 209 (top), 276 (right). Istanbul Museum: page 219 (top). The Jewish Museum, New York: pages 253, 270. E. Jordan: page 203. From Lepsius, *Denkmaeler:* page 43. Univ. of London, Inst. of Archaeology: page 128. Nancy Lapp: page 78. Erich Lessing (Magnum): page 33 (bottom). The Louvre, Paris, pages 110, 155 (Alinari). Herbert G. May: page 245. The Metropolitan Museum of Art, New York: pages 4, 12, 33 (top), 36, 58, 111, 119 (top), 125 (bottom), 135, 136, 158 (top), 212. Mostra Augustea (Alinari): page 252. Museo Aquileia (Alinari): page 167 (bottom). Museo di Antichità, Turin: page 119 (bottom). Museo Nazionale, Naples: pages 152, 156 (bottom). New York Public Library: pages 103 (top), 222. Notre Dame de Sion, Jerusalem: page 214. The Oriental Institute, University of Chicago: pages 31, 44, 80, 82, 106 (bottom), 107, 121 (bottom), 132, 133 (right), 134, 142 (top), 182. Palestine Archaeological Museum, Jerusalem: page 50. From Flinders Petrie, *Tell el-Hesi:* page 11. William L. Reed, courtesy American Schools of Oriental Research: page 192. Theodore A. Rosen, Joint Expedition to Tell el-Hesi: page 8 (bottom left and top right). Scala, New York/Florence: page 271 (top). From C.F.A. Schaeffer, *Syria:* page 52. Gerhard Schlotterbeck: page 92. Leni Sonnenfeld: pages 39, 69, 88, (bottom), 138 (both), 141, 144 (top), 146, 150, 181, 201, 269. Palazzo Spada, Rome (Alinari): page 167 (top). Joseph Stefanelli: pages 29 (bottom), 42, 46 (bottom), 54, 64, 116, 202 (bottom), 225, 228 (top), 232 (both). John C. Trever, courtesy American Schools of Oriental Research: pages 183, 189. Trans World Airlines: page 218. Uffizi, Florence (Brogi): page 166 (bottom). The University Museum, University of Pennsylvania: pages 30 (top), 35, 239. Villa Albani, Rome (Alinari): page 249 (center). Wide World Photos: page 220. Professor Y. Yadin: pages 178 (bottom left), 194 (both).